1983 –
BU Consortium (Tax Ded.)
for Computer Workshop –

The Art and Science of Negotiation

The Art and Science of Negotiation

HOWARD RAIFFA

The Belknap Press of
Harvard University Press
Cambridge, Massachusetts
and London, England

1982

Library of Congress Cataloging in Publication Data
Raiffa, Howard, 1924-
    The art and science of negotiation.

    Bibliography: p.
    Includes index.
    1. Negotiation. 2. Diplomatic negotiations in
international disputes. I. Title.
BF637.N4R34   302.3   82-6170
ISBN 0-674-04812-1   AACR2

Acknowledgments

Ideas are incestuous. They commingle and refuse to sort themselves out so that one can say, "These ideas are his or hers and those mine." I know, however, that many of the ideas in the chapters that follow are the ideas of others, and some of these others can be identified. To no one am I more indebted than to John Hammond.

This book would not have been written if I had not chosen to teach a course in competitive decision making at the Harvard Business School, a course that evolved over more than a decade. In the mid-1960s I taught a doctoral seminar in individual, group, and interactive decisions, and in the early seventies John Hammond incorporated some of the material from that seminar in a pioneering M.B.A. course entitled "Competitive Decision Making." I later inherited that course from John and built on his materials. Although my course evolved into one that was substantially different from John's, he had set the tone; and even when I departed from his work, I had a very comfortable launching pad. Occasionally, when I fell flat, I picked up again from his supporting net.

Now Elon Kohlberg is teaching that course, and his version will certainly be different from mine. Some of his ideas, too, have been incorporated into this book, without credits, because I can't even begin to sort out which ideas are his and which are mine.

So it is with some of my former doctoral students who worked with me at various times during the last five years. Some of me is in their dissertations, and a lot of what is in their dissertations can be found here. I acknowledge the contributions of Kalyan Chatterjee, Zvi Livne, James Sebenius, Timothy Sullivan, and Jacob Ulvila. Jim Sebenius deserves special thanks. Not only did he teach me about the Law of the Sea, but he's a wonderfully supportive and incisive critic—and it's hard to be both.

I have also drawn liberally on ideas discussed during seminars with members of the Harvard Negotiation Workshop. In that group I interacted most closely with Roger Fisher, Bill Ury, Jim Sebenius, Frank Sanders, Larry Susskind, James Healy, and David Lax. Roger and Bill's book, *Getting to Yes,* is full of important insights, and in my weaker moments I thought of such titles for my own as *Before Getting to Yes* or *Beyond Yes.*

Some of the material in this book has been used in various executive programs at Harvard's Business School and Kennedy School of Government, and in various industrial executive training programs. I have collaborated with and observed a master of this type of pedagogy, Paul Vatter, who in innumerable ways has influenced my choice and treatment of subjects.

I have drawn copiously from Mark G. McDonough's cases on international negotiations, which were prepared partially under my supervision. These cases provided rich background material from which I concocted several abstractions. His help was indispensable.

Whenever anyone asks me whether I prefer A or B, I almost invariably answer "Why not both?" When anyone asks me where I learned something and I can't remember, I invariably answer "Tom Schelling," and I think I'm right 69.4 percent of the time.

In the late 1970s I thought about writing a book on negotiation, but I kept postponing the first steps. If Wes Churchman had not invited me to give the 1980 Gaither Lectures at Berkeley on the topic of negotiation analysis, I might still be thinking of those first steps. I am indebted to Wes and his colleagues at Berkeley for focusing my thoughts.

Poornima Ram not only typed and retyped and retyped my evolving manuscript, but her readings of the text helped me tremendously. Whenever she does not understand what I've written, I know that I'm in trouble. It's a pleasure to work with her.

I deeply appreciate the superb quality of the editing of this book; Maria Kawecki's precision imprint is on each paragraph. All remaining grammatical errors are hers, all errors in the symbols are the typesetter's, and my wife agrees to share with me responsibility for the rest.

This book is an elaboration of the H. Rowan Gaither Lectures in Systems Science, delivered November 1980 at the University of California, Berkeley. These lectures are named in memory of one of the founders, and first chairman of the board, of the RAND Corporation. They were established by a gift from the System Development Corporation, formerly a division of the RAND Corporation, and are held under the aegis of the School of Business Administration and the Center for Research in Management of the University of California, Berkeley. The past lecturers were Charles J. Hitch, Charles L. Schultze, Alice M. Rivlin, John W. Macy, Jr., Sir Geoffrey Vickers, Erich Jantsch, and Herbert A. Simon.

Contents

Prologue

In the late 1940s I was a graduate student in mathematics at the University of Michigan, partially supported by a contract enabling me to do work in the theory of games. There was an amazing burst of research activity in this speciality at that time, especially at the RAND Corporation and at Princeton University, where in 1944 John von Neumann and Oskar Morgenstern wrote their classic tome, *Theory of Games and Economic Behavior.* Very rapidly the easier research topics were being appropriated and a fresh crop of Ph.D. students were looking for new fertile ground to explore. I was in a cohort that was beginning to study two-person games where the protagonists did not have strictly opposing interests (the so-called non-zero-sum games). My thinking was very much influenced by a lecture given by William Haber, professor of economics at the University of Michigan, who talked about the role of arbitration in labor disputes. The lecture set me to wondering: If two players of a non-zero-sum, abstract game asked me to act as arbitrator and to determine a joint outcome for their dispute, what would I do? And thus I began some highly abstract mathematical research into this problem—research in the genre of game theory. I was interested in mathematical elegance, and the peers whose opinions I valued were the mathematical community. I certainly was not driven to do empirical work, to see how arbitration actually functioned in the real world; nothing could have appealed to me less.

Receiving my doctorate in 1951, I drifted back and forth between game theory and mathematical statistics for the next six years. After *Games and Decisions,* written with Duncan Luce, was published in 1957, I accepted a joint appointment at Harvard: I was to teach statistics in the newly created Department of Statistics and perhaps game theory in the Graduate School of Business Administration. I didn't know very much about business (a vast understatement) and I began by studying loads of case studies of real-world problems. Practically every case I looked at included an interactive, competitive decision component, but I was at a loss to know how to use my expertise as a game theorist. The theory of games focuses its attention on problems where the protagonists in a dispute are super-rational, where the "rules of the game" are so well understood by the "players" that each can think about what the others are thinking about what he is thinking, ad infinitum. The real business cases I was introduced to were of another variety: Mr. X, the vice-president for operations of Firm A, knows he has a problem, but he's not quite sure of the decision alternatives he has and he's not sure that his adversaries (Firms B and C) even recognize that a problem exists. If Firms A, B, and C behave in thus-and-such a way, he cannot predict what the payoffs will be to each and he doesn't know how he should evaluate his own payoffs, to say nothing about his adversaries' payoffs. There are uncertainties all around besides those that relate to the choices of Firms B and C; no objective probability distributions for those ancillary uncertainties are available. Mr. X has a hard time sorting out what he thinks about the uncertainties and about the value tradeoffs he confronts, and he is in no frame of mind to assess what Mr. Y of Firm B and Mr. Z of Firm C are thinking about what he's thinking. Indeed, Mr. X is mainly thinking about idiosyncratic issues that would be viewed by Y and Z as completely extraneous to their problems. Game theory, however, deals only with the way in which ultrasmart, all-knowing people *should* behave in competitive situations, and has little to say to Mr. X as he confronts the morass of his problem.

For the next ten years I stayed away from game theory and concentrated on a much simpler class of problems: decisions under uncertainty in noninteractive, noncompetitive situations. I worked in a field that has been dubbed "decision analysis."

Between 1968 and 1972, competitive, interactive problems gradually reclaimed my attention, and I became convinced that there should be a marriage between what I was then doing in decision analysis and what I had previously done in game theory. My main preoccupation was with real people in real situations: How could analysis be used to help one party in a competitive conflict situation without assuming excessive rationality on the part of the "others"? My efforts were still marginal.

In 1967 President Lyndon Johnson asked McGeorge Bundy, then president of the Ford Foundation, to explore with the Soviets ways in which science could promote international cooperation. Perhaps a joint scientific undertaking—keeping away from arms control and space exploration—would be appropriate. They weren't sure whether the effort should be bilateral or multilateral, but multilateral seemed more appropriate; if multilateral, it should involve only the advanced industrialized nations. Bundy asked me to be one of his advisers, and for four years I had a taste of international diplomacy and negotiations, continuing in my advisory capacity even after Philip Handler, president of the National Academy of Sciences, took over the leadership of the project in 1970. In 1972 twelve academies of sciences, including five from Eastern Europe —and among these one from the German Democratic Republic, which the United States did not recognize at the time—signed a charter creating the International Institute for Applied Systems Analysis (IIASA), now located outside Vienna. From 1972 to 1975 I was the first director of that scientific institute.

I recount all this because it is relevant to the chapters that follow. I was trained as a decision analyst and game theorist. Did those disciplines help me in my negotiations? Was I properly trained for my role as negotiator or as scientific administrator? Perhaps, because of my training and profession, I thought more conceptually about the problems I was engaged in than I would have without that training, but I never really used the techniques of game theory—concepts and ideas, yes, but techniques, no—in my roles as negotiator and director. And what was frustrating about this was that I was constantly involved in problems that could be loosely classified as competitive and interactive. The concepts of decision analysis seemed to me much more applicable than those of game theory, but not in the way I had taught it. The qualitative framework of thought was repeatedly helpful—not its detailed, esoteric, quantitative aspects. Simple, back-of-the-envelope analysis was all that seemed appropriate. I was constantly impressed with the limitations of iterative, back-and-forth, gamelike thinking. I could try to be systematic, thoughtful, and analytic, but the "others" I negotiated with always seemed to have intricate, hidden agendas. Secretly I thought that if I could really know their true values, judgments, and political constraints, I would be doubly convinced that they were not acting in a coherent, rational way. They certainly weren't satisfying the prescriptive ideals of "rational economic man."

As director of IIASA, I had to balance scientific integrity with political reality. I was continually called upon to structure creative compromises. Researchers pulled in different directions, and since our budget was modest in comparison to their collective appetites, people—good people—had to be disappointed. In most of these disputes I played the role of a mediator, in some the role of an arbitrator.

My actions were subject to the approval of a council, which was made up of one distinguished member from each national member organization. The chairman of the council was Jerman Gvishiani, deputy minister of science and technology of the Soviet Union. And no matter how exalted that title may seem, in reality he was even more powerful than that. I learned about different national negotiating styles, and above all about the importance of timing: one had to keep a fluid agenda and wait for the propitious time to introduce a contentious issue. I learned that even the Soviets are not monolithic and that they occasionally change their minds. I learned how difficult it is to accomplish anything substantial in open meetings when each side has to go on record for the people back home. I learned that money comes from different pockets and that five million dollars taken from the left pocket of a country might be easier to get than five thousand dollars from the right pocket. I learned that if you wait long enough, someone on the other side will vaguely propose what you want, and that it's easier to open negotiations that way. I learned the need of others to feel that they are part of the inner circle. I learned that "gentlemen's agreements" that are not documented are fragile; that a party may be sincere about such an agreement when made, but that they may not be able to withstand internal pressures from objectors at home; and that because negotiators are embarrassed when they have to back away from promises made, they often become more amenable to other compromises. I learned that the boisterous atmosphere of an Austrian tavern often does far more to establish a proper ambience for negotiations than does a sedate cocktail party or dinner.

I came to know Jerman Gvishiani reasonably well, and especially enjoyed those sessions where he coached me in how to bargain with the Austrians and with people of other nationalities. Austrians, perched in a precarious position between East and West, are understandably apprehensive about the Russians. Gvishiani sometimes used his power as a Russian in talks with the Austrians on behalf of the institute, but always in a subtle fashion—the trick was to use the hint of power, rather than power itself. Austrian Chancellor Bruno Kreisky and others in his government realized that the good will engendered in one set of negotiations could spill over and affect other negotiations, and it was this linkage that could be deftly exploited by Gvishiani.

occupied

When I returned to Harvard in 1975 I decided that my primary aim was not to teach what I'd learned, but rather to learn what I should be teaching in the art and science of negotiation.

skills necessary to negotiate

I decided that above all, I needed an experimental laboratory. I wanted to learn how people actually negotiate and, knowing something about how others negotiate, to examine how the side I was advising *should* negotiate. Could simple analysis help? Of course, I could have gone into the field to get vicarious experiences, but that would have been slow and much anecdotal material on negotiations had already been written; also, I knew and could talk to a lot of people who had been in the front lines of negotiation. My advantage was that I was more analytical in approach than most practitioners and that I knew bits of esoteric, mathematical theories that, although not directly relevant, might be made relevant to practice.

I also had to teach, and there was no better way than to get students to learn with me. My idea was to create a quasi-laboratory where students would at the same time be willing subjects in experiments, be interpreters of the empirical findings, and be designers of modified experiments that could be tried with new groups of subjects. Collectively we could test what worked in the laboratory and we could discuss whether our heuristic insights would be applicable in the real world.

I inherited a second-year, elective course developed by John Hammond for students in the Master of Business Administration (M.B.A.) program. Entitled "Competitive Decision Making," it was a perfect launching pad for my interests. The students taking the course were primarily business generalists; most aspired to be business entrepreneurs and negotiators; all had some familiarity with the basic concepts of decision analysis, but most had a low tolerance for theoretical acrobatics. They were eager if properly motivated. Hammond had already collected fascinating cases, many of which I use here. My innovations were to make the course into an experimental laboratory, to make the payoffs in the experiments emotionally gripping by keeping records of individual scores and partially basing grades on these scores, to spend more time on face-to-face negotiations, to emphasize the role of the intervenor, and to test a bit more systematically the potential roles of simple analysis (see appendix to Chapter 2). Hammond kept the course close to real-world cases, while I willingly drifted off into experiments with abstractions of those cases.

In this book I draw heavily on Hammond's cases and on the empirical results of experiments that I conducted in my classes. Some of the accumulated sample sizes of our experiments run into the high hundreds. Data have been collected, in addition, from student-subjects in government and law, from high-level managers and general-grade military officers enrolled in special executive training programs, and from members of the Young Presidents Organization—an international organization made up of presidents of firms who are under the age of forty. An experimental psychologist would be very unhappy with our experimental designs. We kept systematic statistical records only for business students. Experiments were conducted outside class and we did not formally monitor whether our subjects were really obeying the rules; we operated according to an honor system, and sometimes not all are honorable under stress. Some of the observations that follow, therefore, should be understood with this in mind, although a few biased game scores would not alter the basic truth of the messages I want to convey. One may never be able to predict or to simulate in a laboratory setting all the aspects of complex real-world negotiation, but there is no question as to the value of applying decision-theoretic concepts: analysis can help.

traditions
regulations
courts
markets
negotiations

part

I

Overview

There is no shortage of disputes. There are disputes between husband and wife, between siblings, between friends, between indi- *varieties*
vidual and firm, between firm and firm, between developer and en-
vironmentalist, between regions within a nation, between a region
or city or state and the nation, between nation and nation—and perhaps in the far future (who knows?) between planet and planet.

There are many established ways for settling disputes: traditions, ①
regulations, courts, markets (through the laws of supply and de- ②③④
mand), and negotiations. Even the staunchest free-market capitalist ⑤
acknowledges the fact that markets may be imperfect and that governments must often modify the rules of market behavior to achieve
more socially efficient outcomes. But how should the authorities
change these rules? Frequently by the processes of bargaining and
negotiating.

It's important for me to state at the outset that I am not against
conflict per se. Progress is often achieved by engaging uninvolved
individuals in a cause, and the creation of tension and conflict may ✓✓
be a desirable organizing strategy. Some major societal improvements have resulted from conflicts that have been resolved by destructive forces. Competitive sports, parlor games, and card games
are conflicts that are designed to add zest to life. Competition for
advancement in the business world and competition among firms
generate incentives that help the system work more efficiently. All
that granted, this book is concerned with situations in which two or
more parties recognize that differences of interest and values exist
among them and in which they want (or in which one or more are
compelled) to seek a compromise agreement through negotiation.

There is an art and a science of negotiation. By "science" I

7

[handwritten margin notes: art includes: interpersonal skills; ability to convince + be convinced; " to employ many bargaining ploys; wisdom to know when + how to use ploys]

[handwritten margin note: Science of negotiation]

loosely mean systematic analysis for problem solving; and if the phrase "systematic analysis" seems a bit vague, I can only say that its meaning will become clearer as we go on. The "art" side of the ledger is equally slippery: it includes interpersonal skills, the ability to convince and be convinced, the ability to employ a basketfull of bargaining ploys, and the wisdom to know when and how to use them. The art of negotiation has been well documented throughout the ages; the science, on the other hand, is not well developed, and what has been developed is not very accessible to the practitioner. My aims here are to explain in relatively nonmathematical language some of the science (theory) that has been developed by others, to develop a bit more of my own, to sprinkle in a little art, and to show how art and science can interact synergistically.

Often disputes are not settled amicably, and all sides suffer: children fight each other, husband and wife separate, labor and management settle grievances through strikes, and nation-states resolve their differences through wars. Agreements often are not made when they could have been made to the advantage of all disputants. Agreements often are made that are inefficient: others could have been made that would have been preferred by all the disputants.

It is my belief that many disputes could be more efficiently reconciled if the negotiators were more skillful. Other disputes are best reconciled through the efforts of intervenors. In labor-management relations there are reasonably trained—but usually not well enough trained—mediators and arbitrators. Ideally these are impartial, highly ethical, knowledgeable intermediaries who help the disputants negotiate constructively, perhaps by suggesting compromises, and, depending on their role, perhaps by dictating compromises—a bit like a wise parent helping quarrelsome children. Such intermediaries also exist to help counsel families. It is very rare, however, to find well-trained intervenors who can help with serious societal conflicts, such as those between urban interest groups, between developers and environmentalists, between nation-states. Managers likewise seldom receive instruction in negotiating skills as part of their professional education, although they are often called upon to mediate or arbitrate in disputes that occur among their subordinates.

I believe that more training is desperately needed in the art and science of negotiating, and in the art and science of intervening.

Such training would be appropriate for diplomats, military officers, lawyers, politicians, businessmen, and ordinary citizens who may expect at some time or other to be embroiled in situations with serious conflicts of interest among contending parties. It should include instruction not only in the art of interpersonal relations, but also in analytical, problem-solving skills.

This book will therefore blend discussion of the practical side of negotiating with simple mathematical analysis, both of which can be of use to disputants and intervenors alike. We'll begin with a brief look at the various types of disputes and at the ways in which researchers have chosen to explore the field.

game = conflict situation
disputants = "players of the game"   *("many" => 2)*
Strategic analysis = "game theory"

1

Some Organizing Questions

Early in my research I had the grandiose idea of devising a taxonomy of disputes, in which the listing would be reasonably exhaustive and in which overlaps among categories would be rare. This was possible, I found, only after developing a host of abstract constructs —and even then the taxonomy was not very useful. For our purposes here, and to give a flavor of the sweep of topics to be discussed, a partial classification will be sufficient. We'll do this by identifying the important characteristics of each type of dispute.

ARE THERE MORE THAN TWO PARTIES? ①

There is a vast difference between conflicts involving two disputants and those involving more than two disputants. Once three or more conflicting parties are involved, coalitions of disputants may form and may act in concert against the other disputants. Without any intention of being frivolous, many writers talk about a conflict situation (be it economic, political, or military) as a "game," the disputants as "players of the game," and strategic analysis as "game theory." Game theorists have long made a distinction between two-person games and many-person games, where "many" is interpreted as greater than two. The Law of the Sea is one example of a game with many players; the Group of 77 (in reality, some 114 developing nations) is one reasonably stable coalition of players in this game.

There are conflict situations in which the disputing parties are not well specified. Consider a dispute between a developer and a group of disturbed citizens who can organize themselves into negotiating entities but have not yet done so. A group may form, but during negotiations its members may not agree among themselves and

(a)
(b)

11

may splinter into subgroups, each demanding representation in the negotiations.

At other times, well-specified negotiating parties might jointly decide who else should be invited to join them at the conference table; thus, part of the negotiations may be taken up with deciding just who is to negotiate.

ARE THE PARTIES MONOLITHIC?

When U.S. ambassador Ellsworth Bunker negotiated the Panama Canal Treaty with his counterpart from Panama, three agreements had to be made: one across the table (United States and Panama), one within the U.S. side, and one within the Panamanian side. Bunker spent much less time negotiating externally than he did internally within the United States, where there were vast differences of opinion—differences among the Department of Defense, the Department of State, the Department of Commerce, the Department of Transportation, and so on. It is a delicate and highly intricate matter to be able to synchronize external and internal negotiations. On the internal side, the president of the United States and his ambassador play a role not unlike that of a mediator, but a mediator with "muscle" or "clout."

Far from being exceptional, it is commonly the case that each party to a dispute is not internally monolithic: each party might comprise people who are on the same side but whose values differ, perhaps sharply—and even if one side consists of only a single person, that person might still experience internal conflicts. I am not implying that the diversities that exist internally within each team make bargaining more difficult between the teams; indeed, the more diffuse the positions are within each side, the easier it might be to achieve external agreement. But I do wish to emphasize how important it is in discussing negotiation to be aware of internal as well as external conflicts.

IS THE GAME REPETITIVE?

When people haggle in a bazaarlike fashion over such one-time issues as the price of a used car or the price of a home, each disputant may have a short-run perspective that may tempt him to exaggerate his case. Contrast this type of negotiation with those cases in which the bargainers will bargain frequently together in the future and in which the atmosphere at the conclusion of one bargaining session will carry over to influence the atmosphere at the next bargaining session. When bargaining is repetitive, each disputant must be particularly concerned about his reputation, and hence, luckily for society, repetitive bargaining is often done more cooperatively (and honestly) than single-shot bargaining. But this is *not always* so: with repetition there is always the possibility that some inadvertent, careless friction can fester and spoil the atmosphere for future bargaining; this is especially true where there are differences in the information available to both sides. With repetition, a negotiator might want to establish a reputation for toughness that is designed for long-term rather than short-term rewards.

ARE THERE LINKAGE EFFECTS?

When the United States in the 1970s negotiated a contract with the Philippines about military base rights, the negotiators had to keep in mind similar contracts and treaties that were pending elsewhere, such as in Spain and Turkey. One negotiation becomes *linked* with another. Repetitive games also involve linkages that arise from repetitions with the same players over time.

The U.S. Senate, in discussing the SALT II treaty, linked these negotiations to other negotiations on defense spending. In grain negotiations with the Soviet Union, the United States threatened to link food with oil.

One must be aware of the intricacies caused by linkages and, to put it more positively, one must use linkage possibilities to break impasses in negotiations. This is not done creatively enough in most disputes.

IS THERE MORE THAN ONE ISSUE?

In selling or buying a house, a car, or even a firm, the critical issue is the final price of the transaction. This is the case even in some labor-management disputes in which the wage rate may be the overwhelmingly dominant factor. One side wants a higher settlement value; the other side, a lower settlement value. The sides are in direct conflict. Of course, both might prefer some reasonable settlement to no settlement at all.

In most complicated conflicts there is not one issue to be decided, but several interacting issues. There are virtually hundreds that must be resolved in the Law of the Sea conferences. Some of the issues are economic; others are political; others have military considerations. Each side, in comparing possible final agreements, must carefully examine and thrash out its own value tradeoffs—and one must remember that each side may not be monolithic and that these tradeoffs do not usually involve naturally commensurable units. The point is that disputants are engaged in a horrendously difficult analytical task in which there is vast room for cooperative behavior. When there are several issues to be jointly determined through negotiation, the negotiating parties have an opportunity to considerably enlarge the pie before cutting it into shares for each side to enjoy. Negotiations rarely are strictly competitive, but the players may behave as if they were competitive; the players might consider themselves as strictly opposed disputants rather than jointly cooperative problem solvers.[1]

The parties may start their negotiations by trying to decide what will be at stake. But often they may need to be flexible; they may want to introduce new issues or eliminate old ones as part of the negotiation process. Thus, one issue in the negotiations may be to determine just what issues should be included in the negotiations.

IS AN AGREEMENT REQUIRED?

If a potential seller and buyer of a house cannot agree on a price, they can break off negotiations. During negotiations each has a mild threat: he can simply walk away. Contrast this case with the case of a city that is negotiating a complex wage settlement with its police force or firemen. By law a contract must be settled by a given date. True, the parties might delay and miss critical deadlines, but eventually they must settle on an agreement. When contracts have to be made, the parties might be required by law to submit their cases for mediation and arbitration.

If an agreement is not required—or not required at a particular

1. We really are not a zero-sum society—it is not true that what one gains another must necessarily lose. The trouble is that often we act as if this were the case.

stage of negotiation—each party must contemplate what might happen if negotiations were to be broken off. If this were to occur, each party would face a complex decision problem under uncertainty, and the negotiator would have to somehow figure out just how much he must get in the negotiations before he would be indifferent between settling for that amount or breaking off negotiations. This phase of analysis—the determination of a minimal return that must be achieved in negotiations—is usually done very poorly in practice.

Even in those cases where, by law, contracts eventually have to be agreed upon, negotiations may be protracted, and at any stage a negotiator might want to think about a rock-bottom position for acceptability of a contract at that particular point. "If you can't get this much at this time, then break off negotiations until next week"—so go the instructions.

IS RATIFICATION REQUIRED?

Whenever the United States signs a treaty with another nation, the U.S. Senate must ratify it before it becomes binding. Analogously, a union leader might settle on a contract with management, but before it becomes operative the union rank-and-file must ratify the agreement. Further last-minute concessions might be squeezed out of the other side during this ratification process: "salami" tactics— one slice more. What is even more important, the ratification process might strengthen the side requiring it—but, of course, it might also make negotiations much less flexible and less amicable, and might stiffen the resolve of the other side.

In some circumstances, negotiators themselves may artificially create a ratification requirement. For example, a corporation president, while having the authority to commit his firm to an agreement, might say to the other negotiator, "Of course, this agreement is acceptable to me, but my board of directors will have to ratify it." Once again, this ploy might adversely affect the atmosphere of the negotiations.

ARE THREATS POSSIBLE?

If the buyer of a house objects to the price offered by the seller, the buyer can threaten to walk away. This is called the *fixed threat* to go back to the status quo, ex ante. Contrast that situation with the case where a party says, "If you do not agree with my offer, not only will I break off relations, but I will take the following actions to hurt you." Certainly the power of threats can influence outcomes, but if used crassly it can also stiffen opposition. Indeed, it can be demonstrated in laboratory situations that increasing the power of one side (everything else being equal) might empirically result in poorer outcomes *for that side* (and usually for the other side as well). Power is often not used artfully.

Again, these headings are not distinct—since threats by their very nature tend to link problems, and problems are often linked in order to make threats possible and credible.

ARE THERE TIME CONSTRAINTS OR TIME-RELATED COSTS?

When the United States negotiated with the North Vietnamese toward the close of the Vietnam War, the two sides met in Paris. The first move in this negotiation game was taken by the Vietnamese: they leased a house for a *two-year* period.

The party that negotiates in haste is often at a disadvantage. The penalties incurred in delays may be quite different for the two parties, and this discrepancy can be used to the advantage of one side. It can also be misused by one side to the disadvantage of both sides, as we shall see. In some negotiations, the tactic of one side might be to delay negotiations indefinitely. For example, environmentalists can often discourage a developer through protracted litigations. In a civil liabilities suit an insurance company can use delays in bringing a case to court in order to get the plaintiff to accept a more favorable (to the insurance company) out-of-court settlement.

ARE THE CONTRACTS BINDING?

How can the Israelis or the Egyptians be sure that the other side will abide by an agreement after their respective current leaders have passed off center stage? They can't. Any agreement is risky— but so is no agreement.

In many conflicts within a nation-state, agreements can be signed and actions made legally binding. The courts are there to put muscle into agreements. Contrast this situation with the case of a multinational mining company that is negotiating a joint mining venture with a developing country. The multinational is to supply the initial capital and know-how, the developing country the physical resources; and if profits are to be reaped, they might agree to share these profits in certain proportions. Indeed, the agreed-upon proportional amounts themselves might be contingent on other factors, including, for example, the size of the cash flows. But suppose the multinational firm is afraid that the developing country might unilaterally break the contract at some later date (for example, by nationalizing). In order to protect itself, the multinational might bargain harder for a quicker payback period—but, alas, this tactic might hasten the very counterreaction that the firm fears. Uncertainty abounds.

ARE THE NEGOTIATIONS PRIVATE OR PUBLIC?

It's hard to keep secrets nowadays, at least in the public sector. In negotiations involving many issues, a common tactic is to look for compensating compromises: Party A gives in a little on one issue and Party B reciprocates, giving in on another issue. When A gives up a little, A might want to exaggerate what it's giving up, while B will minimize what it's getting—all in preparation for a compensating quid pro quo. But now imagine the prime minister of Israel making a concession to the president of Egypt and making an exaggerated claim of the importance of his concession. How will this be reviewed by the Knesset once his stance is made public?

Public pronouncements (and leaks to the press) can be artfully employed to bolster the credibility of commitments. Public postures of one side can influence the internal negotiations of the other side.

When negotiating parties are not monolithic or when ratification is required, it is critically important to know just how secret the secret negotiations are. It is not easy to negotiate in a fishbowl surrounded by reporters, who themselves feel conflicting desires to both get at the truth and get a spicy, newsworthy story.

WHAT ARE THE GROUP NORMS?

What norms of behavior do you expect of the "others" in your negotiation discussions? Will they tell you what they truly feel? Will they disclose all the relevant information? Will they distort facts? Will they threaten? Will they abide by their word? Will they break the law? Certainly, the modes of behavior you should expect when discussing a point of disagreement with your spouse or your business partner are different from those you can expect to occur between firms or between countries or between extortionist and victim.

In the chapters that follow, I will dwell at length on the problems of *cooperative antagonists*. Such disputants recognize that they have differences of interests; they would like to find a compromise, but they fully expect that all parties will be primarily worried about their own interests. They do not have malevolent intentions, but neither are they altruistically inclined. They are slightly distrustful of one another; each expects the others to try to make a good case for their own side and to indulge in strategic posturing. They are not confident that the others will be truthful, but they would like to be truthful themselves, within bounds. They expect that power will be used gracefully, that all parties will abide by the law, and that all joint agreements will be honored.

I will not deal extensively with the problems of *strident antagonists*, who are malevolent, untrustworthy characters. Their promises are suspect, they are frequently double-crossers, and they exploit their power to the fullest. Sometimes it's not clear whether such a disputant is really a madman or just acting that way. Think of a hijacker, or of an extortionist who is holding an executive's child as hostage, or of those who engage in parlor diplomacy.

I will also not consider the problems of *fully cooperative partners*. Such negotiators might have different needs, values, and opinions, but they are completely open with one another; they expect total honesty, full disclosure, no strategic posturing. They think of themselves as a cohesive entity and they sincerely want to do what's right for that entity. This would be true, for instance, of a happily married couple or some fortunate business partners. Only occasionally do teams of scientific advisers or faculties of universities fall into this category.

My primary subject will be the group norm in the middle: that of cooperative antagonists. Sometimes negotiations start in this category and slide toward stridency. One aim of an intervenor is to prevent this from happening and to nudge negotiations toward the full-cooperation category.

IS THIRD-PARTY INTERVENTION POSSIBLE?

Negotiations are affected by the possible availability of outside intervenors, usually mediators or arbitrators. This is customarily referred to as "third-party" intervention, even when there are more than two disputants. (An alternate, if somewhat pedantic, term might be "(n + 1)-party intervention.") A disputant may say to himself, "If I bargain tough and do not succeed, then I can always submit my case to arbitration." Or: "I'd better be more reasonable, or else an outsider will be brought in and who knows what I can expect." A negotiator must consider if and when to suggest (or to agree with the suggestion of) an outside intervenor. Usually this poses a complex decision problem with vast uncertainties. If an intervenor does enter the dispute, the negotiator has a new set of tactical options: How much should he reveal? How cooperative should he be? How truthful?

The problem can be viewed from the perspective of either negotiator or intervenor. We do each on occasion.

The above set of questions provide a partial checklist of topics that we will consider in the chapters that follow. They give an indication of the complexity, the pervasiveness, and the importance of our subject. The questions are obviously overlapping and are far from exhaustive.

2

Research Perspectives

In order to describe the "is" and "ought" of decision making, consider the case of an oil wildcatter who is poised at a critical choice node: Should he risk his limited financial resources on an oil-drilling venture that has a small chance of a large return? Theorists gaze at such risky choice problems through two sets of glasses. The *describers* examine how real people (wildcatters, bankers, generals, labor leaders, and so on) actually analyze (or do not analyze) such risky choices, how they actually behave, how they think, how they rationalize their choices to themselves. The *prescribers* are interested in how people should or ought to behave, rather than how they do behave. Their aim is to guide the perplexed decision maker in choosing an action that is consonant with the decision maker's "true" beliefs and values. The prescribers perform analysis to help in the selection of a choice to be made; the describers perform analysis to help understand the selection of a choice that has been made.

The "is" and "ought" of decision making get more complicated when there are two or more interacting decision makers, which is certainly the case in bargaining and negotiating. So let's look at sketches of a few research perspectives to give us a base from which to approach the chapters that follow.

SYMMETRICALLY DESCRIPTIVE RESEARCH

A researcher might be interested solely in *describing* the behavior of all the negotiators, without having any interest whatsoever in *prescribing* how they should behave. Such researchers can be very analytical about their subject matter; they can use esoteric descriptive and interactive models of behavior, involving simulations or mathematical models. Some of these researchers are interested in important cases of negotiation from a historical perspective. For example: How do real people, with all their idiosyncrasies and bounded rationalities, actually behave? How do they learn? How is trust created? How is it destroyed? This is the primary interest of storytellers, historians, psychologists, sociologists, anthropologists, political scientists, and positive economists.

SYMMETRICALLY PRESCRIPTIVE RESEARCH

Game theorists—most applied mathematicians and mathematical economists—examine what ultrasmart, impeccably rational, super-people *should* do in competitive, interactive situations. They are not interested in the way erring folks like you and me actually behave, but in how we should behave if we were smarter, thought harder, were more consistent, were all-knowing. Advice is given symmetrically to all parties about how to play certain intriguing games.

Each party has to think about what the other party is thinking about what the first party is thinking about—and so on, ad infinitum. The advice given to all parties must give rise to an equilibrium situation: if the theory says that Party A should choose strategy 1 and Party B strategy 2, then 1 must be a good retort against 2 and 2 must be a good retort against 1; otherwise, the advice would not be self-fulfilling and would be counterproductive.

There is an enormous literature of the symmetrically descriptive variety and the symmetrically prescriptive variety. (See Luce and Raiffa, 1957, for an example of the latter.)

ASYMMETRICALLY
PRESCRIPTIVE/DESCRIPTIVE RESEARCH

The researcher in this area is concerned with studying and understanding the behavior of real people in real conflict situations, so that he can better advise one party about how it should behave in order to achieve its best expected outcome. This type of analysis is *prescriptive* from the vantage point of one party and *descriptive* from the points of view of the competing parties. The advice can range from what to wear and how to present oneself, to intricate analysis of what complex calculations to make. Of course, if all parties are getting such advice, the advice given to one party will have to reflect the fact that advice is also being given to the other parties.

I started my career as a game theorist doing research of the symmetrically prescriptive variety, but later became increasingly involved in advising one party about how it *should* behave, given its descriptive probabilistic predictions about how other parties *might* behave (the asymmetrically prescriptive/descriptive case).[1]

EXTERNALLY PRESCRIPTIVE OR DESCRIPTIVE RESEARCH

One might investigate how in fact *intervenors* behave in negotiation processes. What are the similarities and differences in the descriptive behaviors of these people? My concern here is mainly with determining how intervenors (especially mediators, arbitrators, and rules manipulators) *should* behave in order to help the negotiating parties in some impartial, balanced way. This can be thought of as an externally prescriptive orientation.

A *facilitator* is a person who arranges for the relevant parties to come to the negotiating table. In the international arena a facilitator may use his or her "good offices" to bring the disputants together and arrange the amenities for meetings. In other contexts the facilitator may be a real estate broker who brings together potential buyers and sellers, or an investment banker who identifies firms that might profitably merge. The facilitator may choose not to get involved in the actual process of negotiation, but he may play a facilitating role in implementing the agreement—helping with last-minute legal details, helping with financing, helping with surveillance of the agreements. The facilitator may actually have a short-term asymmetric interest that could lead to biases: for example, a real estate broker gets a percentage fee (from the seller of a house), as does an investment banker who arranges acquisitions

---

1. I am occasionally challenged by people whose ideals I admire about the appropriateness of giving one-sided advice. "Isn't it at the expense of the other side?" And: "If both sides followed your advice, wouldn't society suffer?" If I thought so, I wouldn't be in this game. Most disputes are not strictly competitive—very often good analysis by one side can also be of advantage to the other side. An extreme version of this is: "Let's negotiate instead of fighting."

and mergers. But in such situations the facilitator is playing a repetitive game, and his or her reputation depends on maintaining a balance between the parties that are negotiating deals.

A *mediator* is an impartial outsider who tries to aid the negotiators in their quest to find a compromise agreement. The mediator can help with the negotiation process, but he does not have the authority to dictate a solution. He might not even choose to suggest a final solution; rather, his purpose is to lead the negotiators to determine whether there exist compromises that would be preferred by each party to the no-agreement alternative, and to help the parties select on their own a mutually acceptable agreement.

An *arbitrator* (or arbiter), after hearing the arguments and proposals of all sides and after finding out "the facts," may also try to lead the negotiators to devise their own solutions or may suggest reasonable solutions; but if these preliminary actions fail, the arbitrator has the authority to impose a solution. The negotiators might voluntarily submit their dispute for arbitration, or the arbitration might be imposed on them by some higher authority.

A *rules manipulator* is given the authority to alter or constrain the process of negotiation—or, put another way, to modify the rules of the game. The word "manipulator" might make some people uneasy, but it is used here in a neutral sense. "Rules adjuster" might carry fewer unwanted connotations, but it does not quite capture the flavor of what I have in mind. A simple example might help. Two children are arguing about how they will share a piece of cake. Their mother, acting as a rules manipulator, imposes a procedure for the resolution of the conflict. She designates one child to divide the cake into two parts and the other child to select one part. This is called the "divide-and-choose" procedure. If the prize is not a cake but an indivisible object, the resolution procedure might incorporate time-sharing or possible side payments (not necessarily money). Just such a process was instituted in the Law of the Sea negotiations.[2] Unable to agree on whether deep-seabed mining (for manganese nodules) should be undertaken completely by an international organization or be conducted largely by individual companies and countries, the delegates to the Law of the Sea Conference finally accepted a version of Henry Kissinger's idea that seabed

2. I am indebted to James Sebenius for all I know about these negotiations.

mining take place under a "parallel system." Private and state-controlled entities would mine on one side of the system and a United Nations agency, the International Seabed Authority, would mine the other. Many developing countries feared, however, that the best "minesites" would be claimed early by companies from the industrialized nations. So the following agreement was made: each application for a reserved site would specify a region sufficiently large and of sufficient value to permit two mining operations; the operator (presumably from an industrialized rich country, or countries) would then be required to *divide* the proposed site into two parts, and the International Seabed Authority would have the right to choose which of the two parts to keep for itself.

There are many fair-division schemes more elaborate than divide-and-choose, some involving auction mechanisms. These are seldom used to resolve conflicts because they are even more seldom thought about. A rules manipulator could in fact not only suggest such mechanisms, but could also prohibit the use of various moves (such as threats of unilateral use of power) that could lead to disastrous outcomes. Of course, if this is to work, there must be sufficient power in the hands of the rules manipulator. Government regulation can be viewed as one form of rules manipulation.

An effective intervenor, whether facilitator or mediator or arbitrator or rules manipulator, should understand the negotiation process from various vantage points—the symmetrically descriptive, the symmetrically prescriptive, and the asymmetrically prescriptive/descriptive.

The intervenor has aspirations, ideals, values, judgments, and constraints of his own. Thus, he can be thought of as another player in the game—albeit a special type of player—and he should try to maximize his payoffs. The trick for the other players is to choose an intervenor whose motivations and incentives are compatible with their own.

With the above perspectives on negotiation in mind, we are ready to look more closely at individual bargaining types. The characteristics that define each type of negotiation—number of disputants, number of issues, presence or absence of intervenors, and so on—have a direct bearing on the behavior of all participants. We will analyze the way in which this relationship works, and see how all parties to a dispute, be they negotiators or intervenors, can use such analysis to devise strategies that will be to their best advantage.

Cases and applications will be sprinkled throughout to help motivate and illustrate conceptual points—and, I suppose, to add a bit of spice. Readers interested in one field of application—say, labor-management disputes—will learn more about their own domain of interest by reflecting on the ways in which these disputes are similar to or different from disputes in other domains. The occasional heavily mathematical passage may present difficulties for some readers. Such passages, labeled "analytical elaborations," have been clearly set off from the text. Readers who are nonmathematically inclined can skip over these, without fear that they will be missing something essential. Those of a more analytical bent will find that the digressions add an extra dimension to the argument; for whereas the case studies deal with the particular, the mathematical analyses reveal the universal. It is conceptual formalization that enables one to take what has been learned from one field and use it to solve problems in another.

Appendix: A Course in Competitive Decision Making

Many of the laboratory negotiation simulations that are examined extensively in this book were played by students in elective courses in a Master of Business Administration program and a Master of Public Policy program at Harvard University. The following material (designed for M.B.A. students) describes the philosophy and grading of the course and was distributed to the students before the first class. Students were informed before they enrolled in the course that they would be subjects in competitive and cooperative exercises and that their grades would depend in part on their performances in these exercises. The material is included here to indicate the setting of many of the laboratory findings I shall discuss.

A BIT ABOUT THE PHILOSOPHY OF THE COURSE
AND THE GRADING

There are a host of fascinating and important competitive and interactive decision-making problems that we (students and instructor) will explore in this course: problems in competitive pricing, advertising, expansion, and diversification; problems in competitive allocation of resources; problems in competitive bidding and contract incentives; problems in face-to-face bargaining (buying a house or used car, mergers and acquisitions, settling a liability claim out of court, settling a complex labor-management contract, negotiating an international treaty); problems in environmental mediation; problems in arbitration and fair division; problems with voting procedures; and more abstract problems dealing with justice, fairness, equity, honesty, and ethics. The menu is vast and we'll be forced to push ahead and not get caught up in the intriguing complexities of any single problem type.

The course is called "Competitive Decision Making" (CDM), but in one sense this is a misnomer because in some of the situations we shall discuss, the essence of the problem is cooperation rather than competition. Most problems we shall deal with have a blending of cooperative as well as competitive behavior: you might have to cooperate with others to enlarge the pie that you will eventually have to share competitively.

CDM builds upon the course you had last year in managerial economics, especially the part involving decision making in an uncertain environment. But we will draw upon only the most rudimentary concepts of that course. Unlike most of the uncertainties facing the decision maker in managerial economics, the uncertainties in CDM will stem primarily from the uncertain actions of other decision makers, who are consciously trying to do what is right for themselves, and it is their actions as well as your own that will determine the final outcome. Thus, in most of the interactive decision problems we shall discuss, you (as a participant) will have only partial control in determining what happens. You will have to think hard about what the other disputants are thinking—and to some extent about what they may be thinking about what you are thinking.

Here are some of our aspirations:

1. to introduce you to a wide range of competitive (interactive) decision problems

2. to have you play roles in simplified games and to get you to take these roles seriously
3. to get you to think *actively* rather than passively about such interactive problems
4. to let you see how other people play and think, and thereby help you to learn how you can play your role better
5. to show you how simple analysis can help
6. to lead you to "discover" for yourself concepts that are scattered in the literature
7. to try to glean heuristic insights into real-world problems from experiences with simplified, abstract problems
8. to critique the simplified games played in order to understand where they fall short of reality, and to help design other games that can capture "essences of reality" that have been omitted
9. to get you to experience moral dilemmas relating to questions of ethics, fairness, and honesty.

Here are the steps we would like to follow in this course:

1. We'll start off with some cases of real, interactive decision problems that set the stage for abstractions.

2. We'll discuss the strategic essence of such cases and abstract out this essence in the form of a metaphorical or allegorical game.

3. Each student will be assigned a particular role to play in each of these allegorical games, and the games will be played outside class. Students will be required to complete forms about what happened during each game and to provide information about their analysis of the game.

4. The results of these games will be collected and a statistical analysis will be reported to the class so that each student can see how well he or she fared as *compared with other students playing a similar role.*

5. We'll discuss the lines of reasoning that worked well and those that didn't work well, "discovering" in the process principles and concepts that seem appropriate to guide reasonable behavior. We'll examine the analyses that were done and discuss what should have been done.

6. We'll look at the linkages between the abstract game and the real case. What heuristic insights into the real case can we glean from the abstract game results?

7. Collectively, we'll critique the game analyses and design variations on the theme of the abstract game to arrive at one game

that may be better suited to give real-world insights, or that can be better exploited to test hypotheses about descriptive behavior.

These seven steps cannot always be repeated twenty or thirty times during a semester's course. Often we'll plunge directly into an abstract game—especially where linkages to the real-world problems are pretty obvious. Sometimes we will short-circuit other steps because of a lack of appropriate teaching materials. But mostly our constraint will be *time*. We could, of course, concentrate on fewer situations, but the sweep of different cases is of critical importance and, in this case, breadth contributes to depth.

Scoring the Games

In past versions of this course, the games were not scored and did not contribute to final grades. Students who took these earlier versions of the course suggested, in anonymous questionnaires, that a game-index score be maintained for each student and that each student's final grades be *partially* based on this score. This was done in the fall of 1977, when one-fourth of each student's final grade was based on his or her game-index score. Again, on the basis of anonymous questionnaires the students suggested increasing the importance of the game scores, and in the fall of 1978 the game contribution was increased to one-third. Although many students suggested that this fraction be further increased—indeed, some suggested that we rely on it exclusively—the fraction will remain at one-third.

For the purposes of scoring, there are two types of situations that need to be explained: games in which you play against one or two specified other players, and games in which you play against every player in the class.

Games against specified players. As a prototypical situation of this class of games, let us suppose that you represent labor and have to negotiate a contract with management. Your management partner is Mr. Henry Doe. You and Henry are each given general instructions and confidential instructions "for that player's eyes only." You and Henry then get together to negotiate a contract which is scored by each of you (according to well-specified instructions). Let us suppose that the contract is scored 710 points for you,

36 points for Henry. The game is not strictly competitive (since both labor and management evaluate issues differently and both would rather not have a prolonged strike) and the initial power conditions may be very asymmetric. Hence, it would be meaningless to compare the number 710 with the number 36 to determine who did better. But there are (say) 50 other labor-management pairs playing the same game, each with identical initial conditions, and you can compare your score of 710 with the scores of the other 49 labor players. Let's suppose, then, that the mean of these 50 labor scores is 680 with a standard deviation (a standard measure of spread) of 40. Hence your score is 0.75 of a standard deviation about the mean score: $(710 - 680)/40 = 0.75$. This becomes your standardized score (or z-score) for this game. Now suppose that the mean of the 50 management scores is 34 with a standard deviation of 5, so that Henry gets a z-score of $(36 - 34)/5$ or 0.4. Notice that both you and Henry scored higher than the mean—perhaps you both did well because you worked out a jointly desirable contract. What is recorded for you on this game is the score of 0.75, which is only in part a measure of your own skills: it also depended on Henry, and, as we shall see later, on luck.

During the course your specified partners will change, so that the effects of other persons toward your score will somewhat average out, as will the effects of luck. But these extraneous effects will not average out completely. Hence, you may end up with a final score (averaged over all games) that may not completely and exclusively reflect your "intrinsic" abilities. This is a weakness in the grading scheme—but that's not unusual with grading schemes.

This grading procedure, which looks at how well you have done vis-à-vis others in similar circumstances, is not unlike scoring systems used in duplicate bridge.

Games against all others. There are some simple games that are so highly stylized that you do not need to interact directly with any other player: you could, instead, write down a complete strategy of how you would play that game. Consider a two-person game, in which A plays against B. Suppose that the class is divided into A-players and B-players (50 each) and you, as an A-player, write down a complete strategy of how you would play. Now your strategy will be pitted against each of the 50 B-strategies. Suppose that against the first B-player you get a score of 73, against the second a score of

61, and so on up to the fiftieth player, against whom you score 81. You would then average these 50 scores (73, 61, . . . , 81), and let's say the average is 67. What you are trying to do as an A-player is to maximize this average. This average is meaningless in itself, but it can be compared with all the average scores of the other A-players. Let's say that the average (over all class members) of these average scores is 73 with a standard deviation of 4. In this case, you would be 1.5 standard deviations below the mean, and your z-score would be -1.5: that is, $(67 - 73)/4 = -1.5$.

In some cases you might be asked to play A's role and B's role. In this case, as an A-player you would be pitted against 100 other B-players (including yourself, or we could eliminate having you play against yourself), and as a B-player you would be pitted against 100 A-players.

For each game you will be given a standardized score (z-score). Roughly, your overall game-index score will be the sum of these individual z-scores, restandardized into one overall cumulative z-score. This description is rough because we allow each student to delete one individual game score from his or her total; it seems fair to delete one devastatingly poor game score which could significantly influence the total.

Code of Honor and Ethics

It's easy to cheat. You could, for example, get advice about how to play a given game from a former student of the course. You could, before you "officially" play, find out how other students played in a given game. You could deviate from the specified rules-of-play and collude with your opponent when that is prohibited by the rules. Some of this behavior may occur, but *not very often!* Such behavior is especially inappropriate in a course like this because it would be unfair to others and spoils the fun and excitement for all.

There will be times when you don't know whether a given tactic is ethically appropriate. In such cases, think about the context from which the game was abstracted. How do you think others would behave in a similar situation? What are the norms in that setting? Do you want to behave that way?

One of the aims of this course is to force you to struggle with ethical choice situations: What is it that you should be trying to accomplish or to maximize or to optimize? In general, your aim is not to try to do "better" than the player you are playing with ("better" is often meaningless in games that are not strictly competitive and in which you and your adversary start in very asymmetric conditions); your aim is also not to maximize your probability of winning—even if winning makes sense in a given game. Your concern is with the size of your possible payoffs *and* the probabilities of achieving these. The best practical advice then is: *try to maximize your expected payoff*, which is the sum of all payoffs multiplied by probabilities. Your best bet is not to be risk-averse or risk-prone—just try to maximize your expected payoffs of the raw scores. Don't worry about how these will be converted to z-scores and how these z-scores will form an overall game-index score, and don't worry about how this will be combined with a final exam to get a final grade in the course. That sort of thinking will be nonproductive.

In some games you may be in a position to considerably raise the score of the person you are playing with (not against), and at the same time raise your raw score just a bit. That's a fine thing to do— especially since it's your score that will be pitted against all others in similar circumstances. But how about if you can improve the other person's score without changing your own? Well, that depends on how you feel about that other person. During the play of the game, that other player might have helped you or behaved reasonably and you may wish to "reward" him or her. However, the situation could be just the opposite and your altruism could change to aggressive malevolence. On the whole, you will find that you will do better, and be happier with yourself, if you empathize with your contending player. Sometimes, you may even purposely choose an action that will result in a lower score for yourself and a higher score for the other player because your choice involves an ethical issue. Will this ethically appropriate action be reciprocated? Maybe yes; but if not, is hope of reciprocation the sole reason to help others?

A word of caution: some of your adversaries may believe that the competitive capitalist system works especially well when each actor works in his or her own exclusive interest—within legal constraints, of course. So don't expect in this classroom situation that all your colleagues will think alike: be wary. This does not mean that you should act in ways that you think are competitively inappropriate just because others are doing it. In summary, your aim is to maximize your own expected score—but tempered with your concern to do what's right as you interpret it.

II

Two Parties, One Issue

Two-party bargaining can be divided into two types: distributive and integrative (the latter will be examined in Part III). In the distributive case one single issue, such as money, is under contention and the parties have almost strictly opposing interests on that issue: the more you get, the less the other party gets, and—with some exceptions and provisos—you want as much as you can get. Of course, if you are too greedy or if your adversary is too greedy, or if you both are too greedy, you will both fail to come to an agreement that would mean profits for both of you (that is why I speak of "almost" strictly opposing interests). Benjamin Franklin aptly summed it up: "Trades would not take place unless it were advantageous to the parties concerned. Of course, it is better to strike as good a bargain as one's bargaining position permits. The worst outcome is when, by overreaching greed, no bargain is struck, and a trade that could have been advantageous to both parties does not come off at all."

Two disputants bargain over a price; one wants the price to be high, whereas the other wants it low. One wants to maximize the agreed-upon price, the other to minimize it. Usually the maximizer can be viewed as a seller and the minimizer as a buyer. This interpretation is extremely narrow: the ex-wife who is arguing over alimony in a divorce case does not want to view herself as a seller, and the plaintiff who is suing a negligent party doesn't think of himself as a seller. But still, for the most part, you will not go too far astray if you think of the prototypical problem in Part II as the problem of a seller and a buyer haggling over a single price.

Sometimes the single commodity in contention may be something like time instead of money. The contractor wants more time, the "contractee" less time. A bride-to-be, for instance, may want the proposed marriage to take place in June, so she says April; her fiancé starts the bidding in August and they settle for June. Or the disputed commodity may be a particular amount of effort or attention, or the number of days of someone's vacation, or the percentage of a harvest, and so on. The important thing to remember is that in distributive bargaining only one issue is being negotiated.

We will begin with a very special case, whose strategic elements will reappear in more complicated variations. There are two negotiators, each monolithic; they are engaged in a one-time bargaining situation with no anticipated repetitions with each other; they come to the bargaining table with no former "favors" they have to repay, and this bargain is not linked with others that they are worrying about; there is a single issue (money) under contention; they can break off negotiations and not arrive at an agreement; neither party must get a proposed contract ratified by others; breaking off negotiations is their only threat; there is no formal time constraint (such as a strike deadline); agreements made are legally binding; negotiations are private; and each expects the other to be "appropriately honorable." Finally, the parties do not use the services of an intervenor.

Later we will relax some of these assumptions, but will keep to two negotiating parties and one issue. Obviously we won't be able to cover systematically all possible relaxations of assumptions, although it would no doubt be possible to obtain interesting realistic examples of most of those variations. In addition, we'll examine one aspect of arbitration (final-offer arbitration) and look at the various ways in which an intervenor could become involved.

3

Elmtree House

The following case study is mostly make-believe; one might speak of it as an "armchair" case. It involves a colleague of mine—I'll call him Steve—who, as a professor of business, was quite knowledgeable about finance but not a practitioner of the art and science of negotiation.

Steve was on the governing board of Elmtree House, a halfway house for young men and women ages eighteen to twenty-five who needed the support of a sympathetic group and professional guidance to ease their transition from mental institutions back to society. Many of the residents had had nervous breakdowns, or were borderline schizophrenics, or were recovering from unfortunate experiences with drugs. Located on the outskirts of Boston in the industrial city of Somerville, Elmtree House accommodated about twenty residents. The neighborhood was in a transition stage; some said that it would deteriorate further, others that it was on the way up. In any case, it did not provide an ideal recuperative setting because of its agitated atmosphere. Although the house was small and quite run down, the lot itself was extensive, consisting of a full acre of ground. Its once-magnificent stand of elm trees had succumbed to disease.

The governing board, through a subcommittee, had once investigated the possibility of moving Elmtree from Somerville to a quieter, semiresidential community. Other suitable houses were located in the nearby cities of Brookline, Medford, and Allston, but the financial aspects were prohibitive and the idea of moving was reluctantly dropped.

Some months later, a Mr. Wilson approached Elmtree's director, Mrs. Peters, who lived in the house with her husband and child. Wilson indicated that his firm, a combined architectural and developmental contractor, might be interested in buying the Elmtree

35

property. This was out of the blue. No public announcement had ever been made that Elmtree House was interested in a move. Mrs. Peters responded that the thought had never occurred to her, but that if the price were right, the governing board might just consider it. Wilson gave Mrs. Peters his card and said that he would like to pursue the topic further if there were a chance for a deal.

The governing board asked Steve to follow up on this promising lead. The other board members were prominent individuals in clinical psychology, medicine, vocational guidance, and the clergy; none besides Steve had any feeling for business negotiations of this kind, and since they fully trusted Steve, they essentially gave him carte blanche to negotiate. Of course, no legal transaction could be consummated without the board's formal approval.[1]

Steve sought my advice on how he should approach Mr. Wilson, and we decided that an informal phone call was in order. Steve accepted an invitation to discuss possibilities over cocktails at a nearby hotel. He decided not to talk about any money matters at that first meeting—just to sound out Wilson and find out what he might have in mind. He insisted, I think rightly, in paying his own bill. I assured him that he also did rightly in not even hinting to Wilson that the governing board was looking for other locations.

Based on that first meeting, as well as on some probing into Wilson's business affiliations, Steve ascertained that Wilson was a legitimate businessman of decent reputation. Steve thought that Wilson's company wanted the Elmtree property as a possible site for a condominium. Wilson wished to talk money matters right away, but Steve needed a couple of weeks to prepare for negotiations. He used the excuse that he needed the approval of the governing board before he could proceed to serious negotiations.[2]

During the next twelve days, Steve did a number of things. First,

1. When telling this story in class, I stop at this point and ask the students what advice they would give Steve; I then tell them what he actually did. I repeat this at critical junctures throughout the case study.
2. Queries for students: Are such strategic misrepresentations of the truth an acceptable mode of behavior? Given that Steve has two weeks to prepare (about fifteen working hours), what should he do?
Students are surprisingly tough in their responses to this case study. They generally suggest that Steve invent all sorts of stories because such misrepresentations would seem to be in the interests of a good cause and because the students identify with the housing plight of the residents of Elmtree House. I purposely chose this setting to stir these emotional feelings.

he tried to ascertain Elmtree's *reservation price* or walkaway price —that is, the minimum price that Elmtree House, the seller, could accept. The reservation price was difficult to determine, since it depended on the availability of alternative sites to relocate. Steve learned that of the other sites that had previously been located, the one in Brookline was no longer available but the other two, in Medford and in Allston, were still possibilities—for the right price. Steve talked with the owners of those sites and found out that the Medford property could be had for about $175,000 and the Allston property for about $235,000.[3]

Steve decided that Elmtree House would need at least $220,000 before a move to Medford could be undertaken and that it would need $275,000 to justify a move to Allston. These figures took into account the cost of moving, minor repairs, insurance, and a small sum for risk aversion. The Allston site (needing $275,000) was much better than the Medford site (needing $220,000), which in turn was better than the site at Elmtree. So Steve decided that his reservation price would be $220,000. He would take nothing less, and hope to get more—possibly enough more to justify the Allston alternative. This bit of research took about six hours, or a couple of evenings' work.

Meanwhile Steve's wife, Mary, contacted several realtors looking for alternate properties. There were a few nibbles, but nothing definite turned up.

What next?

Steve next investigated what Elmtree House would bring if sold on the open market. By examining the sale prices of houses in the vicinity and by talking to local realtors and real estate experts, he learned that the Elmtree property was probably worth only about $125,000. He felt that if sold without Wilson in the picture, the house would go for between $110,000 and $145,000 (with probability one-half), and it was just as likely to go below $110,000 as above $145,000. How disappointing! This took another four hours of research time.

---

3. These were not firm figures, but Steve's assessed distributions of these amounts were tightly distributed about these central values; each judgmental distribution had a standard deviation of about $15,000. This means that *roughly* Steve would give 2-to-1 odds that the actual selling price of the Medford property would be within $15,000 of $175,000 and 19-to-1 odds that the actual selling price would be within $30,000 of $175,000. Analogously for Allston.

What next?

What was the story from Wilson's perspective? It was difficult for us to make judgments about the buyer's *reservation price* —that is, the maximum price that Wilson would be willing to offer before he definitely would break off negotiations, not temporarily for strategic purposes, but permanently. Neither Steve nor I had any expertise in the matter. We went for advice to a number of real estate experts (some at the Harvard Business School) and we also queried two contractors in the Boston area. Our experts did not agree with one another, but they all took our question about reservation price seriously, and we were convinced that they understood our problem. A lot, we were told, depended on the intention of the developers. How high a structure would they be permitted to build on the site? Were they buying up other land as well? Steve found out that the answer to the latter question was yes. The matter turned out to be much more involved than Steve or I had imagined it would be. After ten hours of his time and five hours of my time, we decided that we were hopelessly vague about our assessment of Wilson's reservation price. Figure 1 shows Steve's assessed probability density function—all things considered—of Wilson's *RP* (reservation price). As of two days be-

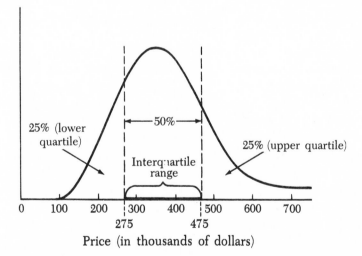

Price (in thousands of dollars)

Figure 1. Steve's probability assessment of Wilson's reservation price for Elmtree House. (Vertical scale is such that the area under the probability density function is 1.00.)

fore the start of real negotiations, Steve would have bet even money that Wilson's *RP* lay in the interval from \$250,000 (the lower quartile) to \$475,000 (the upper quartile).[4]

After all this preparation, Steve and I discussed his negotiation strategy. It had already been decided that the meeting would be at a hotel suite to which Wilson's company had access. Steve and I had no objection to this venue; the dining room of Elmtree House would have been too hectic, and his own university office inappropriate.

Feeling that he needed someone at the discussions to advise him on legal details, Steve decided to invite Harry Jones, a Boston lawyer and former member of Elmtree House's governing board. Jones agreed to participate, and Steve reserved two hours to brief him prior to the meeting.[5]

We also thought it might be a good idea for Steve to bring along Mrs. Peters. She was the person who was most knowledgeable about Elmtree House, and perhaps an appeal to Wilson's social conscience might help. It was agreed that Steve alone would talk about money matters. Mrs. Peters would be coached to talk about the important social role of halfway houses and to argue that it did not make sense for Elmtree House to move unless there would be substantial improvement in the surrounding amenities: "You know how hard it is on kids to move from one neighborhood to another. Just think how severe the effects will be on the young residents of Elmtree House." Mrs. Peters actually did have conflicting feelings about moving, and it would be easy for her to marshal arguments against a move.

What should be Steve's opening gambit? Who should start the bidding first? If Wilson insisted that Steve make the first offer, what should that be? If Wilson opened with *x* thousand dollars, what should Steve's counteroffer be? How far could this be planned in advance? Were there any obvious traps to be avoided?

Steve and I felt that our probabilistic assessment of Wilson's *RP*

---

4. One expert thought that there was a reasonable (over 25 percent) probability that Wilson would go as high as \$600,000; another thought that the chances of this were minuscule (less than 1 percent). Too bad we couldn't have had them bet with each other and taken a brokerage fee for our entrepreneurial efforts.

5. One colleague of mine suggested that bringing a lawyer to the initial negotiations might have hurt Steve's cause: it indicated too much of a desire to do business and to settle details.

was so broad that it would be easy to make a mistake by having our first offer fall below his true reservation price. But if we started with a wildly high request like $900,000—way over what we would settle for—it might sour the atmosphere.

Steve decided to try to get Wilson to move first; if that did not work and if he were forced to make the first offer, he would use the round figure of $750,000, but he would try to make that offer appear very flexible and soft. Steve thought about opening with an offer of $400,000 and holding firm for a while, but we felt there was a 40 percent chance that this amount would be below Wilson's *RP*. If Wilson moved first, Steve would not allow him to dwell on his offer but would quickly try to get away from that psychologically low anchor point by promptly retorting with a counteroffer of, say, $750,000.

I told Steve that once two offers are on the table—one for each party—the final point of agreement could reasonably be predicted to fall midway between those two extremes. So if Wilson offered $200,000 and if Steve came back with $400,000, a reasonable bet would be a settlement of $300,000—provided, of course, that that midway figure fell within the potential zone of agreement, the range between Steve's (the seller's) true *RP* and Wilson's (the buyer's) true *RP*. For starters, Steve thought that it would be nice if he could get $350,000 from Wilson, but, of course, Steve realized that his own *RP* was still $220,000.

We talked about the role of time. Should Steve be willing to walk away from the bargaining table if Wilson's most recent offer was above $220,000? I reminded Steve that there is no objective formula for this. He would be confronted with a standard decision problem under uncertainty, and his assessment of Wilson's *RP* could be better evaluated after sounding out Wilson than it could be with present information. The danger in breaking off negotiations—and a lot depends on how they're broken off—was that Wilson might have other opportunities to pursue at the same time.

As it turned out, the first round of negotiations was, in Steve's eyes, a disaster, and afterward he wasn't even sure that there would be a second round. Mrs. Peters performed admirably, but to no avail; it seemed unlikely that Wilson would raise his offer to Elmtree's reservation price. After preliminary pleasantries and some posturing, Wilson said, "Tell me the bare minimum you would accept from us, and I'll see if I can throw in something extra." Steve expected that gambit, and instead of outright misrepresentation he responded, "Why don't you tell us the very maximum that you are willing to pay, and we'll see if we can shave off a bit." Luckily, Wilson was amused at that response. He finally made his opening offer at $125,000, but first bolstered it with a lot of facts about what other property was selling for in that section of Somerville. Steve immediately responded that Elmtree House could always sell their property for more money than Wilson was offering, and that they did not have the faintest intention of moving. They would consider moving only if they could relocate in a much more tranquil environment where real estate values were high. Steve claimed that the trouble of moving could be justified only by a sale price of about $600,000, and Mrs. Peters concurred.[6] Steve chose that $600,000 figure keeping in mind that the mid-point between $150,000 and $600,000 was above his aspiration level of $350,000. Wilson retorted that prices like that were out of the question. The two sides jockeyed around a bit and decided to break off, with hints that they might each do a bit more homework.

Steve and I talked about how we should reassess our judgmental distribution of Wilson's *RP*. Steve had the definite impression that the $600,000 figure was really well above Wilson's *RP*, but I reminded him that Wilson was an expert and that if his *RP* were above $600,000 he would want to lead Steve to think otherwise. We decided to wait a week and then have Steve tell Wilson that Elmtree's board would be willing to come down to $500,000.[7]

Two days later, however, Steve received a call from Wilson, who said that his conscience was bothering him. He had had a dream about Mrs. Peters and the social good she was bringing to this world, and this had persuaded him that, even though it did not make business sense, he should increase his offer to $250,000. Steve could not contain himself and blurted out his first mistake:

6. A student of mine suggested that during negotiations, obvious modifications could have been made to the exterior of Elmtree House to give the impression that the residents indeed had no intention of moving.
7. A colleague to whom I recounted this story thought that our assessment of Wilson's *RP* should have been updated during the breaks in the negotiations by going back to the experts we had consulted initially; Steve should have been more aware of information he might have obtained from Wilson that the experts could have used to reassess Wilson's *RP*.

"Now that's more like it!" But then he regained his composure and said that he thought that he could get Elmtree's board to come down to $475,000. They agreed to meet again in a couple of days for what would hopefully be a final round of bargaining.

Following this phone conversation with Wilson, Steve told me that he had inadvertently led Wilson to believe that his $250,000 offer would suffice; but Steve also felt that his offer of $475,000 was coming close to Wilson's *RP*, because this seemed to be the only reason for Wilson's reference to a "final round of bargaining." We talked further about strategy and we revised some probabilistic assessments.

Over the next two days there was more jockeying between the two sides, and Wilson successively yielded from $250,000 to $275,000 to $290,000 and finally to a *firm last offer* of $300,000, whereas Steve went from $475,000 to $425,000 to $400,000, and then—painfully—when Wilson sat fixedly at $300,000, inched down to $350,000. Steve finally broke off by saying that he would have to contact key members of the governing board to see if he could possibly break the $350,000 barrier.

Now, $300,000 not only pierced Steve's *RP* of $220,000 (needed for the Medford move), but also would make it possible for Elmtree House to buy the more desirable Allston property. It had at that point become a question of "gravy." I asked Steve whether he thought Wilson would go over $300,000 and he responded that although it would take some face-saving maneuver, he thought Wilson could be moved up. The problem was, he felt, that if Wilson were involved in other deals and if one of these should turn out badly, Wilson might well decide to wash his hands of Elmtree.

Steve did two things next. He first asked Harry Jones to put in place all but the very final touches on a legal agreement for acquiring the Allston property. Jones reported the next day that all was in order but that it was going to cost $20,000 more than anticipated to do some necessary repair work on the house in order to meet Allston's fire standards. Still, $300,000 would meet those needs. Second, Steve worked with Mrs. Peters to find out what an extra $25,000 or $50,000 would mean to Elmtree House. Mrs. Peters said that half of any extra money should definitely go into the Financial Aid Fund for prospective residents who could not quite afford Elmtree House, and that it could also be used to purchase items on her little list of "necessary luxuries": a color television set, an upright piano, new mattresses and dishes, repair of broken furniture, a large freezer so that she could buy meat in bulk, and so on. Her "little list" became increasingly long as her enthusiasm mounted— but $10,000 to $20,000 would suffice to make a fair dent in it, and as Mrs. Peters talked she became even more excited about those fringes than about the move to Allston. She was all for holding out for $350,000.

The next day Steve called Wilson and explained to him that the members of Elmtree's board were divided about accepting $300,-000 (that was actually true). "Would it be possible for your company to yield a bit and do, for free, the equivalent of $30,000 or $40,000 worth of repair work on Elmtree's new property if our deal with you goes through? In that case, we could go with the $300,000 offer." Wilson responded that he was delighted that the board was smart enough to accept his magnanimous offer of $300,000. Steve was speechless. Wilson then explained that his company had a firm policy not to entangle itself with side deals involving free contract work. He didn't blame Steve for trying, but his suggestion was out of the question.

"Well then," Steve responded, "it would surely help us if your company could make a tax-free gift to Elmtree House of, say, $40,000, for Elmtree's Financial Aid Fund for needy residents."

"Now that's an idea! Forty grand is too high, but I'll ask our lawyers if we can contribute twenty grand."

"Twenty-five?"

"Okay—twenty-five."

It turned out that for legal reasons Wilson's company paid a straight $325,000 to Elmtree House, but Wilson had succeeded in finding a good face-saving reason for breaking his "firm last offer" of $300,000.

Lest readers think erroneously that it's always wise to bargain tough, I might suggest another perfectly plausible version of this story: Wilson might have backed out of the deal suddenly, at the time when he made his firm last offer of $300,000 and Steve demanded $350,000. An alternative venture competitive with the Elmtree deal might have turned out magnificently profitable for Wilson.

4

Analytical Models and Empirical Results

With Elmtree House as a basis, we can now simplify and abstract. Later we will begin building up the complexities.

Consider the case in which two bargainers must jointly decide on a determinate value of some continuous variable (like money) that they can mutually adjust. One bargainer wants the value to be high —the higher the better—whereas the other bargainer wants the value to be low—the lower the better. We could label these agents "high aspirer" and "low aspirer," but for our purposes "buyer" and "seller" will be sufficient, even though the context we'll be dealing with is much broader than that consisting of simple business transactions in which there is an actual seller and buyer.

To simplify matters, let's assume that each bargaining agent is monolithic: he or she does not have to convince the members of some constituency that they should ratify the agreement. Let's also assume that the bargaining agents are primarily concerned about this deal only, that linkages to similar problems over repetitive plays, or linkages to other outstanding problems, are minimal—or, better yet, are nil. Setting precedents, cashing credits for past favors, and log-rolling between problems are not appropriate concerns. Time is a more troublesome matter. We shall try at first to deemphasize the role of time, or at most to keep it only informally in mind.

The two agents come together to bargain. The setting, the language, the costumes are all irrelevancies for us. We'll assume that the bargainers are honorable people—at least according to the code of ethics of our time—and we shall also assume that contracts made are enforceable and inviolable. No neutral third-party intervenors are present to assist the bargainers. We'll also assume a single-threat environment: at most, any party can threaten only to break off negotiations and revert to the status quo before bargaining. The bargaining milieu can be classified as nonstrident.

Taking our cues from the Elmtree House illustration, we shall assume that each bargaining party has reflected on the decision problem he or she faces if no contract is made. Each has tried to determine his BATNA, or best alternative to a negotiated agreement.[1] We shall assume that by analyzing the consequences of no agreement, each bargainer establishes the threshold value that he or she needs. The seller has a reservation price, s, that represents the very minimum he will settle for; any final-contract value, x^*, that is less than s represents a situation for the seller that is worse than no agreement. If x^* is greater than s, then we can think of $x^* - s$ as the seller's surplus. The seller wants to maximize his surplus.[2] The buyer has some reservation price, b, that represents the very maximum she will settle for; any final-contract price, x^*, that is greater than b represents a situation for the buyer that is worse than no agreement. If x^* is less than b, then we can think of $b - x^*$ as the buyer's surplus[3] (see Figure 2).

If $b < s$—that is, if the maximum price the buyer will settle for is lower than the minimum price the seller will settle for—there is no possible zone of agreement. However, if $s < b$, then the *zone of agreement* (for the final contract x^*) is the interval from s to b. Suppose that the final agreement is some value x^* where x^* is between s and b; the buyer's surplus value is then $b - x^*$ and the seller's surplus value is $x^* - s$. The sum of the surplus values is $b - s$, which is independent of the intervening x^* value. In this sense, the "game"—if we think of the bargaining problem as a game—appears to be constant-sum (in surplus values). But not quite, because if $s < b$ (where a potential zone of agreement exists), the parties still might not come to an agreement—they might not agree to settle for a mutually acceptable x^* in the zone of agreement. So at most we can only think of this as a quasi-constant-sum game. To make it

1. I am indebted to Fisher and Ury (1981) for this term.
2. In the Elmtree House case, Steve's reservation price, s, was $220,000. The bargainers settled at $x^* = $325,000, so Steve, as the seller, had a surplus of $105,000.
3. In the Elmtree House case we were not privy to Wilson's reservation price. Let us suppose that it was $400,000. Then $b = $400,000 and the buyer's surplus would have been $75,000.

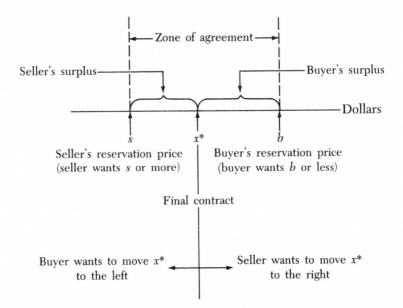

Figure 2. The geometry of distributive bargaining. (Note: If $b < s$, there is no zone of agreement.)

even more "quasi," the players generally do not know the size of the pie, $b - s$, that they have to divide.

In the abstraction we shall develop, each bargainer knows his or her reservation price, but has only probabilistic information about the other party's reservation price. Very often in practice the parties have but an imprecise feel for their own reservation price and make no formal attempt to assess a probability distribution of the other party's reservation price.

If we take the asymmetric point of view of one of the bargainers —say, the seller—the seller would be well advised before the negotiations start to ascertain s and to probabilistically assess $\tilde{b}$.[4] During the negotiation, the seller wants to periodically reassess $\tilde{b}$, at least informally; but he also wants to lead the buyer to think that $\tilde{s}$ is

4. I use the convention of a tilde to denote an uncertain quantity, or random variable. Thus, the seller knows s but assesses a distribution for $\tilde{b}$; the buyer assesses $\tilde{s}$ but knows b. In the Elmtree House case the seller, Steve, knows that $s = \$220{,}000$ and his assessment for the uncertain buyer's reservation, $\tilde{b}$, was depicted in Figure 1. Wilson, the buyer, would know b and assess $\tilde{s}$.

higher than it really is. The seller should also be aware that the buyer may be analogously motivated—that is, the buyer wants to make the seller think that b is lower than it really is. To what lengths a player might be willing to go to mislead his or her quasi-adversary (I say "quasi" since we are not discussing a strictly constant-sum game) depends on the culture. In some cultures, it is acceptable to marshal forcefully, but truthfully, all the arguments for one's own side and to avoid giving gratuitous help to the other side. In other cultures it is acceptable to exaggerate or even to bend the truth here and there—but not too much. In still other cultures a really big whopper, if accomplished with flair and humor, is something to brag about and not to hide after the fact, especially if it is successful.

A simple laboratory bargaining problem can be introduced with less than one page of confidential instructions to the seller and buyer.[5] The context is the sale of a used car, the Streaker, and the setting is dated to justify a seller's reservation price of $300 and a buyer's reservation price of $550. The instructions to each give only the vaguest of hints about the other person's *RP*. The challenge for a buyer is to get a good deal for herself, and she will be judged in terms of how well she has done in comparison to other buyers in an identical situation; the seller is judged similarly, in comparison to other sellers. This is like a duplicate bridge scoring system.

Players who put themselves in the role of one or the other of these negotiators will naturally ask a number of questions. What analyses should be done? What bargaining ploys seem to work? Should I open first with an offer? If I open first, how extreme should I be? Am I better off giving a reasonable value that would yield me a respectable surplus and remaining firm, or should I start with a more extreme value and pace my concessions with those of the other party? What is a reasonable pattern of concessions? Our data indicate that in this situation most pairs of negotiators come to an agreement.

A typical pattern of concessions is depicted in Figure 3, where s_1, b_1, s_2, b_2, and so on represent the prices successively proposed by the seller and buyer. I call this pattern "the negotiation dance." The seller might open with a value of $700 ($s_1$ in the figure); the

5. I am indebted to John Hammond for this example.

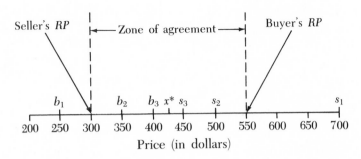

Figure 3. The negotiation dance (x^* = final-contract price).

buyer retorts with b_1 = \$250; then in succession come s_2 = \$500 (breaking the seller's RP), b_2 = \$300 (breaking the buyer's RP), s_3 = \$450, b_3 = \$400, and a final-contract price of x^* = \$425. Would x^* be higher if s_1 were \$900 instead of \$700? If so, why not make s_1 = \$2,000?

Our data yielded a number of interesting findings. First, the final contracts ranged over the entire zone of agreement, from \$300 to \$550. A sprinkling (less than 1 percent) of cases were settled out of the zone of agreement for a value less than \$300 or more than \$550; the subjects in these cases misinterpreted the directions. In some cases, but surprisingly few (around 3 percent), agreement was never achieved.

Second, the average of the final contracts was \$415 with a standard deviation of 52, indicating a surprising spread of outcomes. The average opening offer of the sellers was \$525 (standard deviation of 116); the average opening offer of the buyers was \$261 (standard deviation 112).

Third, the Boulware[6] strategy of making a reasonable opening and remaining firm works sometimes, but more often than not it antagonizes the other party, and many of the no-agreements resulted from this strategy. Advice: don't embarrass your bargaining partner by forcing him or her to make all the concessions.

Fourth, once two offers are on the table (s_1 and b_1), the best prediction of the final contract is the midpoint, $(s_1 + b_1)/2$—provided that the midpoint falls within the zone of agreement. If the mid-

6. Lemuel Boulware, former vice-president of the General Electric Company, rarely made concessions in wage negotiations; he started with what he deemed to be a fair opening offer and held firm. This is commonly referred to as Boulwarism.

point falls outside this zone, then it's hard to predict where the final contract will fall. It is not true that x^* will be near the reservation price that is closer to the midpoint. The reason is that the concessions will have to be lopsided, and it's hard to predict the consequences. Thus, if $b_1 = \$250$ and $s_1 = \$2,000$, with the midpoint being $1,125, the seller is going to be forced to make huge concessions and x^* might end up closer to $300 than to $550.

Fifth, from a linear regression analysis it appears that if the buyer's opening bid is held constant, then on the average adding $100 to the opening bid of the seller nets an increase of about $28 to the final contract. If the seller's opening bid is held constant, then on the average subtracting $100 from the opening bid of the buyer nets a decrease of about $15 from the final contract.

With one group of 70 subjects I ran a variation of the Streaker experiments with some fascinating but inconclusive results. In the variation, the instructions to the buyers were the same: as in the original experiments, they still had a reservation price of $550. But the instructions to the sellers were altered: they still had to get at least $300, but they were told not to try to get as much as possible because of the desirability of later amicable relationships with the buyers. The sellers were told that they would receive a maximum score if they could sell the car for $500 and that every dollar above $500 would detract from their score; a sale of x dollars above $500 would yield them the same satisfaction as x dollars below $500. Thus, for example, a score of $525 would be equivalent to a score of $475. Of course, the buyers were not aware of these confidential instructions to the sellers.

Surprisingly, the sellers did better playing this variation with benevolent intentions toward the buyer than they did with aggressive intentions to squeeze out as much as possible. In the variation, the average price for the car was $457 instead of $415. One reason for this might have been that in the original version, the sellers were told only to get more than $300 and they did not have any target figure. In the variation, they were told that the best achievable value was $500 and this became a target value. Indeed, the sellers' opening offers averaged higher in the variation than in the original exercise ($592 versus $525). In the variation, the sellers came down faster from high values (above $500) but they became more reluctant to reduce their prices as they pierced their $500 aspiration level, thus making it seem to the buyers that they were approaching their reservation values.

Some sellers said that they felt some qualms when they let themselves be bargained back from $600 to $500, knowing that this was the direction in which they wanted to move. Some sellers told the buyers that they thought $500 was the fair price and that they did not want to get a higher value; but the buyers they were bargaining with tended not to believe them, and these sellers on the average hurt themselves.

Analytical elaboration. It would be interesting to run some additional variations, such as the following:

1. Give the seller a specified reservation value of $300. Hint at a "fair" or "reasonable" value of $500, but suggest that getting more would be still better. Let the buyer remain with a reservation value of $550.

2. Go back to the first variation in which the seller needs $300 and wants $500, and in which getting x dollars above $500 is like getting x dollars below $500. Push the buyer's reservation value below $500—to, say, $450. It is likely that some sellers will get confused between what they absolutely need ($300) and what they aspire to ($500).

3. Make the seller's reservation value of $300 more vague. Tell the seller, for example, that if the negotiations fall through he will have to sell the car to a dealer, who will offer him one of the three equally likely values: $200, $300, or $400. Since $300 is the expected value of the alternative, it should serve as the effective reservation value for the present negotiation; but in this case the seller might bargain more aggressively for values over $300.

In distributive bargaining, successive offers by the seller are usually monotonely decreasing, whereas those by the buyer are monotonely increasing. Indeed, one of the principles of good-faith bargaining is that once a concession is made, it is not reversed. The following anecdote depicts an amusing counterexample.[7]

7. I am indebted to Philburn Ratoosh for this anecdote.

Larry M. gazed somewhat disinterestedly at a briefcase displayed in the window of a luggage store in Mexico City. The proprietor, who spoke English, approached him outside the store and said, "Are you interested in that briefcase?"

"No, I'm just window shopping," Larry replied.

"You can have it for $15. That's a good buy."

Larry had a perfectly acceptable briefcase and said that he was not interested.

"All right, you can have it for $14." Declined.

"How about $13? That's a fantastic buy." Declined.

At this point, Larry became interested. He didn't want the briefcase, but he was curious about how far the shopkeeper would lower his price. So he stayed around saying nothing.

"I'll sell it for $12. You can't get anything like this at that price in the States." Declined.

"All right, since you're obviously a tourist with a limited budget, just for you I'll give it to you for $11." Declined.

"My final offer: if you promise not to tell anybody, I'll sell it to you for $12."

"Hey, wait a second," interrupted Larry. "You just offered it to me for $11."

"Did I do that? I made a terrible mistake. I shouldn't have done that. But even a mistake must be honored, so for you and only for you I'll sell it for $11."

Larry bought the briefcase for $11.

Now let's employ the typical mathematician's device: pushing to extreme cases. It might seem that we've already reached the simplest level, but we haven't. Consider the following three special cases.

EACH PARTY KNOWS THE OTHER'S
RESERVATION PRICE

Suppose that the seller and buyer each know their own and their adversary's reservation price. If $b < s$, then there is no zone of agreement: no deal is possible and the parties know it. If $b > s$, then a zone of agreement exists and the parties have a potential gain of $b - s$ to share. Of course, they get nothing if they can't agree on a sharing rule. Instead of carrying around excess symbols, suppose that $s = \$400$, $b = \$600$, and $b - s = \$200$. How should they share that $200 surplus? The obvious focal point would be in the middle ($100 to each), and that's what happens overwhelmingly in experimental negotiations—provided that some care is taken to balance the environment.

In one interesting experiment conducted by Richard Zeckhauser, many pairs of subjects were each asked to divide $2 between themselves; no agreement meant no money. In the symmetrical version, practically all settled on the $1 focal point. In some pairs, one party was secretly prompted to hold out for $1.20 and to hold firm; as expected, the reactions of the opposing parties were also firm—they would rather take nothing than 80 cents. Would this be your preference, too, if you had to share $200 and someone demanded $120?

The subjects were next told to share $2 but they were each penalized 5 cents for every minute it took them to decide on their sharing rule. They quickly jumped to the $1 focal point. Then came an interesting variation: Party A was penalized 5 cents per minute of negotiations, whereas Party B was penalized 10 cents per minute. Clearly Party A had a strategic advantage. But what had become the natural focal point? The surprising thing is that empirically, averaging over many subjects, Party A (the stronger party) in this variation did worse—not better, as might have been expected. Once symmetry was destroyed it invited power confrontations, and the seemingly advantaged Party A ended up, on the average, worse off than he had been in the symmetric case.

There is a famous example used by game theorists: How should a rich man and a poor man agree to share $200? The rich man could argue for a $150-to-$50 split in his favor because it would grieve the poor man more to lose $50 than the rich man to lose $150. Of course, an arbitrator, keeping in mind the needs of the rich man and the poor man, might suggest the reverse apportionment. The rich man could also argue for an even split on the grounds that it would be wrong to mix business and charity: "Why should I be asked to give charity to this poor man? I would rather get my fair share of $100 and give charity to a much poorer person."

Instead of dividing up $200, let's introduce another asymmetry by having two bargainers divide up 200 poker chips; as before, no agreement means no chips to either. Suppose further that Player A can convert the chips to dollars in equal amounts—one chip equals one dollar—but that Player B is given a complicated nonlinear schedule for converting chips to dollars. Figure 4 depicts one possible case. If A gets x chips, then B can cash in the remaining $(200 - x)$ chips for an amount in dollars equivalent to the vertical distance above x from the horizontal axis to the negotiation curve. If Player A argues that the game is symmetric in chips and that each should get 100 chips, Player B would receive $45. If Player B argues that the real currency is dollars, not chips, the symmetric solution would give $58 to each: A would get 58 chips, and B would get 142 chips that are convertible to $58. This is analogous to the rich man's claiming that the real currency involved in his negotiation with the poor man should be after-tax dollars; and because he is in a higher tax bracket than the poor man, he should get more than $100 in a "symmetric" split of $200.

Another way of disturbing an apparently symmetric strategic situ-

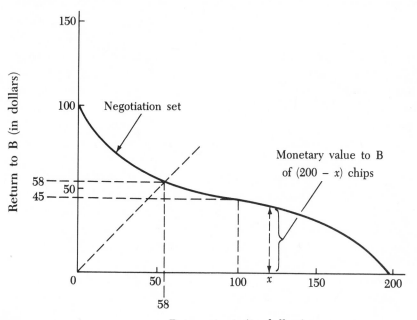

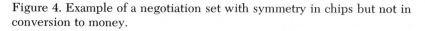

Figure 4. Example of a negotiation set with symmetry in chips but not in conversion to money.

ation is to have different numbers of people on each side of the bargaining situation. A simple case might be one in which Party A and Party B have to divide $200. No agreement means no money. But now let Party A comprise two people (A' and A") who have agreed to their share, and let B represent one person. At one focal point, $100 could go to Party A and $100 to Party B; A's $100 could then be split, $50 to A' and $50 to A". At another focal point, each of the three could get $66.66; each one, after all, has full veto power.

This compendium of possible asymmetries is far from complete, but the examples it presents are instructive: differences in initial endowments or wealth, differences in time-related costs, differences in perceived determination or aggressiveness, differences in marginal valuations (as in tax brackets), differences in needs, and differences in the number of people comprising each side. There are, of course, many others.

The notion of symmetry and focal points is often associated by bargainers with their notion of "fairness." But one person's symmetry is frequently another's asymmetry, and the discussion of what is symmetric can be divisive. Even in the extremely simple case of two-party distributive bargaining, in which each side knows the other's reservation price and in which a zone of agreement is known to exist, there is a possibility that the players might not agree to an apportionment of the potential surplus $b - s$.

ONE PARTY KNOWS THE ADVERSARY'S RESERVATION PRICE

Suppose that the buyer knows the seller's reservation price (s) as well as his own (b); the seller knows s but has only a probability distribution for b. To be less general, assume that in a laboratory situation s is set at $10 and each party knows this. Next, let b be chosen from a rectangular distribution from $0 to $30—that is, all values in the interval from $0 to $30 are equally likely.[8] Suppose that the chosen value of b is $25. How might the players negotiate?

Once the buyer shows an interest in negotiating, the seller can

---

8. This procedure is implemented in experiments by taking thirty-one blank cards; labeling them 0, 1, and so on up to 30; shuffling them; and letting the buyer choose a card at random from the deck. Once the experimenter has shown the card to the buyer, he returns it to the deck.

update his knowledge about the unknown b. He knows that b is not less than 10. The final determination will depend not only on the bargaining skills of the two contenders but on their obstinacy levels. The buyer should be able to push the seller down to a value close to $10. The buyer could act as if b were on the order of 14, rather than 25.

In these simple negotiations, in which only a single number b is unknown to the seller, the behavior of the bargainers will depend critically on whether b will become known to the seller after the negotiations are completed. In most real negotiations a reservation price is not just handed to the players: they have to analyze what their alternatives might be if there is no agreement, and uncertainties are usually involved. When inconvenience, transaction costs, and risk aversion are taken into account, it might never be possible, even after the negotiations, for one party to determine the reservation price of the other. Laboratory results depend to a crucial extent on whether true reservation prices are revealed after the termination of the bargain.

Imagine a case in which a business is acquired for a price of $7.2 million. A couple of months after the transaction is completed the seller asks the buyer, "What was the very maximum amount you would have been willing to pay for my firm?" The buyer's reservation price was $12 million, but if she reveals that high number she might make the seller feel miserable and she might tarnish her reputation. Of course, there are those who might gleefully and boastfully admit to $12 million. More likely the response of the buyer might be, "You did quite well—I might have gone up to $8 million, but I'm not sure." That's not a truthful response, but it's a kind one. The misrepresentation is not offered for the purpose of squeezing out a few extra dollars—at least not immediately—but in a self-serving way it does enhance the reputation of the buyer. The best alternative is probably a truthful but evasive answer: "Sorry, that's a number that just should not be disclosed." Of course, an analytically minded seller might then muse, "Hmm—she wouldn't use that ploy unless she'd really gotten the better of me."

Suppose that the buyer's reservation price happens to be extremely low, either by chance drawing in a laboratory setting, or in a real-world setting because of unexpected exogenous factors. If the buyer reveals this true reservation price—and it may be in her interest to do so—the seller might suspect that this is merely a ploy. The buyer might be better served if she refrained from making such truthful pronouncements, especially if her *RP* appears to be self servingly low: the buyer can actually lose credibility by being honest. In one experiment involving successive bargaining rounds with different, independent, randomly drawn reservation prices for each round, a perspicacious buyer who drew an extremely low reservation price in one round decided to make believe that his *RP* was higher than it actually was; he announced a *b'* that was *higher* than his observed *b*. He was willing to lose money in that round in order not to jeopardize his credibility for further rounds of repeated negotiations.

EACH PARTY HAS PROBABILISTIC INFORMATION ABOUT THE OTHER'S RESERVATION PRICE

The following highly structured bargaining problem might be called the *canonical case of distributive bargaining*. Those who know game theory will recognize it as a formulation based on the work of Harsanyi (1965).

A seller and a buyer each have a probability distribution, one for the seller's *RP* and one for the buyer's *RP*. Both distributions are known to both parties. A random drawing is made to establish the buyer's *RP* and is shown only to the buyer; a second random drawing is made to establish the seller's *RP* and is shown only to the seller. The seller and the buyer then negotiate, face to face, and the payoffs are the surplus values that the parties can achieve. If the random values for *b* and *s* are such that $b < s$, there is no zone of agreement; if $b > s$, there is a zone of agreement and the bargainers have to share the excess, $b - s$. They do not know before they start bargaining whether there is an excess and, if so, how large it is. Since each bargainer knows only his or her own reservation price, each has a different probability assessment of the amount of excess to be shared.

To be specific and to keep the probabilistic elements simple, let *s* be drawn from a rectangular distribution from 50 to 150 and let *b* be drawn from a rectangular distribution from 100 to 200 (see Figure 5). All values between 50 and 150 are equally likely for *s*; all values between 100 and 200 are equally likely for *b*.

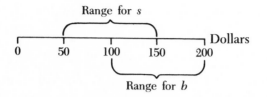

Figure 5. Distribution of reservation prices for the canonical case.

We will assume that the drawings are independent[9]—that the seller's knowledge of the outcome of s does not affect his probabilistic assessments for $\tilde{b}$, and vice versa. A particular joint drawing can be represented by a point (s, b) in the square shown in Figure 6. All points in that square are equally likely outcomes. There is a one-eighth chance that s will be greater than b and that no zone of agreement will exist; there is a seven-eighths chance that a zone of agreement *will* exist.

Subjects are assigned roles and each is given a randomly drawn *RP*. They negotiate outside any experimental setting and follow no structured rules. They can negotiate face to face or over the phone or write notes to each other. They can make up their own rules but they *cannot* show their confidential *RP*s to each other. They are given ample time to negotiate—roughly twenty-four hours, during which they may meet several times, for as little as a few minutes each meeting. They must turn in their negotiation forms at a specified time.

The number of actual agreements reached was surprisingly large. One might think that if there were a small zone of agreement—for example, if $s = 110$ and $b = 115$—the parties often would not be able to agree on a final price. Not so. It is true that the smaller the zone, the longer it may take for the parties to locate it, but they almost always come to agreements when agreements are possible. Inefficiencies occur only when there is a zone of agreement and the parties do not come to an agreement. Informal bargaining, without

9. The laboratory procedure can be implemented as follows. The seller has a deck of 101 cards labeled 50, 51, and so on to 150; one of these cards is drawn at random, shown to the seller and the experimenter, and returned to the deck. The buyer has a deck of 101 cards labeled 100, 101, and so on to 200; one of these cards is drawn at random, shown to the buyer and the experimenter, and returned to the deck. The payoffs to the buyer and seller are made in a confidential manner so that each player never knows the other's *RP*.

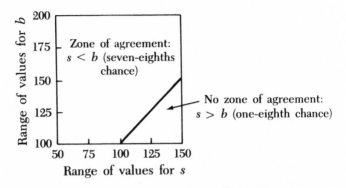

Figure 6. Joint representation of equally likely outcomes.

any imposed structure for negotiations and without tight time constraints, leads to more efficient outcomes than do most formal methods. One proposed structured alternative to informal bargaining is the procedure by which both parties reveal their reservation prices at the same time. This alternative, though appealing, does not work very well, as we will see below.

SIMULTANEOUS-REVELATION RESOLUTION

In any negotiation experiment there will usually be some bargaining pair who decide to devise rules of their own.[10] A seller says to his adversary, "Let's not waste time. My reservation price is $300. What's yours?" What a temptation to a competitive buyer! Let's assume that her reservation price is $550. Should she be honest and say so? Is the seller trying to take advantage of her? Perhaps the true reservation price of the seller is really $200. According to a commonly proposed symmetric resolution procedure, the parties simultaneously disclose their reservation prices: "I'll write down my reservation price if you'll write down yours at the same time. If we're compatible, we'll split." Let these disclosed values be s' (not necessarily the true value s) for the seller, and b' (not necessarily the true b) for the buyer. If $b' < s'$, then negotiations are broken off; of $s' < b'$, the final contract will be $x^* = (b' + s')/2$, the midpoint between b' and s'. (See Figure 7.)

---

10. This section and the following one are fairly technical and can be skipped by nonmathematically inclined readers.

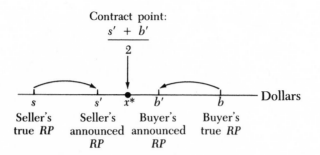

Figure 7. The simultaneous-revelation procedure. (Note: An inefficiency would result if $s' > b'$.)

When this simultaneous-revelation procedure was tried, most parties gave truthful revelations: s' equaled s, and b' equaled b. However, in some cases s' was greater than s, and b' less than b; indeed, in some of these cases, there was in fact a zone of agreement (s was less than b) but the parties did not detect it (s' was greater than b') and an inefficiency resulted.

Suppose that a seller draws a very low s value—say, 60. Should his announced value s' be 60, or a higher value such as 110? Remember that as long as the announced b' is higher than his s', the final-contract price will be midway between these announced values.

In a nonlaboratory, real-world setting a bargainer may have no way of ever ascertaining the other party's true reservation price. In an experimental setting, on the other hand, it's difficult to keep these true reservation prices secret after the fact. Is it "ethically correct" for someone to lie about his or her reservation price when the parties agree to reveal their values simultaneously?[11] Some would say that this behavior was absolutely inappropriate, but others would claim that the purpose of laboratory exercises is to provide vicarious experiences: "In real-world settings most people don't even have firm reservation prices. Besides, it's culturally acceptable to exaggerate a bit in your own favor. What's wrong with that? If my adversary did it to me, I wouldn't be angry. I do to others as I

11. In a debriefing session following one laboratory exercise, a buyer defended her behavior as follows: "My confidential reservation price, b, was 170 and my announced bid, b', was 130. I didn't think of b' as a distortion of the truth but as a strategic bid, not unlike any sealed bid for a contract."

expect others to do to me." We'll look closely at this philosophy later.

Here is a simple exercise. Suppose that the subject playing the role of seller receives a value of s drawn from the interval $50 to $150, and that the subject playing the role of buyer receives a value of b drawn from the interval $100 to $250. All values within these intervals are equally likely. What strategies can the seller devise to determine his value of s' as a function of s (for $50 < s < $150)? Figure 8 depicts three such strategies: (1) a representative strategy where, for example, the seller would say $112 if his actual *RP* were $75; (2) a strategy of truthful revelation, where $s' = s$ for all s; and (3) a strategy of truncated truthful revelation, where $s' = $100 for all $s < $100 and $s' = s$ for all $s > $100.

Each seller must submit a seller strategy and each buyer must submit a buyer strategy. Each seller is then "scored" by pitting his or her strategy against each buyer's strategy in turn; the seller's score is then his average return—averaged over all s values and over all buyer-adversaries. Buyers are scored analogously.[12]

If s and b are the actual *RP*s, and if s' and b' are the revealed values, the payoffs can be formulated as follows:

$$\text{to the seller:} \quad \begin{array}{ll} (s' + b')/2 - s & \text{if } s' < b' \\ 0 & \text{if } s' > b'; \end{array}$$

$$\text{to the buyer:} \quad \begin{array}{ll} b - (s' + b')/2 & \text{if } s' < b' \\ 0 & \text{if } s' > b'. \end{array}$$

The difference between s and s' can be said to be the amount of exaggeration (or distortion) at s. Subjects in general—even those students who helped me design the game—played it very badly: they exaggerated too much. When truthful revelation strategies, or even truncated-truthful revelation strategies (see Figure 8) are pitted against each other, the probability of getting an (s, b) pair with no zone of agreement is .125 (see Figure 6). But averaging over all subject strategy responses and over all (s, b) pairs yielded an extremely large probability, .46, that no zone of agreement (in re-

12. This game has been extensively analyzed by Chatterjee and Samuelson (1981).

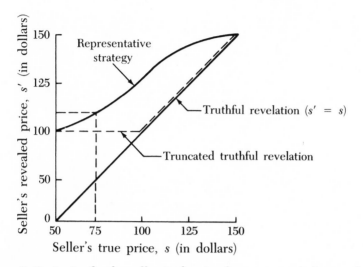

Figure 8. Strategies for the seller in the simultaneous-revelation resolution procedure.

vealed values) would exist! Thus, over one-third of simulated trials resulted in no agreement when in fact a zone of agreement did exist. Not very efficient. This happened because there was so much exaggeration—so much, in fact, that those subjects who used a truncated truthful strategy did exceptionally well comparatively. They found that a good retort against an extreme exaggeration is (truncated) truth telling. If both parties exaggerate a lot, then the chances for an agreement are very poor (see Figure 9).

Thus, although the simultaneous-revelation resolution procedure was devised to eliminate the need for haggling, it is obviously not a very good substitute.

Figures 10 and 11 depict a pair of equilibrium strategies: one for

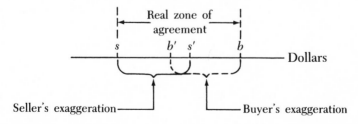

Figure 9. Case in which there is a zone of agreement in real but not in revealed values.

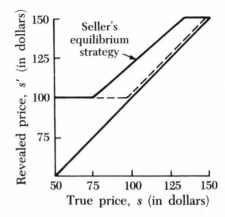

Figure 10. Seller's equilibrium strategy for the simultaneous-revelation resolution procedure.

the seller and one for the buyer. As long as one party adopts his part of the equilibrium strategy, the other would find it to his advantage to do likewise. But the equilibrium pair is not efficient, because for many (s, b) pairs where there is a zone of agreement, the revealed (s', b') pairs yield no agreement. With a pair of equilibrium strategies in contention, 38 percent of all (s, b) pairs result in no agreement. (The empirical percentage of no-agreements was 46.) Two truth tellers do better than two equilibrium strategists.

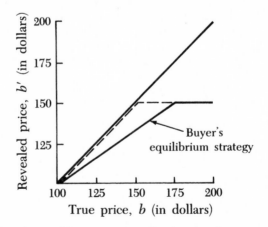

Figure 11. Buyer's equilibrium strategy for the simultaneous-revelation resolution procedure.

Analytical elaboration. What can bargainers do when they know about equilibrium strategies but do not have the analytical skills necessary to compute these equilibrium strategies, or do not have the time to devote to such intricate analyses? Let's take the vantage point of the seller. One simple analysis is to boldly hypothesize a reasonable strategy for the buyer and by trial-and-error figure out a reasonable counterresponse for selected values of s—say, for s = 60, 80, 100, 140; these can be compared with a curve for interpolated values of s by inspection. A second simple analysis seeks the best retort against a truncated truthful revelation strategy; this retort distorts the truth more than the equilibrium strategy. Next, one can seek the best retort against the best-retort-against-the-truncated-truthful-revelation-strategy; this retort distorts the truth *less* than the equilibrium strategy. It can be proved that successive iterations—that is, the best against the best-against-the-best and so on, and finally against the truncated truth—yield a sequence of strategies that converge to the equilibrium strategy, and that these strategies oscillate ever closer and closer around the equilibrium strategy. Two or three stages in that sequence already give a practical approximation of the equilibrium strategy.

The simultaneous-revelation resolution procedure is inefficient because it encourages exaggerations; but it's fast and uncomplicated. If time is at a premium or if one is engaged in many such bargaining problems, then this resolution procedure still has merit —especially if the parties can refrain from undue exaggeration.

A MODIFICATION THAT INDUCES TRUTHFULNESS

The simultaneous-revelation resolution procedure can be altered in such a way as to engender truthfulness.[13] This modified form exists in theory, but no one has yet discovered how to apply it to real-world situations; it would be wonderful if someone could.

It's important to keep in mind that the distributive bargaining

13. The material in this section is based on research done by Chatterjee (1979) and by Pratt and Zeckhauser (1979).

problem being modified is in canonical form: private reservation prices are drawn from commonly known probability distributions. Furthermore, the parties must agree to the modified payoff procedure before drawing their reservation prices. If these assumptions are violated, the modified procedure will not be strictly truth-generating, but it still will encourage less exaggeration.

Suppose that there is a seller (let's call him Jim), a buyer (Jane), and a rules manipulator (George). Imagine that George can induce Jane to make honest revelations: her declared price, b', is the same as her real price, b. How can George get Jim to be equally honest? If Jim's real price is s and if he announces s' while Jane announces b', then let Jim's payoff be $\{[(s' + b')/2] - s\}$ if $s' < b'$ and 0 otherwise (the formula given earlier), *plus* an adjusted amount that Jane will pay him that depends solely on the s' he announces (see Figure 12). Notice that the higher Jim's s' the lower the adjusted payment he will receive from Jane. Hence, with the adjustment there is less incentive for him to exaggerate as much. He will want to decrease s', and now the trick is to manipulate the adjustment function so that if Jane tells the truth by announcing $b' = b$, then Jim's best overall response is also to tell the truth—that is, to announce $s' = s$. Of course, the adjustment function may go too far: it may be so steep that Jim may want to select s' below s. The idea is to adjust it in a way that causes him to announce $s' = s$ for all s. All this assumes that Jim is trying to maximize his expected overall monetary return.

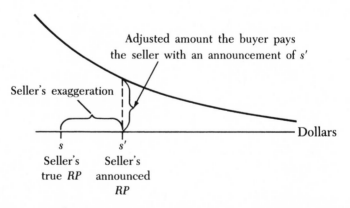

Figure 12. The extra payoff the seller receives as a function of s'

Now, assuming that Jim agrees to always announce $s' = s$, how can we determine the adjustment that Jane will have to pay him? George will induce her to pay this adjustment by reversing the roles and making Jim pay her an adjustment value that depends solely on her announced value b'; he'll manipulate her adjustment function so as to make it most profitable for her (on an expected-value basis) to announce b. Then he'll raise or lower the adjustment function so that Jim's net expected side payment (the amount he receives from Jane: a function of s', less the amount he pays to Jane, which is a function of b') is zero. Her expected net side payments also will be zero.

Can all this be done? Yes, say the experts. But in order to implement this scheme, the seller and the buyer have to agree to it before the seller knows s and b; and in order for the rules manipulator to calculate appropriate adjustment functions, he needs to know the probability distributions that underlie the drawings of s and b. Those are rather restrictive assumptions. But the result is so appealing that it should not be lightly dismissed. With suitable adjustment functions, honest revelations are in equilibrium: each party should tell the truth if the other does. Furthermore, because the equilibrium strategies for the unadjusted game are not jointly efficient, the equilibrium expected payoff from the adjusted game is higher for each than the equilibrium expected payoff of the original game.

5

Settling Out of Court

Ross (1970) asserts that 90–95 percent of all civil liabilities cases are settled out of court. Why? Is this good? Are people of moderate means being taken advantage of by heartless insurance companies? Before discussing these broad questions, let's examine a specific case study—the Sorensen Chevrolet File.[1]

THE SORENSEN CHEVROLET FILE

Mrs. Anderson, a young housewife of nineteen, picked up her automobile from the repair shop of Sorensen Chevrolet not realizing that her left front headlight was inoperative, perhaps through the negligence of Sorensen Chevrolet. On a misty, rainy evening with poor visibility, driving alone in a no-pass zone she "peeked out"— or more than "peeked out"—from behind a truck and had a frightful head-on collision. She was left permanently disfigured, disabled, and blind. Allegedly, she had been traveling at 70 miles per hour in a 50-mile-per-hour zone.

The accident occurred in October 1968, and two years later (not an unreasonable length of time) her lawyer, Mr. Miller, brought suit against Sorensen Chevrolet for $1,633,000. Sorensen Chevrolet was insured with a company we shall call Universal General Insurance (UGI), under a policy that included protection of up to $500,000 per person for bodily injury caused by faulty repairs.

The case extended over more than four years and comprised more than seven hundred pages in UGI's files. The successive steps involved in the suit illustrate what I call "the negotiation dance." In this case it's not a pas de deux, but a pas de trois with

1. Adapted from "The Sorensen Chevrolet File," prepared by John Hammond. See bibliography, under the heading "Case Studies."

66

principals: the lawyer for the plaintiff, the representative of UGI, and, in a lesser role, the lawyer for Sorensen Chevrolet. A greatly abbreviated guide to the main events of this particular negotiation dance (Hammond's own abbreviation consists of eighty-seven entries) is given in Table 1.

According to the case study, "UGI policy required a claims supervisor within thirty days after initial notification to estimate the amount for which the case would be settled, the so-called reserve. This amount was treated as the amount of loss for accounting purposes until modified or until the claim was actually settled. Regulatory authorities required that a part of UGI's assets be earmarked for settling the case. If additional information substantially altered the estimated settlement amount, reserves were to be modified accordingly. The reserve first set in the Sorensen Chevrolet case when the suit was brought was $10,000." That reserve was set aside in November 1970 (see Table 1). On March 12, 1972, Mr. Miller, the lawyer-negotiator for the plaintiff, wrote to Mr. Bidder, the lawyer-negotiator for UGI, saying: "I am aware of the fact that the Defendant, Sorensen Chevrolet, Inc., has liability coverage with the Universal General Insurance Company in the amount of only $500,000. While I think the settlement value of this case is above that $500,000 figure, I will at this time on behalf of the Plaintiff offer to settle this case for the insurance limits available (that is, $500,000), reserving the right to withdraw this offer at any time." Indeed, Miller argued in the same letter that it was "very probable that the jury would return a verdict in the approximate amount of $1,000,-000 to $1,200,000."

As one might expect, Sorensen was extremely afraid that the case would go to court and that the jury would award the plaintiff an amount greater than Sorensen's insurance would cover. Sorensen urged UGI to settle at $500,000. Moreover, they hired counsel to pressure UGI to settle out of court, threatening to sue UGI for bargaining in bad faith if the jury awarded an amount in excess of their insurance coverage. UGI was not impressed.

Let's imagine that it's now the eve of the trial and that one round of negotiations remains. What type of analyses might help each of the protagonists?

First of all, it appears that Sorensen can't do much except reiterate the position that UGI should settle out of court for an amount

TABLE 1. *The negotiation dance: the Sorensen Chevrolet File.*

Date	Event	UGI Reserve (in dollars)	UGI Offer (in dollars)	Plaintiff's demand (in dollars)
October 1968	Accident occurs			
October 1970	Suit brought against Sorensen for $1,633,000			
November 1970		10,000		
November 1970–March 1972	UGI investigates			
March 1972	Demand for out-of-court settlement; Sorensen urges UGI to accept			500,000
April 1972		50,000		
December 1972	UGI wins summary judgment that there is no legal basis for trial; plaintiff appeals			
February 1973			25,000	
September 1973				400,000
October 1973			50,000	
December 1973	Appellate Court reverses summary judgment; case to be tried by jury			
January 1974				500,000
		300,000		
February 1974		500,000		
			200,000	
March 1974			250,000	
				400,000
				350,000

TABLE 1 *continued.*

| | | UGI | | Plaintiff's |
| | | Reserve | Offer | demand |
Date	Event	(in dollars)	(in dollars)	(in dollars)
May 1974				
June 1974–	Large award in			
December 1974	similar case;			
	lawyer for			
	plaintiff loses			
	a different			
	case; lawyer			
	for plaintiff			
	preparing			
	rock-bottom			
	settlement			

less than $500,000 or else be sued for bad faith. Surprisingly, at the last moment before the scheduled trial, Sorensen actually offered to pay a modest amount ($25,000 for openers) of the out-of-court settlement figure. Thus, if UGI agreed with the plaintiff to settle for $350,000, UGI's actual cost would be $350,000 minus x, where x would be Sorensen's contribution. From Sorensen's perspective the higher the value of x, the higher the probability that UGI would agree to settle out of court. Their decision analysis would thus center on the question of how high an x Sorensen could afford. That maximum value would be Sorensen's reservation price in bargaining with UGI.

In a formal analysis, Sorensen must assess: (1) the chance of a settlement out of court without a Sorensen contribution; (2) the chance of a settlement out of court with a Sorensen contribution of x; (3) if there were no settlement out of court, the chance that the plaintiff might win a jury trial; (4) if the plaintiff were to win, the chance that the jury award might be above $500,000; and (5) if the jury award were above $500,000, the chance of winning a bargaining-in-bad-faith case against UGI and the chance of settling that case out of court for various amounts as a function of the jury award to Mrs. Anderson. All these assessments would have to be processed to yield, for each contribution x, a lottery of out-of-pocket payments by

Sorensen. From there, Sorensen could make an unaided choice of x (that is, select the best—or the least bad—lottery) or could compute an optimal choice by first assessing their utility[2] function (reflecting attitudes toward risk) for money and maximizing expected utility. They could even include, besides monetary outcomes, a secondary component of decision-regret in their description of consequences.

Such formal analyses were not done by Sorensen. Indeed, UGI rejected out of hand any contribution by Sorensen because it would adversely affect UGI's business image; from their vantage point, there was a linkage between this problem and other business affairs.

UGI's ANALYSIS

From UGI's perspective, ignoring all costs to date (up to the end of December 1974), what should their reservation price be in the last stage of pretrial negotiations? In a formal analysis, UGI would need to assess: (1) the chance that the plaintiff might win the court case; (2) if the plaintiff were to win, the probability distribution of the award; and (3) if the award were above $500,000, the uncertainties surrounding a secondary negotiation with Sorensen.

Suppose that Mr. Reilly, vice-president of UGI, assesses a .8 chance that the jury will decide in favor of the plaintiff. Conditional on that finding, let Reilly's judgmental cumulative probability distribution be as shown in Figure 13. Roughly, according to his analysis it's just as likely as not that the award (if given) will fall in the interquartile interval from $275,000 to $550,000; if it falls outside that interval, it is just as likely to be below $275,000 as above $550,-000. The judgmental median of the award (if given) is $400,000— that is, the award is just as likely to be below as above $400,000, in the event that one is made. The judgmental probability that an award will be given is .8, and, if one is given, the probability that it will be above $500,000 is .3. The mean (expected value) of Reilly's judgmental distribution is about $360,000, which includes a .2 chance of no payment at all.

Figure 14 depicts UGI's decision tree for the last stage of pretrial

2. Some authors use the term "preference" in lieu of "utility."

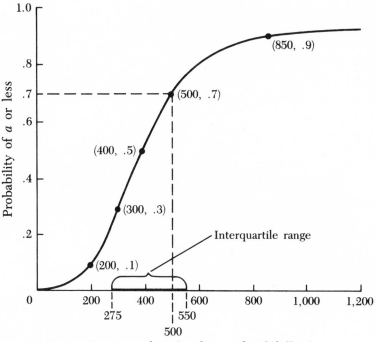

Figure 13. Reilly's judgmental cumulative distribution of the size of the award, in the event that the plaintiff wins.

negotiations. If they do not settle out of court and if they lose, the continuum of possible awards is approximated for convenience by five equally likely awards: $200,000, $300,000, $400,000, $500,000, and $850,000. We shall assume that UGI is concerned with three components: an insurance cost (award to plaintiff), a transaction cost (lawyer's fees), and a penalty for linkages to other problems. Note that if UGI fights the case and wins, this linkage penalty is negative. (Some might want to quibble with these assessments. But let's suppose that UGI has reasons for these numbers. In a more sophisticated analysis it is customary to run sensitivity studies, letting the more controversial numbers roam over plausible ranges; for brevity's sake, we're not going to do this.)

If UGI goes down the do-not-settle path, they assess a .8 chance of losing the court trial. If they lose and if the jury grants an award of $850,000, UGI will have Sorensen to contend with. This might

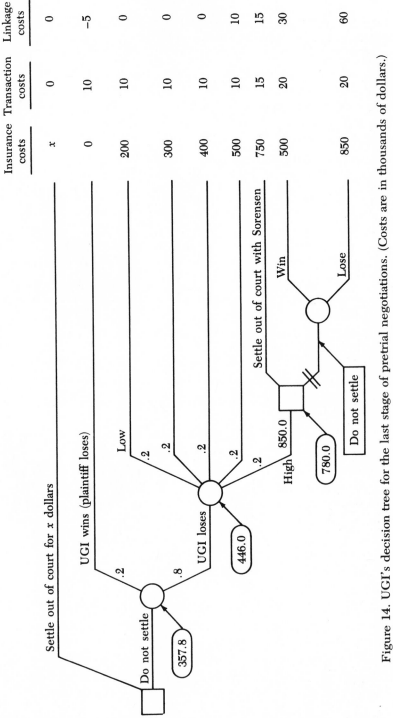

	Insurance costs	Transaction costs	Linkage costs
	x	0	0
	0	10	-5
	200	10	0
	300	10	0
	400	10	0
	500	10	10
	750	15	15
	500	20	30
	850	20	60

Figure 14. UGI's decision tree for the last stage of pretrial negotiations. (Costs are in thousands of dollars.)

prove messy, requiring transaction costs, and it would be a bad precedent for a UGI policy holder to sue them: sympathy would be on the side of the little guy. All things considered, UGI would rather settle out of court with Sorensen if the jury were to award the plaintiff over $500,000. In the decision diagram, UGI assigns a value of $780,000 to the node following an $850,000 award to the plaintiff.

If they choose not to settle and if they lose, they encounter a five-pronged chance node giving equal probabilities to payoffs of $210,000, $310,000, $410,000, $520,000, and $780,000. The expected value average of these payoffs is $446,000, and that's the value that would be assigned to the UGI node. Finally, the chance node immediately following the do-not-settle branch can be assigned a value of $357,000—or, rounded off, $360,000. Hence, UGI from this analysis should want to settle out of court for any value less than $360,000, taking into account future transaction and linkage costs. This analysis uses expected values and makes no allowances for risk aversion—as is roughly appropriate for an insurance company.

THE PLAINTIFF'S ANALYSIS

What should Mrs. Anderson's reservation price be in the last stage of pretrial negotiations? Let's suppose that she has agreed to pay her lawyer-negotiator 30 percent of what she is awarded.

The plaintiff's decision tree is depicted in Figure 15. The consequences are described in terms of the payoff to the plaintiff—she gets 70 percent of the award—and a transaction (anxiety) cost; let's assume that the cost of going to court would be an even $10,000. If the plaintiff were risk-neutral (which she is not), then an expected monetary value analysis would lead to a reservation price of about $350,000, using Reilly's probability assessments.

So we see that if both sides use the same probability assessments, and if both sides are risk-neutral, then there is a small zone of agreement: the plaintiff wants $350,000 or more, whereas the insurance company is willing to pay $360,000 or less. With the assumptions we have made (identical probabilities), it is the transaction and linkage costs on one side and the anxiety costs on the other side that create this small zone of agreement. But it would be surprising if both sides were to agree on the probability assessments.

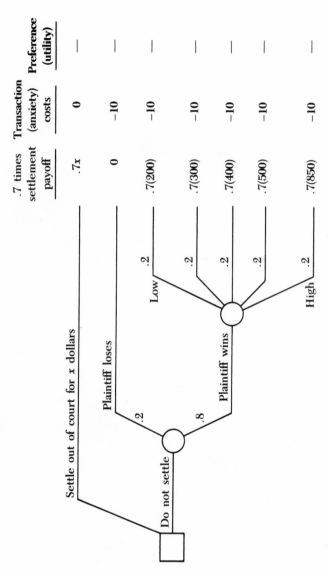

	.7 times settlement payoff	Transaction (anxiety) costs	Preference (utility)
Settle out of court for x dollars	.7x	0	—
Plaintiff loses	0	–10	—
Low .2	.7(200)	–10	—
.2	.7(300)	–10	—
.2	.7(400)	–10	—
.2	.7(500)	–10	—
High .2	.7(850)	–10	—

Figure 15. Plaintiff's decision tree for the last stage of pretrial negotiations. (Costs are in thousands of dollars.)

In experiments dealing with this case, subjects were given identical information and were then assigned roles in this last stage of pretrial negotiations. They were given identical information and were asked to assess, first, the probability that the plaintiff would win the trial, and, second, the conditional distribution of awards. The plaintiffs' median assessment that they would win their case was .75; the defendants' median assessment that the plaintiff would win was .55. And the set of conditional distributions of the size of the award (if given) as assessed by the plaintiffs was displaced to the right from the corresponding set as assessed by the defendants. *Each party tended to view its own chances in court as better than the other side viewed them.* When, as a control, some subjects were asked to assess probabilities before assigned roles were made, their median assessment fell in the middle. It has been noted in other contexts as well that subjects bias their probability assessments according to the roles they play. Furthermore, in this case the displacement was in the direction of *decreasing,* or even of eliminating, the zone of agreement when calculations were based on expected values. Even so, many civil liability cases are settled out of court. I suspect that the reasons for this are primarily risk-aversion and decision-regret, and secondarily the desire to avoid paying lawyer's fees.

Mrs. Anderson and her lawyer, Mr. Miller, probably don't realize it, but they too have an inherent conflict of interest, although the lawyer's incentive structure is designed to motivate him to get as much as possible for his client. Suppose that Mrs. Anderson has a choice between $275,000 for certain, or taking her chances with a jury. Most plaintiffs in Mrs. Anderson's position are probably far more risk-averse than their lawyers. In terms of maximization of expected utility, the plaintiff's utility curve for assets above her current financial position can be expected to be concave (for example, a subject would likely much prefer an additional $300,000 for certain than she would a fifty-fifty chance at an additional $600,000 or nothing). But as Kahneman and Tversky (1979) convincingly demonstrated, the paradigm of expected utility maximization is not a very good prediction of actual behavior: in laboratory experiments, subjects prefer a certain positive reward to an uncertain reward far in excess of what can be explained by the standard theory of expected utility maximization. Mrs. Anderson might ruminate, "How would I feel if I decided to take my chances and lost? I would be plagued with the thought that I had made a terrible error. I would feel such regret that I had been greedy and that I had turned down a *certainty* of $275,000. I would feel far worse in such a situation than I would if no compensation were ever possible. It would be far better to follow the path of certainty now and not risk embarrassing myself." This is the avoidance of anticipated decision-regret.

Risk-aversion and avoidance of decision-regret will also affect the plaintiff's lawyer—but to a considerably lesser degree. One might speculate that the reservation prices of plaintiffs in civil liability suits would tend to be lower than their lawyers', once they fully share their probabilistic beliefs of courtroom uncertainties. If we were to push back the time frame of our analysis from just before the trial to a much earlier stage in the negotiations, the discrepancy in attitudes between the plaintiff and her lawyer would be even deeper: she doubtless would suffer more continuing anxiety than would her lawyer, and she would probably have a greater need for money at an earlier rather than at a later date. This would tend to make her reservation price lower than her lawyer's. The lawyer, for his part, would have to consider the great deal of time involved in handling a court case; but this might be offset by the possible advantages to his career and reputation. Of course, all these concerns to the lawyer are irrelevant for his client, and herein lies a possible conflict.

The insurance company, on the other hand, is far less risk-averse; and insofar as there is a certainty effect such as Kahneman and Tversky describe, it goes the other way: the choice of a definite, certain *negative* amount is less appealing than a gamble with the same expected value. But one shouldn't make too much of this from the insurance company's point of view. They should think in terms of expected value[3]—but allowances should be made for transaction and linkage costs.

It would appear that plaintiffs in civil liability cases are often exploited: when 90–95 percent of cases are settled out of court, a clear bias seems to exist in favor of the big guys. Not only do they have a better "probabilistic feel" for courtroom realities, but they

3. At least the top management of the insurance company will think in terms of expected values—an agent out in the field negotiating the case might be more risk-averse. This generally occurs throughout hierarchical business firms.

can unemotionally afford to play long-run averages, and time works to their advantage. Imagine the feelings of continuing anxiety that are experienced by a plaintiff in a protracted four-year, out-of-court negotiation.

But before automatically taking the side of the risk-averse, regret-prone, overanxious victim, think of the reverse exploitation of the big guy by juries who sympathize with the victim—even if she is partially to blame. After all, doesn't everyone occasionally engage in imprudent excesses? And, the jury might reason, although the cost to an insurance company is passed on to its policy holders, the difference between an award of $500,000 and an award of $1 million is a matter of pennies to those statistically anonymous, faceless multitudes. So even if a case goes to court, it will likely end up as a balance of inequities.

What, incidentally, happened in the real case? On January 10, 1975, Mr. Miller made a last offer—a "rock-bottom" figure of $325,000. Sorensen frantically urged UGI to accept, and made an offer for a contributory payment. But UGI was adamant and prepared for trial. Although Miller claimed to have made a binding commitment that he "could not back down from," UGI learned—literally on the steps of the courthouse—that Miller had been replaced by another counsel who (undoubtedly with Miller's coaching) offered UGI a last-last offer: a rock-rock-bottom price of $300,000.

It had become a game of chicken. Who would back down at the very last second? Would they collide by going to court? UGI graciously agreed to $300,000.

6

The Role of Time

In negotiations conducted in laboratory settings, subjects show an almost uncanny ability to detect even small zones of agreement— but the smaller the zone, and the more offset it is according to their prior expectations, the longer it usually takes them to agree on a solution. As a corollary to this we can surmise that the bargainer who is willing to wait longer, to probe more patiently, to appear less eager for a settlement will be more successful.

Richard Zeckhauser once conducted a negotiation experiment in which Israeli subjects played against American subjects. He found that the Israelis did better because they were less impatient to arrive at a negotiated settlement. The Israelis even asked Zeckhauser how firm he considered the deadline that he imposed on the length of the negotiations. When 8:00 P.M. was the deadline for an all-day negotiation, a lot depended, in their minds, on whether Zeckhauser would accept a settlement executed at 8:02 P.M.

Many Americans are uncomfortable with long pauses in the give-and-take of negotiations. They feel obliged to say something, anything, to get the negotiations rolling. However, it's not what is said in negotiations that counts, but what *isn't* said. Very often the strategic essence of a negotiation exercise is merely a waiting game with self-imposed penalties (embarrassment) for delays.

It is true that during negotiations, real penalties may be incurred by one side or the other with the passage of time; but many unskillful negotiators place a dysfunctional premium on speed. Their concerns are not only anxiety-along-the-way or fear that the other side will opt out or concern that a totally unexpected event will intervene or even politeness, but rather a psychological uneasiness about wasting time. Certainly time is valuable, and sometimes one should be willing to trade money against time. But most people are far too impatient to see a deal consummated.

SEQUENTIAL SEARCH

Let's suppose that a seller has a single item to sell—say, a summer house—and that she has only a broad probabilistic assessment of what buyers would be willing to pay. She knows that she would rather not sell the house for less than $150,000, and she has a month in which to find a buyer before she has to leave for an assignment abroad. There are no realtors involved, and she advertises in the appropriate places: "Secluded summer place on beautiful pristine lake. Asking price $225,000, but not firm." She is then approached by a stream of buyers and haggles a bit with each. The first buyer starts at $120,000 but quickly goes up to $135,000, and the seller feels that *maybe* he could be induced to raise his offer to $150,000. A couple of days later a second buyer offers $160,000. Should she wait? The second buyer intimates that he's looking elsewhere and that if he's not approached soon, he may find something else in the interim. The seller gambles. A third buyer shows up and makes a tentative offer of $170,000. Already twelve of the thirty days have expired.

What are some of the uncertainties that the seller faces? First, she doesn't know how many buyers will show up.[1] Second, she doesn't know the distribution of the prices that the buyers would be willing to pay. Third, she doesn't know whether, if she passes a buyer by, she could resume negotiations with that buyer at a later stage.

In this sequential decision problem, the seller is probing the market and thereby constantly revising her beliefs about the intensity of interest of buyers and the distribution of reservation prices for buyers. Such decision models have been formalized—for example, by Zvi Livne (1979)—and dynamic programming algorithms have been devised to generate numerical solutions. If enough simplifying assumptions are made—such as a fixed number of buyers, an unambiguous determination of each buyer's reservation price, no possibilities of going back to a bypassed buyer—then analytical solutions can also be derived. These models can be thought of as

---

1. This could perhaps be modeled as a Poisson process.

generalizations of that blatantly sexist, but by now classic, "Select the Most Beautiful Woman" problem (successively renamed the "Select the Best Secretary" problem and "Select the Highest Ordinal Value" problem).[2]

In the case where a seller is faced with an uncertain number of sequential buyers, it is likely that once a buyer breaks the seller's overall reservation price (that is, the analogue of the $150,000 in our example), the seller will get impatient because by waiting she's trading in a desirable certainty for a potentially desirable uncertainty, and decision-regret looms large. In such situations most people are overcautious, in the sense that if they had time for deeper, more systematic reflection, they would probably take more chances.

THE STRIKE GAME

Although 90–95 percent of civil liability suits are settled out of court, it is the consideration of what might happen in court that determines the zone of agreement for pretrial negotiations. Most labor-management contracts are settled without the bruising penalties of a strike, but it is the possibility of a strike that often makes men and women more reasonable in prestrike negotiations. If two

---

2. Here's one version of the "Select the Most Beautiful Woman" problem. Ernest is given the task of picking the most beautiful of one hundred women. If two women are presented to him, then he can unambiguously determine who is the more beautiful, but can't say anything quantitatively about how much more beautiful. The one hundred women are to be presented to Ernest in a randomized sequential order. If he passes a woman by and does not declare her the most beautiful, then he can't go back. Suppose he passes the first by. There's already a one-in-a-hundred chance that she is the most beautiful and that Ernest has failed in his quest to find *the* most beautiful woman. There's no reward to him if he identifies the second best. The second woman now presents herself and he compares her to the first. If she is less beautiful, obviously he would not select her; but even if the second woman is more beautiful than the first, he still might want to pass her by and let her be the standard for judging the ones to come. If Ernest lets x women go by, the most beautiful of the first x will represent a level against which to judge the $(x + 1)$st. How many women should he let go by before choosing? What chance does he have of picking the most beautiful one?

The answer is that Ernest should let 38 percent go by (mathematically speaking, this proportion is the reciprocal of the magic number e) and should pick the next woman who is more beautiful than the preceding thirty-eight. If he follows this plan, his chances of selecting *the* most beautiful woman are also 38 percent (or $1/e$). This is a remarkable result. One would suspect at first that achieving as high a probability as .38 would be impossible.

This is only one of a whole genus of search problems. In the real estate version, for example, the chooser can often go back (with some probability) to a previously passed-up option, the payoff is in numerical terms, and the aim is not necessarily to get the very best offer. There is also a transaction cost for each candidate.

sophisticated bargaining parties have to decide on a wage rate, if both parties feel strongly that their side is in the right, and if neither party can walk away from the conflict, then the waiting game is helped considerably by imposing fines on delay. The strike accomplishes this.

In one experiment, subjects were asked to play the role of management or of the union in a highly structured wage negotiation. Management was instructed to hold out for a basic wage of $7.00 per hour, and the union for $8.00 per hour. Equally good arguments could be made for either figure. The issue that the negotiators had to decide was the increment x (in dollars) between 0 and 1.00 that management would pay the union. Management wanted $x = 0$ and the union wanted $x = 1.00$. The situation was asymmetric, however, because the net current value to the union (in wages, fringe benefits, and strategic bargaining position for the future) of $x = 1.00$ was $4 million. To simplify, the union payoff (in millions of dollars) for a settlement of x would be $4x$. Management, on the other hand, was confronted with a different set of realities. They had to worry about their current inventory condition, their competitive position, and so on. The cost to them (in millions of dollars) of a settlement of amount x would be $5x$. There was another asymmetry: the costs of a strike. Such costs escalate slowly at first, but each successive day incrementally costs more. (The daily cost of a strike goes up (quadratically for each side, but with different coefficients—see Table 2.) To terminate the game cleanly, the rules specified that the union could strike for at most twenty days before its treasury was exhausted. Each party was shown his own and the other party's strike costs. The union negotiator did not have to obtain ratification of the final agreement. It would have been easy to complicate the game.

The aims of each side were clearly specified: the bottom line for the union was to maximize its take of $4x$, less its strike costs; the bottom line for the management was to minimize its total costs of $5x$, *plus* its strike costs. Linkages to other problems or to similar wage contracts at a later stage were to be considered already accounted for in the payoff numbers.[3]

3. Of course, there might be times when management would welcome a strike (for example, to reduce heavy inventories) and other times when management or the union would want to strike to teach the other side a lesson for future bargaining. That was not the case in this exercise. All linkage concerns were meant to be captured in the payoffs given to the subjects. Their aims were simply to get favorable scores for themselves in the game.

TABLE 2. *The costs of a strike.*

Days of strike	Cost to each party (in dollars)	
	Management	Union
0	0	0
1	115,000	55,000
2	260,000	120,000
3	435,000	195,000
4	640,000	280,000
5	875,000	365,000
6	1,140,000	375,000
7	1,435,000	595,000
8	1,760,000	720,000
9	2,115,000	855,000
10	2,500,000	1,000,000
11	2,915,000	1,155,000
12	3,360,000	1,320,000
13	3,835,000	1,495,000
14	4,340,000	1,680,000
15	4,875,000	1,875,000
16	5,440,000	2,080,000
17	6,035,000	2,295,000
18	6,660,000	2,520,000
19	7,315,000	2,755,000
20	8,000,000	3,000,000

The subjects could negotiate in any way they desired before the strike deadline, but once the strike began, the negotiations became highly stylized. At the termination of each day of strike, after that day's penalties were imposed, each side simultaneously submitted a settlement offer. Let's denote these offers of management and the union by x_m and x_u respectively. If management's current offer x_m was less than the union's current offer of x_u, then no settlement occurred at the end of that day and the clock was moved ahead one day; if managements's offer x_m was as large as the union's offer x_u, then a settlement was reached at the midpoint $(x_m + x_u)/2$, and the game was terminated.

If, for example, the bargaining parties settled at $x = .40$ at the end of five days of strike, both parties would have fared better if they had settled at $x = .40$ after four days of strike—and still better after three days, after two days, after one day, and with no strike. Any settlement with a strike could not be jointly efficient because there were joint gains to be had with the same settlement and no strike. But with no strike it was impossible to improve the payoff for one protagonist without penalizing the other protagonist. It is in this sense that the jointly efficient set of outcomes was characterized by the simple no-strike condition. Yet despite this obvious character-ization, the subjects did strike—and frequently. Remember that each subject was "scored" not against his or her bargaining adver-sary but against how other subjects did playing a similar role.

There was a wide distribution of outcomes. About 10 percent of the subjects settled with no strike; another 10 percent settled only when the union ran out of money after twenty days; about 40 per-cent settled in one to three days, when the daily cost of the strike was still small; and the remaining 40 percent were sprinkled over the remaining days—more than three and less than twenty. The vast number of settlement values fell between .40 and .60, congre-gating around the obvious focal point of $x = .50$.

The above outcomes were obtained using subjects who were business school students. Middle managers did a bit worse, senior managers still worse, and young presidents of companies even worse than that. Here "worse" is meant in terms of average payoffs. Of course, the results may have been an artifact of the scoring sys-tem, since only with the students did the scores have a real impact, being used as a factor in determining course grades. The students wanted to do well over all the games they played and did not want to do badly in even one game. Still, it is very often the more experi-enced men and women of the world who feel adamant about their insights and thus become less flexible. One should take all this with a grain of salt.

Consider two behavioral anomalies that were exhibited in the game, the first among pairs that took the full twenty days to reach an agreement. These protagonists appeared to have different perspec-tives on the asymmetries of the situation. Each offered a position and held firm, waiting for the other to admit that he had been unrea-sonable. Or else one side was embarrassed into making what he viewed as such unduly large concessions that he became angry, going so far as to subsequently act against his own interests simply in order to get revenge upon his adversary. Meanwhile, the adversary might have felt that her behavior had been quite reasonable, given the way she viewed the asymmetries of the problem. In these cases, during the game there was a shift in the payoff functions: a new psychological component reflecting malevolent attitudes had been added to the monetary component, and this added component became dominant.

The second behavioral anomaly that occurred can be exemplified by the concession pattern shown in Table 3. After the union held fixed at the apparent focal point of .50, management slowed down its concession rate and dug in its heels at .42. There ensued a slow pattern of reciprocal concessions, culminating in an agreement after day nine of $x = .45$. Remember that the costs of the strike had been mounting daily at an increasing rate. For example, on day five, management offered .42 and the union .48. The midpoint between these numbers is .45. But the protagonists did not reach agreement until day nine; and on days seven, eight, and nine, management spent on strike costs a total of .065 + .071 + .077, or .213 in equivalent wage concessions. On day six, management should have said .45—or better yet .49. The union spent on strike costs on days seven, eight, and nine a total of .09375 in equivalent wage conces-

TABLE 3. *A concession pattern in the management-union strike game.*

	Offer made		Daily incremental cost of another day's strike, evaluated in terms of equivalent wage concessions	
Day of strike	Management	Union	Management	Union
1	.30	.60	.029	.01375
2	.35	.50	.035	.01625
3	.40	.50	.041	.01875
4	.42	.50	.047	.02125
5	.42	.48	.053	.02375
6	.43	.47	.059	.02625
7	.44	.47	.065	.02875
8	.44	.46	.071	.03125
9	.45	.45	.077	.03375

sions. On day six, the union should have said .45—or better yet .43. By grudgingly making minuscule concessions, each side incurred substantial strike expenses. Why did they do this? Because each side believed that his adversary should be the one to make the concessions. Does this happen in the real world? It certainly does.

THE ESCALATION GAME

Analysis of the strike game is complicated, because at the close of each day of the strike the parties must decide not just whether or not they should concede, but how much to concede. There is a simpler game which is equally fascinating, involving merely the decision of whether or not to concede at any particular stage. It's called the "escalation game" or the "both-pay ascending auction" (see Shubik, 1971).

For example, two bidders[4] vie for a prize that they value equally in dollar terms. To be perfectly unambiguous about it, let's say that the prize is a $10.00 bill. The bidders in ascending order cry out their bids. The top bidder wins the $10.00 and pays the auctioneer his top bid. But now comes the hook: the second-highest bidder must also pay to the auctioneer the amount of *his* highest bid. So if the first player bids $7.00 and the second bids $8.00, the first can quit and end up with a loss of $7.00 (the other side netting $2.00) or he can escalate to $9.00 with a potential of netting $1.00 and causing the other side to lose $8.00—unless, of course, the other side also escalates.

A coin is tossed to decide who will start the bidding. The designated starter can refuse to play (giving the "follower" a profit of $10.00) or he can bid $1.00. The follower can escalate to $2.00. From there on the starter escalates to odd amounts, the follower to even amounts, each in $2.00 increments. No collusion is allowed between the two bidders or else the game is trivialized: they merely agree that the starter will refuse to bid, and then they share the $10.00 equally. This may be excellent strategy in the real world, but in this case it misses the point of the game.

I once tried a $1.00 version of this (with bidding confined to

---

4. Three or more bidders can start the game—but since eventually the action will come down to just two, it saves time to start off this way.

dimes) with two Harvard Business School colleagues. The opener bid 10 cents; the follower responded hesitatingly with 20 cents; and they continued, still somewhat hesitatingly, up to 50 cents and 60 cents. There was laughter when the players realized that already I, as the auctioneer, was making money. In quick succession came 70 cents, 80 cents, 90 cents. There was a pause, and the follower said, "One dollar," with a note of finality to it. The starter then wanted to clarify a point: "Could I bid $1.10?" I said there was no reason why not.

Rather quickly the bids escalated to $1.60. Another pause for clarification. "Must we pay you with the money we have in our pockets?" I assured them, to their amusement, that I trusted them and would take a check.

The bidding resumed. At $2.50 there was another pause for clarification. "Is this for real?"

"Of course!" I answered. "Wouldn't you have taken my dollar if you had won with a bid of 30 cents?"

The bidding continued with a perceptible change of mood: the players were angry. The dollar bill had become the least of their objectives; each was now intent on winning out over the other.

When the bidding reached $3.10 I became uncomfortable and intervened, persuading them that the game had gone far enough and that I'd be satisfied with collecting $2.00 from each of them. They agreed, with a certain amount of annoyance. It wasn't that they minded losing $4.00 to me—but they were irked that I hadn't let them finish the game.[5]

Similar disturbing results, with much higher final payments, have been obtained by other experimenters. In the literature, the escalation game is sometimes called the "entrapment game" or the "sucker's game." Many subjects who agree to bid in this game know that it can be a trap—that it is often a game that is best avoided. There is, though, a psychological catch: if it makes sense for you not to play, it makes equally good sense for the other bidder not to play—so maybe, after all, you should play. And round and round this line of reasoning goes. Any rationalization you can give

5. I once played the $1.00 version of this game with some students, forgetting to tell them that the first bid had to start at 10 cents. One student smugly announced 90 cents as a starter, feeling certain that it did not make sense for the other party to escalate to $1.00. To his surprise, the movement upward was vigorous.

for yourself you can give for the other player, and maybe therefore you should have $n + 1$ thoughts.

In one laboratory version of the escalation game, students play the game not for real money but for fictitious monetary payments that get translated into real grade points. They are fully briefed beforehand about the entrapment possibilities of the game, and after some discussion they fully realize that if a follower, for example, plans at the outset to escalate up to a maximum of, say, eight dollars, then she should do it with gusto. There's no use hesitating at the six-dollar level, because this hesitation will encourage her adversary to think that she'll finally back down if he goes to seven dollars. After a little reflection, the best strategy becomes clear: bid aggressively up to a maximum cutoff value and then quit.

Subjects are then asked to think hard about the maximum cutoff values they would choose as starter and as follower. Each understands fully that his or her strategy will be pitted against every other person's strategy and that each will be scored according to the average of these payoffs. Suppose, for example, that a subject indicated he would bid, as a starter, up to a maximum of five dollars. He would win nine dollars against each adversary who, as a follower, did not bid at all; he would win seven dollars against those followers whose maximum cutoff was two dollars; he would win five dollars against those whose maximum cutoff was four dollars; and he would lose five dollars to all whose maximum cutoff was six dollars or more.

How can a player analyze what his maximum bid should be? If he knows the proportion of subjects for each of the maximum cutoff values, then he can easily compute an optimum strategy. But how can he assess such a distribution? He might want to think sequentially and conditionally. For example, he might ask himself: Of every hundred subjects who are "alive" at five dollars (that is, who have escalated to five dollars), how many would not increase their bid to seven? If he thinks that more than twenty percent of those alive at five dollars would not go to seven, then he should definitely increase his bid to six. Of those alive at seven dollars, how many would not go to nine? And so on.

In our experiments, using subjects who had not played the game before but who had been briefed about the possibilities of escalating beyond ten dollars and the reasons for it, a starter would have been wise to escalate aggressively to a maximum of thirteen dollars, and a follower to a maximum of fourteen dollars. That would have been good strategy against the empirical mix of the strategies of subjects.[6] Once the subjects had played the game and had seen the results, they realized that a lot of bidders who had used high cutoff maximums had fared well on the average. When given an opportunity to replay the game, many nonbidders became bidders and there was a tendency for cutoff maximums to escalate. At this point, it would have been wise not to bid, or to bid low. Upon repetition, the results vacillated and became more blurred.[7]

Analytical elaboration. This discussion leads naturally to an inquiry into the existence of a pair of equilibrium strategies. To make sense of this, one has to formalize the end-stage game. In the mathematical abstraction, players can simply escalate indefinitely. We could impose a random stopping rule, but let's instead look for an equilibrium pair among so-called invariant strategies. From an expected monetary valuer's perspective, if the bidding has progressed to x dollars and a player is contemplating raising his bid to $(x + 1)$ dollars, then he has already lost $(x - 1)$ dollars, assuming $x > 1$. Ignoring sunk costs (that is, those that have already been incurred), given that he is alive to raise his bid to $(x + 1)$ dollars, he might want to quit, with probability p that is constant for all $x > 1$. This is what is called an invariant strategy: after $x > 1$ a

6. A lot of people find this game confusing. How can it be wise to bid up to thirteen dollars for a ten-dollar prize? The hope, of course, is that many adversaries will quit well below ten dollars. Some will be alive in the bidding at ten or twelve dollars, but a large proportion of them will quit at those points, making it profitable for a player to stay in until thirteen dollars. Why not quit at, say, thirty-three dollars? Because there might be a few obstinate souls who will stick around after ten dollars, and even a few who will have astronomically high quitting values.

7. It would be interesting to try the following variation. Start off with a standard escalation game for ten dollars and choose some pair of bargainers who have escalated their way to high values, such as twenty-three dollars and twenty-four dollars, with the game still in progress. With no previous hint, let the experimenter propose a rules change: the even bidder is told that he can deescalate to, say, twenty-two dollars. The odd bidder, who has announced twenty-three dollars, can now quit and collect ten dollars for a net loss of thirteen dollars (the other would have to pay twenty-two dollars) or deescalate to twenty-one dollars. And so on, backward. It would still remain a both-pay auction. What would happen as they approached ten dollars? As they pierced ten dollars in their downward journey, life would become especially precarious.

player can quit at any stage, with probability p. If his adversary announces a quitting p that is greater than .20, then the player should stay in the game; if his adversary announces a quitting p that is less than .20, then he should pull out; if the announced p is equal to .20, then he could either pull out, stay in, or likewise play p = .20. The pair of strategies according to which (after the game is started) both parties quit at any bid with probability .20 can be said to be in equilibrium.

The both-pay ascending auction is an interesting variation of a regular auction—a variation that's of more than academic interest. Although subjects are fascinated with the game, they at first don't see its relevance to the real world. It takes a while to realize that the game is an accurate reflection of what may occur in arms races, for example, or in wars such as those in Vietnam, Angola, and Eritrea. Gradually, elements of the game become increasingly recognizable in real-world situations, and it can thus be used to teach—albeit in an artificial setting—some very valuable lessons.

First, if you are representing some group or constituency, it may be hard for you to explain sunk costs; once engaged in the negotiations, you may be forced to stay in longer than you want.

Second, if you are challenged to negotiate and you consistently refuse, then a lot of ripe plums will be plucked by the other side.

Third, if you decide to engage up to a certain level, do it with gusto.

Fourth, if critics on your side make it difficult to proceed with gusto, then your apparent misgivings will encourage the other side to escalate further.

Fifth, the leader who engages in an escalation game, probes the other side, and then withdraws as a loser is not to be hastily criticized. It might be a case of good (ex ante) decision with a bad (ex post) outcome.

Sixth, if you are forced to play, avoid announcing a deterministic strategy. If you announce a high cutoff maximum to impress the other side, remember the effect on your own team; if you ask permission to escalate but with a low cutoff maximum, then you're encouraging the other side to go just one step further. Maybe the best thing for you to do is to act naturally confused, somewhat unpredictable.

Last and most important, beware of escalation games—they're treacherous. Think about how you can collude to get out of them.

To tie all this back to negotiations: remember that a strike game may be a particularly vicious form of a both-pay ascending auction game.

7

Acquisitions and Mergers

Business firms often engage in distributive bargaining problems where an entire firm is the prize. An acquiring firm (the buyer) may wish to incorporate another firm (the seller) for a given price. The first part of this chapter shows how complicated even simple mergers can be. We'll look at a controlled laboratory experiment in which a group of experienced executives, all armed with identical information, differed significantly in their appraisals of what a suitable reservation price should be for the firm they were representing. Stripping away some of the rich environment of the acquisition problem, we'll then examine its conceptual essence in terms of a parable that is designed to get our thinking straight about the complexities of the real problem.

Another simulated negotiation will present a highly stylized merger problem where the issues are complex but where each side is given crisp probability assessments of future uncertainties. The problem is so concocted that there is simply no acceptable price the buying firm can pay the selling firm—that is, no zone of agreement exists. But if the negotiators could agree to embellish the types of contracts that they might employ, then they could come to a mutually acceptable agreement. In order to do this, however, they must depart from the model of simple distributive bargaining and try to negotiate a schedule of transfer payments that is tied to the unfolding of future events. These so-called contingency contracts are hard to negotiate if the parties do not share some confidential information with each other and do not try to jointly solve their common problem. Thus, the merger problem of this chapter serves as a bridge to Part III, which deals with negotiations involving several linked issues. The merger problem also provides a transition to the subject of third-party intervention: in Chapter 8 we'll look at a laboratory situation in which the negotiators seeking a merger can use the services of a mediator, who is ready to serve them but knows little of the superior confidential information they possess.

The last section of this chapter deals with salary negotiations for professional athletes. The topic may seem far removed from mergers, but from a conceptual point of view there are common strands. Indeed, parables based on mergers and on salary negotiations have striking similarities, as we shall see. A discussion of salary negotiations is also appropriate here because salaries of baseball players are often set by means of final-offer arbitration, a special form of arbitration that will be extensively discussed in Chapter 8.

HOW MUCH IS A COMPANY WORTH?

A large electronics firm, Magnus, Inc., wanted to acquire a small research-oriented firm, Associated Instruments Laboratories (AIL).[1] AIL was a publicly held company, but the stock was held mainly by a small number of academics who wanted to make money and to be fascinated while doing it. They were at the cutting edge of research but unfortunately could not exploit their talents because they lacked capital, adequate physical plant, marketing contacts, aggressive public relations, and management-for-profit know-how. The real events on which this case was based took place at the beginning of the space exploration era.

Magnus was doing well, but in the eyes of its managers not well enough. The company needed the likes of AIL to make real progress. Magnus, of course, had investigated other alternatives. It had tried at first to produce its own research talent, but to no avail; it had tried buying research talent, but had found that scientists could not be lured by money alone—at least, not by salaries within reason; it had investigated other firms like AIL, but only AIL was just right—not too large and not too small. Magnus anticipated a synergistic, superadditive relationship: the value of the coalition would exceed the sum of its parts.

For tax reasons, Magnus and AIL agreed to confine their deliberations to negotiating an exchange of stock: at the time of the merger, each unit of AIL stock would be traded in by its AIL owner for x

1. See bibliography, under the heading "Case Studies."

units of Magnus stock.[2] How large should x be? That was the point to be negotiated.

Subjects who negotiated this deal in a laboratory setting were inundated with financial information about both companies: book value, a time series of earnings per share, a time series of dividend payments (for Magnus alone, since AIL retained its earnings), a time series of stock prices, and forecasts of the next year's earnings. The stock of AIL was so thinly held that the price at the time of the negotiations—$45 per share—would have been highly volatile if there had been a bit more movement than usual in its market. Magnus' current and past earnings per share far exceeded that of AIL, but AIL's price-to-earnings ratio was an impressive 35, whereas Magnus' was a disappointing (for that time) 12.

Subjects were assigned roles as negotiators for either AIL or Magnus. In one such experiment, twenty-one AIL teams were matched with twenty-one Magnus teams, each team consisting of three subjects.[3] The participants in this case were middle-level managers in their late thirties and early forties who were on their way up the executive ladder; they were experienced, conscientious, and full of participatory spirit. All 126 subjects received the same time-series data about AIL and Magnus before they were assigned roles to play. Each team of three worked out a rough strategy for negotiations and were asked to give careful consideration to three issues.

First, they were told to think of themselves as a disinterested party, not as a partisan to either the AIL or Magnus side. What would be a *fair* exchange rate of Magnus shares for an AIL share? Second, the teams had to determine their walkaway or reservation price. What would be the minimum (maximum) number of Magnus shares for each AIL share that each team would require in any settlement? Third, what exchange rate would each team request in its opening offer?

Magnus team E, for example, required an exchange value of at

2. Unissued stock is kept in a corporation's vaults for just such purposes. Of course, if that stock is issued without proper justification, the existing stock is watered down in value.

3. I am indebted to Paul Vatter for making these data available to me. Other experimenters, including myself, have replicated this simulated exercise several times with different types of respondents; the results reported here are consistent with the total findings.

most 1.0 to come to an agreement; their fair value was assessed at 0.7 and their opening offer was 0.55. AIL team E required an exchange value of at least 1.5; they thought 1.75 was fair and their opening offer was 2.3. The E teams did not consummate an agreement. Only nine out of twenty-one negotiating engagements resulted in a merger, and the exchange rates of Magnus-for-AIL shares ranged from 0.4 to 1.3. With other groups of subjects, the exchange rates went as low as 0.3 and as high as 1.5. Quite a spread of values! When x-values are converted into monetary equivalents, the spread of x from 0.3 to 1.5 gets translated into equivalent selling prices from $3.3 million to $16.5 million.

It is always amazing to see how wide a spectrum of results can be obtained from replicating an identical negotiation with different principal actors; it makes no difference whether the subjects are inexperienced or whether they are senior executives and young presidents of business firms. That is an important lesson to be learned here.

There is an additional point that bears discussion: namely, the wide differences in the distributions of assessed fair values. The fair values as assessed by the Magnus teams centered around 0.75; those of AIL centered around 1.3. Nineteen of the twenty-one Magnus teams assessed fair values below 1.0, whereas only four AIL teams registered fair values below 1.0. Despite the explicit instructions given to the parties—to think of themselves as disinterested when recording a value for what was "fair"—the assigned role biased each team's evaluation. And it was not because they had different information; the information given to each was identical.

There was also a wide variation in the reservation prices recorded by different Magnus teams. Each team chose a reservation price of about 0.3 units above its fair-value price, and thus the wide variation in observed reservation prices among teams could have been caused by the discrepancies in their perceptions of fairness. But the causation direction could be reversed: perhaps each Magnus team decided initially on a reservation value and then subtracted about 0.3 units to obtain a fair value. An analogous situation might have held for the AIL teams.

My impression was, however, that exhorting the negotiators to try to think disinterestedly about fairness did not appreciably alter their reservation prices. Perhaps if the members of each team had been asked to discuss confidentially among themselves what they thought would be fair *before* they were assigned a negotiating role, then this modification in procedure might have yielded more accommodating behavior.

I gained another impression for which empirical support is rather shaky but which I think is important enough to warrant further investigation. It seemed that on the average, teams with several players bargained tougher than did single players. There was a tendency within teams for the members to compromise in the direction of the tougher bargaining stance. It would be interesting to see if this could be verified experimentally.

Despite all the vagueness in the interpretation of the data, one point is clear: negotiators who were given identical information arrived at widely dispersed reservation values, and this argues that in a situation where there are lots of separate deals to be negotiated with different actors, a tough bargainer who is willing to get involved in a lot of abortive negotiations can eventually do well.

In assessing fair values and reservation prices in the Magnus-AIL negotiations, the negotiators used empirical data to rationalize their assessments. Some concentrated on price-earnings ratios, others just on earnings, others on market value, others on book value. The following parable is designed to illuminate these issues.

A Parable

Scientist Anthony Ignatius Lorenzo has an idea with commercial potential. His capital assets (other than brains) are practically nil, so let's say they are nil; his earnings in the last couple of years have been negative, but let's, for simplicity, make them zero. Company M, with 100,000 shares of outstanding stock worth $10 per share, believes—and in this parable let's interpret "believes" as "knows"—that with scientist Lorenzo's idea and know-how for implementation, the value of the company's stock will zoom to $60 per share for a total valuation of $6,000,000. (Forget about Company M's historical time streams of book values, earnings, dividends, and so on.) The company without Lorenzo is worth $1 million and with Lorenzo is worth $6 million. How much should the company pay Lorenzo? First, it must be determined whether there are substitute Lorenzo-types in the wings. Suppose not. Are there any substitutes for Company M in the wings? Suppose not. Lorenzo brings a synergy of $5 million to the deal, and we have a distributive bargaining problem with a focal point of $2.5 million. But the outcome of the bargaining will depend on Lorenzo's skill as a bargainer and not as a scientist; the problem is not unlike that of the rich man and the poor man who have to share $100.

Consider a variation on the above theme. A certain Company N makes it clear that it, too, wants Lorenzo. Company N without Lorenzo is worth $2 million and with Lorenzo is worth $4 million. With Companies M and N both vying for his services, how much should Lorenzo command?

If Lorenzo puts himself up for sale in an ascending outcry auction or in a Vickrey-type sealed-bid auction (high bidder wins at second-highest price; see Vickrey, 1961), then Company M will win Lorenzo's services for a bit over $2 million. But Lorenzo can argue for more. "With Company N in the background," he might say to Company M, "I'm surely worth $1 million without you. You're also worth $1 million without me. Together we're worth $6 million. If we split that $4 million synergy evenly, it's only fair that I get the equivalent of $3 million."

Extrapolating to the Magnus-AIL case, it would be relevant to know whether AIL's stock value of $45 and its price-earnings ratio of 35 reflected the influence of AIL's potential mergers with companies *other than* Magnus or with other companies *including* Magnus. This case well illustrates how the availabilities of outside opportunities (to both parties) affect the reservation prices for negotiations.

There are other instructive variations of the parable. Suppose, for example, that Company M "believes" that it knows (but does not "know") the amount of synergy to be gained by an affiliation with Lorenzo. There are now uncertainties and different perceptions of these uncertainties. Or suppose that Company M is concerned that Lorenzo will lose interest and not contribute as much as he says he will, or even thinks he will, after the merger is consummated. How can incentives be fashioned? A lot can be gained by giving Lorenzo stock in the merged company instead of an outright cash payment. Suppose, though, that Lorenzo is relatively more risk-averse than the widely held Company M should be; in this case, perhaps a mix of some outright payment and some stock (and a mix of types of stocks) would make sense. But notice that now we are no longer talking about simple distributive bargaining. Company M could play to Lorenzo's needs and exact a price from him for fashioning a mix of incentives that is appealing to him. This is especially possible if Company M thinks differently about these matters than does Lorenzo—a situation illustrated by the following merger game.

CONVERTING A SINGLE-FACTOR TO A MULTIPLE-FACTOR CONTRACT

Mr. S is getting on in age and would like to sell his firm to an enterprising buyer, Ms. B.[4] He has examined his other opportunities (such as possible sales to other potential buyers B', B'', and so on); has analyzed the principal uncertainties he faces, his attitudes toward risk, and his preferences for cash flow streams; and has concluded that he would be willing to sell his firm to Ms. B for a minimum of $7.2 million. Any seller's surplus that would result must come from a sale price of over $7.2 million.

Ms. B, of course, does not know S's reservation price of $7.2 million; she suspects, however, that it is considerably lower than that —perhaps $5 million. B has also been busy calculating her opportunities and knows that she has the possibilities of acquiring other firms such as S', S'', and so on. She has done her private analysis, just like S did, but has used different probability assessments of future contingencies, different time discounts, and different risk-aversion factors. B feels that her private breakeven value for acquiring S's firm in light of all considerations is $6.6 million; any buyer's surplus that might result must come from a sale price of lower than $6.6 million. S does not know B's reservation price, but suspects that it is considerably higher than $6.6 million—perhaps $9 million.

S and B start to negotiate. After some genial conversation, B opens the bargaining with an offer of $3.5 million. "Oh, that's much too low," says S. "I'm looking for a buyer who will recognize that my firm is worth at least $10 million." The negotiation dance part-

4. This section is a bit more mathematical than some readers may feel comfortable with. Since getting the flavor of the arguments is more important than understanding all the details, readers should go through this at their normal rate and push on to the discussion of salary negotiations.

ners timidly approach each other, as shown in Figure 16. B leaps from 3.5 to 5.0 to 5.8 to 6.2 to 6.4 (approaching her real reservation price of 6.6); S skips from 10.0 to 8.5 to 8.0 (where he pirouettes for a while), then to 7.7 (approaching his real reservation price of 7.2). They hold out their hands to each other, but no contact is made. They don't realize that there is no zone of agreement. Each feels that the other is holding back more than is appropriate.

Finally, Mr. S suggests that they engage the services of a mediator, Ms. M; if they are more open with the mediator than they are with each other, she will at least be able to tell them whether they have some basis for agreement or whether they are wasting their time. Ms. B agrees.

Ms. M knows practically nothing to start off with. She must glean information about the case from confidential statements given to her by S and B. She would like to arrange an agreement if at all possible, because then she'll get a percentage of the payments going from one side to the other. If—and this is a big "if"—both B and S are completely honest with M, she could find out, first, that no zone of agreement can be reached by means of a straight transfer payment from S to B, but, second, that acceptable contingent contracts which exploit differences in probabilistic judgments and in the time-values of money can be devised that would be acceptable to both sides.

In particular, with full disclosure M could find out that the profitability of the merger will depend heavily on the early reactions of

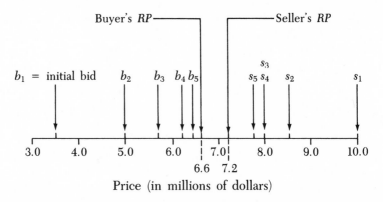

Figure 16. Negotiation dance with Mr. S and Ms. B, showing no zone of agreement.

the market to an invention recently patented by S. Assume that there are four possible reactions, or subsequent states of the world, which we can designate A, B, C, and D. The important point is that S and B assign different probabilities to these states (which are mutually exclusive and collectively exhaustive), and they also have different perceptions of the financial implications of each of these contingencies. With full disclosure M would learn that, conditional on each state prevailing, B and S have different reservation prices for the merger.

So M—or even B and S without M—could readily see the possible desirability of elaborating the usual fixed-amount contract by a contingency contract, according to which B pays S an amount x_0 now, and, depending on whether A, B, C, or D eventuates, B pays S the amount x_A or x_B or x_C or x_D after one year. (For simplicity's sake, we will assume that the resolution of these uncertainties, if a merger takes place, would occur after one year.) A representative contract might be of the form ($x_0 = 4$, $x_A = -1$, $x_B = 0$, $x_C = 5$, $x_D = 8.5$), which would be interpreted: B gives S \$4 million now; if A occurs, S gives back \$1 million a year hence; if B occurs, no further payments are made; if C occurs, S gets an additional \$5 million a year hence; if D occurs, S gets an additional \$8.5 million a year hence. In terms of this notation, a noncontingency contract is one for which $x_A = x_B = x_C = x_D = 0$.

The mediator will learn that B and S have different probability perceptions of A, B, C, and D, have different time-discounts for money, and have different risk attitudes. Each side, in addition, imposes constraints. S, for example, requires that $x_0 \geq 0$; B's board of directors demands that $x_0 + 0.85x_D \leq 11$ (in millions of dollars). With full, honest disclosure the mediator learns that the five control variables x_0, x_A, x_B, x_C, and x_D are jointly subject to constraints. For any feasible contract—that is, any contract meeting joint constraints—S and B are each confronted with a different lottery payoff and each can, in principle, compute or intuit directly a net-present-value certainty equivalent for that contingency contract. The first problem is: Can B and S, with M's help, find a suitable contingency contract such that for each principal the resulting contract is better than the no-agreement outcome? Stated equivalently: In the elaborated set of contingency contracts, is there a joint gain (that is, a gain for each) to be had? As one would suspect, the answer in this case is yes—if both parties share information without distortion. The second problem is: How should they decide which contingency contract, among those yielding joint gains, they should adopt?

When subjects performed this negotiation in an experimental setting, the domain of possible joint outcomes from all feasible contingency contracts was as shown in Figure 17. We'll assume in this case that both principals to the negotiation were risk-neutral, meaning that they used expected values. In the figure, the origin represents the comparison point—the no-contract alternative. The horizontal and vertical axes represent respectively the seller's and the buyer's expected surplus values, "surplus" as compared to the no-contract alternative. Any point below (southwest of) the boundary frontier (line $PQRT$) represents a joint evaluation (in surplus value measured in millions of net-present-value dollars) associated with a

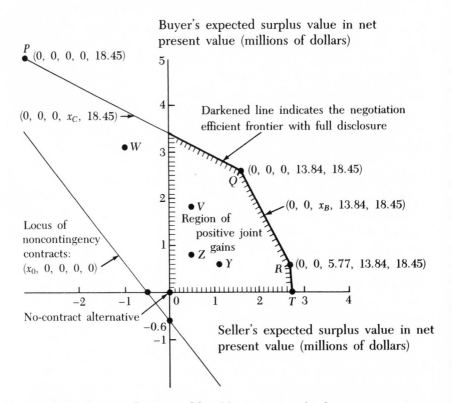

Figure 17. Joint evaluations of feasible contracts. The five components in each configuration represent $(x_0, x_A, x_B, x_C, x_D)$.

feasible contract. Any feasible joint outcome in the interior of the first quadrant (northeast of the origin) represents a contract that has been deemed superior, by each, to the no-contract alternative. A joint outcome such as V is better for each than the no-contract alternative, but V in turn is worse for each than the attainable point Q. The contract giving rise to Q (which can be shown in the numerical details of the case that are omitted here) is associated with the contract that requires payments to the seller only if states C or D occur: $13.84 million for C and $18.45 million for D—each a year hence.

Also depicted in Figure 17 is the locus of all joint payoffs associated with the noncontingency contracts. Since the reservation price of the seller is $7.2 million and the buyer's is $6.6 million, any noncontingency contract has joint surplus payoffs that sum to − $0.6 million. Part III will discuss in detail techniques for discovering feasible contracts in the northeast quadrant and will explore questions of choice within that quadrant.

It's not easy to find points in the northeast quadrant—points with positive gains for each as compared with the no-contract alternative. It requires joint problem solving with some sharing of information. There are distinct cooperative elements but also conflict elements, and care must be taken to determine how much confidential information each side might want to share.

In our experiments, subjects who had been trained in decision analysis, in financial net-present-value analysis, in mathematical programming—in short, who had the analytical competencies to find points in the northeast quadrant—often could not devise contracts with joint positive gains. In conflict situations they were just not used to sitting down with their adversary, laying their cards on the table, and engaging in joint problem solving. Even if their adversary had been willing to do this, would they have trusted him to tell the truth?

Other teams of subjects found points (such as V, Y, Z) in the region with positive joint gains, but still ended up far from the efficient frontier. The aim of each player was not necessarily to achieve an outcome on the frontier; for example, a buyer would have preferred outcome V to R (abstracting away altruistic motivations), even though R could be said to be jointly efficient but V could not. Both could do better than V, but both could not do better than R.

Intuitively, one should be able to see why differences can be exploited to yield positive joint gains: the bigger the differences, the greater the potential for exploitation in the negotiation setting. Suppose, for example, that the seller thinks outcome A is much less likely than outcome D, and suppose that the buyer thinks the opposite. The buyer can agree to give the seller a good deal if D occurs, and as a quid pro quo the buyer can demand and expect to get a compensating gesture if A occurs. For example, in the Law of the Sea negotiations (which we'll discuss extensively in Part IV), multinational mining companies might heavily discount the future, whereas negotiators for developing countries might not be so sensitive to the timing of cost flows; perhaps sharing arrangements could be temporally shifted to the advantage of the former without penalizing the latter, and in recognition of this concession a reciprocal gesture could be sought. Similarly with risk aversion and risk sharing. Indeed, skilled negotiators should seek out differences to exploit. The bigger the differences, the broader the area achievable in the northeast quadrant.

When this negotiation was tried in an experimental setting without a mediator, very few negotiating pairs achieved a contract with positive joint gains. In a subsequent version a mediator was assigned to each buyer/seller pair, but the principal negotiators were not required to use the mediator's services. Only few did. Most felt that the mediator knew nothing of the details, so they saw no advantage in complicating their problem with the inclusion of a third party; believing that their negotiating adversaries would not give truthful information to the mediator, they saw no reason why they themselves should. Those who used the mediator did "better" (in a nonobvious joint sense), but they were surprised to find out that they had done better—after all, everything they had done with the mediator they could have done without the mediator, or so they thought. Mediators who were used felt obliged to be of service, and often initiated an attempt at joint analysis. Some negotiators used the mediator and deftly and strategically misrepresented the truth to their advantage; others did the same, but to their disadvantage.

From this discussion it can be seen that frequently the parties to a negotiation can do better by elaborating the problem and converting a single-factor negotiating problem into a multiple-factor problem. Often the motivation to do so is the fact that without this type of elaboration no agreement can be reached, and the bargaining principals may feel uncomfortable about not reaching an agreement. Equally important—but much less widely recognized—are the cases where agreement on a single factor can be achieved but where further positive joint gains can be realized by an elaboration of the contracts to be contemplated. In Figure 17, for example, suppose that—keeping all else the same—the locus (line) of noncontingency contracts is displaced northeasterly so that it slightly intersects the northeast quadrant. If the principals were to find this jointly acceptable contract—barely acceptable for each—they then might not imaginatively seek out elaborations that might yield still further positive joint gains.

SALARY NEGOTIATIONS IN PROFESSIONAL SPORTS

Not long ago, average salaries for professional baseball players were roughly the same as those for football players.[5] But in 1976 baseball salaries zoomed ahead and subsequently increased to nearly double those of football players. It was not shrewd bargaining but a shift in the *rules* of bargaining that caused this change.

Curt Flood, a $90,000-a-year outfielder for the St. Louis Cardinals, was traded to the Phillies in the winter of 1969. He balked at the trade, filed an antitrust suit, and sat out the 1970 season. In effect, Flood's suit against baseball's "reserve clause"—which bound a player to a team for the entirety of his career—was the first official legal blow delivered in behalf of unrestricted player mobility. The suit was decided in favor of the baseball establishment. It was, however, the last such victory in a major court decision for management in any sport.

Several years later, at the end of an impressive season, Andy Messersmith of the Los Angeles Dodgers requested that his salary be raised from $90,000 to $150,000. Dodger management countered with a take-it-or-leave-it offer of $100,000: "Take the modest increase and forget the no-trade clause, or you'll find yourself playing for another team." Undaunted, Messersmith decided to play the year without signing a new contract. At issue was Paragraph 10a of the uniform player's contract—the so-called renewal clause, which

5. This section was written with the assistance of Andrew Gross.

gave a team the right to renew a player's contract forever without his consent. Messersmith firmly believed that once a player had completed his optional year, he was a free agent. In 1975 the case went to an arbitration panel, with Peter Seitz as impartial chairman. Seitz ruled in favor of Messersmith, a federal court upheld the decision, and the rest, as they say, is history. The Player-Owner Basic Agreement of 1976, arrived at after months of haggling, did little to either clarify or circumscribe the limitations of player mobility. Players could move freely, selling their services to the highest bidder with minimal or nonexistent compensation rules. The only "binding" rule was that players must have six years' experience before declaring free agency. Owners were quick to point out that this arrangement was "experimental."

The most salient contrasts between baseball management and football management revolve around the issues of player mobility, free-agent compensation, and the respective effects of these two factors upon salary structure.

The Andy Messersmith decision of 1975 and the 1977–1980 free-agent drafts were the watersheds. Average baseball salaries, before the first free-agent draft, were estimated to be $52,000; four years later, the average salary for a major-league baseball player was $130,000.

There has been no such explosion of salaries in professional football, for reasons that relate most specifically to the economics of the National Football League (NFL). Pro football operates on a quasi-socialist model: teams share television revenues equally, home teams collect a 60 percent share of gate receipts (in contrast to 80 percent for baseball), and—perhaps most significantly—player movement is strictly controlled by a set of fixed compensation rules. Given fixed profits and sold-out stadiums, there is little motive to chase free agents and lure them with astronomical salaries.

A Parable

Anthony Ignatius Lorenzo is a fabulous athlete who is in demand by two teams, the Ayes and the Bees. To keep matters simple, let's assume that Lorenzo's sport and the position he plays are such that his career lasts only one year.[6] The Ayes and Bees bid for his services. In

---

6. This will avoid having to become embroiled in the dynamics of trading within a period and between periods.

an open ascending auction, the Ayes would bid, if they needed to, up to a maximum of $500,000; the Bees would bid up to a maximum of $900,000. In this situation if Lorenzo could play one team against the other, or if the open ascending auction for Lorenzo were implemented, then he would end up with the Bees with a salary of a little over $500,000.

First wrinkle: the Ayes and the Bees have a binding agreement that gives the Ayes exclusive rights to Lorenzo. These rights, for example, might resemble those of the NFL draft: a losing team in one season gets a preferred draft choice in the subsequent season. The Ayes now offer Lorenzo $100,000 and he signs the contract.[7] Because the Ayes' maximum price was $500,000, they now enjoy a surplus value (or "rent") of $400,000. But before the season starts, the rules allow for trades. The Ayes could trade Lorenzo to the Bees for a price, and this will probably happen. The two teams must engage in a distributive bargaining game where the Ayes have a reservation price of $400,000 (perhaps unknown to the Bees) and the Bees have a reservation price of $800,000 (perhaps unknown to the Ayes). Lorenzo is an ineffective participant in this bargaining —his salary has been set at $100,000. The Ayes are the sellers and want a high value for Lorenzo; the Bees are the buyers. Since there is a wide zone of agreement, Lorenzo will probably end up with the Bees, and the Ayes might get, say, $600,000.

Second wrinkle: the Ayes get modified rights to Lorenzo, meaning that Lorenzo has some power. After being offered a contract with the Ayes, he can try to get more from the Bees; the Bees in this case not only have to pay him, but must *compensate* the Ayes as well.[8] To keep the case simple, let's assume that the Bees must pay as compensation to the Ayes a certain multiple of the salary stipulated in Lorenzo's new contract with them, and to be specific let's

7. If they had offered Lorenzo $50,000, he would have refused and gone to business school or law school instead.
8. In baseball (as of 1980) a player is virtually bonded to a team for six years and then is practically free to move, since compensation requirements are minimal. A football player can, in principle, move after one or two years (depending on the situation) but the compensation regulations (the so-called Rozelle Rule) are so stringent that there is very little player mobility. Even without knowing much about the financial details, with a bit of standard economic theory and common sense one would expect that the owners of football teams could command a larger share of a player's marginal contribution than would be the case with more player mobility and more effective bidding arrangements for the player's services.

make this multiple unity. So if the Bees agree to pay $300,000 to Lorenzo, they will have to pay $300,000 to the Ayes also. With this modification (similar to free agency) the Ayes cannot get away with paying Lorenzo only $100,000. It would be worth it for the Bees to give Lorenzo $200,000 (or more) and give a similar compensatory amount to the Ayes. Actually, the Bees could go up to $450,000 in their distributive bargaining problem with Lorenzo, since their original maximum was $900,000. Notice that the higher the salary the Ayes offer Lorenzo, the higher becomes Lorenzo's reservation price in his negotiations with the Bees. If the Ayes offered Lorenzo an initial contract of $450,000, there would be no zone of agreement in Lorenzo's negotiations with the Bees. Of course, the Ayes and Lorenzo may have misperceptions about the Bees' reservation price.

If the compensation multiple were even more stringent—say, if the Bees had to pay the Ayes twice what they pay Lorenzo—then Lorenzo would lose power to the Ayes. With a compensation multiple of two, the Ayes could pay Lorenzo $300,000 and then he would have no bargaining room with the Bees. Once again, of course, reservation prices may not be known.

Now suppose that the Ayes have a $200,000 contract with Lorenzo and that he gets the Bees to officially offer him a $300,000 contract, with the required matching compensatory amount going to the Ayes. The rules of negotiating behavior may now give the Ayes additional power: the right of first refusal. In this case, the Ayes might be given the opportunity to match the Bees' offer. The rules also might specify that Lorenzo cannot now, in an iterative fashion, go back to the Bees to induce them to raise their offer. Lorenzo can get only one official offer, and the Ayes then have the option to match it.

Let's say that Lorenzo has already exploited his ability to negotiate with the Bees and that his salary with the Ayes has been firmed up at $300,000. Will he remain with the Ayes? He shouldn't if his marginal value to the Bees is more than it is to the Ayes. The Bees will ask the Ayes to trade Lorenzo for a price. Since the marginal value of Lorenzo is $500,000 to the Ayes and $900,000 to the Bees, and since Lorenzo's contract is now $300,000, the distributive bargaining problem has a zone of agreement with a reservation price of $200,000 for the Ayes and $600,000 for the Bees. The Ayes, however, already turned down the compensatory offer of $300,000 when Lorenzo exercised his free-agent rights.

Whatever the rules, as long as the teams can trade, Lorenzo will probably end up with the Bees because his marginal value is greater there. I say "probably" because a bargain need not necessarily be consummated if there is a zone of agreement; one side, for example, may be too greedy or may misperceive the reservation price of the other. But even though Lorenzo will probably end up with the Bees, the amount that he will get depends critically on the compensation magnitude and on whether there is a right of first refusal.[9]

The above discussion abstracts out many essential realities. Foremost among these is the fact that in the real world, negotiations are replicated. The players change from season to season, but the teams stay fixed. It may be in the interest of the teams to enter into a tacit collusion: they agree not to squeeze each other too much or else the players will get an excessively large share of the surplus that the teams themselves could divide. It's easy, of course, for two teams to collude, but somewhat more difficult for twenty-eight—especially when some maverick team might be tempted to break away from a collusion and especially when the others are pledged to remain faithful to that collusion. That's precisely how the dissolution of loose, cartel-like agreements proceeds. Some of the teams remaining in the tacit collusion may not be able to bear the thought that a small minority is profiting at their expense, so they join the parade of defectors. All this is good for the social well-being of the ball players—but not necessarily good for all the negotiating players.

9. The observation that Lorenzo will end up with the team that values him the most, regardless of who is given property rights to him, is a particular instance of a more general result in economic theory, known as Coase's Theorem.

8

Third-Party Intervention

In Part III we'll look quite extensively at the role of third-party intervention. By deferring the discussion until then, we'll have a much richer and more complex set of negotiation problems to draw upon. The topic is important enough, however, to warrant a preliminary discussion at this point. We'll confine our attention to the limited domain of problems where there is a single continuous factor and two monolithic parties, one of which wants more and the other less of the factor to be jointly determined, and where each party is assumed to have only one threat potential: the termination of formal bargaining. In this limited domain, how can third-party intervention help? Following are a number of ways.

By bringing parties together. A mediator can identify potential bargaining pairs, match up a suitable buyer and seller, match up firms for a merger, or initiate discussion. This is essentially a brokerage function.

By establishing a constructive ambience for negotiation. This could include maintaining rules of civilized debate, acting as a neutral discussion leader, helping to set the agenda, suggesting processes for negotiations, smoothing out interpersonal conflicts, giving reticent people a chance to speak, and preparing neutral minutes.

By collecting and judiciously communicating selected confidential material. On the basis of such information, a mediator can determine whether there is a potential zone of agreement.

By helping the parties to clarify their values and to derive responsible reservation prices. This is done by analyzing with each disputant the implications of a no-contract outcome.

By deflating unreasonable claims and loosening commitments.

Mediators can thus minimize excessive posturing and aid in breaking down barriers.

By seeking joint gains. Mediators can devise new compromises and encourage bargainers to be more creative in their search for a solution. They can help negotiators elaborate a single-factor problem into an integrative negotiating problem with several negotiable factors, thereby enabling the negotiators to exploit their differences in judgments and values.

By keeping negotiations going. A mediator can provide bargainers with a face-saving means of holding the channels of communication open while they wait for a better external environment.

By articulating the rationale for agreement. A mediator can publicize the results of the negotiation in such a way as to promote implementation and acceptance.

CONVENTIONAL AND FINAL-OFFER ARBITRATION

The firemen of Podunk City are unhappy: they want more, just like everybody else (especially the policemen and sanitation workers) and they deserve more, so they feel. The city simply can't afford additional expenditures, especially for what it considers to be the outlandish demands of the firemen.

The negotiators for the firemen and for the city have settled the fringe issues, and what remains to be settled is the "basic wage rate," which indexes salaries at all levels. Both sides have made known their ostensibly reasonable demands and are now playing a waiting game. A mediator is brought in to do all he can to promote a settlement—everything from establishing a constructive ambience to helping in the search for creative solutions. He tries to lead (not dictate) both sides to discern what compromise would be to their best advantage; but in this negotiation nothing helps. The sides are adamant, and time is passing. The city cannot lay off the firemen. The firemen, by law, cannot strike.

In such public-service disputes, compulsory, binding, interest arbitration—"compulsory" as opposed to "voluntary," "binding" as opposed to "nonbinding," "interest" as opposed to "grievance"— has been mandated in seventeen states. An arbitrator is appointed and, after determining the facts, must dictate his or her imposed outcome. From a strategic point of view, the arbitrator plays the role of a judge and jury: the contending parties must decide either to settle out of court (that is, to compromise jointly without the arbitrator) or to take their case to court.

Four of these seventeen states (Iowa, Massachusetts, Michigan, and Wisconsin) require what is known as final-offer or last-offer arbitration. With minor modifications, it works as follows. Negotiations are divided into two phases. In Phase 1 the parties bargain directly with or without the aid of an intervenor (mediator). If the parties agree, there is no second phase. If the parties disagree, the negotiations enter Phase 2, at which point the arbitrator enters the scene. In most states the arbitrator does not obtain guidance or information from the mediator present in Phase 1. The arbitrator determines the facts and then demands from each party a sealed final offer. These final offers are submitted essentially simultaneously, and the arbitrator must then, *by law*, select one of these two final offers; no in-between compromises are permissible, and the selected final offer becomes binding on both sides.

As described by Chelius and Dworkin (1980), final-offer arbitration has been used in the resolution of salary disputes in major league baseball. In 1973 it was agreed that, starting with 1974 contracts, final-offer arbitration could be invoked by either players or by clubs in an impasse over salaries; once invoked, it would be binding by both sides. The guidelines for arbitrators were established in the 1973 basic agreement, which states:

> The criteria will be the quality of the Player's contribution to his Club during the past season (including but not limited to his overall performance, special qualities of leadership and public appeal), the length and consistency of his career contribution, the record of the Player's past compensation, comparative baseball salaries, the existence of any physical or mental defects on the part of the Player, and the recent performance record of the Club including but not limited to its League standing and attendance as an indication of public acceptance (subject to the exclusion stated in (a) below). Any evidence may be submitted which is relevant to the above criteria, and the arbitrator shall assign such weight to the evidence as shall to him appear appropriate under the circumstances. The following items, however, shall be excluded: (a) the financial position of the Player and the Club; (b) press comments, testimonials or similar material bearing on the performance of either the Player or the Club, except that recog-

nized annual Player awards for playing excellence shall not be excluded; (c) offers made by either Player or Club prior to arbitration; (d) the cost to the parties of their representatives, attorneys, etc.; (e) salaries in other sports or occupations. (Chelius and Dworkin, 1980, p. 296)

Of special interest here is exclusion (c), which attempts to prevent concessions (or nonconcessions) made in Phase 1 negotiations from influencing the arbitrator in Phase 2 negotiations.

As can be seen from Table 4, final-offer arbitration is quite effective in persuading parties to settle without an imposed, arbitrated solution.

What are some of the strategic aspects of final-offer arbitration? Analysis of a sample negotiation will help here.[1] Suppose that management (M) and the union (U) are at an impasse. They have gone through Phase 1 negotiations without success, knowing full well that they will have to submit the basic wage rate (a single number) for final-offer arbitration. Management submits a sealed final offer, m; the union submits a sealed offer, u. The arbitrator then selects one of these two offers, depending on which value seems more appropriate. How shall we formalize this?

Assume that the arbitrator, after determining the facts, has some ideal value, a, in mind. The arbitrator will elect whichever final offer, m or u, is closer to a. If we imagine m, u, and a to be plotted on some linear scale—say, dollar value (see Figure 18)—it would be easy to see which offer more closely approximates the ideal. It is possible, though, that the arbitrator might have different psychological measurement scales on either side of his ideal; m might be close to his ideal in terms of dollars, whereas u might be closer in terms of some other value. But this complicates our task prematurely. Let's just suppose that in terms of one linear scale, the arbitrator selects the offer that is closer to his ideal. Following is a discussion of three special cases of this situation: first, in which the value of the arbitrator's ideal is known; second, in which there is a commonly perceived probability distribution for the ideal; and third, in which there are differing probability distributions for the ideal.

---

1. The following discussion is based on the work of Chatterjee (1979).

TABLE 4. *Impasse procedures and the incentive to negotiate.*

Domain	Years	Type of impasse procedure	Total number of negotiation cases	Cases employing stated impasse procedure	Procedure usage as a percentage of total negotiation cases
Baseball	1974–1975	Final-offer	1,000	43	4.3
Iowa	1975–1976	Final-offer	372	25	6.7
Massachusetts	1975–1976	Final-offer	548	36	6.6
Wisconsin	1973–1976	Final-offer	549	64	11.6
Michigan	1973–1976	Final-offer	540	88	16.3
Pennsylvania	1969–1974	Conventional	276	83	30.1
New York	1974–1976	Conventional	118	34	28.8
Canadian federal government	1967–1974	Conventional	305	55	18.0
British Columbia schools	1969–1973	Conventional	389	163	41.9
U.S. manufacturing	1969–1975	Strike	3,144	641	20.4

Source: Chelius and Dworkin (1980), p. 298. Reprinted by permission of Sage Publications, Inc.

Arbitrator compares:

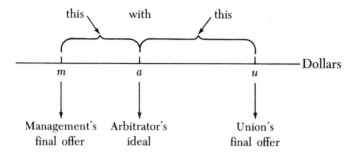

Figure 18. Idealized version of arbitrator's selection procedure in final-offer arbitration. (Arbitrator selects the final offer m or u closest to his ideal, a.)

VALUE OF THE IDEAL IS KNOWN

Suppose that both M and U know the value of a before they submit their final offers. What is the best m against any given u? If, on a linear scale, m is quite a bit closer to a than is u, then the discrepancy between m and the ideal could be even slightly greater and m would still be the superior choice. So it is *not true* that the best retort for M against u is $m = a$. The best retort is to choose a value for m below a that is only slightly closer to a than the distance that u is above a.

To what extent can the parties be sure of their payoffs? If M chooses m below a on the linear scale, then M can guarantee a payoff no worse than $a + (a - m)$. That value would be realized if u were selected at a distance above a that is equal to m's distance below a. Hence, to optimize M's security level (that is, to maximize M's minimum potential payoff), m should be set equal to a. Likewise, to optimize U's security level, u should be set equal to a.

Let's now look at possible equilibria. If U selects $u = a$, then M's best retort is to select $m = a$; conversely, if M selects $m = a$, then U's best retort is to select $u = a$. Hence, the pair $m = a$ and $u = a$ are in equilibrium and, from the analysis above, it is clear that they are the only equilibrium pair.

If a were known, would the players choose their final offers equal to that value? Probably not all; but as the players become more experienced, a exercises a strong attraction.

COMMONLY PERCEIVED PROBABILITY DISTRIBUTION
FOR THE IDEAL

To keep our case specific and simple, suppose that the annual wage rate for a starting fireman and the arbitrator's ideal value as perceived by M and U—which we will designate $\tilde{a}$—could be any value from 16 to 20 (in units of thousands of dollars). Both M and U perceive (and each knows that the other perceives) that all ideal values from 16 to 20 are equally likely for the arbitrator. The median and mean are both 18. Should M and U submit offers that are close to 18?

As a prelude to the analysis, we shall first determine the best retort for U against a known value of m—say, m = 17. Calculations for selected values of u are shown in Table 5. For example, if u were set at 18, then the outcome could either be 17 (at M's offer) or 18 (at U's offer), depending respectively on whether $\tilde{a}$ were less than or more than 17.5. (For this continuous range of a values, we don't have to worry about a being exactly 17.50000.) The probability that $\tilde{a}$ is less than 17.5 is three-eighths, or .375. So under our assumptions if u is chosen at 18, then U will be exposed to a lottery with payoffs 17 and 18 and probabilities of .375 and .625 respectively. An appropriate summary index for a risk-neutral U is the expected value: .375(17) + .625(18) = 17.625.

TABLE 5. *U's expected-value payoffs for selected values of u against* m = 17, *when all values for* $\tilde{a}$ *from 16 to 20 are equally likely.*

Value of u	Possible outcomes	Probabilities	U's expected value
18	17 18	.375 .625	17.625
19	17 19	.500 .500	18.000
20	17 20	.625 .375	18.125
21	17 21	.750 .250	18.000
23	17 23	1.000 .000	17.000

From Table 5 we observe the rather surprising fact that the best retort is $u = 20$ for an expected value of 18.125.

It's not difficult to show that to maximize expected monetary value, the best retort for U against any assumed value of m is the response $u = 20$. This is a strong and remarkable result. Analogously, the best retort for M against any assumed value of u is the response $m = 16$. The pair $m = 16$ and $u = 20$ are in equilibrium, but this is not nearly as strong as saying that $u = 20$ is a best response whether or not M plays its equilibrium value of 16; and $m = 16$ is a best response whether or not U plays its equilibrium value of 20.

Analytical elaboration. Let's say that $\tilde{a}$ is rectangularly distributed between 0 and 1 (no loss of generality). It can readily be shown that U's expected return, as a function of u for fixed m, is:

$$\overline{U}(u|m) = \begin{cases} \dfrac{u + m}{2} & \text{if } u < m \\[2ex] \dfrac{(m^2 + 1)}{2} - \dfrac{(u - 1)^2}{2} & \text{if } u \geq m, \end{cases}$$

which is depicted in Figure 19. Against m the optimum response is $U_m^o = 1$ (for all $m \leq 1$).

If the commonly perceived distribution for $\tilde{a}$ is not rectangular (that is, if all values are not equally likely between some lower and some upper value) but is a more natural distribution as is shown in Figure 20, then against any assumed m the optimum retort U_m^o is higher than the mean of the distribution of $\tilde{a}$—surprisingly higher. And as m approaches the mean (central value), U_m^o *drifts further to the right.* So it is not true that if M makes an offer close to the center of the distribution of $\tilde{a}$, that U should reciprocate. Intuitively, the higher the value of m, the more U can afford to gamble. But also if U suspects that M is risk-averse and will choose an m-value close to the mean, then U can afford to gamble with a higher u-value. All this, of course, depends on U being risk-neutral. If U is risk-averse, then there will be an attractive force toward the center of the distribution of $\tilde{a}$. Conversely, if U is risk-prone, U_m^o will be higher still.

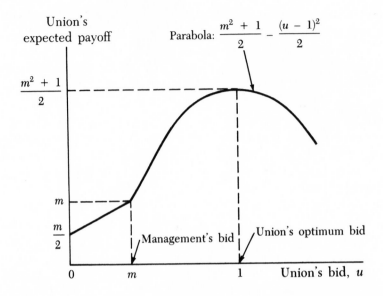

Figure 19. Union's expected payoff as a function of u for fixed m when all values of $\tilde{a}$ between 0 and 1 are equally likely.

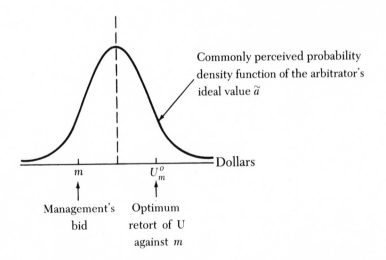

Figure 20. Union's optimum retort against an assumed m when $\tilde{a}$ has a bell-shaped distribution. (Vertical scale is such that the area under the probability density function is 1.00.)

An analogous story holds if we look at M's optimum retort, M_u^o, against an assumed value of u.

DIFFERING PROBABILITY DISTRIBUTIONS FOR THE IDEAL

Some theoretical models show that with complete exchange of information, M's and U's probabilistic perceptions of the distribution of $\tilde{a}$ should be identical. Empirically this does not turn out to be true, however, and very often the distributions are displaced in directions favoring each protagonist (see Figure 21). All of this, of course, is speculative, and it is doubtful whether baseball players, ballclub owners, firemen's unions, or city managers formulate probability distributions. But the distributions shown in the figure would probably be reasonable approximations, especially if both parties voluntarily chose to submit to final-offer arbitration.

If U were to consciously calculate the best U_m^o against m, then U would use its own assessment of $\tilde{a}$, and as is shown in Figure 21 there would be a vast discrepancy between m and U_m^o (tempered somewhat by risk-aversion). But now a further complication is introduced: U might suspect that M's assessment of $\tilde{a}$ will be displaced to the left of U's own distribution, so that U might expect the possibility of very low m-values. Contrary to common wisdom, with the anticipation of low m-values and great uncertainty about $\tilde{a}$, U does not have much security and must be careful. With differing perceptions of $\tilde{a}$ and differing perceptions of perceptions, with risk-

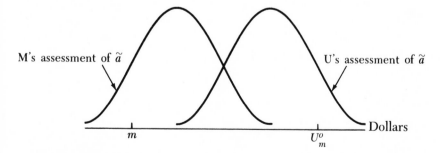

Figure 21. Illustration of case where U and M have different assessments of $\tilde{a}$ and U_m^o is the optimum retort against m. (Vertical scale is such that the area under each assessed distribution is 1.00.)

aversion and differing perceptions of the other party's risk-aversion, with anticipated limited rationality and with expected miscalculations—in short, with full reality, this is a tremendously complicated problem.

Final-offer arbitration should have great appeal for the daring (the risk seekers) who play against the timid (the risk avoiders). As shown in Table 4, it seems that the proportion of cases going to final-offer arbitration is smaller than the proportion going to conventional arbitration. This is often cited as an advantage of final-offer arbitration. Of course, the logic is marred a bit because conventional arbitration preceded by a round of Russian roulette would still do better.

Is it easier for an arbitrator to administer conventional or final-offer arbitration? In both cases he presumably would have to determine the facts. In conventional arbitration, he would have a continuum of choices; in final-offer arbitration, the adversaries—and in this case they really are adversaries—present the arbitrator with a dichotomous choice. It might be an easy choice: if the final offers are close together, it may not make much difference; if they are far apart and one seems ludicrous, again it's an easy matter. But if they are far apart and equally ludicrous, the task may be extremely difficult: the arbitrator might want to settle in the middle, but he can't. He does not have the luxury of being able to make fine distinctions in his judgments. On the other hand, if the arbitrator selects m or u, he does not have to publicly announce how he would have decided for every potential, embarrassingly difficult pair of offers.

In Part III we'll return to final-offer arbitration and look at situations in which there is more than one issue involved. The principal question will be whether it's preferable for the arbitrator to make a simple choice between the composite offer (over all issues) of M and the composite offer of U, or whether it's preferable for him to break down the problem into separate issues and make a choice between final offers on each issue independently.

9

Advice for Negotiators

Now that we've examined a variety of simple bargaining problems, let's consider the personal skills and traits that might improve a negotiator's performance. What attributes, abilities, and behavior patterns could make a bargainer more effective? Are certain types of people better negotiators than others? How do sex roles influence the dynamics of negotiation? And, last, are there any general rules or guidelines that can be of use to all negotiators in distributive bargaining situations?

CHARACTERISTICS OF AN EFFECTIVE NEGOTIATOR

What are the characteristics of an effective negotiator? Opinions differ. John Hammond was interested in how the relative importance of the characteristics of an effective negotiator and attitudes about negotiation varied with occupation. He adapted a list of questions from Karrass (1968) and administered the questionnaire to insurance underwriters, marketers, claims representatives, purchasing agents, salespeople, and bankers, among others. He found, not surprisingly, that purchasing agents and claims representatives had more aggressive attitudes than people in other occupations and that bankers and sales personnel had more accommodating, "satisfy-the-other-side" attitudes.

Table 6 presents the responses of thirty-two senior lending officers of a large U.S. bank; they were asked to rate the importance of thirty-four traits that would characterize an effective negotiator. The list obviously has overlaps: for example, "ability to persuade others" is related to most of the other characteristics. Appropriately for our purposes, "preparation and planning skill" ranks first; undoubtedly labor negotiators would see the negotiating world vastly differently from, say, lawyers that represent clients in civil liability

119

TABLE 6. *Characteristics of an effective negotiator, rated on a five-point scale.*

			Rating			
Characteristic	*Unimportant* (1)	*Mildly unimportant* (2)	*Important* (3)	*Very important* (4)	*Extremely important* (5)	*Mean*
1. Preparation and planning skill	0	0	0	6	26	4.8
2. Knowledge of subject matter being negotiated	0	0	1	10	21	4.5
3. Ability to think clearly and rapidly under pressure and uncertainty	0	1	1	10	20	4.5
4. Ability to express thoughts verbally	0	0	3	12	17	4.4
5. Listening skill	0	0	4	12	16	4.4
6. Judgment and general intelligence	0	0	6	11	14	4.3
7. Integrity	0	0	8	9	15	4.2
8. Ability to persuade others	0	1	6	14	11	4.1
9. Patience	1	2	8	8	12	4.0
10. Decisiveness	0	3	6	13	9	3.9
11. Ability to win respect and confidence of opponent	0	1	12	10	9	3.8
12. General problem-solving and analytic skills	0	2	11	11	8	3.8
13. Self-control, especially of emotions and their visibility	2	3	7	9	11	3.8
14. Insight into others' feelings	1	3	6	13	9	3.8
15. Persistence and determination	0	1	12	15	4	3.7
16. Ability to perceive and exploit available power to achieve objective	0	2	12	11	7	3.7
17. Insight into hidden needs and reactions of own and opponent's organization	0	4	12	10	6	3.6

Item						Mean
18. Ability to lead and control members of own team or group	0	4	11	12	5	3.6
19. Previous negotiating experience	0	3	8	13	8	3.5
20. Personal sense of security	2	3	8	13	5	3.5
21. Open-mindedness (tolerance of other viewpoints)	0	0	3	12	17	3.5
22. Competitiveness (desire to compete and win)	1	2	14	10	5	3.5
23. Skill in communicating and coordinating various objectives within own organization	0	5	15	9	3	3.3
24. Debating ability (skill in parrying questions and answers across the table)	0	6	16	7	3	3.2
25. Willingness to risk being disliked	2	6	13	9	2	3.2
26. Ability to act out skillfully a variety of negotiating roles or postures	2	7	15	4	4	3.0
27. Status or rank in organization	5	7	11	6	3	2.8
28. Tolerance to ambiguity and uncertainty	5	7	14	5	1	2.7
29. Skill in communicating by signs, gestures, and silence (nonverbal language)	5	10	8	6	2	2.7
30. Compromising temperament	5	12	5	7	3	2.7
31. Attractive personality and sense of humor (degree to which people enjoy being with the person)	6	6	12	7	1	2.7
32. Trusting temperament	9	5	12	5	1	2.5
33. Willingness to take somewhat above-average business or career risks	5	10	13	4	0	2.5
34. Willingness to employ force, threat, or bluff to avoid being exploited	6	10	11	3	2	2.5

Source: Adapted by John Hammond from Karrass (1968), pp. 242–244.

suits. More important than the ranking is the list itself, which would be especially helpful if, in a particular case, there were a choice of appointing one of several possible negotiators. The list includes many characteristics that are relevant—just how relevant depends on the particular case and perhaps on the characteristics of the adversaries' negotiators. Certainly characteristics that are ranked low by lending officers in banks might well be extremely important in other situations. Given a specific context in mind, one could generate additional characteristics that would be relevant to that context. Notwithstanding all these limitations, this list of characteristics is thought-provoking and valuable.

A Japanese man who had participated in a laboratory exercise once asked me why Asiatic subjects did better at negotiations than North Americans and Europeans. I asked why *he* thought so. "Oh," he remarked, "we've been brought up that way and we have more patience." I told him a bit ingenuously that I did not keep appropriate records that would enable me to make any such determination; and even if in our small sample the Japanese seemed to do better, the causal relation would not be clear because the Japanese participating in the experiments were undoubtedly special in many ways.

I was asked a similar question by women subjects, and I avoided that one also. But a number of interesting incidents relating to sex roles occurred in our experiments. One man, a generally excellent negotiator, remonstrated to me that he had done miserably in one negotiating game because he had been matched against a woman, and he had been so uncomfortable that he could not negotiate skillfully. "Well, that shows you how important these vicarious negotiating exercises are," I said, as I refused him my sympathies.

A woman subject became extremely upset in one negotiating exercise with a "macho male" (as she described him), who was trying to take advantage of her as a female. Later she learned that the tactics he had used against her had been employed in the same negotiation exercise by male against male and female against female. She subsequently apologized to her adversary.

A group of professional women, who had an average of eight years' work experience and who were enrolled in a mid-career program at Harvard's Kennedy School of Government, once asked me to address a women's group on the role of the woman as negotiator.

Many women, they thought, are uncomfortable negotiating against men, and they asked whether there were any insights I could share with them. I responded that men, too, often feel uncomfortable negotiating against men, and that perhaps these women should take courses in which they could be exposed to negotiating experiences. I refused to address their group—not from a lack of sympathy, but from a lack of knowledge. I did agree, however, to meet a few times with four or five of them to see if we could generate some insights.

In preparation for those meetings I read *The Social Psychology of Bargaining and Negotiation* by Rubin and Brown, who describe what is known in the experimental literature about differences in bargaining skills as a function of age, race, nationality, intelligence, religion, social status, and sex. Their search of the literature "uncovered approximately 100 studies, each of which has focused, at least in part, on the relationship between sex and various aspects of bargaining behavior." It's easy to experiment with sex as a variable. Rubin and Brown examine the many conflicting empirical findings; the considerable variation observed *within* each sexual role masks the differences to be gleaned *between* sexes. However, my impression from reading their book, from talking to professional women, and from the responses of women in experimental exercises is that women are a bit more cooperative than men. When a woman plays against a man, however, and he initiates an aggressive, noncooperative action, she tends to react more forcefully (on average) than a man would. Bixenstine, Chambers, and Wilson (1964) "found that females were initially more trusting and more trustworthy than men but were less willing to forgive violations of trust." I single out these findings from the myriad other findings because I can comfortably rationalize why it might be so—not only for women but for any group whose members feel somewhat self-conscious in their negotiating roles. Before you make too much of this, you should read Rubin and Brown to get a feel for the conflicting evidence.

Many of the psychological experiments they cite use some variation of the Prisoner's Dilemma Game to test for cooperative behavior.[1] A neutral setting of the game involves two players, Mr. Hee

1. See Luce and Raiffa (1957), pp. 94–102.

and Ms. Shee. They see each other but cannot communicate directly. At each round of play, each player has to select one of two options: cooperate or defect. At each round their choices are made independently and (effectively) simultaneously. They receive monetary payoffs at each round that depend on their pair of choices —one choice by each—at that round. Figure 22 shows these payoffs. Thus, for example, if Ms. Shee chooses "defect" and Mr. Hee chooses "cooperate" at a given round, then she receives 10 cents and he loses 10 cents (the experimenter, acting as banker, disburses and collects the payments). If they both choose "cooperate," each receives 5 cents. If they both choose "defect," each loses 5 cents.

Note that if Ms. Shee tries to maximize her return at a given round, with no interest whatsoever in what happens at other rounds, then she is best advised to choose "defect." "Defect" is her best choice against his choice of "cooperate," as well as against his choice of "defect." A similar argument can be made for him: for a single round with myopic behavior, "defect" is best for him. Thus, we see that joint defection seems like the dominant, although unhappy, outcome, with each side losing 5 cents. Hence the dilemma. If Shee and Hee follow this "best advice" (to defect on a single trial), they do poorly; if they reject the advice, they do well. Two individuals who get no advice and are confused may do better than two individuals who are thoroughly briefed. But all this notwithstanding, if you, as a player, are trying to maximize your return, you *should* choose "defect." This game is worth pondering about.

In repeated rounds of play, subjects often enter into a tacit collusion: each plays "cooperate" and each gets 5 cents at every round. Hee, for example, might refrain from taking advantage of Shee at a given round (by switching from "cooperate" to "defect") because in subsequent rounds Shee probably would also switch. So they remain in the precarious cooperate-cooperate state. If there are a fixed number of rounds to play—say, twenty—and each player knows that termination number, then one can expect defection on the rounds near the twentieth. But for our purposes here, Ms. Shee and Mr. Hee are told that the game will be played with some vague indefinite stopping procedure. Most astute subjects quickly learn to cooperate and hold firm.

Studies that are designed to examine cooperative behavior often employ the use of a stooge. (I personally have different pedagogical

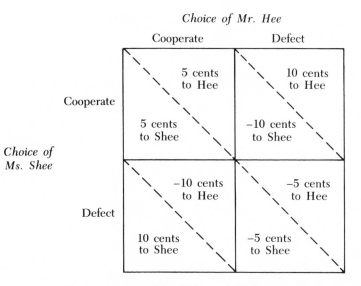

Figure 22. A variation of the Prisoner's Dilemma Game.

and research aims in conducting simulated exercises, and therefore I never use stooges.) Suppose Ms. Shee doesn't know that Mr. Hee is programmed to play according to the experimenter's dictates. Mr. Hee might start out in a cooperative mode to test Ms. Shee's initial behavior. If after a while she locks into a cooperative mode, he might be programmed to double-cross by switching to "defect" in order to test her reactions. "Is this an aberration?" she might think. "Is he just squeezing out a bit more for himself? Or is he taking advantage of me?" If she responds with "defect" at the next round, the stooge might provoke her again or switch back. Once he switches back to "cooperate," how long will it take her to once again resume cooperative behavior? If they are in a "defect-defect" position for a few rounds, will she try to coax him back into a cooperative mode by switching to "cooperate"?

Instead of the stooge being a white male, the experimenter could make the stooge a white female, or a black female, or a black male. The sex and race of the experimenter could also be manipulated. It's easy to be imaginative and to come up with variations on this theme. Many variations have already been tested; these ideas have been around for a long time, and the journals are filled with results of experiments using variations of the Prisoner's Dilemma Game to probe differences in behavior patterns.

A CHECKLIST FOR NEGOTIATORS

Suppose that *you* represent one of two parties that have to negotiate the price of a commodity, the value of a firm, a wage rate, an out-of-court settlement, or the date of a proposed marriage. Based on the discussion of the preceding chapters, what are the things that you will want to keep in mind? Think of yourself for the moment as the seller—or maximizer, if you will—who wants the final contract value to be high rather than low. Your adversary, the buyer (or minimizer), is seeking a low contract value. Assume that you are your own boss and that your side is monolithic, that you do not necessarily have to come to any agreement, that contracts once agreed upon are secure, that negotiations are nonstrident, and that the only threat the parties can make is the threat not to settle.

Preparing for Negotiations

First, *know yourself*. Think about what you need, want, aspire to. Consider what will happen to you if no deal is struck. Search diligently for competing and substitute alternatives. Analyze (or at least think about) your other alternatives, and, all things considered, assign a certainty-equivalent value to your best alternative to a negotiated agreement; this is your subjective evaluation of the no-agreement state. Assess your reservation price for each round of negotiations. Your reservation price—which is based on the value you have placed on the no-agreement state—is the absolute minimum value that you (as the maximizer) would be willing to settle for. Any lesser value would be worse than the no-agreement state; you would walk away from the bargaining rather than settle for a value less than this minimum. Amass your arguments for the negotiations: facts, data, arguments, rationalizations, including arguments about what is fair and how an arbitrator might settle the dispute.

Second, *know your adversaries*. Consider what will happen to them (or he or she, as the case may be) if no deal is struck. Speculate about their alternatives. Examine your perceptions of their reservation price; think about the uncertainties in these perceptions (and, if it is natural to you, encode them into probabilistic assessments). Investigate their credentials, their legitimacy, their integrity. Investigate how they have negotiated in the past.

Third, give thought to the *negotiating conventions* in each context. How open should you be? Can you believe what your adversaries will say? Is it customary to withhold unfavorable information? What number of iterations in the negotiation dance is respectable or customary? Can negotiations be done in stages? If so, what is your reservation value for each upcoming stage? How will each stage of the negotiations affect your continuing relations with your adversaries?

Fourth, consider the *logistics* of the situation. Who should negotiate? Should roles be assigned to the negotiators on your side? Do you need professional assistance, such as representation by a skilled negotiator? Where should negotiations take place, and when? If they will be of an international nature, in what language should the negotiations be conducted, and who should supply the translators?

Fifth, remember that *simulated role playing* can be of value in preparing your strategy. Try to find someone to play the role of your adversaries and give careful thought to what their tactics might be. Arrange for simulated negotiations.

Sixth, iterate and set your *aspiration levels*. Giving consideration to all the above points, what contract value should you strive for? It's easy to say "the more the better," but it's helpful to have some target level that is a reasonable distance from your bottom-line, walkaway price. Your aspiration level might well shift during negotiations, but your reservation price should remain firmer; it too could shift, however, if the other side provides information enabling you to reassess your other opportunities or the value you place on an agreement.

Opening Gambits

Who should make the first concrete offer? Beware of opening so conservatively that your offer falls well within your adversaries' acceptance region. Beware of opening with so extreme a value that you hurt the ambience of negotiations; also, if you are too extreme you will have to make disproportionately large concessions. If you open first, and if your adversaries are ill prepared, you might influence their perception of their own reservation price by your opening offer: your opening offer anchors their thinking about the value of the venture to themselves. Be aware of this anchoring phenomenon if the situation is reversed.

Gauge your reaction to an extreme first offer. Don't get locked in by talking about your adversaries' extreme offer; don't let their offer be the vantage point for subsequent modifications. The best strategy in this case is to either break off negotiations until they modify their offer, or quickly counter with an offer of your own. When two offers are on the table, the midpoint is a natural focal point, so think about this when you make an initial counteroffer. Compare the midpoint of the two offers with your aspiration level.

Protect your integrity. Try to avoid disclosing information (such as your reservation price) as an alternative to giving false information. Use phrases like "This is what I would like to get" rather than "This is what I *must* get," when your "must" value is not really a must.

The Negotiation Dance

The pattern of concessions. The most common pattern of concessions (for a maximizer) is monotone decreasing—that is, the intervals between your decreasing offers become successively smaller, signaling that you are approaching your limit (which does not necessarily have to be your reservation price; it could be your readjusted aspiration level). The number of concessions that you should be prepared to make depends on the context. Your concessions should be paced and linked to those of your adversary.

Reassessing perceptions. During the negotiations, reassess your perceptions about your adversaries' reservation price. Remember that they might want you to infer that their reservation price is lower than it really is. Conversely, you might want them to believe that your reservation price is higher than it really is. How aggressive should you be in this game of deception? Again, it depends on norms, on the extent to which you guard your integrity, on whether you will be continuing relations with your adversaries, on your (probabilistic) perceptions of their reactions, on your attitudes toward risk, on how you empathize with the needs of the other side, and on what you think is "fair."

Your adversaries may have information that is relevant to an evaluation of your own reservation price; part of your negotiating strategy may be to ferret out some of this information. But be careful of possible deceptions on their part, such as selective disclosure of information.

As you go along, reassess your aspiration levels. This is hard to do analytically, but you should nevertheless keep such reassessment in mind. Your adversaries are doing the same.

End Play

Making commitments. For sincere or possibly insincere reasons, you might want to signal that some value is as far as you can or will go. How can you convince your adversaries that you really mean it? That your stance is not merely a bargaining ploy? For example, you might threaten to break off negotiations, leaving it somewhat vague as to whether negotiations could start up again; or you might make statements that limit your further flexibility.

Breaking a commitment gracefully. How can you disengage from a commitment that didn't work? You can get new instructions from the interests you represent. You can add new issues (as we will see in Part III). You can get new information. You can be replaced by a new negotiator for your side. And so on.

Helping your adversaries to break a commitment gracefully. It may be to your advantage to let your adversaries disengage from an agreement without too much loss of face. You could, for example, imply that the situation has changed when it really hasn't. Or you might imply that they were not well organized to begin with and it's reasonable for them to change their mind. Conversely, if you would like to free yourself from a commitment, you might want to give your adversaries the opportunity to help you.

In the abstract, these games of deception may sound somewhat immoral. But in concrete situations they do not seem so at all. In the case of Elmtree House, it seemed quite proper and natural for Steve to engage in such behavior—for example, by suggesting that Wilson's company donate some construction work or make a contribution to a scholarship fund. These ploys were designed to provide Wilson with a face-saving means of breaking his absolute top, irrevocable offer.

A commitment is really not a commitment if both sides realize that it can be easily broken. So it may be necessary in some contexts to escalate the rhetoric in order to achieve "real commitment" or a "real-real commitment." This is akin to the situation described in the Sorensen Chevrolet case: the lawyer for the plaintiff offered a rock-bottom price of $350,000; on the steps of the courthouse a new lawyer for the plaintiff offered the rock-rock-bottom price of $300,000. Maybe in the judge's chamber the plaintiff herself might have overruled her lawyers and offered the REAL FINAL offer of $250,000.

Introducing an intervenor. If you suspect that your latest rejected offer is well within your adversaries' acceptance region and if you refuse to move still lower toward your own reservation price, you might have to give up and break off negotiations. Before doing that, you might suggest bringing in a mediator or even an arbitrator. Both you and your adversaries might be willing to disclose more confidential information to an intervenor than to each other.

The important decision of whether or not to engage the services of an intervenor and how much sovereignty to give him should be given long and careful thought. Formal analysis can sometimes help. The Sorensen Chevrolet case gives a good idea of the type of analysis that could be done.

Broadening the domain of negotiation. In the end, there may be no zone of agreement, or—because of stated commitments—there may be no way of achieving a solution even if there is one. But if the domain of negotiation is enlarged to include more complicated exchanges (for example, contingency arrangements) or to include additional issues, then a mutually profitable contract may be possible and desirable for both parties.

A final word of advice: don't gloat about how well you have done. After settling a merger for $7 million, don't tell your future partners that your reservation price was only $4 million; that won't make them feel good. You might be tempted to lie for their benefit and make a vague claim to a reservation price of about $6.5 million— but lies, even beneficial ones, generate their own complications. Some confidential information should remain confidential even after the fact.

III

Two Parties, Many Issues

We have already seen that although a buyer and a seller may share no zone of agreement, they still might be able to negotiate a deal if they enrich the menu of possible contracts by introducing contingency payments at different time periods. Such flexibility can enable both parties to exploit their different perceptions of the future, their different attitudes toward risk, and the different ways they feel about money now versus money in the future. They are, in essence, converting a single-factor problem into a multiple-factor problem. Such bargaining—in which there are two parties and several issues to be negotiated—is called integrative bargaining. The parties are not strict competitors. It is no longer true that if one party gets more, the other necessarily has to get less: they both can get more. They can cooperate in order to enlarge the pie that they eventually will have to divide.

To take another example, suppose that Mr. Hee and Ms. Shee are engaged in two separate negotiations, each negotiation involving a single continuous issue. On the first issue, one of money, Mr. Hee needs a value of $60,000 or more to settle, whereas Ms. Shee needs a value of $50,000 or less to settle. He wants higher values while she wants lower values, and there's no zone of agreement. On the second issue, one of time, Mr. Hee needs a settlement value of thirty months or less to settle, whereas Ms. Shee needs a settlement value of thirty-four months or more to settle. He wants lower time values while she wants higher time values, and again there is no zone of agreement. Mr. Hee and Ms. Shee are involved in two separate, frustrating, distributive bargaining problems, neither of which permits an acceptable compromise.

Now let's see what happens if we link the two problems. She has refused his last offer of $63,000. He has refused her last offer of thirty-six months. But he might be willing to accept thirty-six months on the time issue if she would be willing to accept $63,000 on the money issue. She might also be willing to accept this linked proposal. They might, in fact, have different tradeoff rates for money and time, and the linkage of these two problems would allow them to exploit these differences. For him, the money issue may be more important, so that if he gets more of his way in terms of money, he might be willing to give up more in terms of time. She might feel that time is the more important issue and would be willing to give up a lot in terms of money to get more of what she wants in terms of time. A deal *could* be struck, but will it? How can they communicate their complicated preferences to each other without disclosing too much confidential information? Thus far we have discussed situations in which the parties have engaged in face-to-face negotiation; in this case, however, the bargainers may have to engage in what Roger Fisher has termed "side-by-side" joint problem solving, in order to squeeze out potential joint gains. In Part III we will explore the various ways in which this can be done.

10
AMPO versus City

The case of Associated Metropolitan Police Officers (AMPO) versus City, another armchair negotiation, involves the settlement of a wage contract between a police union and the administration of a fictitious municipality.[1] The two parties are trying to settle nearly a dozen different bargaining issues, some with continuous ranges and others with two or three possible settlement levels. In our experiments, the parties were treated as monolithic—differences of opinion within each side, for example, were viewed as negligible—and it was therefore convenient to have just one subject represent each party. Players were instructed to worry about future relations so that bargaining was reasonably cordial; the payoff structures were made clear to the negotiators and were designed to include linkages between problems; contracts jointly agreed upon were inviolable and did not require ratification by erratic constituencies. Negotiations were to be completed (unless broken off) within twenty-four hours, and the possibility of using outside intervenors was not an option.

Each subject was given appropriate confidential information for his or her role. In face-to-face interchanges much of this confidential information was shared—perhaps selectively and perhaps with exaggerations—but the rules of the game prohibited the negotiators from revealing to each other these confidential instructions. After all, in the real world, such written instructions would not even be available and certainly, if available, almost never disclosed. Both sides received the same background data describing the setting of

1. This chapter is based on an exercise developed by Edwards and White (1977) and modified by Jacob Ulvila. See also the bibliography, under the heading "Case Studies."

the problem (resembling an amalgam of the realities of New Orleans and Atlanta) and then each was given confidential scoring information.

The issues to be settled were the following:

1. starting salaries for police officers
2. maximum salaries for police officers
3. vacation for officers with less than five years' service
4. vacation for officers with more than five years' service
5. the status of fourteen officers under suspension
6. the percent of two-man patrol cars
7. creation of the rank of corporal
8. expansion of the number of sergeants
9. the fate of the police commissioner, Mr. Daniels
10. the status of the Police Civilian Review Board.

Table 7 shows the possible levels of agreement on each of these ten issues and the associated scores for City and AMPO. On the reinstatement issue, for example, if the resolution was "Yes, with back pay," the City got − 70 points and AMPO got zero points. Players knew their own scoring schedule only, but they could surmise the direction of increase for their adversaries. It was obvious to City, for example, that AMPO wanted higher salaries, more vacation, and so on. The resulting scores from the resolution of each of the issues were added for each side, and the performance of each protagonist was judged by his or her total score. If a given pair of City and AMPO players ended up respectively with total scores of − 113 and 1,570, then (since the scoring schedules were completely independent of each other) nothing could be gleaned by comparing − 113 with 1,570. But the score of − 113 for that particular City negotiator could be compared with the scores of other City negotiators playing the same role with different adversaries. Likewise for the AMPO score of 1,570.

It can be seen from the table that the scores for salaries were not *strictly* monotonic (for example, for any increase in starting salary from $501 to $599 the City negotiator got a constant − 4 points) and that there were jumps at symbolic points (AMPO got, for example, a jump in points from 550 to 700 by increasing the starting salary from $599 to $600). Though admittedly this was not realistic, the scoring had to be accepted by the players as given—it was not negotiable.

AMPO ideally would have liked two officers to every patrol car; City wanted only one. The compromise positions were two officers in high-crime areas, and two officers at night. At some previous time there had been an unauthorized wildcat strike on this issue, and fourteen officers had been suspended. The issue now was whether they should be reinstated, and, if so, with or without back pay. AMPO had a reservation price on this issue: no reinstatement meant no contract, no matter what else.

AMPO wanted to create the new rank of corporal; City was against it, mainly because they believed it would lead to an escalation of their costs.

Both the AMPO and City negotiators wanted to fire Commissioner Daniels (as can be seen from the joint payoffs). But AMPO *did not know* beforehand that the mayor was secretly disgusted with his political appointee and was looking for an excuse to get rid of him. AMPO assumed that City wanted to retain Daniels.

The issue concerning the Police Civilian Review Board was a bit complicated. At the time of the negotiations there were no police on the board, and a vote for censure of an officer had to be unanimous. AMPO wanted the board disbanded; failing this, they wanted to add police officers to the board—but not if the voting rules were changed.

Reservation prices existed for City on vacation days, on two-man patrols, and on the number of sergeants; AMPO had a reservation limit on the reinstatement issue. City could not agree to an increase of starting salary over $1,000; AMPO was required to get an increase in maximum salary of at least $500. Most confidential of all: City negotiators had to get a total score of -250 and AMPO negotiators a total score of 600.

ARRIVING AT AGREEMENTS

The final contract arrived at by each pair of negotiators was evaluated by a score for City and a score for AMPO, which can be plotted as shown in Figure 23. If City scored -113 and AMPO 1,570, then that joint evaluation $(-113, 1,570)$ would be represented by point X. A sample of nineteen other joint evaluations are depicted. Five of the nineteen pairs scored better than point X for both players. The negotiating pair that scored -113 and 1,570 could have ob-

TABLE 7. *Scoring schedule for AMPO and City.*

Issue	Setting	Payoff (in points)	
		City	AMPO
Increase in salary:	$0–99	0	0
starting	100–199	0	100
	200–299	0	200
	300–399	0	300
	400–499	0	400
	500	0	550
	501–599	−4	550
	600	−4	700
	601–699	−8	700
	700	−8	850
	701–799	−16	850
	800	−16	1,000
	801–899	−32	1,000
	900	−32	1,150
	901–999	−64	1,150
	1,000	−64	1,300
	1,000+	NA	1,300+
Increase in salary:	$0–499	0 to −12	NA
maximum	500	−12	0
	501–600	−24	2–200[a]
	601–700	−48	202–400[a]
	701–750	−96	402–500[a]
	750+	NA	500+
Increase in vacation:	0 days	0	0
less than 5 years'	2	−3	40
service	3	−6	60
	4	−10	85
	5	−15	110
	5+	NA	110+
Increase in vacation:	0 days	0	0
more than 5 years'	1	−2	0
service	2	−6	60
	3	−14	85
	3+	NA	85+
Bonus if increase in vacation for all officers is held to zero		+10	

TABLE 7 *continued.*

Issue	Setting	Payoff (in points)	
		City	AMPO
Reinstatement	No	0	NA
	Yes, without back pay	−50	−100
	Yes, with back pay	−70	0
Two-man patrols	Status quo	+15	−25
	Less than 20% increase	−5	25
	Greater than 20% increase, but less than strictly two-man patrols	−5	50
	Strictly two-man patrols	NA	100
Create rank of corporal	No	+5	0
	Yes, limit of 20	−15	50
	Yes, unlimited	−20	50
Increase number of sergeants	0	+5	0
	1	−2	10
	2	−4	20
	3	−6	30
	4	−8	40
	5	−10	50
	6	−13	60
	7	−16	70
	8	−19	80
	9	−22	90
	10	−25	100
	10+	NA	100+
Commissioner Daniels	Fire	+40	200
	Keep	0	0
Police Civilian Review Board	Disband	−100	250
	Add police, no vote change	−20	150
	Add police, change vote	+20	100
	No police, no vote change	0	25
	No police, change vote	+20	−25

Note: If the City and AMPO failed to reach agreement on a sufficient number of issues (which were specified in the confidential information sheets), the City representative received a *total* score of −250 and the AMPO representative received a *total* score of 600. These scores were City's and AMPO's reservation prices.

NA indicates that such a setting was not acceptable as part of the agreement. A City representative who agreed to a setting that was not acceptable to City received a *total* score of −250, and an AMPO representative who agreed to a setting that was not acceptable to AMPO received a *total* score of 600.

a. For these settings, the AMPO representative received 2 points for every dollar over $500.

137

tained a higher score for each player: that is, they left "potential joint gains" on the bargaining table. There was plenty of achievable space northeast of their evaluation at X. Indeed, it can be shown that holding AMPO fixed at 1,570, City could have achieved an additional 100 points; and holding City fixed at − 113, AMPO could have achieved an additional 600 points. Of course the X-pair of negotiators might have been content with their achievement, since

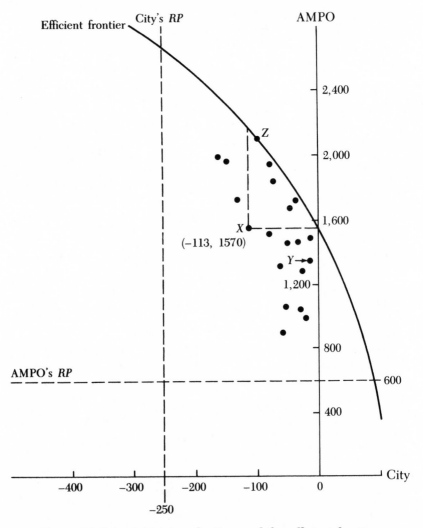

Figure 23. Selected joint evaluations and the efficient frontier.

both amply achieved their reservation prices (−250 for City and 600 for AMPO). But when they negotiated the values −113 and 1,570 they might not have realized that it was possible for each to do better. Ignorance sometimes is bliss.

The Y-pair of negotiators, scoring −4 (City) and 1,315 (AMPO), left little in the way of potential joint gains on the table. They were more efficient than the X-pair. But the AMPO player for the X-pair did better than the AMPO Y-player. Each negotiator was aiming not for joint efficiency, but rather for a personal score that was as high as possible—consistent, of course, with his or her ethical standards of negotiating behavior.

The efficient frontier—sometimes called the Pareto Optimal Frontier, after the economist Vilfredo Pareto—is defined as the locus of achievable joint evaluations from which no joint gains are possible. Thus, at point Z on the efficient frontier (see Figure 23) AMPO's score could be improved only at the expense of decreasing City's score, and vice versa. We shall see later how that efficient frontier can be determined; it requires information from each side, and thus cannot be computed by an AMPO player or a City player acting alone.

Overall, the results of negotiations by the subjects were quite spread out and usually fell below the efficient frontier. Considering the complexity of the problem, however, the joint evaluations were surprisingly close to the efficient frontier; undoubtedly this was so because the scoring system for each negotiator was laid out so clearly and in such an easy-to-use fashion that it was easy for the negotiators to seek joint gains.

Most subjects admitted unabashedly that they had arrived at their negotiating solutions by just "thrashing around." Some started with a "strategy"—in a very loose sense of the term—but their adversaries had incompatible ideas of their own. Despite protestations to the contrary, most subjects followed some sort of system, but one that was often discernible only after the fact.

A few started by offering a complete package—of course, favorable to themselves—and the adversary would respond with a counteroffer package. There would then ensue a dance of complete packages, as shown in Figure 24. Few pairs pirouetted adroitly enough to achieve closure. For example, the AMPO negotiator might initially offer a package such as that scored at point A_1; City

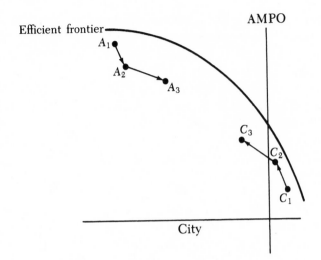

Figure 24. A dance of complete packages.

might offer a counterpackage such as that evaluated at C_1; AMPO might respond with A_2; and so on. Somewhere along the line the negotiating pair would give up the orderly procession and thrash around, trying jointly to devise an entire package. Mostly to no avail.

More successful was the technique of building a package from the bottom up with successive compromises. After thrashing around, some negotiating pairs began systematically by choosing some issue with a few levels—issues like reinstatement, or two-man patrols, or creation of the rank of corporal—and would compromise on a central focal point. If an issue had three levels (high, medium, and low), it was fairly certain that they'd start at medium. Many subjects were astute enough to select two issues for joint compromise: one party would get his way on one issue for a reciprocal gesture on the other issue. Most subjects proceeded tentatively: agreements made at early stages were not treated as irrevocable, but were reviewed later as the package evolved and grew in complexity. Each negotiator would keep his own score along the way and would test at each stage to see if the partial package seemed destined to clear the reservation-price hurdle (-250 for City and 600 for AMPO). Each side may have complained that he

was not getting enough, but most subjects, like most real-world negotiators, were embarrassed not to make progress, and time was at a
premium. So compromises were made and a package would result.

In order to get a more specific idea of how these pairs of negotiators might have arrived at their agreements, we can imagine a conversation between two hypothetical negotiators: Mr. A (representing AMPO) and Ms. C. (representing City). Table 8 shows an
abbreviated scoring schedule depicting possible beneficial tradeoffs. Mr. A and Ms. C have already built up a compromise contract
and now they are looking for jointly beneficial improvements. In
building up the contract package issue by issue, they have tentatively agreed to a $600 increase in starting salary, to a five-day in-
crease in vacation for officers with less than five years' service, and
to a greater than 20 percent increase in two-man patrols.

After a few suggestions for joint improvement have been offered
and rejected, Ms. C says, "How would you feel about increasing
starting salaries from $600 to $700 and simultaneously lowering our
agreed increase of vacation days from five days to three? This
would be a rough standoff for me [not quite true], but if it would
offer advantages to you I would go along with it, provided that you
would then try to help *me* out." Actually, Ms. C gains a modest 5
points for this simultaneous change, whereas Mr. A gains 100
points.

TABLE 8. *An abbreviated scoring schedule for Mr. A and Ms. C*
(a dot indicates the level of a tentative agreement).

Issue	Level	Ms. C	Mr. A
Increase in salary: starting	• 600	−4	700
	700	−8	850
	800	−16	1,000
Increase in vacations:	3	−6	60
less than 5 years' service	• 5	−15	110
Two-man patrols	Status quo	+15	−25
	• Greater than 20% increase, but less than strictly two-man patrols	−5	50

"That's something of an improvement for me," he responds cautiously. "But how about going from $700 to $800 in starting salaries? Then I could possibly go back to the status quo on the two-man patrol cars."

Ms. C at first sounds very dubious. "Well, that's an awfully high starting salary. On the other hand, I do hate to see so many two-man patrols in these financially hard-up times. City Hall might not like this, but—all right, it's a deal." So she nets an increase of 12 points and he an increase of 75 points. And the migration continues northeasterly.

STRATEGIC MISREPRESENTATIONS

The art of compromise centers on the willingness to give up something in order to get something else in return. Successful artists get more than they give up. A common ploy is to exaggerate the importance of what one is giving up and to minimize the importance of what one gets in return. Such posturing is part of the game. In most cultures these self-serving negotiating stances are expected, as long as they are kept in decent bounds. Most people would not call this "lying," just as they would choose not to label as "lying" the exaggerations that are made in the adversarial confrontations of a courtroom. I call such exaggerations "strategic misrepresentations." The expression is not my own invention; it was used by game theorists and mathematical economists long before I adopted it.

Let's say that in the course of negotiations, Mr. A demands in no uncertain terms that Commissioner Daniels be dismissed. Ms. C protests equally strenuously that her side will never agree to such a move. This is a strategic misrepresentation: City indeed wants to get rid of Daniels, but AMPO doesn't know it. Ms. C later "reluctantly" backs down (picking up a positive 40 points for doing so) and gets Mr. A to make some concessions in addition. In our experiments, the payoffs achieved by City players depended to some degree on how they handled the Daniels issue. What behavior is appropriate in such a situation? I am not a cynical person, but I suspect that in the real world most City negotiators would exact a price from AMPO for getting rid of Daniels.

Some experienced practitioners may argue that Daniels, not

being part of the contract, should never have been part of the contract issues to be discussed. Perhaps so, but we could have concocted some other issue that would have presented the same strategic possibilities. The ethical dilemma cannot be sidestepped so easily.

Some lawyers might want to argue like talmudic scholars: although it would be inappropriate for Ms. C to *say* that she wants to keep Daniels, it would be all right for her to *intimate* that she wants to keep him, as long as she doesn't actually come out and say so. "So you want to get rid of Daniels? Well, let's talk about that later." Or: "If you're willing to give in on those inflationary two-man patrols, then I guess I could go along with you on the Daniels issue." Is this sort of misrepresentation any more acceptable? I myself would not feel comfortable engaging in such deceptions, either by direct statement or by intimation; but I might do so in a real-world context if the cause I was representing were important enough. If I were a subject in an experiment and were competing merely for points, I would not misrepresent in this case. A lot depends on the stridency of the negotiations and on the desire to maintain good relations for the future.

The Daniels issue raises a related question about advice. Common wisdom says that one should start negotiations by trying to settle easy questions first. What could be easier than an issue for which each negotiating party prefers the same outcome? But even in this case, if one party feels very strongly about this outcome and the other party is almost indifferent, then the latter can extract a concession from the former by acting strategically. Bargainers are often advised that they should purposely add to the negotiation agenda issues that they do not really care about, in the hope that the other side will feel strongly about one of these superfluous issues— strong enough to be willing to make compensating concessions in return for dropping the offending issue. This questionable strategy can, of course, poison the atmosphere of the negotiations, with detriment to both parties.

Strategic misrepresentation can also cause inefficiencies. Consider a distributive bargaining problem in which there is a zone of agreement in actual, but not necessarily in revealed, reservation prices. An inefficiency can arise only if the parties fail to come to an agreement. By bargaining hard the parties may fail to come to an agreement, even though any point in the zone of agreement would yield a better outcome for both than the no-agreement state. Still, one cannot conclude from this observation that a negotiator should unilaterally and truthfully reveal his or her reservation price.

Contrast this situation with an integrative bargaining problem, in which it may be possible for the negotiators to enlarge the pie before cutting it. In order to squeeze out potential joint gains, the negotiators must do some joint problem solving. If both sides strategically misrepresent their value tradeoffs, then inefficient contracts will often result. In complicated negotiations where uncertainties loom large, there may be contracts that are far better for each negotiating party than the no-contract alternative, but it might take considerable skill at joint problem solving to discover those possibilities. Without the right atmosphere and without some reasonably truthful communication of values, such jointly acceptable contracts might never be discerned. It is my impression from observing many negotiation exercises that each negotiator is well advised to behave cooperatively and honestly (for example, by disclosing tradeoffs) in seeking joint gains, but to bargain more toughly when it comes to sharing the jointly created pie.

In general, I would advise negotiators to act openly and honestly on efficiency concerns; tradeoffs should be disclosed (if the adversary reciprocates), but reservation prices should be kept private. Like most similar pieces of advice, this could be called into question by a stark counterexample, like what to do about Commissioner Daniels; but still, on balance, I think this is a good way to proceed—even on the Daniels issue.

Ms. C—or any other negotiator, for that matter—should try to maximize her score. But she does not necessarily do better for herself if she hurts AMPO. (I'm assuming here that relevant aspects of altruism or malevolence are already embedded in her scoring scheme.) Indeed, if she empathizes with Mr. A and he reciprocates by empathizing with her, then she might gain overall. Manifestations of concern for the other person may be a good strategic way for you, as a negotiator, to enhance your own score. And if, in addition, you gain pleasure by helping someone else, then so much the better. (Actually, your scoring system should be modified by incorporating this altruistic embellishment.) The other person might be thinking analogously; and it may be to your selfish advantage for you to encourage this reciprocated respect for the other's needs.[2]

THE VALUE OF EXPLICIT TRADEOFFS

In integrative negotiations where there are many issues to be settled, especially when some of these cannot readily be evaluated in monetary terms, the negotiators may have only rough qualitative tradeoffs. In AMPO versus City, the tradeoffs were quantified and crisp. What happens if, as very often is the case in practice, quantitative scores are not generated prior to negotiations? This question prompted a modified version of the confidential instructions to City and to AMPO.[3] Let's call the original sets of instructions, with numerical scoring systems, the quantitative version. In the modified version, we deleted all *quantitative* scoring information and substituted instead *qualitative* comparisons of tradeoffs across the issues. We wanted to remain faithful to the quantitative version and thus tried to use words that conveyed the information of the deleted numbers. The qualitative version did not have tidy numerical summaries of the scoring systems.

We conducted four types of negotiations: (1) quantitative City versus quantitative AMPO—the control group; (2) qualitative City versus quantitative AMPO; (3) quantitative City versus qualitative AMPO; and (4) qualitative City versus qualitative AMPO. We obtained results for about thirty negotiating pairs for each of the three experimental types, and considerably more for the control group. Subjects who played according to the qualitative instructions were numerically scored by using the numbers in the original quantita-

2. It would be interesting to try the following experiment. Take an exercise like AMPO versus City and fully disclose to both sides the scoring system, but not reservation prices. Let half the subjects (the control group) negotiate under this arrangement. For the other half (the experimental group), privately tell each City player that he will be scored by how well he does, but that he will receive, in addition, a small fraction of the score of his AMPO adversary. This would formally build in the empathy factor. The fraction could probably be so adjusted that City players operating according to this altruistically modified incentive structure would actually do better than the control group, even if the comparison were made without the empathy component of the score for the experimental group.

3. This version was devised with the assistance of Jacob Ulvila.

tive version (on which the qualitative version was based). The results were as follows.

First, when both sides negotiated from qualitative instructions the outcomes were extremely variable and, comparatively speaking, most inefficient: the negotiated agreements fell far from the efficient frontier and the negotiators left a lot of potential joint gains on the table. Second, each side was better off with quantitative instructions, no matter whether the other side had qualitative or quantitative instructions. Third, and somewhat unexpectedly, if a City player had qualitative instructions, she was better off playing against an AMPO adversary who had quantitative rather than qualitative instructions.

How can this last result be rationalized? First, players with quantitative information were able to take the analytical lead in seeking joint gains for both sides and could do this fairly efficiently. Second, players with only qualitative information felt uncomfortable when their adversaries did all sorts of numerical calculations and seemed to know more thoroughly what was going on; so their bargaining grew tougher as they became more uncomfortable.

Interestingly, this observation seemed to hold only for City players: when AMPO players had qualitative information, they were not helped when their adversaries got quantitative information. Still, some AMPO players claimed that when they were in the inferior (qualitative) information position and playing against a quantitative City player, they also tended to bargain more vigorously.

More research clearly needs to be done. Our experiment showed conclusively only that (1) quantitative information helps the recipient of that information, and (2) it is better for both players to have quantitative information than for both not to have it—"better" in terms of higher scores and lower variability of scores.

In the process of trying to sort out these conflicting results by means of interviews with the disadvantaged players (that is, players with lesser information), I learned something else that could use further investigation. Some players with qualitative information claimed that they bargained harder and longer in this exercise than in others because they did not have clear reservation prices. Thus, they did not experience the inner conflict that many negotiators do when they realize during negotiations that they have surpassed their reservation hurdles. "It's difficult to exaggerate with an innocent face," one stated, "when you know quite well that the numbers say otherwise." I mentioned this result to an experienced negotiator who then claimed that this is one of the reasons why negotiators are often not told, and do not want to know, crisp reservation prices. Think of the ethics of that one.

11

Tradeoffs and Concessions

In preparing for negotiations, either bilateral or multilateral, each side should try to sort out its own preferences. Bargainers are continually asked during negotiations whether they prefer one constellation of outcomes to another: Would they rather end up with this or that? Not only must they decide what they ultimately want, but they also must determine what they would be willing to give up in order to achieve their goal. How can a negotiator assess the values of various tradeoffs, and what effect do these values have on the dynamics of negotiations?

Suppose that you are the administrator of the Environmental Protection Agency and that you must choose between Policy A and Policy B. Your staff has prepared a table listing the attributes that are of concern to you (some involving economic efficiency, some economic equity, some health indices, some environmental indices, some political indices) and has evaluated the two policies on these attributes. A is better than B on some attributes and worse on others. How can you think systematically about such composite sets of evaluations? This issue arises not only in negotiations, but more broadly in decision and policy making.

The problem is mind-boggling in its complexity, but formal analysis can help bring some order to the morass. One approach is to try to generate scoring systems that assign points to various levels within each attribute and that quantify tradeoffs between issues. This is not easily done, but values can be probed by observing preferences between simple hypothetical choices for which all but two or three attributes have identical scores, and then by invoking some intuitively plausible consistency requirements. Most decision and policy makers are skeptical and suspicious of this whole approach. They just don't see the need for formalization, believing that the decision maker can simply make a subjective choice among the real alternatives when they are presented at the time of the decision. But now let's change the setting. Suppose that you as the EPA administrator have to give instructions to a representative who must negotiate a complex contract with industry representatives. Several issues are involved and compromises will have to be made during negotiations. What's more, you must handle dozens of these same kinds of negotiations simultaneously. At this point, the desire to establish the equivalent of a formal scoring system becomes more compelling: without it, the representative would be at sea, with no way of knowing how to make tradeoffs between issues, and you would not be able to delegate your authority.

THE ADDITIVE MODEL

Assume that prior to its negotiations with AMPO, City listed the ten issues to be discussed and the possible levels on each of the issues. The City negotiators were concerned about money, real and perceived security of its citizens, security of the police, symbolic consequences with possible ramifications for other wage negotiations, political image, and so on. Suppose that they started out monetizing various issues, such as starting salaries, maximum salaries, vacations, creation of the rank of corporal, number of sergeants; but that they found it hard to put a price tag on the reinstatement of suspended officers (there was a principle at stake), on two-man patrols (lives were at stake), on the Police Review Board (justice and alienation were at stake), on the police commissioner (the mayor's job may have been at stake). How could they put a dollar figure on what happened to the Police Review Board? One way to do this would be to imagine a situation in which everything was settled except the issues of the Police Review Board and the starting salary level. The negotiators could then decide how they would be willing to trade one against the other—in effect, acting as if they were placing a monetary value on various Police Review Board options. It's the structure of the problem situation that essentially forces this evaluation.

When we turn our attention to other applications (such as international treaty negotiations), reducing everything to money may not be convenient or appealing. Some abstract scoring system may be easier to work with. In the case of AMPO versus City we could have evaluated City's reactions for nonmonetary issues in terms of equivalent salary concessions, and thereby monetized these nonmonetary concerns. This might, in fact, have been the more "natural" approach. But the introduction of abstract scores for City served a useful purpose: they will be easier and more comfortable to handle when we deal with subsequent examples like the Panama Canal Treaty and the Camp David negotiations.

In the laboratory experiment, we assumed that City and AMPO assigned a specific point score to each outcome level on each issue and then added these to get an entire contract evaluation. We'll call this an *additive scoring system* — although there was one small deviation from this system. Remember that if City held AMPO to zero additional vacation days for all officers, City achieved a bonus of 10 points. In this case we simply could not add up City's score for these two issues. The bonus introduced what is known as an *interaction effect* between the vacation issues. If we combined the two separate vacation issues into a single composite issue, then we would have strict additivity among the nine resulting issues.

Considering just two issues — starting salary and number of sergeants — suppose that the other seven issues (treating vacations as a composite issue) are already fixed. We're now investigating tradeoffs between starting salary and sergeants only. In the scoring system we are using, notice that any tradeoff comparisons between levels on these two issues do *not* depend on the levels of the remaining seven issues: the tradeoffs between starting salaries and sergeants can be said to be *preferentially independent* of the levels of the remaining issues. Indeed, it can easily be seen that with an additive scoring system, the tradeoffs between the levels of any two issues are preferentially independent of the levels of the remaining issues. It can also be seen (but not so easily!) that the converse is true: *if there are more than two issues, and if the tradeoffs between the levels on any two issues are preferentially independent of the remaining issues, then an additive scoring system is appropriate.*

Let's look at one particular technique for obtaining scores for the additive case, using a fictitious situation that is just complicated enough to illustrate the complexities I wish to address. Suppose that you, the manager of an expanding business, are entering into negotiations with a building contractor for the construction of a fac-

tory. You are concerned about three factors: cost, time to completion, and quality. From preliminary discussions you limit the
ranges of these factors to, respectively, $3.0–4.5 million, 250–400
days, and a "best" value of 1 to a "worst" value of 5 (on an ordinal
scale). You would most prefer a cost of $3.0 million, a time of 250
days, and the best quality (an index of 1). But you realize that it's
highly unlikely you will be able to negotiate such a deal.

Assume that your tradeoffs between the levels of any two factors,
keeping the level of the third factor fixed, do not depend on the
level of this third factor. For example, your tradeoffs between cost
and time do not depend on quality, as long as the level of quality is
held fixed. So it's legitimate in this case for you to seek an additive
scoring system. You agree for normalization purposes to give the
best contract ($3.0 million, 250 days, quality 1) a score of 100 points
and the worst contract ($4.5 million, 400 days, quality 5) a score of
zero points. This is like an exam with three questions, in which the
scorer must decide how much weight should be given to each question and how many points should be given to each partially correct
answer. You decide to score individual factors in the same way
(100 = best, 0 = worst), and to combine the scores with proportional weights that sum to 1. For example, suppose that you give a
weight of .5 to factor C (cost), a weight of .3 to factor T (time), and a
weight of .2 to factor Q (quality). Suppose that the internal component scoring is as shown in Figure 25. A contract that gives you $4
million, 350 days, and quality 2 would then receive—multiplying
weight times score for each factor—a total score of $(.5 \times 50) + (.3 \times
25) + (.2 \times 80)$, or 48.5 points.

How should you determine the weights of the factors (reflecting
the importance of each) and the component scoring within each factor? Following are some observations that should provide insights
into these questions.[1]

Starting from the worst case ($4.5 million, 400 days, quality 5), if
you have the choice of improving one factor from the worst to the
best level, let's suppose that you would most prefer to improve the
cost factor first, the time factor second, and the quality factor third.
This reflects the ordinal ranking of the weights. Suppose, furthermore, that you would be indifferent between improving the cost

---

1. For a systematic discussion, see Keeney and Raiffa (1976).

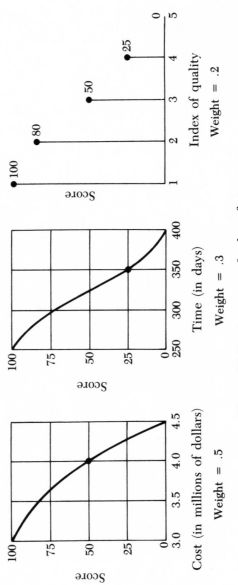

Figure 25. Scoring system for three factors.

factor alone and improving both the time and quality factor together, reflecting the fact that .5 = .3 + .2. Using the exam analogy: getting the cost question perfect and the other questions completely wrong would be as desirable as getting the cost question completely wrong and the others completely right.

The cost factor. The more you spend, the more important it is that you save a given increment of money. Reducing your costs from $4.5 million to $4.0 million is just as important as reducing your costs from $4.0 million to $3.0 million, which accounts for the shape of your cost function.

The time factor. Improving the time value from 400 days downward is not very important at first, but improvements become more important as the value goes from 350 days to 300; thereafter, the value of time reductions decreases (which accounts for the shape of your time function).

The quality factor. Going from one quality index to the next is approximately worth the same as moving between any other two indices, except that quality index 2 is closer in value to quality index 1 than to quality index 3.

Roughly, the way to go about constructing any scoring system is to formulate some rough guidelines, and then to tune the system by manipulating numbers and curves and by testing the implied results. There are fancier and more systematic methods, but the task should be approached in the same way one would grade an exam with several questions. If you are solely responsible for giving a grade and you don't have to explain your grading to anyone else or to the student, then you might want merely to respond intuitively and impressionistically to the entire exam. But if you want someone else to do the grading for you, then some scoring system, even if it is not perfect, can be a great help. A case can also be made for adopting some formal system of grading even if you are not accountable to anyone and do not plan to delegate authority to an agent. A formal scheme of your own devising might help you decide how to grade each question separately and how to combine the scores of different questions.

An additive scoring system sometimes falls far short of what is reasonable. This may be a result of the interdependence between factors, an extreme example being the case where preference ranking of levels within one factor depends on the level of another factor. For example, the better the military defenses of an ally of Country X, the better off Country X will be; however, X's preferences for the ally's military defenses (the more the better) might *reverse* (to the less the better) if the level of their friendship slips below some critical point.

Factors may also be interdependent when there is a need for balance or equity. Suppose that you are a negotiator, acting in a benevolent way so as to favor two groups (A and B) internal to your side. For any contract you negotiate, you are primarily concerned with the benefits to groups A and B. For political reasons you must make sure, however, that the benefits to A are commensurate with those accruing to B. The value of an increase in benefits to A may depend critically on the level of benefits to B; indeed, if benefits to B are at a very low level, the increase in already high benefits to A may be deemed undesirable. An additive scheme that scores the benefits independently for A and for B and adds these together misses the need for balance.

In cases such as these, a *nonadditive* scoring system can be used. Nonadditive systems are not too difficult for current state-of-the-art measurement, but they are too difficult and too involved to be discussed here. Suffice it to say that often there may be many factors under consideration, but only a few will be interdependent; negotiators can derive advantage from grouping them together and treating them as one composite factor in an otherwise additive scheme.

VALUE AND UTILITY FUNCTIONS

Researchers sometimes distinguish between a *value* scoring scheme and a *utility* scoring scheme (see Keeney and Raiffa, 1976), but this distinction is not standard. In the case involving cost, time, and quality, the scoring system, as we have seen, allows you to assign an overall numerical value to any contract. The scoring system has been tuned in such a way that contracts with higher scores are preferred. No uncertainties are involved. Such a system can be called a *value* scoring system.

Now suppose that you must decide between a compromise contract ($4 million, 350 days, quality 2) and a gamble in which, with equal probability, you could end up with the best contract ($3 million, 250 days, quality 1) or with the worst contract ($4.5 million,

400 days, quality 5). The value scores of the best and worst contracts are, respectively, 100 and 0, and therefore the gamble has an
expected value return of 50. But regardless of what the numbers
imply, you might strongly prefer the certainty of the contract with a
score of 48.5 to the uncertainty of the gamble with the higher expected score of 50. This is not surprising, because the scoring system was constructed on the basis of nongambling tradeoff options:
the derived numbers do not reflect any attitudes toward risk. Here
is where the advantages of utility scoring become apparent. Such
techniques enable one to find suitable scoring procedures that not
only reflect preferences under certainty, but that appropriately use
expected utility calculations as guidelines for choices between lotteries with well-specified probabilities.[2]

In negotiations, probabilities may become relevant in several
ways. The consequences associated with an agreed-upon final contract might involve uncertainties not under the control of the negotiators. Differences in probability assessments might be exploited
in terms of contingency contracts. But even in idealized cases
where there are no external uncertainties outside the control of the
negotiators, each negotiator is uncertain about what his adversary
ultimately will do. Should Steve hold out for $350,000 in the Elm-
tree House sale, instead of settling for $300,000? Should a union,
which can secure a given contract from management, refuse to
accept the contract and submit to the uncertainties of voluntary
arbitration?

A well-developed theory of utility analysis has been devised to
handle both uncertainties and multiple attributes, but the theory,
while operational, is not easy to use and requires a level of co-
herency that few individuals, and still fewer groups, achieve. Most
people, even in simple risky situations, don't behave the way the
theory of utility would have them behave. There are a few researchers who prefer to trust the recommendations of formal utility
analysis rather than their own intuition, even though this behavior
would not occur without the existence of the theory. A larger num-

2. Many analysts assume that a value scoring system—designed for tradeoffs
under uncertainty—can also be used for probabilistic choice (using expected
values). Such an assumption is wrong theoretically, but as I become more experienced I gain more tolerance for these analytical simplifications. This is, I believe, a
relatively benign mistake in practice (see Bell and Raiffa, 1980).

ber of analysts who understand the theory simply don't trust it; they point to examples of situations (the Allais Paradox, the Ellsberg Paradox, the experimental results of Kahneman and Tversky)[3] in which they, even knowing the theory, would deliberately act out of accord with it. Some are probably confused and will eventually see the value of utility analysis. Some are not confused, but have deep psychological concerns; they may anticipate that a given act might lead to an unfortunate outcome, which will result in persistent, deeply felt pangs of regret. Such psychological concerns are usually not accommodated in applications of the theory of utility, but in principle they could be—with further complexities in the theory.

Even though you, as a negotiator, might want to act reflectively, coherently, and rationally, your adversaries in all likelihood will act with very limited rationality. Don't be naive and expect them to behave like you may want to behave. However, if they are prone to the gambler's fallacy, to an excessive zeal for certainty, to an excessive avoidance of potential ex post regret, to misperceptions of small probabilities (one could come up with a litany of so-called nonrational, descriptive behaviors), then you might be able to exploit such behavior in negotiations.

TRADEOFFS WITH TWO CONTINUOUS ISSUES

Mr. Hee and Ms. Shee are negotiating over two continuous issues: cost and time. The ranges under discussion are $3.0–4.5 million and 250–400 days. He wants high dollars and high days; she wants low dollars and low days. Figure 26 indicates by means of indifference (iso-value) curves their respective tradeoffs. He, for example, deems contracts V, Q, and P equally desirable, and thus they are on his same iso-value curve; he prefers contract R to any of the value-equivalent contracts V, Q, and P, and hence R is on a higher iso-value curve. He wants to go northeasterly; she southwesterly. Let's suppose that they have tentatively settled on a contract agreement of $4.0 million and 275 days, which is depicted as point P and which is scored 20 for him and 50 for her (see Figure 27).

Notice from Figure 26 that if the final contract were to be moved from point P along Mr. Hee's iso-value contour (along the arc PQV),

3. See Raiffa (1968) and Kahneman and Tversky (1979).

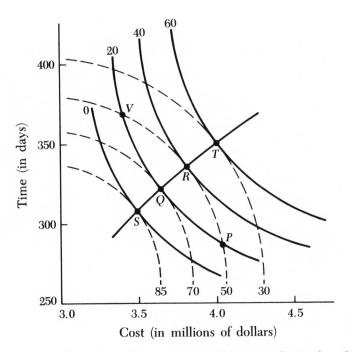

Figure 26. Iso-value curves for Mr. Hee (solid lines) and Ms. Shee (broken lines). Her direction of preference is southwest; his is northeast.

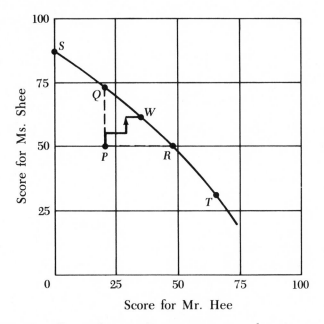

Figure 27. The efficient frontier. (Point P represents the joint scores for a contract agreement of $4.0 million and 275 days.)

his score would remain at 20 but her score would start at 50 (point P), gradually rise to 70 (point Q), and then gradually fall again to 50 (point V). Thus, if the negotiators were to try to search for joint gains starting from P, and if Mr. Hee were to indicate that he is indifferent about moving along the curve from P to Q to V, and if he invited Ms. Shee to choose a point on this curve, then she would want to select Q as the contract that best meets her needs. If, on the other hand, she were to announce that she remains indifferent for movements along curve PRV (her 50-point indifference curve), then he would most want to move to R, yielding him a return of 40. See points Q and R in Figure 27.

Observe that any point within the lens-shaped region PQVRP represents an improvement over P to him and to her (Figure 26). Also observe that any point along the curve SQRT is jointly efficient (Figure 27). His and her iso-value curves are tangent to each other whenever they pass through a point on this efficient curve, as demonstrated at points S, Q, R, and T. The efficient curve through these points is also called the "contract curve."

Let's assume that the negotiators have tentatively agreed on P, that they are looking for joint improvements, and that each party knows only his or her own iso-value curves. Following is one way that they can squeeze out joint gains. Mr. Hee starts by announcing a few points on his iso-value curve through P, but near P—say, P' a little northwest of P, and P'' a little southeast of P. Ms. Shee says that P'' is worse for her than P but that P' is an improvement. She then reciprocates: she announces points close to P' for which she is indifferent and he selects an improvement for himself. By going back and forth in this way, they each gradually improve their own scores and eventually end up with some point on the contract curve between Q and R. Figure 27 shows this as point W, and depicts their joint scores as they move from P to point W on the efficient frontier. Of course, the parties recognize that they have arrived at the efficient frontier only when they can no longer squeeze out any further improvements.

Here is another method that the negotiators can use to squeeze out joint gains. Assume that the parties do not have their own prepared iso-value curves in front of them. The aim is to jointly improve upon P. An intervenor or one of the negotiators suggests that they seek an improvement on P at some higher level of days—say, at 325 days rather than the 275 days of the tentative agreement (see Figure 28). The negotiators now try to seek a cost figure x such that a contract of x million dollars and 325 days is preferred by each party to a contract of $4 million and 275 days. The case now becomes a simple one of distributive bargaining. Along the line 325 days, Mr. Hee prefers higher x-values with some reservation price —say, $3.6 million. In other words, if he can't do at least as well as $3.6 million, he would prefer to stay at the status quo, P. The point (3.6, 325) would be on the same iso-curve as the point (4.0, 275), but we are not now assuming that he has drawn such curves. Along the line of 325 days, Ms. Shee prefers lower x-values with a reservation price of, say, $3.8 million. These reservation prices would have to be decided upon by the protagonists in the context of the problem. As in distributive bargaining, each party might be reluctant to unilaterally disclose his or her reservation price. As Figure 28 shows, there is a potential zone of agreement from 3.6 to 3.8. An appealing procedure would be to have each negotiator simultaneously submit

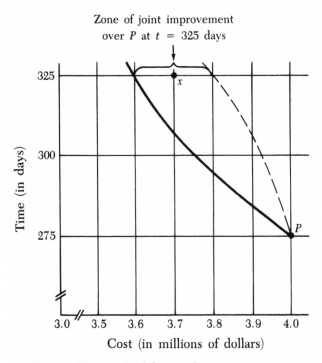

Figure 28. A method for jointly improving upon P.

a sealed offer; his would indicate what minimum x-value he would need in order for him to move from P; hers would indicate what maximum x-value she would need in order for her to move from P. With compatible offers (his offer lower than hers), they would split the difference evenly and move from P to that midpoint (recall our discussion of simultaneous-revelation resolution). Thus, if he acted nonstrategically and offered 3.6 and if she acted likewise and offered 3.8, then they would move from a contract of $4.0 million and 275 days to one of $3.7 million and 325 days. The negotiators would continue to seek joint gains from the newly arrived-at joint agreement. In this context—where improvements are sought over a given contract, where there might be a series of intervening, self-generated, distributive bargaining exercises, and where time is a factor in the search for elusive joint gains—there is a great deal of incentive for each party to act honestly and nonstrategically.

THE EFFICIENT FRONTIER WHEN BOTH SIDES USE ADDITIVE SCORING SYSTEMS

Given that both parties to a negotiation are using additive value systems, how can they reach the efficient frontier? What are the implications for the dynamics of negotiations?

Let's again assume that Mr. Hee and Ms. Shee are negotiating the issues of cost and time.[4] The additive value scoring systems for both negotiators are shown in Figure 29. Generally each protagonist would know only his or her own value system, so let's say that they both truthfully disclose their scoring systems to an intervenor. Suppose that they choose the midpoint on each issue: $3.75 million and 325 days. From Figure 29 we see that Ms. Shee will obtain a cost-component score of 50 points, which we can write as $C_S(3.75) = 50$, and a time-component score of 75, which we can write as $T_S(325) = 75$. Ms. Shee weights the cost and time factors with values .7 and .3, so for this contract she has a total value V_S of:

$$V_S(3.75, 325) = .7C_S(3.75) + .3T_S(325)$$
$$= (.7 \times 50) + (.3 \times 75)$$
$$= 57.5.$$

4. This section is more technical than conceptual. Readers who are getting bogged down may wish to skip to Chapter 12.

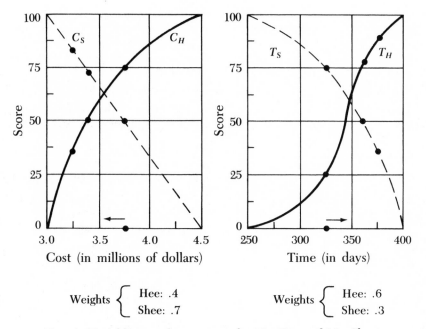

Figure 29. Additive value systems for Mr. Hee and Ms. Shee.

Mr. Hee has a cost-component score of $C_H(3.75) = 75$ and a time-component score of $T_H(325) = 25$. Since his importance weights are .4 for cost and .6 for time, his total value V_H for this contract is:

$$V_H(3.75, 325) = .4C_H(3.75) + .6T_H(325)$$
$$= (.4 \times 75) + (.6 \times 25)$$
$$= 4.50.$$

The joint scores for this contract, 45 for him and 57.5 for her, are plotted as a point in Figure 30, along with joint scores for eight other possible contracts. We see from Table 9 that the contract (3.75, 325) is inefficient: both negotiators are better off with either (3.0, 400) or (3.4, 360). Of these latter two, he would prefer (3.4, 360) and she would prefer (3.0, 400).

It should be apparent by now that, in general, Mr. Hee gives high importance weight to time and Ms. Shee to cost. So if we start with the central compromises of $c = 3.75$ and $t = 325$, then it makes joint sense to slip c to the left and t to the right. He gains as t moves from 325 to 360, both because his T_H curve is sharply increasing in this

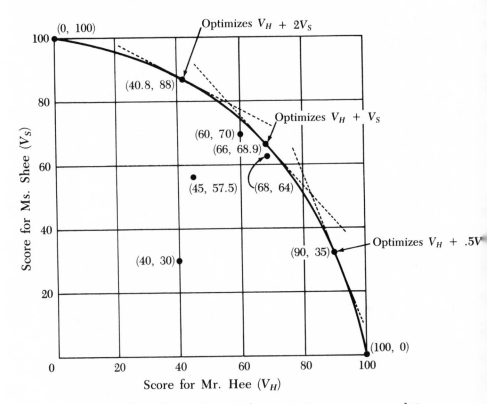

Figure 30. The efficient frontier for negotiations over cost and time.

range and because time is important to him. She also picks up some points because she gives a lot of weight to cost improvements.

Suppose that the intervenor wants to find suitable c and t values that will maximize the sum of the total scores for the two negotiators. For any (c, t) contract, the payoffs scores are as shown in Figure 31. Notice that there are four summands. The intervenor's task is to choose c and t in order to get the maximum overall total. This can be accomplished by choosing c to maximize the subtotal of the two contributions controlled by c (which are enclosed in the left-hand box), and by choosing t to maximize the subtotal of the two contributions controlled by t (in the right-hand box). Using a finer grid to do these tasks, it is possible to show that the value of c that maximizes the cost contributions is a c-value of 3.25, yielding $C_H(3.25) = 30$ and $C_S(3.25) = 83$. Recall that a c-value of 3.25 does

TABLE 9. *Evaluations of selected contracts.*

Contract		Mr. Hee			Ms. Shee		
		C_H	T_H		C_S	T_2	
Cost	Time	(Wt. = .4)	(Wt. = .6)	V_H	(Wt. = .7)	(Wt. = .3)	V_S
3.75	325	75	25	45.0	50	75	57.5
3.00	250	0	0	0.0	100	100	100.0
4.50	400	100	100	100.0	0	0	0.0
3.00	400	0	100	60.0	100	0	70.0
4.50	250	100	0	40.0	0	100	30.0
3.40	360	50	80	68.0	70	50	64.0
3.25	375	30	90	66.0	83	36	68.9
3.75	400	75	100	90.0	50	0	35.0
3.00	350	0	68	40.8	100	60	88.0

not maximize $C_H(c) + C_S(c)$, but rather maximizes $.4C_H(c) + .7C_S(c)$. Similarly, a t-value of 375 maximizes $.6T_H(t) + .3T_S(t)$, yielding $T_H(375) = 90$ and $T_S(375) = 36$.

The contract (3.25, 375) gives Mr. Hee a total score of 66.0 and Ms. Shee a score of 68.9, for a combined total score of 134.9 (see Table 9). No other (c, t) contract can yield a combined total score greater than this.

Obviously, the joint evaluation (66.0, 68.9) must lie on the efficient frontier. There is no way of squeezing out additional joint gains. If simultaneously he could get more than 66.0 and she could get more than 68.9, their combined scores would be more than 134.9, which is the maximum achievable; hence (66.0, 68.9) is efficient.

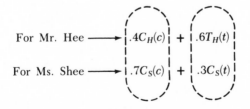

Figure 31. Payoff scores for the contract (c, t).

The intervenor now knows three points on the efficient frontier: (0, 100), (100, 0), and (66.0, 68.9). How can he find a point on the frontier that would yield Mr. Hee a higher value? Instead of choosing c and t to maximize the combined total, the intervenor can choose c and t to maximize Mr. Hee's score plus half of Ms. Shee's, thus giving her less weight. Since her full contribution is $.7C_S(c) + .3T_S(t)$, her .5 weighted contribution is $.35C_S(c) + .15T_S(t)$. Hence, the intervenor should now choose c to maximize $.4C_H(c) + .35C_S(c)$, and choose t to maximize $.6T_H(t) + .15T_S(t)$. Once again, by means of a finer grid, it would be possible to show that a c-value of 3.75 is best and a t-value of 400 is best. The contract (3.75, 400) yields a total score of 90 for Mr. Hee and 35 for Ms. Shee, with a weighted average of $90 + .5(35) = 107.5$. No other joint evaluation will yield a weighted average ($V_H + .5V_S$) higher than 107.5. Thus, a joint evaluation of (90, 35) is on the efficient frontier.

In a similar manner, it can be demonstrated that the contract (3.0, 350) maximizes $V_H + 2V_S$ (see Table 9 and Figure 30). The procedure should now be clear. These ideas can be generalized to more than two issues, provided that the scoring system remains additive; for a detailed analysis, see below.

Appendix : Generalizing to More Than Two Issues

Let i (for $i = 1, 2$) designate a negotiator; let j (for $j = 1, \ldots, J$) designate an issue; let x_j be a generic value of the jth issue with domain $[a_j, b_j]$ (for $j = 1, \ldots, J$); let $V_{ij}(x_j)$ be the component score of negotiator i on j at x_j; let w_{ij} be i's importance weight on issue j where $\Sigma_j w_{ij} = 1$ (for $i = 1, 2$); let i's total score for contract $x = (x_1, \ldots, x_j)$ be given by

$$V_i(x) = \sum_j w_{ij} V_{ij}(x_j).$$

If we weight V_1 by 1 and V_2 by λ (which we will vary to get different points on the efficient frontier), we observe that

$$V_1(x) + \lambda V_2(x) = \sum_j w_{1j}V_{1j}(x_j) + \lambda \sum_j w_{2j}V_{2j}(x_j)$$

$$= \sum_j [w_{1j}V_{1j}(x_j) + \lambda w_{2j}V_{2j}(x_j)].$$

Hence, if we want to choose x to maximize $V_1(x) + \lambda V_2(x)$, then we merely have to choose x_j in $[a_j, b_j]$ to maximize

$$w_{1j}V_{1j}(x_j) + \lambda w_{2j}V_{2j}(x_j),$$

for $j = 1, \ldots, J$. Let $x_j^{(\lambda)}$ be an optimum for that λ and let $x^{(\lambda)} = (x_1^{(\lambda)}, \ldots, x_j^{(\lambda)}, \ldots, x_J^{(\lambda)})$. The joint evaluation $(V_1(x^{(\lambda)}), V_2(x^{(\lambda)}))$ will be a point on the efficient frontier whose supporting tangent line is the locus of (V_1, V_2) points for which

$$V_1 + \lambda V_2 = V_1(x^{(\lambda)}) + \lambda V_2(x^{(\lambda)}).$$

The analysis is easily generalizable to more negotiators by letting $i = 1, \ldots, I$ and in lieu of $V_1(x) + \lambda V_2(x)$ using

$$\sum_{i=1}^{I} \lambda_i V_i(x)$$

for a set of $(\lambda_1, \ldots, \lambda_I)$ weights. In this case $x_j^{(\lambda)}$ is a maximizer of

$$\sum_i \lambda_i w_{ij}V_i(x_j),$$

and all goes through as before.

12

The Panama
Canal Negotiations

Negotiations concerning the Panama Canal can be divided into two
separate sets. The first took place at the turn of the century, when
the United States decided on Panama rather than Nicaragua as the
site for an isthmian passage between the Atlantic and Pacific. The
second set occurred in the mid-1970s, when a treaty was at last produced that the U.S. Senate considered acceptable for ratification.
We will concentrate on the more recent of these two sets of negotiations, since it presents interesting complexities for analysis. There
were many issues under discussion, and the parties to the negotiations were not monolithic: external negotiations had to be coordi-
nated with internal negotiations. John Dunlop, former secretary of
labor and a formidable negotiator, once remarked that bilateral negotiations usually require three agreements—one across the table
and one on each side of the table. In the case of the Panama Canal
discussions, this requirement caused seemingly endless delays and
difficulties.

THE BATTLE OF THE ROUTES

The story of the earlier stage of the negotiations is a fascinating one,
and has been chronicled by a number of historians.[1] For our purposes, it will be sufficient to give a brief outline of the main events
relating to the negotiations themselves.

1. For an excellent account, see McCullough (1977). The description given here is
based on McCullough's book.

166

1847	A treaty with Colombia (at this time known as New Granada) grants the United States right of transit over the Isthmus of Panama, guarantees Panama's neutrality, and recognizes Colombia's rights of sovereignty over the Isthmus (formerly part of Spain).
1850	Clayton-Bulwer Treaty is signed. Great Britain and the United States declare "that neither one nor the other will ever obtain . . . for itself any exclusive control" over any ship canal over Nicaragua, nor "exercise any dominion over . . . any part of Central America."
1881–1889	A French company headed by Ferdinand de Lesseps, the Compagnie Nouvelle du Canal de Panama, begins work on a canal but goes bankrupt eight years later. Capital lost: approximately $287 million (more than the cost of the Suez Canal). Lives lost: approximately 20,000. An overwhelming disaster.
1899	The third Isthmian Canal Commission (the Walker Commission), under the chairmanship of Rear Admiral John G. Walker, is created by the U.S. Congress to study the choice of routes. (The first commission was created in 1895; the second in 1897.) The United States is convinced that the canal is a necessity.
1900	The first Hay-Pauncefote Treaty is signed, permitting the United States to build and maintain an isthmian canal (but without the right to fortify it) and providing for its neutrality in peace or war. The treaty is rejected by the Senate in its original form; amended by the Senate on December 20; then rejected by Great Britain.
1901	In November the Walker Commission, like the two preceding commissions, comes out in favor of the Nicaraguan route. The commission's report is submitted *in secrecy* to President Theodore Roosevelt. Two days later the second Hay-Pauncefote Treaty is signed, giving the United States free rein to build and fortify an isthmian canal and superseding the Clayton-Bulwer Treaty.

Negotiations between the United States and the Compagnie Nouvelle extended over many years. Although the negotiations involved various issues, the principal concern was the amount of money that the United States would pay the French for their holdings in Panama. These holdings were considerable: 30,000 acres of land; the Panama Railroad; 2,000 buildings (offices, living quarters, storehouses); hospitals in Panama City and Colon; surveying instruments and medical supplies; and an immense amount of machinery (tugs, launches, dredges, excavators, pumps, cranes, locomotives, railroad cars), which had already excavated over 36 million cubic yards of earth. The Compagnie Nouvelle reportedly thought that these assets were worth $109 million; the Walker Commission claimed they were worth no more than $40 million.

One can imagine the two sides bargaining—the French asking $140 million, the Americans offering $20 million, and gradually each side easing to, respectively, $100 million and $30 million. Knowing that the United States desperately wanted an isthmian passage and aware that the U.S. strategy was to play Nicaragua against Panama, the French, too, devised a ploy: theirs was to hint at deals with the Russians and the English for financing continued French involvement in the canal's construction. They were therefore extremely agitated when, on November 21, 1901, the *New York Journal* leaked details of the Walker Commission's secret report to the president. Although the report made a strong case for Panama, the cost of buying out the Compagnie Nouvelle was claimed to be prohibitive, and the commission recommended the Nicaraguan path between the seas. On December 19 the U.S. House of Representatives declared itself ready to consider the Hepburn Bill, which called for a Nicaraguan canal.

Two days later a storm broke in Paris. The president of the Compagnie Nouvelle resigned, and rioting took place at a stockholders' meeting. Sell at any price to the United States! The French offer came tumbling down overnight to a mere $40 million when they received further leaks that this amount might be acceptable. It was indeed acceptable to Roosevelt, but he had a lot of convincing to do. On January 10, 1902, a day after the House had voted favorably on the Hepburn Bill, Roosevelt called each member of the Walker Commission separately into the Oval Office and twisted arms. A week later there was a new Walker Commission report favoring Panama. But the campaign to convince the French of the United

States' preference for Nicaragua had done its job only too well: many senators had also been convinced. The debate in the Senate was heated. The vigorous efforts of one of Panama's supporters, Senator Mark Hanna, succeeded in changing a few minds (some began calling the project the "Hannama Canal"), but a week before the Senate vote there still were not enough Panamanian enthusiasts. At this point, a decisive role was played by a Frenchman named Philippe Bunau-Varilla, an engineer and investor who was dedicated to defending France's interests in Panama. Three days before the deciding vote, he sent each senator a pretty Nicaraguan stamp showing a railroad wharf in the foreground and, in the background, Momotombo in magnificent eruption. "What have the Nicaraguans chosen to characterize on their coat of arms and on their postage stamps? Volcanoes!" Bunau-Varilla made his point. On June 19, 1902, Panama won in the Senate—by the uncomfortably narrow margin of eight votes.

In this story, the Battle of the Routes has been portrayed as a two-party distributive bargaining problem in which both sides tried to make credible commitments by nurturing credible alternatives. But where was Colombia in all these negotiations? The Colombians were basically ignored until the Americans and the French had decided their own affairs. After a treaty had already been drawn up, U.S. Secretary of State John Hay offered a deal to the Colombian chargé d'affaires, Thomas Herran: sign the treaty that the United States was offering Colombia, or else the United States would commence negotiations with Nicaragua. Communications were not very reliable between Washington and Bogota, and Herran, acting without orders from home, succumbed to the pressure. On January 22, 1903, the Hay-Herran Treaty was signed, giving the United States the right to lease a six-mile-wide strip across the Isthmus for $10 million and an annuity of $250,000. This treaty, however, was rejected by the Colombian senate in August.

Rumors of a revolution in Panama were already in the air. On November 2, in order to maintain "free and uninterrupted transit" across the Isthmus, Roosevelt ordered warships to proceed to Panama—thus guaranteeing the success of the projected revolt. The revolutionary forces seized power the following day in Panama City, while U.S. ships prevented the interference of Colombian troops.

The independence of the Republic of Panama was proclaimed.

In an unusual move, the new republic named the Frenchman Bunau-Varilla as its minister to the United States. On November 18 the United States and Panama signed a new agreement, the Hay–Bunau-Varilla Treaty, which set forth the same provisions as those of the Hay-Herran Treaty. Needless to say, the new treaty was ratified by the U.S. Senate.

In 1914 the Panama Canal was opened.

ELLSWORTH BUNKER AND THE PANAMA
CANAL TREATY

Relations between the United States and Panama became distinctly less cordial in the decades that followed. In 1939 the Hay–Bunau-Varilla treaty was amended, eliminating the right of the United States to intervene in Panamanian affairs. In 1959 mobs of Panamanians invaded the Canal Zone to protest U.S. sovereignty and to demand complete revision of the treaty. Things went from bad to worse during the 1960s and 1970s:

1964   Riots break out in the Canal Zone as Panamanians protest U.S. failure to abide by an agreement calling for simultaneous display of Panamanian and American flags. Relations with the United States are broken off, but are resumed after three months.

1967   Negotiations with Panama are initiated by President Lyndon Johnson. Three draft treaties are negotiated; none is ratified by either side.

1968   In a military coup, Panama's National Assembly is dissolved and constitutional guarantees are suspended. Colonel José M. Pinilla is sworn in as provisional president.

1969   Brigadier General Omar Torrijos Herrera, one of the instigators of the coup, emerges as the nation's leader.

1971   Panama asks the United States to withdraw its Peace Corps. Negotiations are resumed, but are unsuccessful.

1973   The U.N. Security Council proposes a resolution guaranteeing "full respect for Panama's effective sovereignty over all of its territory." The resolution is vetoed by the United States.

President Nixon being preoccupied with the Watergate scandal, it was Secretary of State Henry Kissinger who appointed a new negotiator to deal with Panama. The man chosen was the highly respected Ambassador-at-Large Ellsworth Bunker, fresh from his intensive involvement in the negotiations leading to U.S. disengagement from Vietnam. Bunker's task was to reconcile somehow the emotionally charged demands of the Panamanians with the interests of various U.S. parties: the Department of Defense, Congress, and nongovernmental interest groups, to mention only a few.[2]

To do this, Bunker had not only to come to some agreement with the Panamanians, but to bring antagonistic forces within the United States to some grudging compromise position. The Department of Defense, clearly, would have to be allowed a role in the negotiations: in return for relaxing their rigid adherence to the status quo, the hardliners would have to be given a voice in formulating the U.S. negotiating position. The hardliners, who were against any alteration of the Hay–Bunau-Varilla Treaty, consisted of two groups: the "Zonians" and the "Southern Command." To facilitate Pentagon participation, Bunker set up a "Support Group" in the Department of State to help prepare possible U.S. positions. The Support Group included representatives from the Department of State (Panama Desk, Legal Section, and so on) and members from a Department of Defense ad hoc group that was responsible for developing and coordinating Department of Defense positions on the Panama issue. Formed by Secretary of Defense Melvin Laird and called the Panama Canal Negotiations Working Group (PCNWG), this ad hoc group included representatives from the Office of the Secretary of the Army (which in turn represented the interests of the Zonians), the Office of the Assistant Secretary of Defense for International Security Affairs, and the Office of the Joint Chiefs of Staff (representing the interests of the Southern Command). For a long time, the PCNWG was chaired by the deputy undersecretary of the Army, who was sympathetic to the Zonians.

Members of Congress were aware of a general opposition in the country to any treaty that would entail significant U.S. concessions.

2. The descriptions of the setting of the problem and its denouement are drawn from "Panama Canal Treaty Negotiations," a case study prepared by Mark G. McDonough under the joint supervision of Douglas Johnston and myself. See the bibliography, under the heading "Case Studies."

The American public had indicated in several polls that it regarded the Canal as a symbol of American ingenuity, a piece of peculiarly American property that should by no means be given up to Panama. Also, in the aftermath of the Vietnam War, a majority of Americans seemed to want to avoid a U.S. withdrawal from another area of strategic and economic interest. By the time of Bunker's appointment, a number of resolutions had been proposed in both the House and the Senate opposing the negotiation of a treaty that would dispose of U.S. sovereign rights in the Canal Zone. Senator S. I. Hayakawa summed it up prettily when he proclaimed that the Canal belonged to the United States because "we stole it, fair and square."

Besides the concerns of the general public, Bunker had to consider the commercial and parochial interests of a variety of groups with powerful lobbies on Capitol Hill. The American Institute of Merchant Shipping, for example, was very apprehensive about the possibility of the Panamanians' gaining control over the pricing structure of Canal services, which in the long run would mean higher toll rates for the use of the Canal and might eventually make U.S. intercoastal trade through the Canal unprofitable. Another group, the Canal Zone Central Union (which was affiliated with the AFL-CIO) represented the interests of the U.S. employees of the Panama Canal Company; any new treaty that enlarged the Panamanian role in the administration of the Canal Zone would lead to a gradual displacement of U.S. employees by Panamanian nationals and the elimination of special commissary privileges and retirement benefits. To gain an understanding of the problems facing these interest groups, Bunker and other government officials participated with them in a number of seminars run by independent think tanks such as the Brookings Institution.

In his first meeting with Panama's foreign minister, Juan Antonio Tack, on November 26, 1973, Bunker received the impression that an agreement was possible. Before negotiating specific points, however, he felt that the two sides should agree on some general principles to guide their exploration of specific alternatives. In a round of negotiations that took place January 1–6, 1974, the two sides agreed on a United States–Panama Joint Statement of Principles, which Kissinger and Tack signed in Panama on February 7. (Commentators accorded Kissinger's presence a "symbolic importance" to Panama, because it suggested an equality between the negotiating parties.)

The principles agreed on by the United States and Panama read as follows:

1. The Treaty of 1903 and its amendments will be abrogated by the conclusion of an entirely new interoceanic canal treaty.
2. The concept of perpetuity will be eliminated. The new treaty concerning the lock canal shall have a final termination date.
3. Termination of United States jurisdiction over Panamanian territory shall take place promptly in accordance with terms specified in the treaty.
4. The Panamanian territory in which the canal is situated shall be returned to the jurisdiction of the Republic of Panama. The Republic of Panama, in its capacity as territorial sovereign, shall grant to the United States of America, for the duration of the new interoceanic canal treaty and in accordance with what that treaty states, the right to use the lands, waters, and airspace which may be necessary for the operation, maintenance, protection, and defense of the canal and the transit of ships.
5. The Republic of Panama shall have a just and equitable share of the benefits derived from the operation of the canal in its territory. It is recognized that the geographic position of its territory constitutes the principal resource of the Republic of Panama.
6. The Republic of Panama shall participate in the administration of the canal, in accordance with a procedure to be agreed upon in the treaty. The treaty shall also provide that Panama will assume total responsibility for the operation of the canal upon the termination of the treaty. The Republic of Panama shall grant to the United States of America the rights necessary to regulate the transit of ships through the canal, and to undertake any other specific activity related to those ends, as may be agreed upon in the treaty.
7. The Republic of Panama shall participate with the United States of America in the protection and defense of the canal in accordance with what is agreed upon in the new treaty.
8. The United States of America and the Republic of Panama, recognizing the important services rendered by the interoceanic Panama Canal to international maritime traffic, and bearing in mind the possibility that the present canal could become inadequate for the said traffic, shall agree bilaterally

on provisions for new projects which will enlarge canal capacity. Such provisions will be incorporated in the new treaty in accordance with the concepts established in principle 2.[3]

By the end of June 1974, after two rounds of negotiations, the United States and Panama agreed on a definition of major issues relating to the Joint Statement. The issues were: (1) *duration:* the length of time before a new treaty would expire and all rights would revert to Panama; (2) *jurisdiction:* the number of years before the United States would give up certain jurisdictional rights in the Canal Zone, such as those of criminal jurisdiction and police authority—rights not directly related to Canal operation; (3) *defense role of Panama:* the degree to which Panama would assume responsibility for Canal defense; (4) *land and water:* the percentage of the Canal Zone that was to be turned over to Panama when a new treaty was ratified; (5) *expansion rights:* the deadline for a U.S. decision on whether to expand the Canal by adding a third set of locks or a new sea-level canal; (6) *expansion routes:* possible routes that could be used by the United States in the event it decided to build a new sea-level canal; (7) *use rights:* the jurisdictional rights required by the United States for the efficient operation of the Canal; (8) *compensation:* the amount of money the United States would pay to Panama for the right to operate and defend the Canal; (9) *U.S. defense rights:* the resources (facilities, personnel, and so forth) that the United States would be permitted to retain to defend the Canal, and the extent to which it would be allowed to guarantee the neutrality of the Canal (some form of a post-treaty relationship); (10) *U.S. military rights:* the degree to which the United States could retain military rights not directly related to local defense of the Canal.

In June 1974 Bunker prepared for another round of negotiations with the Panamanians. What might have gone through his mind at that time? The issues had been clearly designated and grouped into ten categories. For each category, Bunker had some idea of the bargaining ranges involved. For example, on the issue of compensation, Panama might have been seeking an annual fee of about $75 million, while the United States was considering $30 million. Drawing an analogy between this negotiating problem and AMPO,

3. U.S. Department of State (1974).

Bunker might reasonably have wanted to get a much more precise feel for tradeoffs between issues: How much should the U.S. side be willing to give up on Issue X for a given incremental change on Issue Y? But who was "the U.S. side"? Was it Bunker, the Department of State, the Department of Defense, the Department of Commerce? The tradeoffs of a military man with a mission are likely to be very different from the tradeoffs of a representative of the Department of State: one cannot expect that high-level officials from different branches of government will attach the same value to certain issues. Bunker attempted to devise a comprehensive value function (implying tradeoffs) for the U.S. position that he could use in external bargaining, but he could not reach an internal consensus. Worse, guardians of special interests all want to establish reservation values on those issues of primary concern to themselves. If Bunker formally asked each constituent representative for a reservation value on each issue separately, then we could guess what might have happened. The guardian of Issue X would stake out a bargaining position and exaggerate his needs; so would the guardian of Issue Y, exaggerating her needs. If the former exaggerated and the latter didn't, then when they were both compelled by higher-ups to relax their demands, the guardian of Issue X would end up better off. But the guardian of Issue Y, anticipating this, would likewise play the internal negotiating game. It's in the nature of the situation that if a compromise has to be settled externally, some internal faction will be disappointed with the result.

It may not always be desirable for a collective U.S. team to agree to a proposed treaty: a reservation value should be established for the overall contract, but not necessarily for each issue. Bunker would have been severely hobbled if he had had reservation values for each of the issues separately—especially if the set of all reservation prices would have yielded a composite contract that was completely unacceptable to the Panamanians and was merely wishful thinking on the U.S. side. The secretary of defense might have wanted to consider defense issues as a composite and might have been unwilling to trade military preparedness for, say, a gain in commerce. He might, however, have been exasperated with individual members of the Joint Chiefs of Staff for wanting to put separate reservation values on the needs of the Navy, Air Force, Army, or Marines.

At about this time, the U.S. negotiators enlisted the aid of a consulting firm, Decisions and Designs Incorporated (DDI), to help them formulate a negotiating strategy. The DDI analysts interviewed members of the U.S. negotiating team, including Ambassador Bunker, and on the basis of the responses concocted a point scoring system (a value function) for the U.S. side. This was done with slight modifications, very much as we did in Chapter 11. For ease of analysis, an additive scoring system over the issues was used without any real checks to see if there were interactions that would render the additive form inappropriate. The analysts should ideally have checked for preferential independence before blithely using an additive scoring system, and they probably would have discovered some dependence between issues; but it is likely that the additive form provided a good, convenient approximation.

There is no evidence that Bunker cleared the resulting additive scoring system with the Support Group, the PCNWG, or congressional committees. The scoring system reflected the tradeoffs that Bunker's personal negotiating team deemed appropriate, with all viewpoints and pressures informally incorporated; a consensus, if attempted, would not have been achieved, but Bunker and his team wanted a means of articulating some of their tradeoffs because they anticipated a need for such knowledge in the external negotiation process.

Besides assessing component value functions over each of the issues and assigning importance weights for the U.S. side—a task that would have been divisive if done in conjunction with interested parties within the government—Bunker's team also recorded their own perceptions of the Panamanian positions. That assessment task, although fuzzy, would probably not have been divisive if it had involved the contending factions on the U.S. side; but it was not openly discussed.

Table 10 lists hypothetical importance weights for the United States and Panama. Keep in mind that importance weights very much depend on the bargaining ranges of the issues being considered. Thus, for example, if the U.S. side assigned an importance weight of .22 to U.S. defense rights and if the bargaining range of those rights were changed from 10–25 percent to 15–20 percent, then the importance weight might drop to perhaps .10. Pairs of

TABLE 10. *Hypothetical importance weights for the United States and Panama.*

Issue	Units	Range	Importance weights United States	Panama
U.S. defense rights	Percent to be given up	10–25	.22	.09
Use rights	Number of rights	20–30	.22	.15
Land and water	Percent to be given up	20–70	.15	.15
Expansion rights	Years	5–30	.14	.03
Duration	Years	20–50	.11	.15
Expansion routes	Nominal	3 choices	.06	.05
Compensation	Millions of dollars	30–75	.04	.11
Jurisdiction	Years	0–20	.02	.07
U.S. military rights	Percent to be given up	10–25	.02	.07
Defense role of Panama	Percent to be given up	10–25	.02	.13
Total			1.00	1.00

Note: Importance weights for Panama are as perceived by the United States.

issues with unbalanced importance weights and with opposing tilts between the negotiating parties represent golden opportunities for log-rolling between issues.

The consulting analysts, using the additive scoring systems devised, generated the efficient frontier of possible treaties and constructed a dozen or so efficient treaties—that is, treaties whose joint evaluations fell on the efficient frontier.

Members of the Bunker team were then assigned roles, and simulated bargaining sessions were conducted in order to develop a feel for the upcoming negotiations. Apparently the team did not use scoring systems or formal analysis during the actual negotiations— these were purely preparatory devices. Also, it seems that DDI did not specify reservation values for the U.S. side or guess at reservation values for the Panamanian side. It is likely, though, that any discussions of reservation prices would have been highly confidential—especially because they would have been so internally divisive if they had become known.

The Course of the Negotiations

In an effort to keep the course of negotiations smooth, the Panamanian and U.S. negotiators decided to concentrate initially on those issues that would be easier to resolve, and negotiate the harder ones later. The Panamanians asked that compensation be discussed last, although they very much wanted favorable terms on this issue. (One observer commented that, for domestic political reasons, the Panamanians did not want to be perceived as having sold out to the United States during the early stages of the negotiations.)

For the round of negotiations scheduled for November 1974, the U.S. negotiators had prepared a package that they believed would go far toward meeting Panamanian demands on issues of comparatively minor significance to the United States. The package (agreed to by Bunker's team and the Department of Defense representatives) included the return of some jurisdictional rights to Panama within a period of less than five years after the treaty went into effect, and also included terms to increase Panamanian participation in the administration and defense of the Canal. In return, the U.S. negotiators were expected to get a Status of Forces Agreement[4] with the Panamanians and the unilateral right of the United States to be guarantor of the security of the Canal when the treaty expired. On the question of use rights, the U.S. negotiators were to seek Panama's assurance that the administrative entity operating the Canal would be a U.S. government agency and that the American civilian employees in the Canal Zone would enjoy the same exemptions and privileges as would military personnel under a Status of Forces Agreement. (Department of Defense officials maintained that these provisions were critical for the efficient operation and defense of the Canal.)

In the session of November 6, Bunker encountered strong Panamanian resistance to the package. To avoid risking a break-off of the negotiations and to demonstrate the good will that would be necessary for later Panamanian concessions, he decided to concede some issues to Panama without insisting on a quid pro quo. Thus, that

---

4. This is a series of administrative agreements governing the conditions under which a foreign military force is subject to, or exempt from, the laws of the country in which it is stationed. The issues under agreement generally include criminal jurisdiction, tax laws, customs laws, and so on.

same day, Bunker and Tack initialed three "threshold agreements" on jurisdiction and on Panamanian participation in the defense and operation of the Canal.[5] The threshold agreement on jurisdiction stated that the United States would transfer police authority and criminal jurisdiction to Panama within three years after the treaty went into effect. In regard to defense, it was agreed that the United States would bear the main responsibility for defending and protecting the Canal for the life of the treaty, but with the increased participation of Panama; a "joint board," composed of an equal number of high-level Panamanian and U.S. military representatives, would be established as a planning and advisory body. Both parties committed themselves to guaranteeing the neutrality of the Canal. The threshold agreement on administration provided for the creation of a new administrative body that would manage the Canal and that would implement programs for training Panamanian citizens to operate the waterway.

According to the U.S. negotiators, the priorities of the two sides changed during the discussions that led to the three threshold agreements. For the United States, the "post-treaty relationship" aspect of U.S. defense rights assumed much more importance, while the importance of the land and water issue declined. (The U.S. negotiators assumed that they could persuade the Department of Defense to give up more on the latter issue by demonstrating that it was not really relevant to the operation and maintenance of the Canal.) On the Panamanian side, the issue of jurisdiction had become one of paramount importance. The Torrijos regime wanted to assure its public that Panama would have substantial control over her territory under any new treaty. On the other hand, the United States commitment to return some jurisdictional rights within a very short period of time, as reflected in the threshold agreement, tended to soften Panama's position on use rights and U.S. defense rights. The Panamanian negotiators now seemed confident that the United States was serious about negotiating a fair treaty and was not trying to mislead or trick them. Consequently, they apparently felt that they could grant the United States the use and defense rights it was seeking, without running much risk that these rights would be abused.

5. U.S. House of Representatives (1975), p. H9713. Subsequent material and quotes are taken from the same source.

Internal Conflict

Following the initialing of the threshold agreements, Bunker requested presidential guidance to proceed with the negotiations. This guidance was expected to emerge from a series of National Security Council (NSC) meetings, which were to serve as a forum for the presentation of the positions of the Department of State, the Department of Defense, the Central Intelligence Agency, and so on. As it turned out, however, these NSC meetings brought into the open the Department of Defense's strong resentment about Bunker's concessions and its dissatisfaction with its negotiating role in general.

The first NSC meeting, in April 1975, was acrimonious and revealed major differences between the State Department and Defense Department positions. The Pentagon representatives argued that the U.S. negotiators, just to keep the talks going, were conceding too much too soon without receiving much in return: although Bunker's team had initialed a draft Status of Forces Agreement with Foreign Minister Tack on March 15, Deputy Secretary of Defense William Clements felt that the Panamanian concession on this issue was minimal compared to those (on jurisdiction, canal operation, and canal defense) which the United States had made. Also, the Pentagon officials complained that Bunker, in making the concession on canal defense, had acted independently and had overridden the final U.S. negotiating position agreed upon by the two departments.

At issue was the clause of the threshold agreement that stated that the United States and Panama would "commit themselves to guarantee the permanent and effective neutrality of the interoceanic canal . . . and . . . make efforts to have this neutrality recognized and guaranteed by all nations." The Department of Defense had agreed to a package that would give the United States the *unilateral* right to guarantee the permanent neutrality of the Canal. In addition to emphasizing the security risks involved in the multinational agreement, Clements maintained that without the unilateral right, the treaty would not stand a chance of being ratified by the Senate and would become a political issue in the presidential primaries of 1976. Clements also suggested that the Defense Department's representation on the mid-level State Department Support Group was inadequate for the protection of its interests and that some other arrangement would have to be made.

Bunker's team and the State Department, on the other hand, contended that the Pentagon's complaints derived from an unwillingness to accept the negotiating parameters set forth in the 1974 Kissinger-Tack principles, which stated the intention of "increasing Panamanian participation in the defense of the Canal." Since military leaders regarded internal civil disturbances and acts of sabotage as a much more credible threat to the Canal than any attack by a foreign power, they were reluctant to place much faith in the reaction of Panamanian forces in the event of sabotage or attack by extremist Panamanian nationals. The State Department argued in response that any treaty agreement that met basic Panamanian nationalistic concerns would defuse motivation for sabotage,[6] and also maintained that the Defense Department was being needlessly unyielding on the issue of land and water by insisting that almost all of the lands and waters in the Canal Zone were needed to operate and defend the Canal. (The U.S. negotiators judged that large sections of the territory under question were irrelevant for these purposes.)

To gain support for their position, Pentagon officials leaked the substance of the intragovernmental conflict to the press and thus stimulated congressional opposition to the negotiations. By June 1975 Senator Strom Thurmond "had already gathered 37 Senators on the 1975 model of his resolution to block a new treaty and had personally warned Kissinger not to send up a treaty."[7] In the House of Representatives, Congressman M. G. Snyder offered an amendment to the State Department's appropriation bill which provided that none of the appropriated funds would be used for negotiating "the surrender or relinquishment of any U.S. rights in the Panama Canal Zone." Although neither piece of legislation passed, they indicated the opposition that any future agreement would face in the absence of Defense Department support.

Looking back over the negotiations thus far, one can see that they were conducted in stages. When a treaty cannot be resolved it is

6. Duker (1978), p. 14.
7. Rosenfeld (1975), p. 7.

nevertheless important, for international political reasons, to avoid risking a complete break-off and to demonstrate good will; thus, representatives of the two sides may agree on face-saving partial agreements. This was done with the Tack-Kissinger agreements in the early part of 1974 and with the three threshold agreements at the end of that year. One of the difficulties in settling the easier issues first is that there remain fewer opportunities for log-rolling with the residue of tougher issues. Critics often protest that too much is given away in these interim agreements, but what these agreements buy has linkage value in foreign policy: sometimes a government desperately needs some peace and quiet so that its leaders can concentrate on more important problems. Of course, the other side might be aware of this need and might exploit it.

After signing the three threshold agreements, Bunker and his team faced new internal problems. The remaining issues were repackaged and the bargaining ranges on the unresolved issues were shifted somewhat. The tradeoffs, too, shifted, and Bunker's team went through the exercise of reassessing component value functions and importance weights for the two sides. Once again this exercise was used to prepare for the next round of negotiations, but once again the results were not used in any formal way during those negotiations, and apparently no formal analysis was done on reservation values.

The Panama Canal talks present an interesting view of the way in which internal conflicts are continually mediated throughout the negotiation process. Let's look more broadly at the pressures that are brought to bear on the external negotiator. Often he cannot get a clear set of internally generated instructions suitable for external use and consequently must feel his way along, buffeted by external and internal pressures. Occasionally, in an internal deadlock, someone has to back down. How does this happen?

Suppose that in the course of some international treaty negotiations the Joint Chiefs of Staff dig in their heels and absolutely refuse to make further concessions. The external negotiator, an ambassador, has no power to push them further and must enlist the aid of higher-ups (in Bunker's case, these would have been President Ford and Henry Kissinger). The president can try to cajole the Joint Chiefs to yield a bit, but as guardians of a mission they sincerely believe that any further concessions would be detrimental to the security of the country. The president, with wider perspectives to balance, thinks otherwise. He can try to convince the Joint Chiefs, but he cannot comfortably fire or threaten to fire his top staff; they'll withdraw from the government and lend their support to the opposition party. So the president's power, too, is limited. But he knows that, although the military firmly believe in the value of their demands, perhaps an extra aircraft carrier or two or maybe some additional Army funding might counteract the perception of weakness in the proposed treaty. In other words, the mediation of internal conflicts can be resolved by linkages with other problems.

These sorts of linkages are made frequently, and can be useful and effective strategies: they are the very art of compromise. Of course, if a president is weak and "buys" the acquiescence of his staff with outlandish side payments, then he might encourage a contest among potential recipients to see who can get the most. Such payments are only appropriate within reason. If one argues that each problem should be resolved unto itself, that log-rolling between issues is reprehensible, then one seriously curtails potential zones of agreement. It is far better to negotiate acceptable deals through linkages than to resolve conflicts one by one through sheer exercise of power. The president of a country, the chief executive officer of a state-owned enterprise, the head of a firm, and the president of a university all frequently act as mediators in internal conflicts—"mediators with clout" whose power comes from their ability to link problems.

Appendix : The Philippine Military Base Negotiations

In 1978 the United States and the Philippines entered into negotiations over the status of U.S. military bases on the islands.[8] The case raises some of the same analytical issues as the Panama Canal case, but in the Philippine talks the divisions of opinion within the

8. The account given here draws extensively from cases written by Jacob W. Ulvila and Mark G. McDonough, entitled "U.S. Philippine Military Base Negotiations" and "Philippine Base (Supplementary Case)." See the bibliography, under the heading "Case Studies."

United States were relatively mild, and formal analysis could there-fore be used more directly in preparing for and in conducting the negotiations.

On April 29, 1978, Vice-President Walter Mondale left on a twelve-day trip to the Philippines and four other Pacific nations. He decided to include the Philippines in his itinerary even though some U.S. government officials argued that a visit so soon after an allegedly fraudulent Philippine election would make a mockery of the Carter administration's commitment to human rights and free elections. Mondale and other officials thought that Philippine pres-ident Ferdinand Marcos might be so affronted by a decision to by-pass the Philippines that he might call a halt to the ongoing negotia-tions over continued U.S. use of military bases on Philippine territory.

On May 4 Marcos and Mondale issued a joint statement to the press in which they declared that U.S. use of the bases benefited both countries and that amendments to the Military Bases Agree-ment should be negotiated. They agreed that these amendments should reflect certain specified principles:

1. The United States reaffirms that Philippine sovereignty ex-tends over the bases.
2. Each base shall be under the command of a Philippine base commander.
3. The United States shall be assured effective command and control over United States personnel, employees, equipment, material, the facilities authorized for their use within military bases, and unhampered military operations involving their own forces, as provided for in this agreement.
4. In every fifth anniversary year from the date of the amend-ments and until the termination of the agreement, there shall be begun and completed a complete and thorough review and reassessment of this agreement, including its objectives, its provisions, its duration, and the manner of implementation to assure that the agreement continues to serve the mutual inter-ests of both parties. In order to expedite the conclusion of such amendments, the two sides will designate representatives to develop means of giving concrete manifestations to these principles.

Shortly after Mondale's trip was completed, Richard Holbrooke, assistant secretary of state for East Asian and Pacific affairs, was given the responsibility of completing the negotiations. These differed in important respects from the Panama Canal negotiations, in which a treaty was at issue and in which there were severe differences of opinion within the U.S. side. The Philippine negotiations merely involved amendments to a current agreement scheduled to extend to 1991, and the Philippine representatives preferred to use the term "discussions" rather than "negotiations." But the Philippine case, like that of Panama, dealt with such issues as command-and-control, criminal jurisdiction, number and extent of facilities, security commitments, length of agreements, and amount of compensation. Just as in the Panama case, the analysts (1) specified ranges for the issues; (2) assessed an additive value scoring system for both sides, using U.S. perceptions of the other side's desires; (3) derived the efficient frontier; and (4) generated different contractual packages that fell along this frontier. Once again, U.S. negotiators and analysts did not appear to formalize reservation values for the entire package or for separate issues. In the Philippine discussions, however, there seemed to be a very good consensus among the diverse interest groups within the United States about tradeoffs between issues.

Ken Bleakely, one of the analysts working with Assistant Secretary Holbrooke, indicated in an interview with Jacob Ulvila that formal analysis had been of great help during the negotiations. He personally used it primarily to explore alternative packages of issues and, with the aid of quantitative analysis, constructed verbal arguments for and against various proposed sets of contractual arrangements; the results of these analyses greatly influenced his recommendations, presentations, and way of thinking. With the help of a small computer that he took with him to the Philippines, he charted the progress of ongoing negotiations and the movement and pattern of concessions. Analysis helped him use information acquired during the negotiations to modify his perceptions of the Philippine tradeoffs (especially importance weights) and also helped him identify and define the issues.

Most important, inducing staff analysts to formalize their assumptions and tradeoffs helped *generate creativity.* "It gets people to think about the integrative aspects of bargaining, not only the distributive ones," said Bleakely. "Typically, people approach a negotiation thinking only about their own position, about how to defend it, and (if they must) about compromise without actually giving up anything. The analysis draws people into thinking about how they can improve their own total score by trading off asymmetric interests."

13

Risk Sharing and Insecure Contracts

Mr. George is an oil wildcatter. His past diligence and business acumen have assured him a good reputation, and he now enjoys the right to drill for oil at a given site. The trouble is that he has liquidity problems: most of his money is tied up in other risky ventures and his credit rating at the bank is not favorable. The cost of drilling is uncertain, but he has the possibility of taking seismic soundings at the site which will yield some information—but not perfect information—about the possibilities of finding oil. He could plunge all his financial resources into this deal and go it alone; or he could borrow more money at the bank; or he could cut others into the deal, either by means of a straight proportional sharing of profits and losses or, perhaps, a different proportional sharing on the up and down sides of the deal. Let's assume for the moment that all contingent, financial sharing arrangements are *secure*—that all contracts are inviolable both in law and in the intent of the protagonists—and look at one way in which this problem can be abstracted into a risk-sharing negotiation problem. The terrain we're about to enter into is so vast, including as it does financial markets, equity financing, insurance, and reinsurance, that we must be careful not to get lost in its intricate byways.

Mr. George approaches Mr. Lloyd, a speculator, to share his risky venture with him. They examine their options and identify one strategy that appears promising, but the payoffs are uncertain: these depend on the (uncertain) cost of drilling, on how much oil is down there, on how easy the oil is to recover, on future regulations, on future oil prices, and on a lot more. To simplify, we'll say that they depend on which one of five states of the world—A, B, C, D, or E—

TABLE 11. *Potential outcomes and sharing rules.*

	Probabilistic assessments		Net present value (in thousands of dollars)	Sharing amounts	
State	George	Lloyd		George	Lloyd
A	.07	.05	−70	A_G	A_L
B	.13	.20	−20	B_G	B_L
C	.30	.50	30	C_C	C_L
D	.40	.20	80	D_G	D_L
E	.10	.05	200	E_G	E_L
Total	1.00	1.00			

will prevail. (If we were to be more realistic, we might use something like five thousand states of the world.) Mr. Lloyd consults his own experts and obtains probabilistic assessments of the five potential outcomes; these differ from Mr. George's assessments as shown in Table 11. All assessments are kept confidential.

George and Lloyd, however, do agree on the financial implications of the deal, conditional on a given future state prevailing.[1] A dry hole (state A), for instance, would lead to a loss of $70,000, or an abortive attempt after a negative seismic sounding (state B) would lead to a loss of $20,000.

George and Lloyd have to agree on how to share the financial proceeds in each of the five states. If state A unfortunately occurs, then the team will lose $70,000. George, who is short of funds, will want Lloyd to assume most of this loss. But, of course, Lloyd is not going to agree with this unless his own shares are sufficiently high for the states C, D, and E. He also might want George to share in some of the losses if A or B occurs, just to keep George honest—or, more felicitously put, to give George the right incentives.

George and Lloyd have to decide how to share the loss of $70,000 if state A occurs. In order to keep our notation symmetric (which makes it easier to generalize to more than two risk sharers at a later

---

1. If they were to disagree on the financial consequences associated with a given state, then they could decompose that state into two or more states with differing probabilities. Our present format (including additional states) is thus quite general. For example, if George thinks the payoff in state C is $30,000 and Lloyd thinks it is $50,000, then state C could be split into two states, C' and C", with payoffs $30,000 and $50,000, respectively. George may assign probabilities of .3 and zero to C' and C", whereas Lloyd may assign probabilities of zero and .5 to C' and C", respectively.

stage), let's suppose that George and Lloyd have to select two numbers: A_G, the payoff to George if A occurs, and A_L, the payoff to Lloyd if A occurs (all payoffs are in thousands of dollars). We then require that $A_G + A_L = -70$. They have to decide analogously on the splits in cases B, C, D, and E. So overall, George and Lloyd have to decide on ten numbers: $A_G, A_L, \ldots, E_G, E_L$ (see Table 11), subject to the following set of five constraints:

$$A_G + A_L = -70,$$
$$B_G + B_L = -20,$$
$$C_G + C_L = 30,$$
$$D_G + D_L = 80,$$
$$E_G + E_L = 200.$$

For any determination of these ten numbers, George and Lloyd will each be confronted with a lottery. George's lottery will yield financial prizes $A_G, B_G, \ldots, E_G$ with probabilities .07, .13, . . . , .10, respectively; Lloyd's lottery will yield financial prizes A_L, $B_L, \ldots, E_L$ with probabilities .05, .20, . . . , .05, respectively. Their reactions to these lotteries will depend on their attitudes toward risk taking. It could be that a specific risk-sharing plan (determined by a specific setting of the ten numbers)[2] is inefficient in the sense that the ten risk-sharing numbers could be changed to improve the lottery for each party (in that party's subjective opinion). In other words, there may be opportunities for joint gains. Figure 32 depicts graphically what could occur. For a specific risk-sharing plan, Q (which arises through the specification of ten legitimate numbers), George might assign a certainty equivalent to his resulting lottery of $5,000, and Lloyd might assign a certainty equivalent to his resulting lottery of $13,000. However, as depicted, the risk-sharing plan Q is not efficient: they both can improve, since there are joint evaluations of risk-sharing deals that fall northeast of Q.

George controls the ownership of the deal and can remind (threaten?) Lloyd that there are other speculators who would love to join in the venture. Lloyd could counter that he, too, has a choice of other potential drilling deals. They also can remind each other about the transaction costs of starting negotiations with other part-

2. Because of the five financial constraints, these ten numbers have really five degrees of freedom: once we determine what Lloyd gets in each state, George gets the complement.

ners and how nice it would be to work on other deals together in the future. The point of all this is that Lloyd and George are involved in a negotiation that bears strong similarities to other negotiations we have considered. This is not the place to discuss details about how such sharing procedures are made or could be made more efficiently. As in most negotiation processes, the protagonists have to worry about their alternatives if they find it impossible to come to an agreement. Each must consider the other external opportunities available to him before he can arrive at a reservation price for the present set of negotiations.

Suppose that George will deal with Lloyd only if he can get a certainty equivalent of at least $15,000 from a mutually agreed-upon risk-sharing deal; in other words, George's reservation price is $15,000. As shown in Figure 32, it may be possible to satisfy George and still get a positive return for Lloyd, but there's not much leeway. They may never find sharing arrangements that are mutually acceptable, even though such agreements might exist.

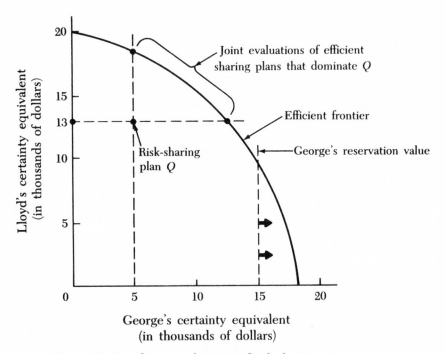

Figure 32. Set of joint evaluations of risk-sharing agreements.

The more structured the market, the easier it becomes to assess objectively these externally driven reservation prices. We do not engage in much haggling with our insurance companies when we obtain collision insurance for our automobiles. But the owner of an oil tanker entering into troubled waters might have some negotiating leverage with his insurance suppliers, and vice versa.

OPERATING WITH INSECURE CONTRACTS

We are assuming throughout this discussion that George and Lloyd can make binding contracts with each other. Suppose that Lloyd agrees to a risk-sharing contract in which $A_L = -\$60,000$ and $A_G = -\$10,000$, and in which Lloyd gets the majority share of the positive outcomes at other states (for example, $C_L = \$25,000$ and $C_G = \$5,000$). Now suppose that A does in fact occur. Lloyd is unhappy and says that it's unfair for him to pay $60,000 of the $70,000 loss, that George withheld information about the likelihood of A. "Nonsense," retorts George. "A deal is a deal and I'm going to hold you to our official contract." Lloyd can complain, but the court system is on George's side. What happens, though, if the court system is ineffective?

Let's look at a starkly simple risk-sharing mining venture between an international mining company (conveniently labeled IMC) and a developing country (labeled DC). Assume that IMC and DC agree on the following simple structure for a joint mining venture. There are two possible outcomes, bad (B) and good (G), and these states have probabilities .6 and .4, respectively (jointly agreed upon by IMC and DC). If state B occurs, the consortium of IMC and DC will lose $10 million; if state G occurs, they will jointly gain $30 million. After a lot of negotiating, IMC and DC agree to the risk-sharing agreement shown in Table 12. We see that IMC agrees to a penalty of $8 million if the venture turns bad, but gets a reward of $20 million if all turns out well. DC would prefer to share the deal with IMC, even though with sharing its expected-value return is $2.8 million and without sharing its expected-value return is $6 million. The sharing procedure limits DC's potential loss to $2 million.

Now things become a bit more complicated. Suppose that the IMC negotiators need to gain ratification of the agreement from

TABLE 12. *Risk-sharing agreement between IMC and DC.*

| State | Probability | Outcome (in millions of dollars) | Shares (in millions of dollars) | |
			IMC	DC
	.6	−10.0	−8.0	−2.0
	.4	30.0	20.0	10.0
Expected values		6.0[a]	3.2[b]	2.8[c]

Note: Probabilities sum to 1.
a. The expected value of the joint venture is $(.6 \times -10) + (.4 \times 30) = 6.0$.
b. IMC's expected value for its share of the lottery is $(.6 \times -8) + (.4 \times 20) = 3.2$.
c. DC's expected value for its share of the lottery is $(.6 \times -2) + (.4 \times 10) = 2.8$.

their home office, and some skeptics back home are dragging their heels. "Look," they say, "we are risking a loss of $8 million for a potential gain of $20 million and the chances are less than fifty-fifty that we'll come out ahead. If the venture turns out favorable, DC may want to renegotiate the contract. They may argue that it's unfair for us to get twice as much as they do, that it was clear all along the deal would be good and that we've exploited them." An argument ensues within IMC as to whether DC will in fact try to renegotiate the contract if the outcome is good. And to keep matters from getting *too* complicated, suppose that they collectively agree that in the case of a good outcome, there is a fifty-fifty chance for a renegotiation; and if renegotiation takes place, IMC will get only $10 million instead of the original $20 million that was promised in the original contract.

Table 13 gives the revised anticipated breakdown. Notice that the state "Good," which formerly had a probability assignment of .4, has been broken into two states: "Good without renegotiation" and "Good with renegotiation." We can see that even if IMC believes that DC might force a renegotiation, the company might nevertheless want to execute the deal. IMC's expected value for this agreement is $1.2 million, and it might still clear a hurdle rate if risk-aversion were added. Of course, numbers could be altered

TABLE 13. *Risk-sharing agreement between IMC and DC with possibilities for renegotiation.*

State	Probability	Outcome (in millions of dollars)	Shares (in millions of dollars)	
			IMC	DC
Bad	.6	−10.0	−8.0	−2.0
Good, without renegotiation	.2	30.0	20.0	10.0
Good, with renegotiation	.2	30.0	10.0	20.0
Expected values		0.6[a]	1.2[b]	4.8[c]

Note: Probabilities sum to 1.
a. $(.6 \times -10) + (.2 \times 30) + (.2 \times 30) = 0.6$.
b. $(.6 \times -8) + (.2 \times 20) + (.2 \times 10) = 1.2$.
c. $(.6 \times -2) + (.2 \times 10) + (.2 \times 20) = 4.8$.

such that the deal would turn out to be unfavorable if there were a strong possibility of renegotiation.

Now DC proposes an alternate agreement. They want IMC to put up all the initial capital in return for a larger share of the profits. DC proposes the risk-sharing formula shown in Table 14. Notice that this sharing rule is more favorable than that of Table 12 for IMC (based on expected values), and that it has more appeal to DC because of their aversion to risk: it requires no penalty for DC if the bad state occurs. But IMC might in this case assess a higher probability that the deal would be renegotiated if the good state occurs. This is because the four-to-one payoff in favor of IMC in the good state might be politically intolerable (*after the fact*) to DC. The second part of Table 14 suggests one final set of assessment numbers; these illustrate the point that although the risk sharing of Table 12 is worse for IMC than that of Table 14 without the consideration of renegotiation, the relationship reverses once the possibilities of renegotiation are assessed. Although the impetus for renegotiation does not depend *fully* on the details of a contract, it may *partially* depend on those details. The important thing to remember is that what appears to be fair ex ante might not appear to be fair

TABLE 14. *An alternate risk-sharing agreement between IMC and DC.*

State	Probability	Outcome (in millions of dollars)	Shares (in millions of dollars) IMC	DC
Without renegotiation				
Bad	.6	−10.0	−10.0	0.0
Good	.4	30.0	24.0	6.0
Expected values		6.0	3.6	2.4
With renegotiation				
Bad	.6	−10.0	−10.0	0.0
Good, without renegotiation	.1	30.0	24.0	6.0
Good, with renegotiation	.3	30.0	8.0	22.0
Expected values		6.0	−1.2	7.2

Note: Probabilities for each case sum to 1.

ex post—especially if the cast of characters changes during the period of the resolution of uncertainty. Also, any state that actually does occur after the contract is signed can easily be rationalized, ex post, to have been given far too low a probability of occurring ex ante. Hindsight is a great clarifier.

SECURING INSECURE CONTRACTS

During the 1960s and 1970s there were hundreds of cases in which developing countries expropriated the holdings of international companies, and there were even more cases of forced contract renegotiations. Any less-developed country (LDC) might argue that it is in its interest to renegotiate a given contract. But when an LDC renegotiates a contract, this may affect decisions by firms to invest in that LDC and in others. If international mining companies feel that the probability of renegotiations is increasing, they will try to squeeze out more from contracts in the early days (for example, by requiring a faster payback period for their investments), and these actions, in turn, will precipitate those very renegotiations that they are trying to avoid. The result is that a growing mistrust develops, and investments in LDCs decrease—to the mutual disadvantage of LDCs and investment companies. There has been a dramatic reduction of mining company expenditures in LDCs, and oil companies are most reluctant to drill exploratory wells in countries that they perceive as financially unstable.

In the initial stages of negotiation, an international company has a strong bargaining chip: it simply can refuse to invest. But once a large investment takes place, the company's bargaining power gradually dissipates; it becomes hostage to its own sunk costs, and the bargaining power shifts to the host country. Both parties know this in advance, and if it is the anticipation of this possibility that is preventing agreement, then it may be in the interest of *both sides* to try to make these insecure contracts more secure. What can be done?

Somehow the incentives for renegotiation must be changed. Penalties must be imposed on parties that break contracts. In colonial times, an investing firm could use military intervention in order to continue to exploit weaker partners; unfortunately, there are still vestiges of that practice today. Many colonial powers chose purposely not to train indigenous laborers in the intricacies of the modern technology they employed. As a result of the continued need for highly trained experts, whose loyalties were with the investing firm, a dependency was maintained—one that was also based on the continued need for spare parts. This is not unlike the way in which the United States and the Soviet Union supply countries with modern weapons but withhold from them stocks of spare parts.

All this sounds as if industrialized countries (the big guys) have to find ways to constrain the LDCs (the little guys), who later might want to show their power. But it's also sometimes in the interest of the LDCs to assure investors that they have every intention to remain in a nonthreatening state; they might even want to be inventive about finding ways to make themselves seem weak. The more they can convince investors that they should have no worries about unilateral changes in agreements at a later stage, the more they can demand from those agreements in the early stages.

To take the situation in the Middle East as an example, the Israelis are rightly concerned that if they make concessions to the Palestinians on the issue of the West Bank, at a later stage new Palestinian leaders might violate those agreements. But it may be in the interest of the Palestinians themselves to figure out ways to prevent that from happening. They might want to make current agreements less vulnerable to later unilateral abrogation in order to get more sweeping concessions from the Israelis initially. There may be a mutuality of interest for both sides to devise schemes for securing contracts.

As another example, the United States would like to extract from countries lacking nuclear weapons an agreement that they will not reprocess spent nuclear fuel or build breeder reactors, the aim being to diminish incentives for nuclear proliferation. But countries who are sincerely against nuclear proliferation may still not want the insecurity of energy dependence; and hence, for perfectly innocuous reasons, they may want to reprocess their nuclear wastes. They, in turn, should understand that the United States might be suspicious of their motives—or the stability of their motives. Again, it may be mutually advantageous for both sides to devise ways of securing contracts. Countries might want to be inventive about convincing others of the sincerity of their future intentions.

In contracts with other countries regarding nuclear issues, the United States has not always been a reliable partner, sometimes reneging on agreements to furnish assured supplies of enriched uranium for light-water reactors. To be sure, U.S. government officials felt that they had good reasons for reneging, but in any case the United States is not always a model of probity. Indeed, some countries believe that the United States violated the spirit of the Nuclear Non-Proliferation Treaty with its reluctance to share the type of information it had agreed to share at the time of the agreement. In a volatile world, what made sense earlier may not make sense today, and it is hard to account for all contingencies in a contract or treaty. As another example, one could cite the numerous treaties with American Indian tribes that the United States unilaterally abrogated—although it can be argued that the U.S. government from the very beginning had no intention of honoring some of these treaties.

Let's consider the matter of making credible promises and enforcing promises with reference to ourselves. Think of all those sincere New Year's resolutions—about eating less, drinking less, smoking less, studying more and so on—that have been broken. Many of us anticipate not being able to do what we now sincerely want ourselves to do, and we sometimes try to invent penalties to impose on ourselves if we break our promises. One trouble is that the penalties we concoct are not formalized, not severe enough, and not enforceable enough.

Let's imagine that there is such a thing as a Personal Enforcement Agency (PEA), which provides a counseling and enforcement service. Bill, who is overweight, desperately wants to lose forty pounds, so he discusses his problem with representatives of PEA and establishes a weight-loss plan. He puts up a bond of $1,000 with the idea that parts of the bond will be forfeited if he does not keep on target, and that all will be forfeited at the end of a year if he does not fulfill his own proposed contract. Periodically he weighs in at the PEA offices. In order to increase incentives for Bill, PEA might agree that if he fulfills his contract, they will not only return his $1,000 (less, say, a $50 transaction fee), but they will let him share in PEA's profits. Bill might get $1,200 at the end, the bonus coming from all the other people who forfeited their bonds. An ingenious variation: let each applicant choose the institution that he or she most dislikes, and then require that a percentage of any forfeited amount go to that institution.[3] Bill, for example, a liberal, agrees that if he forfeits his $1,000, then $100 of this bond will automatically go to the American Nazi Party. John, a member of the Moral Majority, will be forced to give part of his forfeited bond to the Cuban Communist Party.

To return to international issues, how can a host country credibly promise an investing firm that it will not expropriate that firm's holdings or force a renegotiation of a contract when it later turns out to be in its interest to do so? It could, for example, set up an escrow account outside the country with some financially responsible institution, and deposit enough funds to secure its credibility; the understanding would be that these funds are forfeited to the investor if the host country forces a renegotiation of the contract. A major flaw in this proposal is that the host country in all likelihood would not have sufficient capital to do this.

It might, however, be possible to use a variation of the escrow

3. Suggested to me by David Lax.

account scheme. Imagine that the host country is dependent on a steady stream of capital from some international bank. The bank might agree to lend the host country sufficient funds to set up the escrow account, and the investing firm might agree to pay the bank's interest charges. The firm is buying security in return for that interest payment. If the host country reneges on its contract, it penalizes the bank—and it might not want to do that. There would be serious problems in implementing this idea, one of them being that it is impossible to foresee all contingencies: unanticipated grievances might well arise in the future. If the firm can dictate a resolution of these grievances because it has ultimate financial leverage (the escrow account), then power tilts too far one way. The obvious remedy is to set up a mechanism for compulsory grievance arbitration, and the question then becomes: Who will appoint the arbitrators?[4] It's complicated, and perhaps not resolvable; but the point here is that it may be in the interests of both parties to think imaginatively about enforcement techniques.[5]

The best way to secure a contract, when there are no binding, legal, enforcement mechanisms, is through the linkages of continuing involvements. If it is to the advantage of the host country that the investing firm start new business ventures on a regular basis, then reneging on old contracts would jeopardize the creation of new contracts. A weaker form of this also works: if the host country reneges on a contract with Firm A, then it might jeopardize the host's future contracts with Firms B, C, and D. Indeed Firms A, B, C, and D might have a formal agreement that none of them will renew investments if the host country attacks any one of them; and in order to secure this supercontract, they might stagger over time their new investment projects. Tacit collusion among investing firms often suffices to achieve the same end—that is, to make it unprofitable for a host country to force renegotiation on any one of them.

In the Middle East the Egyptians and Israelis have been negotiating a nervous truce. Each side might gain by not disrupting the Camp David agreements because there are still mutually advantageous concessions to be made (such as further Israeli withdrawals

4. A possible way would be to have each side appoint an arbitrator and then have these two collectively appoint a third, thus forming a three-person arbitration panel.
5. See Lax and Sebenius (1981).

from the Sinai and more extensive normalization of bilateral trade). The United States is there, too, on the sidelines, cajoling each side to behave as it promised. If either side reneges on its promises to the other side, it also reneges on its promises to the United States, and this may be deemed quite serious. But despite their dependence on the United States, life in the Middle East is so volatile that we can easily imagine events that could upset past agreements. Israel and Egypt might begin bonding their relationship over time by jointly investing in some common projects (water resources development or joint medical projects); future rewards would be forfeited by both if one side reneges. Any benefit/cost analysis of such a joint venture should factor in the benefits to both of stable relations.

Some of the above ideas can be examined in terms of a simple game, depicted in Figure 33. At stage 1, Ms. Shee must choose *up* or *down*. If she chooses *up*, Mr. Hee subsequently can choose *up* or *down*; he has no choice if she chooses *down*. The payoffs are as shown in the figure. The players are concerned solely with getting the highest payoff for themselves—there are no elements of altruism or malevolence involved.

Suppose, to begin with, that the players are fully informed of the rules, that the game is to be played once, and that there is no communication between the players. She might ponder: "If I choose *down*, I will get zero. If I choose *up*, he will certainly choose *down*, since he would rather get 2 than 1. Hence, if I choose *up*, I'll get − 1. I'm better off choosing *down*. It's too bad we can't talk to each other and agree that we both should choose *up*."

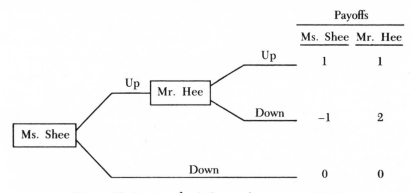

Figure 33. A game depicting an insecure contract.

Now let's allow the players to communicate, but let's assume that any agreement is nonbinding and that the culture is such that promises are often broken. "It doesn't make sense for you to choose *down*," he begins. "If we both choose *up*, we'll get 1." She responds: "True enough. But if I commit myself and choose *up*, you might choose *down*. How do I know that you won't do that? If you somehow could convincingly bind yourself to the *up*-choice, I'd be delighted to choose *up*." He promises her that if she chooses *up*, he will do likewise.

She now has a problem. Can she trust him? He may mean well— but at a later stage, when he has to act, he might be under pressure to choose *down*. He might think that if the roles were reversed, she certainly would choose *down*. So she says: "I think you might be sincere now, but when the time comes for you to act I know you will be under terrific pressure from your side. For all I know, someone else might replace you in the interim. It's too dangerous for me to place my fate in your hands when I know that you will want to take the *down* alternative when you have to choose at a later stage. I'm going to take the *down* alternative—*unless* you can take some binding action now to reduce that payoff of 2 units to a value below 1 unit. In order to convince me, you must change your real payoffs so that it is clear you would prefer *up* to *down* if I were to take *up*. In this culture, where promises are often broken, a promise is not enough."

Rather than try to convince her of his trustworthiness, it might be easier for him to take at the beginning some action that, if she chooses *up*, effectively reduces the value to him of the choice *down*. The trick for him is to convince her that he *has* done something to ensure this.

Ms. Shee might be willing to trust Mr. Hee if the game were repeated an indefinite number of times. She knows that he knows that if he responds *down* to her choice of *up* at a given stage, then she will certainly choose *down* at the next stage. But now suppose both parties definitely know that the game is to be repeated a fixed number of times—say, exactly five times—instead of an indefinite number of times. She can think ahead as follows: "At the fifth and final iteration he would probably choose *down* if I took *up*; so I'd better take *down* at stage 5. But if he knows that I'll choose *down* at stage 5, then why should he take *up* at stage 4 if I were to give him the choice by going *up*? He probably will double-cross me at stage 4 if I

TABLE 15. Possible scenarios for the five-fold iterative game.

	Scenarios											
	A		B		C		D		E		…	Z	
Round	She	He	She	He	She	He	She	He	She	He		She	He
1	Up	Up	Up	Up	Up	Up	Up	Up	Up	Up		Down	—
2	Up	Up	Up	Up	Up	Up	Up	Up	Up	Up		Down	—
3	Up	Up	Up	Up	Up	Up	Up	Up	Up	Down	…	Down	—
4	Up	Up	Up	Up	Up	Up	Up	Down	Down	—		Down	—
5	Up	Up	Up	Down	Down	—	Down	—	Down	—		Down	—

give him the opportunity. I'd better choose *down* at stage 4. But arguing this way from 4 to 3 and then 3 to 2 and then 2 to 1 leads me to the conclusion that I should start at stage 1 and choose *down*. This is terrible."

Suppose that in a definite five-fold iteration, she discloses to him her apprehensions and the logic that leads her to the conclusion that she should take the *down* alternative each time. "That's nonsensical reasoning," he retorts. "You could argue the same way if we were to play the game a thousand times, as long as that number were definitely known. Would you want to forgo a possible profit of 1,000 units in payoffs? You're too paranoid; and although I understand that you might be suspicious of my actions, I'm not going to act so as to hurt myself." Table 15 depicts some scenarios of what might take place after this dialogue. Which ending seems the most reasonable to you? What would *you* do?

In this game it is never disadvantageous for the players to discuss their joint problem, and the possibility of repetitive play improves matters; also, they are better off if they can make binding agreements. This need not always be the case. Consider the two-player matrix game shown in Table 16. In this game, the two players must choose simultaneously. If, for example, he chooses *down* and she chooses *right*, then he gets a payoff of zero units (say, the status quo) and she loses 50 units. Notice that he prefers *up* if she chooses either *left* or *right*. Hence, if the game is to be played just once without any communication, he should choose *up* and she should choose *right*, yielding him a payoff of 1 and her a payoff of 3. Should she want to come to the conference table? At the conference table he can threaten to do her harm (by choosing *down*) unless she promises to choose *left*. If binding commitments can be effective,

TABLE 16. *A two-player matrix game.*

His choice	Her choice	
	Left	Right
Up	(5, 0)	(1, 3)
Down	(0, −100)	(0, −50)

Note: The left coordinate is his payoff; the right coordinate is hers.

this is no empty threat, and she may have to succumb to the pressure. Indeed, if the game is repetitive without any communication — if they both learn about the outcome at the end of each round — he may "teach" her to choose *left* by selectively choosing *down* at the next trial when she chooses *right*. From her point of view, discussions with binding agreements or repetitive plays are a disaster.

STRIDENT OR UNPRINCIPLED NEGOTIATIONS

We have thus far avoided discussing negotiations in which a promise is not a promise, contracts are insecure, and players pride themselves on devious behavior; but our observations on insecure contracts lead naturally to the subject of strident, unprincipled negotiations. At least two or three of the ten current bestselling novels deal with negotiations of this type. Bargaining with terrorists and extortionists is a popular theme.

Take kidnapping for ransom, as an example. An extortionist kidnaps a child and demands $200,000. The parents in this case are not worried about precedent; they are not worried that if they pay the ransom and their child is returned, this might encourage other kidnappings. Indeed, if there were a law against paying ransom, the parents might want to break the law and would be most reluctant to confide in the police. There are four possibilities: the ransom is or is not paid, and the child is or is not killed. There have been real examples in each of these four cells. But certainly, paying the ransom increases the empirical probability that the child will be released. Between 1946 and 1976 there were only 647 kidnappings for ransom in the United States — roughly twenty a year (Jenkins, 1974). In comparison to other crimes, that is a surprisingly low number. By and large, ransoms have been paid; but kidnapping is not a profitable crime in the United States. All but three of the 647 cases were solved, and over 90 percent of the criminals were apprehended. Conviction rates were high and the punishments severe.

Since hostages are sometimes killed before ransom is paid, it is reasonable for the extortionist's victim to stall for time and demand proof that the hostages are alive and well. This gives an opportunity for government investigators to act. Extortionists prefer bank executives as targets because they usually can get ransom money quickly; delays cause problems for extortionists.

Will the extortionist actually carry out his threat if his demands are not met? Another pertinent question: Will he do as he promises if his demands *are* met? If he acts too irrationally, he might raise the credibility of his threat but lower the credibility of his promise. One tactic of the police, who may be coaching the victim, is to suggest that the victim demand more proof of the credibility of the extortionist's promise: "Prove to me that my son is still alive and that you will do as you say."

When terrorists hold governments hostage, the calculus becomes trickier. Consider the case where several diplomats of Country X are threatened and where the terrorists demand ransom money and the release of incarcerated saboteurs. Country X must not only worry about the well-being of the hostages but the security of other diplomats in the future, the ensuing terrorist activities of the released prisoners, the possible nefarious uses of the ransom money, the encouragement of other terrorists, its image in the eyes of the world, the possible alienation of its own people, and so on. The tradeoff is often between losing known, identifiable lives immediately and losing a larger expected number of as-yet-unknown lives in the future. Society tends to empathize far more with tangible faces than with anonymous statistics, and this works to the advantage of terrorists.

Why can't countries announce, as irrevocably as they can, that they simply will not negotiate with terrorists or pay ransom? This will certainly deter some terrorist activities—but the terrorists, in desperation, might decide to raise the stakes and threaten still more destructive acts. They could hijack luxury liners with thousands of people, or hijack tankers filled with oil and other pollutants, or threaten water supplies. For a more imaginative set of possibilities, consult the fictional bestseller lists. Sometimes the primary motives of the terrorists are best served if they can dramatize their cause by actually carrying out their threats after their "righteous" demands have been spurned. It's too simplistic to assert that the best policy is *never* to submit to blackmail. Even the Israelis, who say they will not negotiate with terrorists and who most of the time abide by this rule, occasionally have to show more flexibility. Perhaps, as in the case of kidnappings, the most effective deterrent is not necessarily a hard line during a crisis, but a determined, vigorous action afterward, both against the terrorists and against any group, faction, or country that lends support to them.

14

The Camp
David Negotiations

The historic Camp David negotiations will be used here to illustrate the role of a third-party intervenor with mediating clout, and as a basis for discussing a recently developed technique for structuring the negotiation process—a technique that employs what is known as a "single negotiating text."[1]

In early 1977 President Jimmy Carter and Secretary of State Cyrus Vance, abandoning Henry Kissinger's step-by-step approach to mediating the Egyptian-Israeli conflict, tried to convene another Geneva Conference to be jointly chaired by the United States and the Soviet Union. Several key parties, however, were reluctant to attend: Syria because of the Palestinian issue; Israel because it did not want to deal with the Palestinian Liberation Organization (PLO); Egypt because it had reservations about an increased Soviet role. In an effort to impart momentum to the stalled peace process, Egypt's President Anwar-el Sadat on November 19, 1977, made his celebrated trip to Jerusalem, and conferred with Israel's Prime Minister Menachem Begin on Christmas of that year at Ismailia, Egypt.

Sadat, insisting that he was acting as spokesman for all Arab interests, asked for the return of all occupied territories (Egypt's Sinai Peninsula, Jordan's West Bank, Syria's Golan Heights) as well as for the return of East Jerusalem, in exchange for peace and normalization of relations with Israel. His inability, though, to evoke from Begin a "grand gesture" comparable to his own caused mounting

---

1. The historical account in this chapter is based extensively on "Middle East Negotiations—Camp David Summit," a case study prepared by Mark G. McDonough. See the bibliography, under the heading "Case Studies."

opposition from his fellow Arabs. Sadat was not deterred by the vociferous opposition of the "steadfast front" of Arab states allied against him, but he was undoubtedly angered by the terrorist operations of the PLO, some of which he believed were directed against him.

Begin appeared to be pleased with the prospect of direct negotiations with Egypt, as long as they focused on bilateral issues and addressed the Palestinian issue only in broad terms. A separate peace with Egypt would give Israel military advantages relative to its other Arab neighbors and would avoid the security risks involved in the return of the Golan Heights to Syria and the West Bank to Jordan. Nevertheless, there were indications that in return for peace, Sadat would attempt to get Israel's agreement to a set of principles that would give the Palestinians wide-ranging autonomy rights on the West Bank and Gaza Strip. The nature of these rights evoked the possibility that a Palestinian state might evolve out of the accords. This sort of provision would help Sadat defend himself against charges that he had sold out his brethren by making peace with Israel.

The United States was surprised by Sadat's trip to Jerusalem, but soon saw the merits of this initiative and offered its mediating services. Carter's effort to bring about a settlement, on which he had staked so much of his domestic and international prestige, depended in large measure on Sadat's ability to carry it off. The United States, in playing its mediating role, was bound to be extremely sensitive to his problems and his needs. But its decision to support Sadat's bilateral initiative and renege on its commitment to a comprehensive approach ran a high risk of antagonizing the other Arab states—including Saudi Arabia, upon whom the United States was depending for political support not only for its Middle East peace efforts but also for its own national energy requirements. Furthermore, the United States was taking a calculated risk in excluding the Russians from the negotiating process. It was becoming obvious that the Soviet Union was working with the rejectionist Arab states in an effort to sabotage U.S. initiatives. Nevertheless, the United States was still hoping that the principles of any agreement it helped to mediate would eventually draw in the Arab states that were now boycotting the negotiations.

In order to simplify the negotiation process, Sadat and Begin agreed at Ismailia to convene two ministerial-level committees. A Military Committee would deal primarily with Egyptian-Israeli bilateral issues (especially Israeli withdrawal from the Sinai) leading to a peace treaty between the two states. A Political Committee would address the multilateral Arab-Israeli issues, including the form of Palestinian autonomy on the West Bank and Gaza Strip, and would design a Declaration of Principles that could serve as a "framework" for peace negotiations.

On January 10, 1978, the Military Committee convened in Cairo, but bogged down rapidly when the Israelis demanded at the outset that they be allowed to retain civilian settlements and military air bases in Sinai, while giving sovereignty to Egypt. Starting on January 16 the Political Committee, with Vance in attendance, had an abortive two-day meeting. Sadat recalled his delegation because of (in his view) Israel's hard line.

Acrimony developed between Sadat and Begin. In February Sadat was invited to Washington and received U.S. backing for his contention that Israel should agree to give up all the territory it had gained in the 1967 war. The Israelis, though, remained adamant about the West Bank and Gaza Strip, which Begin regarded as an integral part of Israeli territory.

The following month Begin came to Washington, where he and Carter differed strenuously about the territorial issues. Part of the problem was the interpretation of United Nations Security Council Resolution 242. This resolution, which had been approved unanimously by the Security Council on November 22, 1967, called for: (1) the withdrawal of Israeli forces from occupied Arab areas; (2) an end to the state of belligerence between the Arab nations and Israel; (3) acknowledgment of and respect for the sovereignty, territorial integrity, and political independence of every nation in the area; (4) the establishment of secure and recognized national boundaries; (5) a guarantee of freedom of navigation through international waterways in the area; and (6) a just settlement of the refugee problem. Since the United States had repeatedly said that it interpreted Resolution 242 as requiring Israeli withdrawal on all fronts from Arab territories occupied in 1967, Sadat apparently hoped that as a "full partner" in the negotiations, the United States could pressure Israel into giving up the territories. On the other hand, Israel, wary of this interpretation, insisted that the U.S. role remain that of mediation and therefore opposed the presentation of "American peace plans."

On July 18, 1978, Vance met with Moshe Dayan, foreign minister of Israel, and Mohammed Ibrahim Kamel, foreign minister of Egypt. Vance was encouraged by their flexibility and reported this to Carter. After meeting with his senior policy advisers, Carter decided that without his presidential intervention the Egyptian-Israeli peace process would collapse, and that given Vance's report about glimmers of flexibility, a three-nation summit would be a reasonable gamble.

On August 4 Vance flew to the Middle East in an effort to break the impasse that had developed during the previous few months. His trip, however, had a more specific purpose than the American public was led to believe. In an attempt to revive the momentum toward peace that had been created by Sadat's visit to Jerusalem, Vance carried with him personal invitations from Carter to Begin and Sadat to join him at Camp David, Maryland. On August 8, the White House issued the following statement: "The President is pleased to announce that President Sadat and Prime Minister Begin have accepted an invitation to come to Camp David on September 5 for a meeting with the President to seek a framework for peace in the Middle East . . . Each of the three leaders will be accompanied by a small number of their principal advisors and no specific time has been set for the duration of the meeting."

To prepare for the upcoming U.S. mediating effort, Carter set up a task force that included Zbigniew Brzezinski and William Quandt of the National Security Council, and, from the State Department, Harold H. Saunders and Alfred L. Atherton, Jr. (both assistant secretaries for Near Eastern and South Asian Affairs), as well as Vance. The task force was to derive methods or tools of mediation to be used by the president, to "invent" solutions, and to identify compromise language acceptable to both Egypt and Israel.

What were the United States' interests in the upcoming summit discussions? In 1975 a report entitled *Toward Peace in the Middle East,* prepared by a Brookings Institution group that had included Brzezinski and Quandt, had presaged the Carter administration's comprehensive approach to the settlement of the conflict in that region. The report had reached five main conclusions. First, the

United States had a strong moral, political, and economic interest in the resolution of the Middle East conflict. Second, unless the core issues of the Arab-Israeli dispute (such as the Palestinian issue) were addressed soon, the risk of another war would increase. Third, future negotiations should make use of informal multilateral meetings or a reconvened Geneva Conference. Fourth, the United States, "because it [enjoyed] a measure of confidence on both sides and [had] the means to assist them economically and militarily," should remain actively involved in the settlement. Fifth, the United States "should work with the U.S.S.R. to the degree that Soviet willingness to play a constructive role [would] permit." The report had also suggested guidelines for accords on seven specific issues:

a. *Security.* All parties to the settlement commit themselves to respect the sovereignty and territorial integrity of the others and refrain from the threat of the use of force against them.
b. *Stages.* They withdraw to agreed boundaries and that the establishment of peaceful relations be carried out in stages over a period of years, each stage being undertaken only when the agreed provisions of the previous stage have been faithfully implemented.
c. *Peaceful relations.* The Arab parties undertake not only to end hostile actions against Israel, but also to develop normal regional and international political/economic relations.
d. *Boundaries.* Israel undertakes to withdraw by agreed stages to the June 5, 1967, lines with only such modifications as are mutually accepted. Boundaries will probably need to be safeguarded by demilitarized zones supervised by UN forces.
e. *Palestine.* There should be provision for Palestinian self-determination, subject to Palestinian acceptance of the sovereignty and integrity of Israel within agreed boundaries. This might take the form either of an independent Palestine state or of a Palestine entity voluntarily federated with Jordan.
f. *Jerusalem.* The report suggests no specific solution for the particularly difficult problem of Jerusalem but recommends that, whatever the solution may be, it meet with the following criteria: there should be unimpeded access to all of the holy places and each should be under the custodianship of its own faith; there should be no barriers dividing the city which

would prevent free circulation throughout it; and each national group within the city should, if it so desires, have substantial political autonomy within the area where it predominates.

g. *Guarantees*. It would be desirable that the UN Security Council actively endorse the peace agreements.

At the time of the Camp David meeting in early September 1978, the idea of a reconvened Geneva Conference with a Soviet role was a thing of the past.

PREPARATIONS FOR NEGOTIATIONS: THE U.S. ROLE

The members of the team advising Carter were not new to the Egyptian-Israeli situation. They had already thought deeply about their preferred solutions. They knew what issues had to be debated at Camp David and they knew how the Military Committee and the Political Committee had already structured the issues dividing the two sides. In addition, the members of the U.S. team were familiar with the Israeli proposal of December 31, 1977, called the "twenty-six-point self-rule plan," as well as the Egyptian proposal of July 5, 1978, called the "six-point plan." They knew a lot about both sides; they could have assessed—but evidently did not assess—a multiattribute value function for each side and even one for the United States, as well as reservation values on packages and on individual issues. Keep in mind that the set of negotiators from each side did not have a monolithic position—to say nothing about the contending factions back home—and that there were many concerned parties on the fringes: the Arab states, the PLO, the Soviet Union, and a number of oil-starved developed and developing nations. Crisp formalization was hardly the crucial issue.

Carter and his team decided that progress could not be made in a fishbowl atmosphere: privacy during the negotiations was vital. Carter also tried desperately (futilely, as it turned out) to create a cordial ambience for negotiations and to get the contending parties to approach the problem as a joint problem-solving exercise. In addition, it was critical for the world, and especially the political forces within Israel and Egypt, to know that three very important world figures were isolating themselves from all other duties in order to devise a compromise accord—an accord that could only be acceptable to Egypt and Israel if it did not come easily. Any quick, realistic agreement was destined to meet trouble at home.

The U.S. mediators did not want both sides to come to the negotiating table with fixed packages. A dance of packages had already been tried, and the gaps were formidable. The mediators tried initially to get the principals to construct a package on an issue-by-issue basis, but they expected that this strategy would not work. It didn't. By day two Begin and Sadat would not talk to each other. What could be done?

The conflict was mediated through the use of a single negotiation text (SNT), a device suggested by Roger Fisher of Harvard Law School, who knew some of the key U.S. players (Atherton, Quandt, and Brzezinski). The use of some sort of SNT is often employed in international negotiations, especially with multiparty negotiations. The U.S. team devised and proposed an entire package for the consideration of the two protagonists. They made it clear that the United States was not trying to push this first proposal, but that it was meant to serve as an initial, single negotiating text—a text to be criticized by both sides and then modified and remodified in an iterative manner. These modifications would be made by the U.S. team, based on the criticisms of the two sides. The SNT was to be used as a means of concentrating the attention of both sides on the same composite text.

Neither side formalized its value tradeoffs; but if they had, then the United States might have generated a set of feasible joint evaluations and an efficient frontier, as shown in Figure 34. Assume that the ranges on each of the issues have been specified in advance; that each side has scored the worst possible agreement for its side at zero and the best agreement as 100; and that both sides have monolithic preferences. It is not necessarily true that the agreement that is worst for Israel is best for Egypt, or vice versa.

The United States starts the ball rolling by offering its first single negotiating text (point SNT-1 in the figure). Both Begin and Sadat protest that the proposal is ridiculous, whereupon the mediators reassure them that SNT-1 is not intended as a serious final settlement, but as a document to be criticized and improved upon: Why, they ask, is it so unacceptable? The mediators know very well why each side is so vehement in its rejection of SNT-1. This is part of the

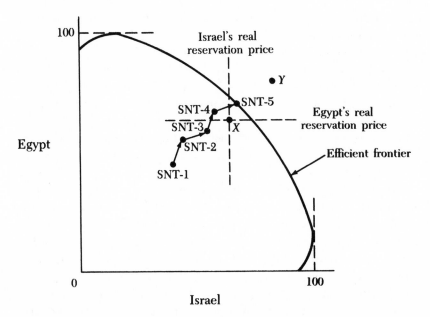

Figure 34. A hypothetical march of joint evaluations of successive SNTs.

ritual. After some of the most egregious flaws have been pointed out by each side, the U.S. team comes up with SNT-2. Begin and Sadat, although they may agree that this text is marginally better than SNT-1, still claim that it's so far from being acceptable that they feel they're wasting their time. Sadat packs his bags and gets ready to go home, but Carter persuades him to stay for a few more rounds.

After SNT-2 United States offers a new SNT, but the Israelis feel that this "improved" text is marginally a step backward—and a step backward from a hopelessly unfair starting point. So the United States comes up with a revised SNT-3; then with SNT-4 and SNT-5. Now let's imagine that the improvement from SNT-3 to SNT-4 was a critical jump for the Egyptians because the transition pierced their real reservation value—that is, Egypt truly preferred no agreement to SNT-3, but preferred SNT-4 to the no-agreement state. There still may be joint gains to be had, and if Egypt announces that SNT-4 is acceptable whereas Israel does not, then the ensuing gains are going to be tilted toward the Israeli side. That would not be a disaster for Egypt if that's the only way Israel can get over its reservation hurdle, but Sadat might think that the Israelis are already satisfied and are just trying to squeeze out more at Egypt's expense. So he still maintains that SNT-4 is unacceptable, but his protests are less vehement than before.

With the proposal of SNT-5, Israel's reservation value, too, is pierced. Will Begin announce this? Probably not, for the same reasons Sadat did not. But now it is no longer possible to squeeze out additional joint gains. If SNT-5 is modified to the advantage of one side, it is only at the expense of the other side. In Figure 34, SNT-5 is on the efficient frontier and no achievable joint evaluations are northeast of it. Point X represents a composite reservation value: Egypt would rather have no agreement than any deal that yields an evaluation south of X; Israel would rather have no agreement than any deal that yields an evaluation west of X; both sides would prefer to have any point northeast of X rather than the no-agreement state. But each, acting strategically, does not announce that SNT-5 is better than no agreement. Of course, if the composite reservation value were at Y rather than X, then they would be acting sincerely in their rejections of SNT-5. We're dealing with idealizations here. The reservation values are vague, and a politically acceptable agreement is usually one that has been difficult to negotiate.

Assume that both sides claim that they cannot settle for SNT-5, and that it proves impossible for the mediating team to squeeze out further joint gains. What now? The mediators are very discouraged, since the United States, too, has a stake in the negotiations. It may now be propitious for President Carter to give up something. Perhaps Israel could accept SNT-5 if the United States funded the construction of new airfields in Israel to replace those of the Sinai. No? Well how about some oil guarantees also? And might Egypt accept SNT-5 if the United States provided some financial aid for Egypt's ailing economy? So the president applies pressure and offers sweeteners, and a deal is struck.[2]

Did Egypt and Israel expect the United States to sweeten the pie? Did they gamble by declining SNT-5 in anticipation of a U.S.

---

2. In reality, the negotiations at Camp David were a bit different from those described here. The number of iterations of the single negotiation text was not five, but more like twenty-five. Magnanimous U.S. offers to each side were not made exclusively at the end of the play; they were sprinkled along the way to keep the protagonists from quitting the negotiating game.

contribution? Did the United States anticipate that it might have to offer inducements to each side in order to generate an agreement? In preparing for the meetings, did all three sides think hard about what the United States could offer and about their tradeoffs and reservation values with potential U.S. contributions? Did Egypt and Israel agree to come to Camp David because this would put pressure on the United States to get an agreement? Did the U.S. team know that they were thinking this way? Did they know that the mediators knew that they knew? Did Egypt and Israel engage in tacit collusion to squeeze the United States?

Most of these questions probably have affirmative answers, at least to some degree. Is this morally wrong? Some might be tempted to say that it is, because they are not pleased with the outcome of the Camp David accords. But trying to leave that aside, would it be morally reprehensible, in principle, for statesmen to behave so strategically? My general answer is that it is not morally reprehensible—that leaders who do not act strategically may not be behaving in the best interests of their constituencies. But—and this is an important "but"—strategic misrepresentations can lead, as we have seen, to inefficiencies in outcomes and to ensuing mistrust. So the challenge is: How can we devise negotiating processes that will encourage more honest revelations and less strategic behavior?

GENERATING A SINGLE NEGOTIATING TEXT

Let's look at how a negotiator or mediator might successfully combine a number of issues into a single composite text for discussion.

Suppose that Negotiator B persuades his adversary, Negotiator A, to *tentatively* consider an opening package that B himself has suggested as a point of departure for potential improvement. The joint evaluation of B's proposal is represented by point SNT-1' in Figure 35. Actually, B lures A into this position by arguing that it is easier for them to talk about a single negotiating proposal (text) than about two proposals simultaneously. Although SNT-1' is certainly not acceptable to A, Negotiator B suggests that no harm will be done if they jointly try to see if it could lead to some acceptable conclusion. The first improvement to SNT-1' favors A. Then A and B become so involved in generating successive improvements that A forgets where they started from (B's opening proposal); or perhaps A runs out of time. Figure 35 depicts what might happen: the negotiations starting from SNT-1′ end up with a joint evaluation at X. If the roles were reversed and if A started with proposal SNT-1″, they might have ended up at Y.

The conclusion should be clear: where one ends up depends in large part on where one starts. The question that remains is how to go about getting started—how to generate an SNT.

At Camp David the U.S. team generated an SNT. They probably tried not to start too close to the efficient frontier, aiming for a starting point that would appear to be "neutral" (as interpreted by the U.S. team). If the mediators had privately informed one side of the U.S. negotiating strategy, that side might have tried to influence the United States to start with an alternate SNT more favorable to themselves. A lot depends on the starting point.

Here are some ways in which an SNT can be generated. Suppose that A and B negotiate through a dance of packages. In Figure 36 successive offers by A are denoted as A_1, A_2, A_3, and by B as B_1, B_2, B_3. The offers seem to be converging on some package X, but the

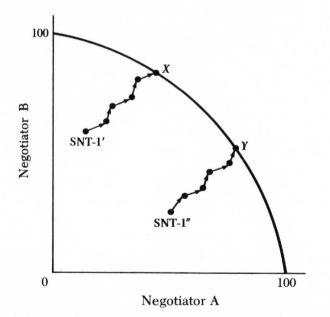

Figure 35. Dependence of final outcome on the choice of the SNT.

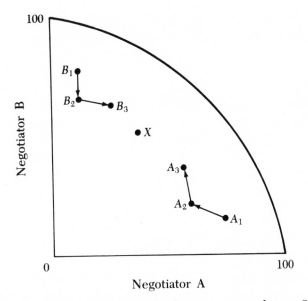

Figure 36. A dance of packages leading to an agreed-upon SNT.

negotiators each want more. As a tactic, they might agree to accept X as their SNT and look for successive joint gains from that vantage point. Or A and B might agree to negotiate cordially and loosely on all issues and not to log-roll while looking for joint gains; this results in a joint *tentative* package, X, that is treated as the starting SNT. As a variation on this theme, the negotiators themselves might identify a bargaining range for each factor. They then agree to choose a focal point (for example, the mid-value on each continuous factor). They might have to haggle a bit in the process; but they know that they are not haggling about a final contract, but a starting point for the pursuit of joint gains.

Suppose there are a host of small issues, all of secondary importance and all of comparable magnitude of importance. If one issue seems to loom large, it might be broken into separate issues or staggered over time. Or the importance of an issue might be lessened by the parties first narrowing the range of possible outcomes on that issue. The parties might then agree to resolve each issue separately by the toss of a coin. Or they might agree to take turns, each resolving the issue of its choice, of those remaining, in its favor (within mutually agreed-upon bounds, of course). A coin might be tossed to designate the starter. For example, the coin falls heads and A starts. She selects issue 17 and resolves it in her favor—but within a range preset by both before the process starts. B goes next, choosing issue 12 and resolves it in his favor. And so on. The parties, of course, first have to negotiate bounds on each issue or else the outcome might depend critically on who goes first.

There is no reason why the parties can't agree on a composite scheme for determining an SNT. Some issues can be settled by using central values; some by a random process; some by the parties' taking turns. The parties can be ingenious about the schemes they devise. The important thing is that this process appear to be fair to both sides and not be divisive. The parties should keep in mind that they are agreeing merely on the SNT which, in turn, will only loosely influence the final outcome.

Recall from our discussion of final-offer arbitration how the process works with a single continuous issue (distributive bargaining): if A and B can't settle, the arbitrator calls for final offers from both negotiators simultaneously and then chooses one of these. The same procedure can be used when there are several issues. One way to do this, which has been adopted by some states, requires each side to submit a final-offer *total package;* the arbitrator selects one of these two packages. A second way, adopted by other states, allows the arbitrator to break up packages—to accept A's final offer on some issues and B's final offer on other issues. Some arbitrators try to look at each issue separately and to resolve each in isolation without log-rolling, in their minds, between issues. It's easy to see how these procedures could be jointly inefficient, because the essence of squeezing out joint gains lies in log-rolling between issues. Perhaps the best method would be to encourage both sides to use the arbitrated solution as an SNT for an ensuing round of negotiations, perhaps with a mediator; if they can't agree on how to squeeze out further joint gains, the arbitrated solution holds. If an SNT were to be generated by a final-offer arbitration process, then it would probably be better if the SNT were created by using final-offer resolution on each issue separately, rather than on the package of issues collectively.

15

Mediation of Conflicts

On the subject of mediation of negotiations, there exists quite a lot of good literature; but I believe that not enough has been written about the potential value of analysis in the mediation process.

Mediators are not supposed to dictate solutions to the disputants, as arbitrators do. The distinctions between mediation and arbitration, however, are sometimes fuzzy. Strong mediators may suggest solutions or use their prestige to push disputants toward certain solutions. Also, mediators might want to think about what would be a fair solution and let these reflections partially govern their mediating behavior. Although third-party intervention may be extremely helpful in dispute resolution, an extraneous third party can sometimes exacerbate differences rather than minimize them.

Sometimes an intervenor may not be the invitee but the inviter. Parties might be engaged in an escalating fracas and refuse to negotiate; an offer by one side to negotiate may be interpreted as a sign of weakness. In such cases a discerning, well-meaning, noninvolved party may identify the disputants that have a stake in a negotiated agreement and invite them to the conference table. The intervenor might ensure that all legitimate disputants are represented in the ensuing negotiations. Sometimes, in multiparty disputes, the intervenor may select which parties should negotiate, when it would be embarrassing for a given disputant to make such a selection. It may also be up to the intervenor to suggest the key issues to be negotiated.

There is a continuum of roles, from weak to strong, that a mediator can play. On the weak side, the mediator may be just a convenor of meetings or a nonsubstantive, neutral discussion leader; he or she might simply maintain rules of civilized debate or occasionally give a reticent speaker a chance to interject some comments. In more complex negotiations, the mediator might prepare neutral minutes of the discussions and summarize or articulate any consensus that can be gleaned. A mediator might refuse to get involved in the process or substance of the discussions, but might help in implementing agreements: by preparing well-written public relations documents that explain the necessity for compromise, by giving a stamp of approval to compromise agreements, by attesting that both sides negotiated in good faith and that no hidden agreements were secretly arrived at, by helping with the verification of agreements, by helping with grievances that might arise in the future because of ambiguities in the contract. The mediator may want to do more. He or she may want to improve the ambience of the negotiations, assist with personal problems by stabilizing and controlling emotions, and help the disputants understand that the conflict is not a contest to be won but a conflict to be solved.

When disputing parties join a mediator in an open, honest, collegial, joint-problem-solving quest for a reasonable compromise solution, they are often confronted with an analytical problem of some complexity. In problems of comparable complexity with a single decision maker, various analytical skills are frequently employed. But somehow when a problem has a tinge of competitiveness to it, attempts at joint analysis tend to be shunned. It's my belief that in a great number of such cases, joint gains could be realized if only the contending parties were willing to yield up enough sovereignty to allow a mediator to help them devise creative alternatives and to help them analyze their joint problem.

HOW ANALYSIS CAN HELP

If two contracts, A and B, are proposed and analyzed, an astute mediator, by examining those factors that favor A and those that favor B, can often generate a new strategy, C, that combines the best of both worlds. If two disputants differ in their preferences for contracts A and B, and if a mediator understands how each protagonist weighs the multiplicity of factors in arriving at his or her preference, then the mediator may be in an ideal position to devise and propose a compromise contract.

The set of decision options may be constrained by technological, financial, and political considerations. Each side of the dispute, having only partial information and partial control, may not be in a position to perform the types of analysis that would be possible with a joint problem-solving effort. This joint effort may require the sharing of delicate information, value tradeoffs, and reservation values; it may require willingness to coordinate actions. The protagonists to a dispute may be more willing to enter into a joint problem-solving activity if a reputable mediator is there to accumulate information from each in a balanced way. The mediator might also provide analytical, problem-solving skills that are not available—at least not in equal abundance—to all protagonists. If one of the parties to a dispute performs an analysis that is supposedly applicable to all, it might be held in suspicion by the other parties; analysis done by an impartial mediator has more of a chance of being accepted.

The word "analysis" has a Greek etymology, and means a loosening or dissolving or breaking up of any whole into its parts. Any joint problem-solving effort that decomposes a problem into its component parts can run into difficulties, because the disputants may not agree on the structure, or on the prognostication of uncertainties, or on synergies and interactions within and between these component parts. In other words, analysis and decomposition will tend to highlight differences in judgments about uncertainties and in opinions about value tradeoffs. But this is precisely what a mediator can exploit in fashioning compromise agreements.

Complex negotiations can often be resolved by compromises that exploit the role of time. Not everything must be decided here and now. Some actions can be deferred to a later time and be made contingent on information learned along the way. Such contingency arrangements may require a deep understanding of the problem's uncertainties, which can often be better understood by modeling the dynamic interacting effects. An intervenor may be ideally suited to supervise such modeling efforts.

The mediator might prepare a single negotiating text and then successively modify it after the disputants have criticized it separately and collectively. In the search for joint gains, the mediator might want to help each side separately to clarify its own value tradeoffs. By gaining an understanding of the differences in their value tradeoffs, the mediator might be better prepared to suggest joint improvements to the current single negotiating text.

In seeking to devise other ways in which a third party could help disputants come to an agreement, I once invented a role for a rather unorthodox type of intervenor, whom I called a "contract embellisher." Suppose that two parties are involved in a complex negotiating deal. At some early stage in the negotiations, when both sides fully understand the issues they are negotiating, the contract embellisher interviews each side separately, confidentially, and in depth about its needs, perceptions, value tradeoffs, and so on. He then seals this information and retires from the scene until normal contract negotiations are terminated. Knowing a great deal about each side's beliefs, values, aspirations, and constraints, he is in a position to ascertain whether they have arrived at an efficient contract—a contract that will not permit further joint gains. If they have not, the contract embellisher attempts to devise an alternate contract, which according to his calculations they would both prefer. But there may be slippage and it is possible that he could be wrong. So next he asks each side privately if it would prefer his suggested contract to the one already negotiated. If both sides separately indicate that they would prefer his proposal, then the change is consummated. There is no haggling about the proposal: the parties can either take it or leave it. After presenting his suggestions, whether they are accepted or not, the contract embellisher destroys the confidential information he has received from each side. As a fee for his services, he might collect, say, one-fifth of the value added by the embellished contract over the negotiated contract— as perceived by each of the parties.[1]

The contract embellisher is a strange type of intervenor, not quite mediator and not quite arbitrator. In the parlance of this book, we can describe contract embellishment as follows. The parties, unaided, come to some agreement; among other things, this final agreement establishes a single negotiating text; the embellisher, knowing the values, beliefs, and constraints of both sides, then seeks an efficient contract that both sides would prefer to the SNT they have created. In Chapter 17 we'll discuss the myriad contending principles of fairness that could enter into the embellisher's choice of a particular efficient contract.

1. There is no assurance, of course, that the protagonists would tell the embellisher their true values. But a substantial majority of a large sample of senior executives indicated that in such a context they would not act strategically.

MORE ON DYNAMIC COMPROMISES: THE MEXICO
CITY AIRPORT

In the early 1970s Ralph Keeney and I were asked by the Mexico City ministry of public works, the Secretaria de Obras Publicas (SOP), to help prepare its case for the development of a new airport for the city. The SOP wanted to construct a new airport at Zumpango, twenty-five miles away, whereas the ministry of communication and transport, the Secretaria de Communicaciones y Transportes (SCT), advocated modernizing the existing inadequate airport in Mexico City. At one time the existing airport had been outside the city; but as the city grew, the airport had "moved" to be just outside and then to be quite a bit inside the city limits.

The SOP and SCT acted as adversaries or disputants, each trying to convince Mexico's President Luis Echeverria Alvarez that its proposed master plan was best for the country. Any plan had to be evaluated on the basis of a number of conflicting attributes: capacity of the airport to handle passengers and freight; costs of land, construction, and capital improvements; operating costs; safety; noise; commuting times to and from the airport; dislocation of people; national and municipal prestige; impacts on other developments; effect on the military; and so on. Alternative master plans were developed with thirty- or forty-year horizons—that is, what would happen in 1975, 1985, and 1995, and a glimpse at what could be expected to happen beyond the turn of the century. Of course, there were confounding uncertainties: Mexico's ability to pay; future demand for air travel, including the impact on low-cost tourist travel from the United States to Mexico; the cost of land; projected improvements in aircraft noise control; projected improvements in airplanes that would enable them to fly different takeoff and landing patterns; projected improvements in construction techniques that would make it economically feasible to build landing fields on marshland; projected changes in international safety standards; and so on. No one could be sure how these uncertainties would be resolved over time, but the SOP and SCT each had different probabilistic projections that naturally favored their preferred solution.

Keeney and I were asked to do an honest decision analysis of the two alternatives, and not to bias our analysis in favor of the SCT's preferred alternative: a new airport at Zumpango. The SOP authorities, for their part, were convinced that an impartial analysis would vindicate them. I proposed an alternative procedure: rather than using the current heated and suspicious adversarial mode, have the president appoint a blue-ribbon, impartial mediating panel to supervise the analysis and to structure the debate in a joint problem-solving atmosphere. The SOP thought that this was a fine idea, because they were sure that their proposals would win. The SCT, on the other hand, was suspicious of a suggestion coming from an SOP consultant, and in the propaganda battle of adversarial politics, they felt that they had an advantage. So my idea was not implemented.

With ample help from specialists within the SOP, Keeney and I did an analysis that concentrated on Echeverria's decision problem —not on what Mexico should do in 1985 and 1995, but on what should be done during Echeverria's six-year term of office. Of course, we had to look at the long-run future to see how the future would reflect back on the present. We argued that Mexico need not adopt a definitive master plan; it could base its future decisions on the critical information learned along the way. Surprisingly—to all parties involved—we convinced the SOP to advocate a compromise proposal that would only partially commit Mexico to a new airport, and to make modest improvements in the old airport. This analysis came as a shock to our clients, who had earlier been adamant in their support of Zumpango; but they convinced themselves that our analysis was responsive to their inputs—inputs about uncertainties and about value tradeoffs—and they adopted our advice.

What insights about mediation can be drawn from this example? There are a lot of problems like the one involving the Mexico City airport, in which two parties argue vociferously about what should be done not only now but far in the future. They may have different initial perceptions about how future uncertainties will unfold, and in the course of adversarial debate they may exaggerate their perceptions. We saw earlier how a compromise can sometimes be generated through the use of contingent payoffs that depend on which future event occurs. That idea can be extended in an important way: not only can *payoffs* be made contingently, but *future actions* can be made contingently. The parties might agree now on what future joint actions they will adopt if certain events occur. This opens up a vast domain of possible compromise agreements.

Take the 1981 baseball strike as an example. Both the team owners and the players wanted the sport continued; neither wanted an excessive concentration of player talent located in a few rich teams; both wanted the sport to remain competitive and to appeal to the American public; neither wanted teams to go bankrupt because of excessively large salaries. Both sides agreed to all this, but they couldn't agree on what to do about it. They could not be certain about the long-range implications of any complex agreement, such as compensation for free agents. And because of these uncertainties, each side demanded a bit more, for the sake of prudence. Perhaps they could have agreed on desirable levels for a set of indicators that would have reflected the health of the professional baseball industry; and then perhaps each side might have been willing to give up some sovereignty to a group that could have fine-tuned the system over time (for example, tightening or loosening compensation rules year by year, depending on the current dynamics). This would have been a little like the Federal Reserve Board's method of controlling monetary supply, to balance myriad factors that cannot all be foreseen. With regard to compensation rules in professional sports, it is difficult to make precise predictions of the dynamic effects of various actions. Inevitably there will be surprises, and it's hard to account ex ante for all contingencies. Contending parties, therefore, might find it advantageous to argue not about actions but about indicators of a healthy industry; they might debate on the guidelines or constraints to be put on a committee that will be asked to control the system using an adaptive feedback philosophy of control. The controllers could be thought of as dynamic arbitrators who will be constrained in their actions by a set of guidelines mutually agreed upon—perhaps through a mediation process. To make an analogy with a different sort of system, the courts can be seen as a control mechanism for fine-tuning justice, a mechanism whose actions are constrained by the Constitution and guided by a heritage of past legal cases.

Analysis, of course, is not a panacea. In many cases, compromises are reached because both sides are so vague about the issues that they can settle for almost any agreement, and ambiguity might help sell that agreement to their constituencies back at home; in such instances, joint analysis can make the parties comprehend for the first time just how competitive they really should be. But in many other cases, where compromise agreements have *not* been achieved, a careful dissection of the interests of both sides, a careful articulation of value tradeoffs, a careful assessment of uncertainties, and a careful examination of intricate contingency contracts can provide the key to resolution.

A little analysis on the part of one disputant can go a long way. Often there is no time to do more than a little analysis. More often a lot of analysis is self-defeating because it's hard to do depth analysis and because there is a tendency to attribute excessive rationality to the other side. A little analysis can also be of value to the mediator. But sometimes the mediator can gain the cooperation of all the protagonists, and—armed with more complete information and a better balance of interests—may profitably invest more time in doing deeper analysis.

THE JUDGE AS MEDIATOR

Of the 85,420 federal civil cases that were filed in the United States in 1975, only 9 percent were disposed of by trial.[2] In our discussion of the Sorenson Chevrolet File, we saw some reasons why litigants settle out of court: the cost of litigation, the anxiety caused by delay, the need for early resolution, the reluctance to risk the vagaries of a trial process with potentially extreme outcomes, the "vindication" enjoyed by both parties with a compromise solution, and the economic motives of lawyers who can process more cases without actual court trials. Since only a small fraction of suits can be tried, given the limited resources of the court, out-of-court settlements are encouraged. Some states, such as California, enable a party making a settlement offer to recover subsequent litigation costs if the opposing party fails to obtain a judgment better than the offer.

The judge has important roles to play outside the courtroom in settling disputes. First, he or she can *facilitate negotiations.* Since each litigant may be averse to being the first to suggest a possibility of settlement, the judge can bring the opposing parties together. The Federal Rules of Civil Procedure allow pretrial conferences, which serve to create an atmosphere conducive to settlement.

Second, since litigants may be reluctant to hasten the completion

2. This section is based largely on Shallert (1980).

of protracted negotiations, the judge can *impose firm deadlines* for completion of negotiations and thus expedite an agreement.

Third, the judge, acting as mediator, can *reduce adversaries' differences* by helping to deflate extremely unrealistic aspirations. Some judges have adopted a "Lloyds of London" technique, whereby the judge privately leads the attorneys for the plaintiff and defendant to do expected-value calculations: they are each asked to estimate (a) their chances of winning, and (b) the conditional expectation of the dollar amounts of damages that a jury would award. These two factors are then multiplied together to get an overall expected value. A deduction is made for the incremental costs of litigation, and perhaps for risk-aversion. The judge acts as an analytical consultant by helping each side obtain a realistic, ballpark estimate of the worth of their case. If the gap between estimates is small, the judge might want to leak this information to the litigants, as neutrally as possible, and encourage them to settle out of court.

Fourth, the judge, after preliminary fact-finding in pretrial conferences, might *suggest avenues for agreement.* If both sides announce their offering prices, the judge can preach the fairness of a split-the-difference compromise, or possibly hint at another compromise point that then serves as a basis for ensuing negotiations.

Fifth, the judge can *help implement agreements,* by ensuring that the terms of agreements made outside the courtroom (under his guidance) will be faithfully executed. Here the record of the courts is impressive.

The judge, wearing mediator's robes, is nevertheless somewhat restricted; at some stage, the judge might have to don the robes of juridical arbitrator. Care must be exerted that the mediation process does not prejudice the courtroom outcome, if by chance the case does go to trial.

THE CHIEF EXECUTIVE OFFICER AS MEDIATOR

Business executives like to think of themselves as negotiators, since they do a lot of it in different guises. Very few see themselves as mediators or arbitrators. But when one analyzes what mediators and arbitrators do in settling disputes, one realizes that a lot of these same skills are employed by business executives in their role as managers. Managers are constantly called upon to help settle disputes among lower-level executives. Sometimes these managers play the role of mediator-with-clout; other times, the role of arbitrator. Very often these disputes can be settled by appeal to the bottom line: profits to the firm. But there is far more to business than making money, and some heated disputes within business firms cannot easily be resolved by monetary accounting alone. Let's look at a hypothetical example.

Charles Edgeworth Osgood is the newly appointed chief executive officer of a fictional state-owned enterprise (SOE).[3] He was chosen by a government minister, the titular head of the SOE and himself a recent appointee, who sought guidance from the SOE's board of directors in making his choice. No internal candidate seemed to be suitable and, in an act of desperation, they picked Osgood, a professor of management.

Traditionally the board has taken some part in the operational decision making of the SOE, and in the past there has been considerable tension between the CEO and the board over operational jurisdiction. The theory has been that the board should have its say on broad strategic policy questions, but that the CEO should have considerable flexibility on purely operational matters. (The jurisdictional conflict reminds one of the classic joke that asks: Who is to decide whether this question is a big or a little question?) Osgood has been told to expect that there would be shifting coalitions within the board, depending on the nature of the issue.

It is clear to all that the board structure has never reflected the organizational needs of the SOE. Several present board members were each appointed to be the guardian of the rights of some specific constituent group, and unfortunately some of these members do not have an appreciation of the enterprise as a whole. Indeed, many board members are prominent men and women with other outside responsibilities, so that their knowledge about the enterprise they are governing is somewhat lopsided. They themselves are aware of this and feel guilty about their own inadequate grasp of the complexities of the enterprise; but despite their good intentions, they simply do not have the time to learn the intricacies of the business.

The board plays a key role. It encompasses a broad range of polit-

3. This case is adapted from Raiffa (1981).

ical and business acumen. The members, although each might have a pet hobbyhorse, want the enterprise to do well. They act as a political buffer between the supervisory ministry (and other ministries) and the CEO, thereby protecting the enterprise from too much outside interference. They represent and protect the interests of the SOE in higher governmental circles and in broad national planning; they help the CEO open some doors and they collectively know the right people.

Osgood, very early in his tenure, decides to seek advice from Martin Bryan, one of the members of the board, who served under Osgood's predecessor and who is one of the few members possessing a broad vision of the functions of the SOE.

> *Osgood:* I hope I don't end up being just an ineffective figurehead. I want to be viewed as an imaginative and effective entrepreneur.
>
> *Bryan:* So did your predecessor. He meant well, but nothing meaningful was accomplished. There are just too many conflicting objectives in this organization, and it paralyzes innovation.
>
> *Osgood:* Do the board members have a grasp of the full array of objectives?
>
> *Bryan:* Well, it seems that at every board meeting someone, once again, states the full panoply of objectives that we would like to accomplish. These objectives are packaged in different ways by different members, but surprisingly there's no disagreement about the objectives we should be thinking about. It's how to think about compromises among these objectives that causes the problem. We're simply great at preparing taxonomies and checklists.
>
> *Osgood:* Let's stay on this issue for a while. Has anyone ever tried to formalize tradeoffs between objectives?
>
> *Bryan:* I'm not quite sure I understand what that means. Do you mean putting numbers on various potential levels of achievement and getting a formula to operate this enterprise? If so, no. And furthermore, I don't think it can be done. There are just too many qualitative variables, intangibles, and fragile values. And besides, members would simply disagree about the tradeoffs, even if it could be done.
>
> *Osgood:* Well there's a lot of room between running the enterprise by a formula and getting first-cut approximations of some critical tradeoffs. But let me push on. Can you give me an ex-

ample of what you consider a significant proposal and tell me how the board and the CEO dealt with it?

Bryan: As you know, ours is an aging enterprise and we are trying to keep our losses down while fulfilling important social roles. Your predecessor rightly asked the board to consider a range of possible ways to turn losses into profits. These possibilities involved change and enlarging our product mix, diversifying into less-related businesses, and vertically integrating our operations. Oh, there were some minor functional shifts in our production line, but the board couldn't agree on any significant change.

Osgood: Let me see if I understand. The CEO would propose some significant change in policy, and his analytical staff would project the implications of this proposal, presumably on the objectives of concern. Am I right so far?

Bryan: Close enough. Sometimes, I or someone else on the board would suggest the change, but the CEO's staff would be responsible for doing the analysis.

Osgood: And none of these proposals would work because someone on the board would block it?

Bryan: It's not that simple. There's a reasonable amount of give and take. The original proposal is often modified and remodified to meet the objectives of the board members, but all too often a blocking coalition develops.

Osgood: Are these always the same people? And how many blockers does it take?

Bryan: No, the coalitions shift and it's hard to give numbers. If a member of the board representing another ministry objects, the deal is usually dead. If several members object, and if they represent different concerns within our own ministry, then numbers do count. But if a quarter or more defect, then politically it's just not feasible to go ahead.

Osgood: Am I right in thinking that most board members want to make some meaningful changes, but not changes that will hurt their special interests?

Bryan: That pretty well captures it, except for a few ideologues who never seem to want to change anything.

Osgood: Let's see if I have it right. You're saying that if I want to get anything significant through the board I'm going to have to educate, to influence, and to twist arms with the help of the minister. I'm going to have to fight. Is that right?

Bryan: More or less.

Osgood:: The task as I see it, is that I must fashion a proposal that makes eminently good sense to me and then sell it to the board. Many of the board members will have cutoff constraints on the objectives of their particular concern, and you're saying that if I'm not resourceful and influential, these constraints will collectively kill my proposal.

Bryan: That's right! And you can be sure that in the in-fighting that goes on, each guardian of a right will exaggerate his objective. He'll say he needs more protection than he really needs. But each will have a fallback position below which he won't go. Trouble is, you'll never know what that position is without testing it.

Osgood: This is a tough question and I don't see how it can be answered precisely. But do you think that if I were to play the role of an effective mediator and were to push those recalcitrant members back to their bottom-line absolute minimum positions, this would allow us room for possibly achieving some meaningful changes?

Bryan: Sure, for simple functional changes—but not for anything as profound as unrelated diversification or partial divestiture. Anything that requires a change in our charter will involve a major confrontation.

Osgood: Well, as I see it, I would like to try my hand at achieving something significant, and I would like to enlist the aid of the minister himself to push back those rock-bottom positions of the guardians of special interests.

Bryan: That won't be easy for the board members who are here under the protection of other ministries. Our minister will have to log-roll his interests with the interests of the other cabinet ministers. And for board members in his own ministry that are under his control, he will have to fashion lots of side deals.

Osgood: Tell me, what are the criteria that the board uses to judge the performance of the CEO?

Bryan: Pardon me if my answer is a bit cynical: the trick is to stay out of trouble. Any direct, discernible harm you do to any identifiable group will cause you political difficulty. Secondary and tertiary dynamic effects of your policies, especially if they are not traceable unequivocally back to your actions, will be discounted by the public and, therefore, by the board. It's fine if some program directly improves regional development, for example; but if the improvement is indirect and only partially attributable to your policy, don't expect any credit for it.

Osgood: Are you also saying that long-range programs, no matter how good, will be undervalued by the board?

Bryan: Well, that also happens in the private sector; but in my opinion, the diversity of objectives of a public enterprise tends to diminish the importance of basic research and development in new ventures. We have no bottom line to keep our eyes focused on. We don't make enough hardheaded calculations of our future needs. Politics tends to be dominated by short-term interests, by the here-and-now.

Osgood: How about uncertainty and risk? Does the board ever take chances?

Bryan: You're going to be evaluated by the quality of the outcomes of your decisions and not by the quality of your decisions themselves. As a government-owned business, we should not be too risk-averse, but certainly we are.

Osgood: Is this because the board, the CEO, and the minister are worried far more about the effects of decisions on themselves rather than on the public at large?

Bryan: There's nothing new in that. It's hard in the public sector to balance minuses with pluses. Unfortunately, it's a lot easier to propagandize about the negative than the positive. So this SOE, like others, tends to be conservatively managed.

Osgood: But if most of the board members feel as you do, why don't they collectively join forces and share the risk by standing by each other?

Bryan: Ah, but that takes leadership—and leadership is a rare commodity.

In this case, Osgood will be "mediating and managing" those who are organizationally above him. We could easily change the context to one in which a manager at one level of a hierarchically organized enterprise must mediate and arbitrate the conflicts that boil up from below; in such a role, it is the manager who has the clout, whereas Osgood has to rely on the government minister for that support. The manager, acting as intervenor, of course has objectives of his or her own. But the manager also must act to keep subordinates fulfilled and happy—and that means having to incorporate into the payoff function the payoff values of those others being "managed."

QUALITY RANKING OF MEDIATORS

Some mediators are clearly better than others. Can we articulate why? What are the criteria we should use to judge whether a mediator is doing a good job? We could, perhaps, score mediators on how well they perform various roles, and then use these scores to evaluate their relative appropriateness for a given type of dispute.

A well-known mediator, William Simkin, described and commented extensively on the desirable qualities of a mediator (Simkin, 1971). In a jocular mood, he wrote that a mediator should have:

1. the patience of Job
2. the sincerity and bulldog characteristics of the English
3. the wit of the Irish
4. the physical endurance of the marathon runner
5. the broken-field dodging ability of a halfback
6. the guile of Machiavelli
7. the personality-probing skills of a good psychiatrist
8. the confidence-retaining characteristics of a mute
9. the hide of a rhinoceros
10. the wisdom of Solomon.

And, in a more serious vein, he added the following:

11. demonstrated integrity and impartiality
12. a basic knowledge of and belief in the collective bargaining process
13. firm faith in voluntarism, in contrast to dictation
14. a fundamental belief in human values and potentials, tempered by the ability to assess personal weaknesses as well as strengths
15. a hard-nosed ability to analyze what is available, in contrast to what may be desirable
16. sufficient personal drive and ego, qualified by a willingness to be self-effacing.

In an experimental setting, it is difficult to determine how to score subjects who are playing the role of mediator. Are there any objective standards one can impose? Suppose that the dispute involves several issues, some monetary and others nonmonetary, and suppose that the mediator is not paid a contingent fee that he or she is trying to maximize. How should one score mediators in those cases?

Let's simplify. Suppose that Disputant A and Disputant B have confidential scoring systems: A knows only his and B knows only hers, but both are known to the experimenter, and neither is known to the mediator, M. Consider the case in which five such groups—

each consisting of two disputants and a mediator—participate in the same laboratory exercise. In Figure 37, let the resulting joint evaluations of the final contracts be labeled V, W, X, Y, and Z, where V is not shown because the disputants did not come to any agreement.

The mediator involved in outcome Y achieved maximum efficiency: he left no potential joint gains on the table. The mediator involved in outcome X left lots of potential gains on the table. But from an equity point of view, X might be "fairer" than Y. This raises the question that we will consider in Chapter 17: What is fair? Outcome Z is clearly better than X for both disputants; but even here it is hard to argue that the mediator involved in Z did a better job than the one involved in X. It may be that the Z outcome would have been achieved by that particular pair of disputants without their mediator, whereas the disputants involved in the X outcome would have achieved no agreement without their mediator. Furthermore, the disputants in the Z outcome might have the impression that they could have done a lot better, or that they could have done

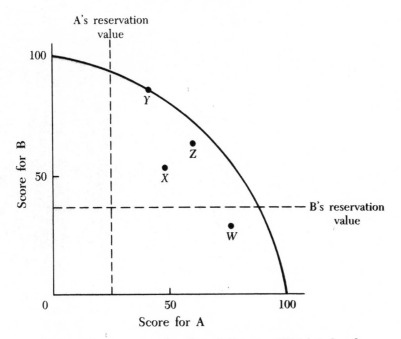

Figure 37. Outcomes of mediated disputes: Which is best?

better with another mediator. On the other hand, the disputants involved in the X outcome might feel they did really well; they might have felt comfortable with their mediator and would enthusiastically recommend her to others.

The mediator involved in outcome W might have cajoled Disputant B into accepting an outcome that is clearly not in B's interest; B would have been better off with no contract, but she was unable to perceive this—perhaps because the mediator in her dispute did not explain things clearly enough. Another mediator failed altogether to lead his disputants to an agreement. But from the vantage point of an impartial intervenor, the no-agreement outcome might have been better than the W outcome, where Disputant B might later have realized that she would have been better off with no agreement.

Obviously, evaluating the performance of a mediator is never simple, even in simple cases. And we still have not come to grips with the question: "What is fair?"

16

Arbitration of Disputes

Two disputants are negotiating, but to no avail. An arbitrator intervenes to settle the dispute—not to lead or to suggest to the disputants what they might do, but rather to dictate the terms of the final contract. The dispute could be quite unrestricted in scope, involving many issues and including the possibility of intricate contingent contracts that exploit different perceptions of uncertainties. The parties are not disputing an interpretation of a previously negotiated contract, as would be the case in grievance arbitration, but are trying to negotiate a contract where none existed before, or where one existed but has expired. For the time being we'll keep it ambiguous as to whether the parties volunteered or were compelled to submit their dispute for arbitration.

The arbitrator must dig out the facts, must probe the desires and values of both sides, must seek external guideposts or norms that will constrain his or her choice. Let's assume that the arbitrator is impartial and wants to do what is right and fair for the disputants.

Certainly the arbitrator would not *purposely* choose an inefficient contract—one for which an alternate contract exists that both would prefer. But the disputants may not have crisp value tradeoffs, and the arbitrator may only very vaguely know what those vague tradeoffs are. The arbitrator, therefore, might very well dictate a final contract that is not truly efficient, even though it might be *perceived* as efficient. The designated arbitrated solution, although perhaps inefficient, may be far preferred by each disputant to no outcome; efficiency, while desirable, is not critical.

We would all agree that letting each side propose a wish list and letting the arbitrator toss a coin to decide who gets all would be a ludicrous procedure—one that would treat both sides equally in an ex ante sense, but that is not in any ex post sense "fair" to the losing side. How can one approach the issue of fairness in the context of negotiation?

There is a literature in the theory of games on the abstract notion of fairness; it's doubtful, however, whether it has made much of an impact on arbitrators. Let's look at a hypothetical dialogue between a sophisticated arbitrator and an analyst who knows something about this literature as they work together on a concrete case of arbitration. The arbitrator must decide the case, but the analyst is there to dig out the facts, to perform calculating chores and, where appropriate, to tell the arbitrator what some theorist has written about critical issues that he is struggling with. To simplify, we'll assume that each disputant has crisp and consistent preferences and that, with the help of the analyst, each side has formalized its trade-offs: it can associate with each potential contract a payoff value— a single number that reflects the desirability of that contract. Each side has adjusted its payoff scale so that the no-agreement alternative for each disputant is scaled at zero. As we get deeper into this

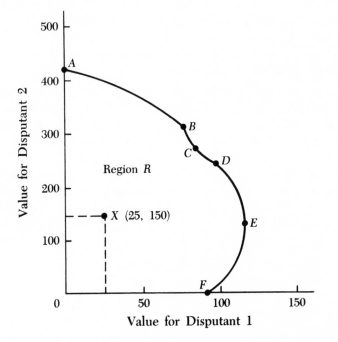

Figure 38. Set of feasible joint evaluations.

problem, the payoff scales will be further clarified. Particularly important in this case will be interpersonal comparisons of values and utilities—questions, for instance, pertaining to whether one disputant prefers a particular alternative more than the other disputant. Interpersonal comparisons are natural to think about in the context of fairness, but they are difficult—some would say impossible—to formalize.

Suppose that the arbitrator tells the analyst to prepare for him a display of all potential joint evaluations. The analyst does so, without specifically identifying the two disputants, Ms. Sharon and Mr. Henry. For example, as in Figure 38, final contract X might specify a complete description of one way in which all issues can be resolved, possibly including monetary side payoffs from one disputant to the other, and perhaps a schedule describing what each side will have to do in the future, depending on how circumstances unfold. In other words, a final contract such as X can be quite complex. Suppose that Disputant 1 subjectively evaluates X as being worth 25 points, and Disputant 2 evaluates X as being worth 150 points. This joint evaluation (25, 150) is plotted in the figure. The arbitrator consults with the analyst about the implications of the data.

Arbitrator: At this point I don't know if Disputant 1 is Mr. Henry or Ms. Sharon.

Analyst: Do you really want to know?

Arbitrator: Well, I guess not. That's one way to force myself to be neutral. Maybe later I'll want to know the identities of the two sides. Let's look at that joint evaluation at X. Since 150 is larger than 25, does this mean that Disputant 2 prefers X more than Disputant 1 does?

Analyst: That conclusion would be unwarranted because 2's scoring system is independent of 1's—except that I forced each to score the no-agreement point at zero. If, for example, Disputant 2 divided all points by 10, then X would be scaled at 15 rather than at 25. If you want to make interpersonal comparisons, you will have to get additional information not shown in the figure. Do you want me to probe whether one side prefers X more than the other side?

Arbitrator: I'm not sure I understand what that means, but I'd rather not for the time being. Let's see if I understand your figure. For each potential contract that will determine what Henry or Sharon will get, you have scored his and her evaluations. But you are keeping me in the dark, so far, about who is who. If I want to know the details of X, you could provide them. You could also presumably give me the details of those contracts whose evaluations are on the northeast frontier.

Analyst: Yes.

Arbitrator: How do you explain the shape of the boundary from F to E?

Analyst: Well, along the arc from F to E, Disputant 2 gets increasing concessions from 1, and 2's satisfaction improves. But 1 also is happier at E than at F, even though I might get fewer tangible payoffs at E than at F.

Arbitrator: I can see how that can happen—a desire to maintain good future relations between the parties, for example. Now tell me about that strange dip that occurs between B and D.

Analyst: It just happens that way.

Arbitrator: Could it happen that each disputant would prefer a fifty-fifty chance[1] at C and D rather than E?

Analyst: I'd have to check further.

Arbitrator: Well, at this point I know that I would not arbitrate this conflict by taking a point within the region R of potential joint evaluations. I certainly would confine myself to the considerations of points along the boundary from A to E. I'm still confused, though, by the scales. For example, Disputant 1 prefers E to D to C to B to A. As they are laid out in the figure, does this mean that Disputant 1 would prefer going from A to B more than going from C to D? It's not an *inter*personal comparison I'm asking about, but an *intra*personal one.

Analyst: I'm not sure.

Arbitrator: Well this is important to me. The way you've arranged it, I can think of Disputant 1 getting paid off in blue chips and 2 in white chips. At X, Disputant 1 would get 25 blues and 2 would get 150 whites. Isn't it important for me to know how those chips get cashed in for psychic pleasure? All you're telling me now is that each party prefers more chips. Why don't you go back to the drawing board and come up with a better display, so that I can think more meaningfully about the payoffs. But still keep me in the dark about the identity of the parties, and try not to make interpersonal comparisons.

---

1. Granted that not many arbitrators would think of randomizations; but this arbitrator is quite special.

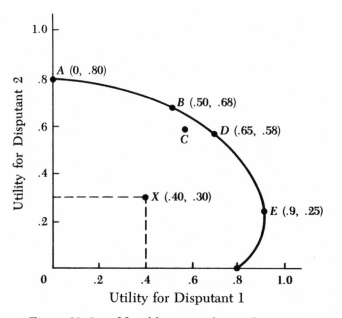

Figure 39. Set of feasible joint utility evaluations.

The analyst consults with several game theorists (who have been worrying about this problem for more than three decades),[2] goes back to the two parties for a bit of further information (for example: Would a given party prefer the contract leading to *C* in Figure 38, or take a fifty-fifty chance on *B* or *D*?), and comes up with a new presentation, as shown in Figure 39.

Analyst: I hope this new figure will better meet your demands. Notice that the coordinates are now in terms of *utilities* rather than *values*.

Arbitrator: What does that mean?

Analyst: Following the advice of game theorists who have tried to address the concerns you raised in our last conversation, I elicited further information about the preferences of each of the two disputants separately. Let me talk about Disputant 1, since 2 went through a similar procedure. For Disputant 1, I chose some idealized contract that was better than *E* — a con-

2. See Nash (1950), the seminal paper on this problem; Raiffa (1953); and Roth (1979).

tract that could not be achieved. I used that idealized contract as a "reference prize." Let's call it *REF*-1.

Arbitrator: Should I know any of the details of *REF*-1?

Analyst: No, unless you want to compare *REF*-1 with the reference prize for Disputant 2 (that is, *REF*-2) and then make interpersonal comparisons.

Arbitrator: Maybe later, but not now. Go on.

Analyst: Well, contract *X* was deemed by Disputant 1 to be just as desirable as getting a .40 chance at *REF*-1 and a complementary chance (that is, .60) at the no-agreement alternative. Disputant 1 was indifferent between getting contract *B* and a .50 chance at *REF*-1 and a complementary chance at the no-agreement alternative.

Arbitrator: Those seem like quite hard questions to answer. Did you always compare alternatives like *X* and *B* against a lottery with prizes *REF*-1 and no agreement?

Analyst: In fact, no. I also asked questions like: Is *B* closer to *D* than to *A*? Would you rather have *C* than a fifty-fifty chance at *B* and *D*? Sometimes Disputant 1 gave inconsistent answers, but after some probing I think I fairly caught 1's preferences.

Arbitrator: Is it all right if I think that Disputant 1 values *B* as worth a .50 chance at *REF*-1 (and a complementary chance at the no-agreement alternative), values *D* at a .65 chance at *REF*-1, and values *E* at a .90 chance at *REF*-1?

Analyst: Exactly.

Arbitrator: And Disputant 2 values *A* at a .80 chance at *REF*-2, values *B* at a .68 chance at *REF*-2, and so on.

Analyst: Yes. If you want to cut corners further, you can say that Disputant 1 has a *preference* for *B* of .50, for *D* of .65, and so on.

Arbitrator: Can we say that for Disputant 1 it's less valuable to go from *B* to *D* than from *D* to *E*? I'm asking this because *B* to *D* is .15 units and *D* to *E* is .25 units, in 1's preference units.

Analyst: From what I understand, you can say the following: for Disputant 1, since *D* is three-eighths the distance from *B* to *E* in preference units, you can say that 1 is indifferent between *D* and a lottery that yields *E* with a three-eighths chance and *B* with a five-eighths chance.

Arbitrator: Why is *C* no longer on the efficient frontier?

Analyst: Because using lotteries, each party prefers a fifty-fifty chance at *B* and *D* than getting *C* outright.

Arbitrator: Tell me, for Disputant 1, why didn't you use the actual best contract, E, as 1's reference prize and use A as 2's reference prize?

Analyst: Because the other reference prizes seemed more natural at the time. But the change is trivial to make. All you have to do is to change 1's coordinates by dividing by .9 and 2's coordinates by dividing by .8. For example, for D with coordinates (.65, .58) you would have the new coordinates (.65/.90, .58/.80) or (.722, .725). You can see this in Figure 40.

Arbitrator: From Figure 40 it looks like if I select contract D as my arbitrated solution, then each party would get a contract that it deems worth a .72 chance at its most desirable contract. That seems equitable.

Analyst: Well, yes—but contract A may mean a lot more to Disputant 2 than contract E means to Disputant 1. Remember also that REF-1 and REF-2 could be quite different in importance to the two disputants.

Arbitrator: That could be; but should such subjective interper-

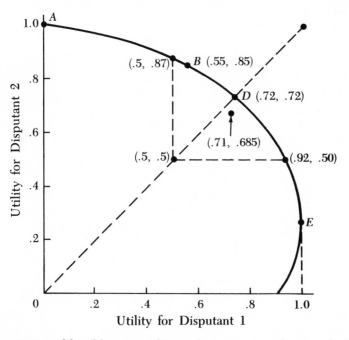

Figure 40. Set of feasible joint utility evaluations, normalized such that the best contract for each party is 1.00.

sonal comparisons—whatever they might mean—be part of my deliberations? In arbitrating this conflict, should I consider the wealth position of the two parties? I'm not sure. I don't think so. Should I, for example, take into consideration the fact that one party may have been disadvantaged in the past? I think not. That would be overstepping my role as arbitrator. I judge only what is fair in this situation. Tell me, are there other suggested solutions in the game theory literature?

Analyst: Nash [1953] gives a beautiful axiomatic rationale for choosing a point on the frontier of Figure 40 that maximizes the product of the payoffs. I can discuss later why this is so, if you want. For example, point B yields a product of .55 × .85, or .4675; point D yields a product of .72 × .72, or .5184. In fact, it appears that in this case the Nash solution is also very close to D. To really understand the different rationales, it's instructive to look at a few examples where different proposed solutions lead to radically different arbitrated solutions.

Arbitrator: Let's see some such examples, so I can intuitively decide what I think is reasonable in those cases.

In experimental situations, I have used this dialogue to help prepare subjects for their roles as arbitrators. They are then asked to select arbitrated values for various regions of joint utility evaluations, where each region is exhibited in the format style of Figure 40.

How would you select an arbitrated value for the region in Figure 41? Obviously it should be some point along the efficient frontier from B to F. But what is equitable? Would you choose B, the Nash solution that maximizes the product of the two components? Would you choose D, the point that equates utility values (when each party norms its utilities by giving zero to the no-agreement point and 1.0 to the best contract)? How about E, which is halfway between B and F?

The following argument produces point C. If there is no agreement, each party ends up at zero. Each can get a maximum of 1.0. So a "fair share" for each should be at least .5. If each gets .5, we are led to point G and we see that each can get still more. Disputant 1 has a potential excess of (.75 − .50), or .25; Disputant 2 has a potential excess of (1.0 − .50), or .50. Let's give each of them half of their potential excesses over and above point G. This yields the joint

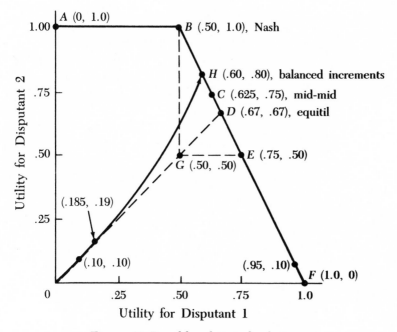

Figure 41. Possible arbitrated solutions.

evaluation (.625, .75), which for convenience we can refer to as the "mid-mid" solution.

If I were the arbitrator, my own preferences thus far would be C over D over B over E. What would your preferences be?

Another argument produces arbitrated solution H, a bit above C toward B. Start at the origin and ask how much each side can maximally gain. The answer is 1.00 for each. If we go one-tenth of the way[3] for each and proceed to point (.10, .10), how much can each side maximally gain now? Disputant 1 can go from .10 to .95—observe that (.95, .10) is on the boundary—for a maximal gain of .85, whereas 2 can go from .10 to 1.0 for a maximal gain of .90. If we give each one-tenth of their maximal gains, the next point we arrive at is (.10 + .085, .10 + .09), or (.185, .190). Proceeding in this fashion, we'll approach point H, with coordinates (.60, .80), which lies on the frontier just a bit higher than C. This might be called the "bal-

3. Instead of one-tenth of the way we could go one one-hundredth or one one-thousandth, and finally we would discover the differential calculus.

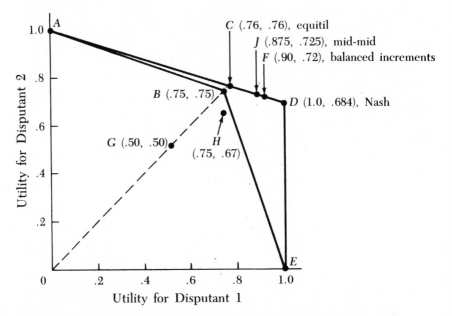

Figure 42. How arbitrated solutions are affected by an increase in the feasible region.

anced increments" solution. I suggested this solution in 1951, and it's still my favorite.

Let's examine another case, as shown in Figure 42. First consider the symmetric region (around the 45-degree line through the origin) whose frontier is given by the points A, B, and E. The symmetric arbitrated solution in this case is at point B, which gives each party a return of .75. (All the rationales leading to the different arbitrated solutions B, H, C, D, and E in Figure 41 would converge on point B in Figure 42, with frontier ABE.) Now let's enlarge the region of potential joint evaluations to $ACDE$. Both parties seem to have increased potential. How might some of the different arbitration schemes deal with region $ACDE$?

The scheme that leads to D in Figure 41—the "equitil" point that equates utilities after each party has been scaled using the full range from zero to 1.0—leads in Figure 42 to point C, with joint evaluation (.76, .76). The Nash procedure (which led to B in Figure 41 and which maximizes the product of the payoffs) leads in Figure 42 to point D, with joint evaluation (1.0, .684). Notice that with Nash's resolution, Disputant 2 is *worse off* in region $ACDE$ than in region ABE, scoring .684 instead of .75. It could be argued that this is not reasonable—that each party should profit if region ABE is enlarged to $ACDE$. What do you think?

Consider the mid-mid scheme that gave rise to C in Figure 41. Start off by giving each party one-half of what it can maximally get without hurting the other party; this leads to point G, with joint evaluation (.50, .50). Since there are joint gains to be squeezed out, once again give to each party one-half of what it can maximally get starting from point G; this leads in Figure 42 to point H, with joint evaluation (.75, .67). Repeating, we approach the limit J, with values (.875, .725). If we repeated that same process giving to each one-tenth (or, in the limit, successively smaller and smaller fractions) of what that party can maximally gain without hurting the other party, then the analogue of the trajectory that led to H in Figure 41 would lead to point F in Figure 42—the balanced increments solution. Notice that at point J or F in Figure 42, Disputant 2 is worse off than at point B, and is thus disadvantaged when region ABE is enlarged to $ACDE$.

Arbitrator: I think I understand the figures thoroughly now. Can you give me some feeling as to why the Nash scheme is so popular? What's its rationale?

Analyst: Consider the efficient boundary GBF in Figure 43. For that region, point B would be the symmetric, arbitrated solution. All the schemes we have discussed thus far would lead to B. Now suppose that region AGB is eliminated so that the region under consideration becomes ABF, and that point B is still available in the smaller region. Since B is deemed to be the best in the bigger region and since B is still available in the restricted region, shouldn't B be considered to be best in the restricted region? Nash relies on this principle to argue his case.

Arbitrator: Let's see: the region bounded by ABF is exactly the same, with change of units for Disputant 2, as the region we considered in Figure 41. There were several rationales leading to points H, C, D, and E, all violating that principle evoked by Nash. Can you say more about why B should be retained as the solution if we eliminate those possibilities from G to B—but still keep B itself available?

Analyst: Suppose you go into a restaurant and glance at the menu and decide to order braised beef. You give your order to the waiter and then ask him, "What do those asterisks mean next to

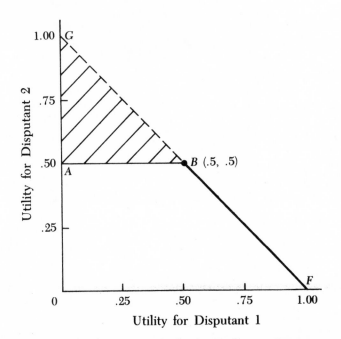

Figure 43. The rationale for the Nash procedure.

several items on the menu?" The waiter responds, "Those items are not available today." Suppose that braised beef (alternative *B*) is not starred. You deemed it best for you on the full menu. Shouldn't it be deemed best by you on the restricted menu, given that it's still available? In Figure 42, *B* is best when you have the menu from *G* to *F*. Shouldn't it be best for you when you have the restricted menu *B* to *F*?

Arbitrator: That's fascinating, but is the argument convincing in the context of arbitration? After all, excluding the possible agreements from *G* to *B* could change Disputant 1's aspirations; and shouldn't I, acting as arbitrator, be responsive to that reasonable feeling?

Analyst: I feel confused by all this, but luckily you've been asked to select an arbitrated solution in Figure 40, and all the solutions we've discussed come out close to point *D* in that figure. So we're fussing about trivial differences.

Arbitrator: Well, that's a comfort to me. But I'm still curious. In order to get marked differences among the various arbitrated solutions, there is a need to present highly asymmetric regions, like the one shown in Figure 41. But are such regions plausible? Would a point like B arise in practice? There should be some way that Disputant 1 could make a side payment to 2 in money or in physical goods, so that 2 could do better than at point B and still not totally penalize Disputant 1.

Analyst: You mean that with the possibility of side payments with divisible goods (like money) there should not be any sharp points on the frontier where the slopes to the left and right of that point are vastly different.

Arbitrator: That's it. I would expect in practice that the frontier would be rather smooth and, if I understand you right, this would have the effect of making the distinctions between the different arbitrated solutions of minor concern—that is, in practice but not in theory.

Analyst: I suppose so. I'm still bothered by the fact that you don't know the identities of Disputants 1 and 2. Should it make any difference to you that one of the parties is wealthier than the other? How, for example, would you divide up $1,000 between a rich man and a poor man? Suppose that they can't decide between themselves and that you have been appointed as arbitrator.

Arbitrator: Did they voluntarily agree to abide by my resolution, or were they forced to agree?

Analyst: Let's say that arbitration is compulsory.

Arbitrator: Well, first show me counterparts to the figures we've been discussing.

Analyst: In Figure 44 I exhibit how $1,000 could be shared between the two recipients. I thought you might want to see what happens in both before-tax and after-tax dollars, assuming that the rich man pays taxes at a marginal rate of 50 percent.

Arbitrator: You just tipped your hand: you've told me that the rich man is Disputant 1, since he can only get 500 after-tax dollars.

Analyst: That's right. But when I made up Figure 45 I tossed a coin to decide whether the rich or poor man should be designated Disputant 1. Do you want to know who's who?

Arbitrator: Not yet. The efficient boundary in Figure 45 seems quite symmetric around the 45-degree line. Does it have to be that way?

Analyst: No it doesn't. But I chose reasonable utility functions for the two parties and it came out looking quite symmetric; with a little fudging I made it symmetric.

Arbitrator: Why did you do that?

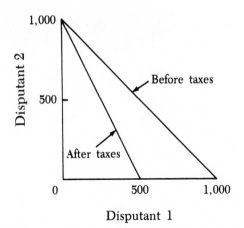

Figure 44. Payoffs before and after taxes (in dollars) to rich man and man.

Analyst: Well, since the shape of the region is symmetric, the different solutions we talked about before—the Nash solution, the equitil solution, the mid-mid solution, and the balanced increments solution—all get resolved at point *A* with utility .8 for each.

Arbitrator: Now let's see if I understand. At point *A* the rich man will get an amount that he thinks is just equivalent to a .8 chance at his best outcome of 500 after-tax dollars, and the poor

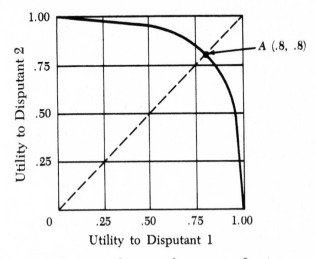

Figure 45. Utilities to rich man and poor man of various payoffs.

man will get an amount that he thinks is just equivalent to a .8 chance at his best outcome of 1,000 after-tax dollars. In some sense that's equitable: they get the same equivalent chance at their best prizes. But your point, I take it, is that the best prize to the poor man is worth more to him than the best prize to the rich man. That's an interpersonal comparison that I'm not sure I should be making. At point A how much actual money does each get?

Analyst: At point A the rich man gets $800 and the poor man gets $200—that's before taxes.

Arbitrator: Why? That's surprising.

Analyst: Well, the rich man is risk-neutral and he thinks that $800 for certain is worth a .8 chance at $1,000 and a .2 chance at nothing. The poor man, on the other hand, needs the money desperately. He would just as soon settle for $200 for certain as get a lottery with a .8 chance at $1,000 and a .2 chance at nothing. I could have concocted even more extreme numbers and come out with a split of $50 for the poor, risk-averse, desperate fellow and $950 for the risk-prone playboy.

Arbitrator: What bothers me, as arbitrator, is that I must split the $1,000 between them with no probabilities or gambles involved. Why should their attitudes toward risk get involved? Why should I care if the poor man is risk-averse? Isn't that irrelevant?

Analyst: Many game theorists argue that attitudes toward risk do enter the picture because they do get involved in the dynamics of bargaining. The rich man says, "If I don't get $800 there will not be any deal." The poor man can settle for $200 now or take a *chance* at possibly getting more but possibly getting nothing. Each side in that setting is making threats or backing off from threats; it's a highly uncertain environment. The fact that the rich man is more risk-neutral gives him more bargaining power.

Arbitrator: I'm not convinced of that point. It seems to me that this is what would happen in the real bargaining problem if the rich man tried to squeeze hard: he would say, "$200 is more important to you than $800 is to me, so let's settle here or not at all." The threat is credible. But my trouble is that I don't like it when people use power that way. As an arbitrator, should I dictate a solution that reflects that kind of raw power? Earlier in our conversation I intimated that it might make a difference to me if the arbitration process was initiated voluntarily or compulsorily. If I, as an arbitrator, minimize the realities of relative bargaining power, then those disputants with power will refuse to arbitrate their controversies with me. Who wins then?

As an arbitrator, should I try to predict how the negotiators would settle their controversy without my services, and then try to do better for each? I think not. Should I give preferential treatment to a party who acts more irresponsibly and irrationally because this gives that party more power? I think not. Should I imagine how reasonable negotiators *should behave* and then impose that solution on them? That's coming closer, but it's not very operational.

Analyst: So now, how would you settle the split of $1,000?

Arbitrator: If the setting were appropriate for me to take power into consideration, I would fudge a little. I would give each the same after-tax benefits. That would mean giving one-third to the poor man, one-third to the rich man (after taxes), and one-third to the government. That would be understandable. I wouldn't like to base my analysis on utilities because the less risk-averse the poor man is, the more he'll get; and this gives him an incentive to hide his true feelings.

Analyst: But there are always incentives for the disputants to exaggerate their claims to the arbitrator. Presumably that's why you first try to find out the facts. How would you settle the case if arbitration were compulsory?

Arbitrator: I guess I would give each $500; but I would be sorely tempted to give the poor man the whole $1,000 and to fine the rich man for being such a mean character.

Analyst: But what would you do if the rich man wanted to give the poor man $500 at the outset and the poor man wanted more because of the principle involved? What if that were the reason they came to you?

Arbitrator: I see that you're agreeing with me. The context of the dispute and my role as arbitrator in that dispute are of paramount importance, and while the abstraction brings out a lot of nice fine points, it abstracts away too much to be of direct use.

We shall return to questions of fairness at several points in Part IV, particularly in our discussion of the Mariner space probes.

part

IV

Many Parties, Many Issues

For the purposes of this discussion we will, like members of a primitive society, count "one, two, many." There's a world of difference between two-party and many-party negotiations. We've already looked at special classes of negotiating problems with more than two parties: for example, when one of the two parties is not monolithic, or when a mediator in a two-party dispute has strong views, or when a seller maneuvers one buyer against another buyer. But now we turn to a richer class of disputes in which each of the many parties is a bona fide participant in the negotiation process. The parties could be several members of a disputing family, or the many members of a firm's board of directors, or the many firms in an industry, or the many nations in a trade dispute. The parties may be of different types: a consumer interest group, a union, an environmental group, a firm, a state, a government agency—all in contention.

Throughout this book we've been simplifying and abstracting, as mathematicians are wont to do. When approaching real-world problems, it helps to start with the simplest of cases and then consider complications, one at a time; so we began by analyzing two-party disputes. Now, what are the salient conceptual differences between many-party and two-party disputes? Some of these alleged differences are complexities only in degree, which can just as well be explicated in two-party negotiations. Can some of the real salient differences, once identified, be captured and explicated in terms of starkly simple many-person games?

Imagine that you are one party in a multiparty dispute. In this case, as in two-party disputes, you'll want to know the issues that should be included in the negotiations, how you'll feel about certain outcomes, and what your tradeoffs are among the issues. In particular cases, this may be an emotionally difficult, time-consuming, and analytically complex task. But to some extent this would be the case whether you had one or more than one negotiating party to contend with.

In many-party disputes it is sometimes the case that the parties are not well specified. It may be that your antagonists are so diffuse and poorly organized that you might have a hard time knowing even with whom you can or should negotiate. And some of these parties, once organized, might shift and split apart during negotiations. This presents a new conceptual wrinkle. But even here some of this flavor could have been captured in the discussion of two-party negotiations. You might erroneously think that you are pitted against a monolithic, single "other side" when in fact you might be facing other *sides,* and these sides could fuse or fractionate.

In order to set your reservation price, you must think hard about how the world will look to you if you do not come to an agreement with the other side or sides. What is your best alternative to a negotiated agreement (BATNA), and how much will you need as a minimum from the upcoming negotiations in order to match in desirability the prospects of the no-agreement state? Are there conceptual distinctions here between two-party and many-party negotiations? Game theorists emphatically answer yes.

If you decide not to come to an agreement with all of your adversaries, you might still forge an agreement with a subset of the other parties. In other words, you can still cooperate with a coalition of some of the others. If there is only one other party, this complexity can't be formulated. But even if there are two other negotiating parties—say, B and C—you might consider what you could do with B alone, or with C alone, or with both. You must also contemplate what B and C could do without you. If you plan to enter eventually into negotiations with B and C, should you first approach B and compromise some of your differences with B before jointly approaching C? What should be your reaction if B and C collude before you can get into the act? Should you try to upset this coalition by trying to woo away B? How much do you have to give in to B so that B will not be vulnerable to enticements from C? How much can you inveigle from B by threatening to go to C and squeezing out B altogether? The complexities can become surprisingly rich with just three players, even if we concentrate on the polar extreme where each party faces a world of certainty and where there is only one issue involved. The two-party version of this three-party polar case would be the distributive bargaining problem in which each party knows the other's reservation price—not a very interesting case with two parties.

Assume now that your adversaries have been identified and that the multiple issues are known to all. You have considered your own tradeoffs, your BATNA if you go it alone, and the BATNAs you face with various coalitions; you have thought about the motivations of other parties—about your adversaries' BATNAs both alone and in coalitions. You are about to enter into negotiations with all the parties. What should be your opening gambit? Should you prepare an opening package—a complete contract that resolves all issues? With regard to two-party, face-to-face negotiations, we discussed three dynamics for negotiating contracts: (1) engage in a dance of packages; (2) build up the contract issue by issue; and (3) generate a single negotiating text and seek northeasterly modifications. Do these dynamics make sense in many-party negotiations? Yes, but with variations—some of which falter because of their complexity. Consider the dance of packages. Before a meeting takes place with all parties, a subset of the parties might get together and concoct a package to be offered by their loose coalition. At a later stage two separate coalitions, offering different opening packages, might join forces and devise a compromise package. If there are fifteen parties, there may on the table initially be six packages, which may fuse to four and then to three. Packages change continually: some fuse; others fractionate and come together with shifting coalitions. Likewise, building up a contract issue by issue gets harder and harder to do when parties are added.

I personally engaged in one protracted international negotiation with many parties, which culminated in October 1972 in the signing of a charter for the newly formed International Institute for Applied Systems Analysis (IIASA). Those negotiations took three years to complete. There were twelve signatories to the charter, representing twelve scientific institutions from twelve nations, but there were three principal negotiators: Jerman Gvishiani, representing the Soviet Academy of Sciences; McGeorge Bundy, followed by Philip Handler, of the U.S. National Academy of Sciences; and Sir Solly Zuckerman of the British Royal Society.

Negotiations started in a diffuse manner, as the representatives sounded each other out on the issues, resolving none but getting some sense of the realistic bounds on each. When progress appeared to be going too slowly, Zuckerman, acting as the formal convenor of the informal negotiating enterprise, suggested that the National Academy of Sciences draw up a sample charter for discussion—a single negotiating text, if you will. It was supposed to represent not only what the United States wanted, but insofar as possible the interests of other countries as well. The negotiating parties then discussed this text and the Soviets modified it—not in a way that all parties approved, but in a way that favored their side. Then Zuckerman's team modified the text; then the National Academy of Sciences; and so on. Occasionally representatives from Italy, France, or the Federal Republic of Germany would insist on some modifications, and their concerns were reflected in successive drafts. There was no relentless march upward in desirability for all; rather, there was a big improvement for some and a little worsening for others, followed by an improvement for those who were hurt the most, and so on. Since all parties desired to complete the charter, successive drafters, in the spirit of compromise, made fewer and fewer substantial changes. The process converged. Certain issues were resolved by resorting to ambiguous language, so that the parties were able to go back home and interpret these ambiguities to their own side's advantage—a process that I call "creative obfuscation." Other irresolvable issues magically became non-issues, and nothing more was said about them. These are effective but not necessarily good tactics to adopt for the long run; it depends.

I have talked extensively to professional negotiators, who have reinforced my conclusion based on personal observation: many-party negotiations are often too diffuse to be effective unless they focus on a single negotiating text. In the international sphere, as we will see in Chapter 18, this is frequently done by technical committees in such a way that the principal negotiators are not personally committed.

Many-party negotiations can be chaotic unless some structure is imposed either externally or internally. So all that we have noted about the constructive roles of external intervenors (facilitators, mediators, arbitrators) for two-party negotiations apply with more force as the number of parties increases. In many-party negotiations, one of the minor negotiating principals—someone who is perceived to hold moderate views—may be designated to chair the meetings; this chairperson may effectively play the role of facilitator or mediator or generator of a single negotiating text. This ploy is usually impossible to implement in two-party disputes.

When established groups repeatedly make collective decisions—groups such as boards of directors, legislatures, university faculties, courts with several judges—it is indispensable to have well-specified procedures for orderly discussion and for collective action. Robert's Rules of Order and various voting schemes are common, but auctions, competitive bids, and some limited market-type mechanisms can be effectively employed. We will explore how some of these mechanisms work in such problems as settling an estate, allocating costs to several cooperating parties, and mediating environmental disputes. We'll see that many procedures that elicit values from involved parties may be subject to improper manipulation from individuals and from coalitions of individuals. Recall, for example, the two-party distributive bargaining problem where a seller and buyer have privately held reservation prices. In the laboratory, informal haggling usually results in a trade when there is a zone of agreement. A simultaneous-disclosure mechanism, while impersonal and quick, tempts the parties to behave strategically, and empirically it turns out to be inefficient: too many trades are not made that should be. In the two-party case, informal haggling, while personally uncomfortable to some, is relatively easy to execute. But as the number of parties increases, it becomes more difficult to resolve disputes by unstructured haggling. There is a need for many-party generalizations of simultaneous-disclosure procedures (or variations thereof); but many of these procedures may be flawed—for example, they may invite extreme misrepresentations of individual values that lead to group inefficiencies. We will consider these ideas in the chapters that follow. But first let's turn to the fundamental difference between two-party and many-party negotiations: the interplay among shifting coalitions.

17
Coalition Analysis

Significant conceptual complexities arise when even a single new party is added to a two-party negotiation: coalitions of two parties can now form. Game theorists, starting with the seminal contribution of Morgenstern and von Neumann (1944), have investigated these complexities under the heading of "n-person games in characteristic function form." This chapter sets the stage for our discussion of multiparty bargaining by introducing the problem faced by three cement companies who can form a cartel: How should they split the synergies they would create? Based on the motivation of that real-world example, we'll abstract out the essence of the game for laboratory experimentation, first focusing on the strategic problem facing a given player and then on those facing the intervenor concerned with fairness.

THE SCANDINAVIAN CEMENT COMPANY

The Scandinavian Cement Company (SC) is the leading producer of cement in a nameless country. It has traditionally shared the market in a cartel arrangement—perfectly legal in that country—with two other producers, the Cement Corporation (CC) and the Thor Cement Company (TC). The cartel arrangement is about to expire, and the three companies are contemplating a formal merger.[1] The companies call in an independent consultant, Loran Chat, to prepare a preliminary analysis of the problem.

Loran Chat's analysis is summarized in Table 17. With the pres-

---

1. This armchair case is an adaptation of an adaptation of an adaptation. The original article was Lorange (1973). Lorange wrote a version of this case in a seminar that I conducted. My former research assistant, Kalyan Chatterjee, adapted Lorange's article for M.B.A. classroom use. I now simplify further.

ent arrangement—all firms separate, but with a cartel understanding—their earnings are 32 million, 23 million, and 6 million (net present value) monetary units for SC, CC, and Thor respectively. (For convenience, we'll call the monetary units dollars.) If they join in a total merger, they can do better than the sum of their earnings ($61 million): they benefit from synergies that add $16 million, for a total of $77 million. But Loran Chat also points out that there will be synergies involved if any two merge; for example, SC and CC together can command $59 million rather than $55 million (32 + 23) whereas Thor in this case would be reduced from $6 million to $5 million.

The SC representative argues that the $16 million synergy should be allocated according to size:

$$\frac{32}{32 + 23 + 6} \times 16 = 8.39 \quad \text{to SC,}$$

$$\frac{23}{32 + 23 + 6} \times 16 = 6.03 \quad \text{to CC,}$$

$$\frac{6}{32 + 23 + 6} \times 16 = 1.57 \quad \text{to Thor.}$$

This proposal would result in the following payoffs:

$$32 + 8.39 = 40.39 \quad \text{to SC,}$$
$$23 + 6.03 = 29.03 \quad \text{to CC,}$$
$$6 + 1.57 = 7.57 \quad \text{to Thor.}$$

The payoffs would total $76.99 million.

"That's just not reasonable," argues the Thor representative. "I should end up with a lot more than $7.57 million."

"I don't see why," responds the SC representative. "We're all getting about a 26 percent increase in our worth because of the merger."

"I'll tell you why. According to Loran's figures, if my company, Thor, joins with CC the two of us can get $39 million—we would get more than you want to give us in the three-way merger. And in the case that Thor joins CC, SC would end up with $30 million and not the $40.39 million you want." Thor then turns to CC and says: "If you join me we can command $39 million; you could take $30 million and I would take $9 million."

TABLE 17. *Net present value of earnings for each merger.*

Type of merger	Earnings (in millions of dollars)
All firms remain separate	
SC	32
CC	23
Thor	6
Two merge, the third remaining separate	
SC, CC	59
Thor separate	5
SC, Thor	45
CC separate	22
CC, Thor	39
SC separate	30
Total merger	
SC, CC, Thor	77

SC protests loudly. "You fellows are bringing in an irrelevancy. Are we in this together or not?"

"I'd rather go it alone than with the two of you," says Thor, "and only get $7.57 million. It's my company that's generating the synergy."

The CC representative enters the fray: "I think $7.57 million is a fair payoff for you, Thor, but $29 million is a bit low for me. Remember: if you don't join us, you'll end up with only $5 million."

"Yes, but you two will get only $59 million together, and I doubt that you, CC, will be able to get $29 million out of SC. Furthermore, if you two join as one entity and get $59 million while I get $5 million, then together we would total $64 million. So if we then joined all together, we could produce a synergy of $13 million [77 − 64] and it would then be fair to share that synergy evenly: half to your combined firm and half to me.

"Are you saying, Thor, that you want $11.5 million? If you are, you're being completely unrealistic."

And so the argument goes. Finally, they agree to ask Loran Chat what he thinks. Loran, being mathematically inclined, starts off by saying that he's being asked to find three amounts X_{SC}, X_{CC}, and X_{TH} that divide up the total of $77 million:

$$X_{SC} + X_{CC} + X_{TH} = 77. \tag{1}$$

These three amounts should, as a minimum, also satisfy additional inequalities:

$$X_{SC} \geq 30, \tag{2}$$

$$X_{CC} \geq 22, \tag{3}$$

$$X_{TH} \geq 5, \tag{4}$$

$$X_{SC} + X_{CC} \geq 59, \tag{5}$$

$$X_{SC} + X_{TH} \geq 45, \tag{6}$$

$$X_{CC} + X_{TH} \geq 39. \tag{7}$$

Inequalities (2), (3), and (4) state what each firm can get alone against a coalition of the other two; inequalities (5), (6), and (7) state what pairs of firms can get if they form coalitions.

"The first thing," says Loran, "is to see if we can find three numbers that will satisfy requirements (1)–(7). If so, we will then try to describe all feasible sets of three numbers that do the trick. And after that we can talk about ways to decide, among these feasible triplets of numbers, if we have a plenty of riches."

Loran plots these inequalities in a rather strange way (see Figure 46). He uses a horizontal axis for X_{SC}, a vertical axis for X_{CC}, and equation (1) to account for X_{TH}. Requirements (2) and (3) are plotted directly. Inequality (4), when combined with (1), implies

$$X_{SC} + X_{CC} \leq 72. \tag{4'}$$

Inequality (5) is plotted directly. Inequality (6), coupled with (1), implies

$$X_{CC} \leq 32; \tag{6'}$$

and inequality (7), coupled with (1), implies

$$X_{SC} \leq 38. \tag{7'}$$

Inequalities (6') and (7') are also plotted. The points that satisfy all inequalities lie in the shaded area and each of the vertices of that

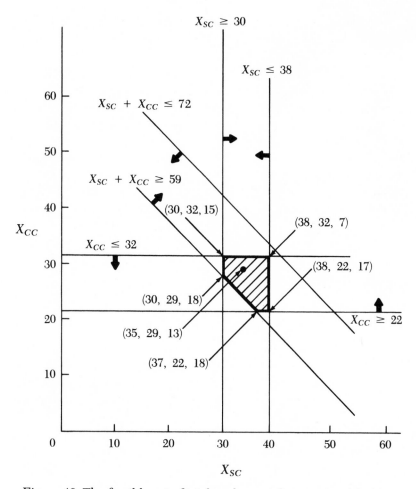

Figure 46. The feasible set of triplets that satisfy equations (1)–(7).

region is labeled with three numbers: a value of X_{SC}, of X_{CC}, and of X_{TH}. For example, the most northeasterly vertex has coordinates 38 for X_{SC}, 32 for X_{CC}, and—because of requirement (1)—7 for X_{TH}. We see that lots of triplets of numbers are feasible, in the sense that they satisfy requirements (1)–(7).

The parties ask Loran to suggest a solution. "One possibility," he responds, "is to take some point near the center of the feasible region. Estimating roughly, I would suggest 35 for X_{SC}, 29 for X_{CC}, and 13 for X_{TH}."

"I don't like your suggestion at all," says SC. "I represent the biggest firm and I get an increment of $3 million, while Thor is ending up with a $7 million increment."

"Let's compromise," says the CC representative. "We have SC's original suggestion and Loran's suggestion. I get 29 in each case. Let's split the difference. I suggest that SC get midway between 40.39 and 35, or 37.69; I'll take 29.02; Thor will get midway between 7.57 and 13, or 10.29. How's that?"

The SC representative scowls. "I don't like it, but for harmony's sake I'll go along."

The Thor representative smiles. "I don't like it either, but I don't know how to convince you that I deserve more. So I'll go along, too."

We'll come back to this story later. But first let's discuss a related problem that serves to highlight some complexities in the dynamics of coalition formation.

A PURE COALITION GAME

Let's abstract away the context of the cement industry and consider a simply explained game (this is not the same as saying that it is a simple game) in which Loran Chat can find no solutions to the counterparts of equations (1)–(7).

Instructions. The game has three players: A, B, and C. You will be assigned one of these roles. Your aim is to join some coalition that commands a positive payoff (see Table 18), to negotiate how

TABLE 18. *Payoffs in a pure coalition game.*

Coalition	Payoff
A alone	0
B alone	0
C alone	0
A, B	118
A, C	84
B, C	50
A, B, C	121

the joint payoffs should be split, and to try to maximize your own payoff. You will be scored according to how well you do: your payoff will be compared with the payoffs of others playing a similar role.

For example, if a coalition of A and C were to form, they would command a joint return of 84 units. They might jointly agree to give 50 to A and 34 to C. Of course, C might want more from the coalition AC and might threaten A by courting the favors of B. After all, if B does not join any coalition at all (or remains as a one-party coalition), then B gets nothing. So B will be desperately trying to join A and C in a grand coalition ABC (commanding 121), or else to break up AC and join one of them.

The idea of the game is for you to maneuver about and eventually join a coalition that will offer you the best return. Of course, what you might demand from one coalition depends on what you can add to that coalition and what you potentially could obtain elsewhere. You should have no prior communication with the other two players (except for arranging for a meeting place) before the negotiations start. You are allowed thirty minutes for negotiations, but are free to complete negotiations sooner. All three of you should arrange yourselves in symmetrical positions at the beginning. If any two players want to arrange for a private meeting, the third must not interrupt for at least a two-minute period. [*End of instructions*]

To start off, players examine the table of possible payoffs and devise the beginnings of a strategy. After being assigned roles, but before discussing the game with the other two players, subjects are asked to describe their strategy in writing. As they play the game, they record the outcome of the negotiations and the sequence of tentative agreements that were made along the way. After the negotiations have been completed, the three players discuss exactly what happened during the game.

There are various ways in which players can jockey for inclusion in a coalition. Suppose that A rushes out and makes a private offer to B. "Let's join together without C and split the 118. Since I am obviously stronger than you, a reasonable split would be 78 to me and 40 to you."

"I don't think that's reasonable," B responds. "I don't care who my partner is, but my aspirations are far higher than 40. I can go to

C, who is now out in the cold, and offer her 4, and take 46 for myself."

"If you offer 4 to C," warns A, "I'll woo C away with an offer of 8."

"But if you do that," argues B, "then you'll end up with only 76, which is worse than the 78 you unreasonably demanded from me."

With the above conversation as background, let's investigate how players can make offers that "cannot readily be refused" (see Table 19). What do we mean by "cannot readily be refused"? If, for example, C offers 42 to B, keeping 8 for herself, then B cannot go to A and try to get more than 42 without A being vulnerable to an effective counteroffer from C that would both beat B's offer to A and yield C more than 8. Restated more slowly, if C offers 42 to B and if B threatens to go to A and request, say, 44 (leaving A with 74), then C in turn could go to A and offer him 75, which would permit C to keep 9 for herself—an improvement over her original 8. Thus, C can say to B: "My offer to you of 42 is not readily vulnerable. If you are wooed by A who offers you more, I can outbargain you with A and you'll end up with nothing, while I will get my 8."

Here's a tactic that B can use. B muses at the very start: "I can make offers either to A or to C that cannot readily be refused, and in each case I would get 42. But A can make similar offers that would yield him 76 and C can make offers that would yield her 8. Yet all three of us cannot command 76 + 42 + 8, or 126. As a grand coali-

TABLE 19. *Offers that cannot readily be refused.*

| Offer | Payoff | | | |
	A	B	C	Total
Offer of A to B	76	42	—	118
Offer of A to C	76	—	8	84
Offer of B to A	76	42	—	118
Offer of B to C	—	42	8	50
Offer of C to A	76	—	8	84
Offer of C to B	—	42	8	50

Note: 76 + 42 + 8 = 126, which is greater than 121—the amount that the grand coalition can demand.

tion we can only get 121. So it's critically important that I not be left out in the cold: it's imperative that I prevent a coalition between A and C. Should I approach A or C first? I think that I'm better off with C; and to make C really tied to me, I'll start off with a magnanimous offer: I'll offer her 10 units, 2 units more than she should expect from a two-way coalition that includes her. If C understands what I am doing and if she remains faithful to me, then we as a firm bargaining unit can then approach A. In that bargaining problem with A, there would be 71 points to share $(121 - 50 = 71)$ and our firm BC coalition should get 35.5 units of that. I'll suggest to C that we split this 35.5 units evenly between ourselves. So C will end up with $10 + 17.75$, or 27.75 units, which should far exceed her reasonable aspirations. I'll end up with 57.75. Not bad, eh? Let's see how she responds."

C is favorably impressed and she agrees to the plan. The BC team then approaches A, who is shocked by their cold calculation. A refuses to negotiate for the 71 points that could be divided between himself and the BC coalition. "Once I start down that path," A ponders, "I'm a goner. My best bet is to try to woo C away from her partnership with B."

So A approaches C confidentially. "It just does not make any sense for you and B to share 50 between the two of you," he says to her. "I'm not going to join with you under those circumstances. If we brought in an impartial arbitrator, don't you think my *fair share* would be much more than B is suggesting that I get? How much is he offering you of that 50? I bet it's a lot less than half. If you agree to come with me, I'll give you 30 points. The principle and morality is all on our side. It was B that started the intriguing."

C now sees a possibility of getting 30 from A, rather than a secure 10 from B with a decreasing hope of an additional 17.75. But still, C has made an agreement with B. She wavers and says that she'll have to think about it. Quickly A goes to B and informs him that C is about to sign an agreement with him, but that there is still time for B to join with him. A offers to give him 45 of the 118 points they can command together. And so the jockeying continues. Those who try to foresee outcomes in situations like this should not be too dogmatic about their predictions: anything can and does happen in such uncharted terrain.

This coalition game was played by subjects under two very different interactive conditions. In an early version, subjects negotiated face to face. In a later series of experiments, conducted by Elon Kohlberg, subjects communicated via computer terminals; they did not know the real identities of their adversaries, and their messages tended to be much more circumscribed than those of the earlier set of subjects.

In the face-to-face negotiations,[2] two of the three parties in each group occasionally talked to each other in the presence of the third party; other pairs arranged for private meetings. Over 90 percent of the triplets ended up in a three-way coalition, splitting the entire 121 units available. In about 80 percent of the contests that ended up with three-way coalitions, however, the players got involved in some two-way coalitions at some time during the negotiations. In the other 20 percent of cases that ended up in a coalition of the whole, the players never formed any two-way coalitions during the negotiations—they merely suggested successive changes in how the 121 total points should be divided. For face-to-face negotiations the average payoffs were roughly 69, 40, and 10 for A, B, and C, respectively—including the groups that formed two-way coalitions.

A strikingly different set of statistics resulted when the interactions were computerized. Outcomes for sixty-seven triplets were recorded. Three triplets did not settle at all, and only *three* of the sixty-seven achieved a three-way coalition. Of the remaining sixty-one cases that involved two-way coalitions, twenty were between A and B, twenty-two were between A and C, and nineteen were between B and C. The average payoffs in the sixty-seven contests yielded 49 to A, 27.8 to B, and 5.7 to C—not a very efficient set of performances. On the average, all three parties fared far better in face-to-face negotiations.

How can we account for these differences? They are so striking that no statistical tests of extreme hypotheses need be conducted: they are not a statistical fluke. People probably find it easier to act tough if they are not looking at the other negotiators—if the "others" are anonymous. It's hard to squeeze out someone else from a coalition when that person is looking at you. Each of the parties seem to do far better (on the average) in the softer, more personal atmosphere of face-to-face negotiations; but the results were

2. Or, more accurately, face-to-face-to-face negotiations.

not conclusive. Perhaps the interactions via computer simply required more time. More experimentation certainly needs to be done. It would be interesting to include an intermediate case where negotiations are done by telephone via a three-way conference hookup. It might also be interesting to give subjects a choice as to whether they want to interact face-to-face or by means of a less impersonal mode. On the evidence thus far, it would likely be to their advantage to choose personal contact.

RATIONALITY, FAIRNESS, AND ARBITRATION

What would you do if you were asked to arbitrate this pure coalition game? What's fair? Subjects were all asked that question. One would-be arbitrator argued that each player alone gets nothing, whereas all three together get 121; so each should get one-third of 121, or 40.33. Others objected that this solution was unreasonable —that it ignored the power relations that accrued to the players because of two-party coalitions. The equal-shares advocate maintained that an arbitrator should not be concerned with that sort of power and intrigue. Most subjects, however, strongly believed that the payoffs for two-party coalitions *should* influence the division of the 121 total units—that the potential power of the negotiators should be considered by the arbitrator. We'll proceed with this assumption.

Paralleling the treatment of the Scandinavian Cement problem, several subjects tried to find sharing values X_A, X_B, and X_C for A, B, and C, respectively, that satisfied the requirements:

$$X_A \geq 0, \quad X_B \geq 0, \quad X_C \geq 0, \tag{8}$$

$$X_A + X_B \geq 118, \tag{9}$$

$$X_A + X_C \geq 84, \tag{10}$$

$$X_B + X_C \geq 50, \tag{11}$$

$$X_A + X_B + X_C = 121. \tag{12}$$

No one succeeded in finding a triplet (X_A, X_B, X_C) that satisfied requirements (8)–(12) because no such triplet exists. To prove this, we can argue as follows: Suppose that (X_A, X_B, X_C) satisfies requirements (9), (10), and (11). Adding these three equations together, we would have

$$2(X_A + X_B + X_C) \geq 118 + 84 + 50,$$

or

$$X_A + X_B + X_C \geq 126,$$

which contradicts equation (12). Hence, we see that any allocation of 121 units among A, B, and C will have to violate requirement (9) or (10) or (11). In this example, there is no allocation of the grand total that will simultaneously meet the demands of all two-party coalitions.

Some astute subjects argued that if the grand coalition commanded 126 units instead of 121 units, then there would be a triplet that would satisfy requirements (8)–(11), with 12 modified by the replacement of 121 by 126. The solution would be

$$X_A^o = 76, \qquad X_B^o = 42, \qquad X_C^o = 8,$$

where the superscript o is used to connote "optimal." The suggestion was made that a "reasonable and fair" solution would back off from these values to satisfy the 121 requirement. This is achieved by reducing each value by five-thirds, or 1.67. The resulting suggested triplet is then:

$$X_A^* = 74.33, \qquad X_B^* = 40.33, \qquad X_C^* = 6.33. \tag{13}$$

Subjects in earlier games learned an important tactical trick in negotiations: most people want to be fair, and they can be persuaded somewhat by fairness arguments. So it makes sense for you, as a negotiator, to step back from the fray and ask what an arbitrator might impose. In the course of negotiations, if you seem to be getting less than what you deem to be fair, then you could use this argument in your support. (The obverse of this stratagem is more controversial: you should temper your aspirations toward fairness and should not try to get much more than your fair share.) One complication with this suggestion is that normally there is more than one seemingly fair solution. Of course, astute negotiators will select those principles of fairness that favor their side. If several parties engage in these tactics, then a strange thing happens: instead of focusing on substance, the arguments shift to debates about fundamental principles—which often is a good thing. But the setting is somewhat corrupting, since the parties are persuaded by the implications for their own payoffs as well as fairness in the abstract.

A few subjects, without any prompting, computed the fairness solution given in requirement (13) and used this to temper and guide their initial aspirations. Some used it quite openly and passionately when the negotiations were developing adversely from their vantage point.

Another so-called fair solution for this negotiation exercise is known extensively in the literature as the Shapley Value, after game theorist Lloyd Shapley. Consider a hypothetical model of the dynamics of coalition formation in which one player starts out singly, then is joined by a second player, and then by a third. With three players there are six possible dynamic formations of the grand coalition of all three players. In the first line of Table 20, we see how a grand coalition forms in the sequence A then B then C. In this sequence, A alone commands zero; when B joins A, B contributes 118; when C joins A and B, she adds 3 to bring the grand total to 121. In the last line of the table, C starts and brings zero; B joins C and adds 50; A then joins with C and B and adds 71. The Shapley arbitrated solution averages the contributions added by each player. Thus, according the Shapley's scheme, A would get a fair share (or arbitrated value) of 57.33, which is the average of the six

TABLE 20. *The Shapley Value of the pure coalition game.*

Order of players forming the grand coalition	Incremental value added by each player			
	A	B	C	Total
ABC	0	118	3	121
ACB	0	37	84	121
BAC	118	0	3	121
BCA	71	0	50	121
CAB	84	0	0	121
CBA	71	50	0	121
Average	57.33	40.33	23.33	121

Note: The Shapley Value (for A, B, and C) is the vector quantity (57.33, 40.33, 23.33).

TABLE 21. *Another arbitrated solution of the pure coalition game.*

Starting two-party coalition	"Reasonable" payoff			
	A	B	C	Total
Coalition AB	76.0	42.0	—	118
Synergy	0.75	0.75	1.5	3
Total	76.75	42.75	1.5	121
Coalition AC	76.0	—	8.0	84
Synergy	9.25	18.5	9.25	37
Total	85.25	18.5	17.25	121
Coalition BC	—	42.0	8.0	50
Synergy	35.5	17.75	17.75	71
Total	35.5	59.75	25.75	121
Average	65.83	40.33	14.84	121

numbers in the column under A. Notice how the Shapley arbitrated values (57.33, 40.33, 23.33) differ sharply from the values in equation (13), namely (74.33, 40.33, 6.33).

What would I do if I were the arbitrator? Even though the Shapley Value has some deficiencies, I am persuaded by many of its merits.[3] But in this case I would suggest my own peculiar brew, which exploits a hodgepodge of the ideas we have touched on. Start with the analysis in Table 19 exploiting the idea of offers that cannot readily be refused. Add the possibility that any two-party coalition can bargain with the remaining party, and divide that synergy in half; take the half received by the existing coalition of two parties and divide that in half. Then average the results over the three different starting two-party coalitions.[4] All this is systematically done in Table 21. Suppose, for example, that we start off with the coalition AC, which commands 84 units. If A receives 76 and C receives 8 units, then this decomposition is not readily vulnerable to B's offers to A or C. This idea goes back to "offers that cannot readily be refused." Coalition AC alone commands 84, and B alone gets nothing. If, however, they join together they create a synergy

3. See Luce and Raiffa (1957), pp. 245–252.
4. I have not investigated how this would generalize to situations with more than three players.

of 37 units. For this arbitration scheme we imagine that B is given 18.5 of this synergy and that coalition AC shares its 18.5 equally. So if coalition AC forms first, the 121 units are divided as follows: 85.25 to A, 18.5 to B, and 17.25 to C. The solution shown in Table 21 averages the partitions of the 121 units. Notice that in this case C gets 14.84.

We can now return to the Scandinavian Cement Company case and investigate other arbitrated solutions for that problem. The Shapley Values are (35.5, 28.5, 13), as shown in Table 22. My preferred arbitrated values, shown in Table 23, are (34.916, 28.416, 13.66). Both these solutions fall close to the center of the shaded region of Figure 46.

Let's look at an extremely simple example and compare the solutions obtained by using various methods. Assume that there is one strong player, A, and two weak players, B and C. Their coalition payoffs are as follows: each player alone commands 0; coalition AB and coalition AC each command 10; coalition BC commands 0; all three together command 10. We see that A, the strong player, can play B against C; he needs only one of them. If we set up the following requirements:

$$X_A \geq 0, \qquad X_B \geq 0, \qquad X_C \geq 0, \qquad (14)$$

$$X_A + X_B \geq 10, \qquad (15)$$

$$X_A + X_C \geq 10, \qquad (16)$$

$$X_B + X_C \geq 0, \qquad (17)$$

$$X_A + X_B + X_C = 10, \qquad (18)$$

then there is only one triplet of values that satisfies all of these, namely:

$$X_A^0 = 10, \qquad X_B^0 = 0, \qquad X_C^0 = 0.$$

Is this a fair solution? The power resides in A; all A has to do is to get B or C to join him, and he can play one against the other. Think of A as the employer and think of B and C as workers. The obvious tactic is for the workers to unite and present themselves as a unified front to A, since without B or C player A is impotent. B and C should not squabble among themselves, because they're symmetrically constituted. It's easy for them to decide allocations: divide equally.

TABLE 22. *Shapley Values for the Scandinavian Cement Company case.*

Order of players forming the grand coalition	Incremental value added by each company			Total
	SC	CC	TH	
SC, CC, TH	30	29	18	77
SC, TH, CC	30	32	15	77
CC, SC, TH	37	22	18	77
CC, TH, SC	38	22	17	77
TH, SC, CC	40	32	5	77
TH, CC, SC	38	34	5	77
Average	35.5	28.5	13	77

TABLE 23. *Another arbitrated solution for the Scandinavian Cement Company case.*

Starting two-party coalition	"Reasonable" payoff (in millions of dollars)			Total
	SC	CC	TH	
SC, CC	32.5	26.5	5.0[a]	64
Synergy	3.25	3.25	6.5	13
Total	35.75	29.75	11.5	77
SC, TH	32.5	22.0[a]	12.5	67
Synergy	2.5	5.0	2.5	10
Total	35.0	27.0	15.0	77
CC, TH	30.0[a]	26.5	12.5	69
Synergy	4.0	2.0	2.0	8
Total	34.0	28.5	14.5	77
Average	34.916	28.416	13.66	77

a. These are the values that can be obtained by the company alone, remaining outside the two-company coalition.

The core—that is, the set of triplets that satisfies individual and coalitional demands as given by requirements (14)–(18)—contains in this case only a single triplet (giving all to A). Yet this resolution does not have compelling predictive value: B and C do join together in the laboratory setting.

The Shapley Values for this game are 6.67 for A, and 1.67 each for B and C. The counterpart to the arbitrated solutions in Tables 21 and 23 would yield in this case 8.33 for A, and 0.833 each for B and C.

Now let's consider this same game structure with one dominant player (A, the "employer") and instead of two weak others introduce twenty-five weak others (B, C, D, . . . , Z). Assume that A and any single "other" can get 10 units. The core, which gives all to A and nothing to anyone else, seems to be a reasonable prediction, because it would be very hard for those twenty-five others to remain unified. Should a fair arbitrated solution reflect this reality? Should A get more and more as the number of others increases? The Shapley Values do this, but the core solutions do not.

It is not easy to suggest a compelling set of "fairness principles " that deserve to be universally acclaimed as *the* arbitrated solution. The more you think about this, the more elusive the dream becomes.

MOVING TOWARD REALITY

As a reminder of how very restrictive our discussion about coalition games has been, consider the way in which the discussion specializes to two-party negotiations. Instead of players A, B, and C we would have only players A and B. There is no loss of generality if we assume that each player alone commands zero and that as a coalition they command one unit of reward. The problem thus boils down to: How should A and B share 1 unit of reward? Obviously the focal point is .5 for each, which would be the Shapley Value. But the core in this case is embarrassingly rich: any division whatsoever of the unit reward—as long as each party does not get a negative amount—is a solution in the core. The two-player version of the pure coalition game is simply a distributive bargaining problem with openly disclosed reservation values—not a very interesting case. But how very rich in conceptual complexity this trivial game becomes when we go from two to three or more players!

The fascinating part of two-party distributive bargaining arises from the fact that the negotiators do not know each other's reservation prices; indeed, they may have to work hard to determine their own. All these considerations are abstracted out in the simple coalition games. When Scandinavian Cement and the Thor Cement Company are deciding how they should divide up their spoils (the net present value of future profits) if they were to form a two-way coalition, they are engaging in two-party distributive bargaining. It is the presence of that third company that brings a richness of detail to the situation. We can think of the three-party pure coalition game in part as a set of interlocking two-party distributive bargaining games, where each of the players in any such game has a reservation price that is determined to some extent by the other negotiations that can take place. To top things off, there is also the complexity of a three-way coalition. Matters get even more intricate when we include a fourth and fifth player.

Now let's add further reality to the potpourri. Increase the number of issues and let some of these be noneconomic, with nonobjective tradeoff rates between the levels of the different issues. The parties are not necessarily monolithic and each party may not have a clear picture of its own value structure. There are uncertainties and asymmetries of information. In a case such as this, teams of analysts would have to work awfully hard with their clients, separately and collaboratively, in order to reduce the complexity of a real, multiparty, multi-issue negotiation problem to the format of a simple coalition game, in which each coalition has a numerical payoff made up of a decomposable commodity (like money) that can be traded. And after all this simplification takes place, after the players have really come to understand the strategic structure of interlocking coalitions, the bargaining dynamics can become especially bruising. To some extent, the complexity of the real situation softens the intensity of the bargaining dynamics. The parties are not clear about what is in their own interests, and their knowledge about the interests of others is likewise vague. Compromise is often easier to arrange in a situation of ambiguity. In this perverse sense, the complexity of reality yields simplicity: many real-world negotiations are happily not as divisive as starkly simple laboratory games, because in the real world it is difficult to see clearly what is in one's own best interest.

18

The Law of the Sea

Nobbly, coal-like lumps called manganese nodules are strewn in vast quantities over much of the deepsea floor.[1] The nodules contain commercially promising quantities of copper, cobalt, nickel, and manganese. For the United States, the treasure trove on the ocean floors is of strategic importance, since there are only a few—possibly unreliable—land sources for these critical minerals. Who should be allowed to pick up these nuggets, and how fast? "Go slow" say Zaire, Belgium, and Zambia, which now supply the United States with 90 percent of its cobalt; Canada, which supplies the United States with 77 percent of its nickel, joins them, as do South Africa and Gabon, which have strong mining positions in manganese.

The richest and most abundant nodule grounds lie outside the limits of any one nation's jurisdiction, and as a result of this the question of nodule "ownership" took on increasing importance as their commercial potential emerged. In July 1966 President Lyndon Johnson warned: "Under no circumstances, we believe, must we ever allow the prospects of a rich harvest of mineral wealth to create a new form of colonial competition among the maritime nations. We must be careful to avoid a race to grab and hold the lands under the high seas. We must ensure that the deep seas and the ocean bottom are, and remain, the legacy of all human beings."[2] This phrasing was echoed by Arvid Pardo, the Maltese delegate to

---

1. This chapter draws extensively from Sebenius (1980). Sebenius served, under Ambassador Elliot L. Richardson, as a formal member of the U.S. delegation to the Law of the Sea Conference, and also as an informal staff assistant to Ambassador T. T. B. Koh of Singapore. Koh at that time was chairman of the LOS Negotiating Group on Financial Arrangements, and subsequently became president of the entire LOS Conference.
2. Luard (1977), p. 84.

the United Nations, who in a 1967 speech proposed that the seabed beyond the limits of national jurisdictions be declared the "common heritage of mankind" and that nodule exploitation be undertaken on behalf of the international community. In 1970 the United Nations General Assembly adopted this common-heritage principle and proposed the creation of an international regime for the seabed, which would ensure "equitable sharing by States in the benefits derived therefrom."

The increasing frequency of ocean use for commercial and military navigation, fishing, energy production, and scientific research led repeatedly to frictions and conflicts, emphasizing the inadequacies of the existing international laws of the sea. To address this situation, the General Assembly in 1973 convened the Third United Nations Conference on the Law of the Sea (LOS). As an integral part of their lengthy and complex agenda, the participants faced the task of giving substance to the "common-heritage" principle.

By 1978 these negotiations—the largest, the longest running and, according to Henry Kissinger, one of the most important international negotiations ever to have taken place—had reached agreement on about 90 percent of the contentious maritime issues under debate. The fate of the proposed treaty was expected to turn on the resolution of seven issues that were designated as critical by members of the conference, the most important of these being the system of financial payments to the international community (fees, royalties, and profit shares) that would be required of future miners in return for the right to mine. A linked issue was the means by which the first operation of an international seabed mining entity would be financed. Together, these two questions were termed the "financial arrangements" for seabed mining.

According to experts, the nickel, cobalt, and copper that is recoverable from the sea floor with current technology exceeds known land-based supplies. Collection methods are still in a developmental stage, even though mining consortia have invested more than $265 million in research and exploration. The business, political, and legal risks in mining are still formidable, and giant companies like Kennecott, Lockheed, and Royal Dutch Shell have joined to form several international consortia.

In June 1980 the U.S. Congress passed a seabed-mining law that permitted the Department of Commerce to start using mining licenses; but the law prohibited commercial mining before 1988 in order to give the Law of the Sea Treaty a chance to be ratified. The 1980 law and similar laws pending in other industrialized nations posed a threat to the United Nations negotiators; they said, in effect, "Be realistic in settling the financial terms, or else we'll go it alone."

By the end of the summer of 1980, in fact, the tired negotiators had hammered out what was generally agreed to be a nearly final agreement on the entire text. Under this draft of the proposed Law of the Sea Treaty, the industrialized countries would give roughly a billion dollars in loans and loan guarantees to establish the International Seabed Authority, which would be responsible for licensing exploration by private companies and which would undertake its own mining efforts through its commercial arm, the Enterprise. A sophisticated system of financial payments by private miners would be set up. The Authority would also administer a formula to limit nodule production in order to partially protect the land-based suppliers of seabed minerals.

It's truly amazing that 160 countries could reach a consensus on anything as intricate as the proposed financial arrangements for deep-seabed mining. Elliot Richardson, head of the U.S. delegation to the LOS Conference, said that it was all but certain that the text would be ready for signing in 1981. "Historians looking back on this session of the conference," he added, "are likely to see it as the most significant development of the rule of law since the founding of the United Nations itself" (*New York Times*, August 30, 1980, p. 1). Time and electoral fortunes, however, can play havoc with the most confident projections. With the coming of a new U.S. administration, the entire tentative agreement came under sudden and serious review in March 1981. It is uncertain what the full implications of this sharp action will be.

Personally, I concur wholeheartedly with the spirit of President Johnson's warning that the deep-sea treasures are the "common heritage of mankind" and should not be prematurely exploited by those who happen to be ahead in the technology race. But if technology is to work for mankind it has to be encouraged and rewarded. My purpose here is not to guess what will happen or to take sides in the dispute, but to describe how 160 nations came as far as they did toward a consensus. From an analytical point of view, it's a real success story.

THE PARALLEL SYSTEM OF MINING

In the early days of the LOS Conference, developed countries that expected to mine the seabed expressed a preference for a broad-based, international seabed-mining framework over one composed of only a few mining nations. At that time they argued strongly for a seabed "authority" that would primarily register claims and permit the orderly development of mining. Some revenue from the mining operations would be shared with the world community, in deference to the common-heritage principle. At the outset of the LOS negotiations, however, many Third World representatives wanted an international body as the sole exploiter of seabed resources. Since this idea was in opposition to the claims registry concept espoused by most of the developed world, early negotiations were soon deadlocked.

By 1976 the Conference participants had begun to coalesce behind a split-the-difference compromise which became known as the "parallel" system. On one side of the system private and state organizations would mine, while on the other side an international mining entity—the Enterprise—would be established to mine directly on behalf of the international community. For this compromise to have meaning, it was necessary to ensure that the Enterprise could in fact undertake seabed mining. Among other things, it needed access to mining areas, technology, personnel, and sources of financing.

Many delegates were concerned that the prime minesites—the areas of 40,000–60,000 square kilometers necessary to support individual mining operations for their expected 20–25-year lives—would early be snapped up by developed countries with technological leads. This would saddle the Enterprise with lower-quality operations. The solution to this dilemma involved an ingenious method similar to the "I cut, you choose first" method of dividing a piece of cake fairly. States or companies making application to the International Seabed Authority to mine on the private side would be required to submit two prospective sites. The Authority would reserve or "bank" one of them for later Enterprise operations, and the applicant would mine the other.

Two financial aspects of seabed mining were the subject of intense negotiation. The first was the scheme of required payments to the Authority by miners operating on their side of the parallel system. The Authority would decide how much of the funds to distribute directly to member countries and how much to reinvest in Enterprise mining operations. The second financial issue concerned the sources of funding required to ensure that the Enterprise had an initial mining operation.

Sebenius (1980) described the interests of the various disputants: the interests of the developed countries with the technological advantages; of the developing countries, who were not producers of the relevant minerals; of the Eastern Bloc countries, who were not ready themselves to exploit the deep-seabed treasures and who wished to gain the favor of some developing countries; of the land-based producers of the relevant minerals, both developed (like Canada) and developing (like Zambia). Most countries, like the United States, had internal differences of opinion about the financial arrangements for deep-seabed mining. Furthermore, the negotiations on the financial arrangements were intimately linked with other issues being debated: for most of the developing countries, financial arrangements were linked to ideological struggles for a "new international order." Strange coalitions formed. Some countries formed cohesive negotiating units on some issues, only to find themselves as members of contending coalitions on other issues— all within the deepsea-mining debate. The developed countries exploited the fact that in the LOS, the Group of 77 (made up of developing countries) could be fractionated.

Sebenius also examined relevant trends in other mineral-agreement negotiations—for example, contracts between multinational mining companies and host countries. How are risks and rewards shared? Contingency contracting is employed to some extent, but more commonly there are periodic contract renegotiations, with all the uncertainties that they present. How are the initial capital costs shared? Are payments to the hosts made from gross revenues or from net profits? How should the parties share downstream profits that come from a highly vertically integrated enterprise?

Six negotiating sessions were held in the New York and Geneva facilities of the United Nations during the 1977–1980 period. Detailed debate on the financial arrangements did not begin until the 1977 New York session. At the time, there was no general agreement on the likely economics of seabed mining. Available studies were highly aggregated, were typically based on industry sources, and produced highly varied results. Many representatives from developing countries took it as an article of faith that mining would be profitable—so profitable, in fact, that front-end payments from private miners could get the Enterprise under way and at the same time could be a virtual engine of Third World economic development. Representatives from developed countries seemed to expect more modest economic results.

At the 1977 New York session the United States and India offered starkly contrasting packages, which reflected opposing philosophies on nearly every dimension. The United States proposed no front-end fees; India suggested a $60 million payment. India proposed a 20 percent *ad valorem* royalty (percentage of gross revenues), plus an effective $15 million yearly charge (five dollars per ton of nodules mined, for a three-million-ton-per-year operation); the United States offered no provision for either kind of payment. The United States suggested a profit-sharing system that was progressive with the accounting rate of return on assets, with rates ranging from 15 percent on low-return projects to a 50 percent marginal rate on high-return projects; India wanted a profit share of 60 percent, once 200 percent of the investment costs were recouped. These specific figures are not in themselves important, but they do indicate the great distance that existed between two representative parties near the outset of the negotiations. India argued, moreover, that revenue shares ought to be levied on the basis of the *entire* operation, from nodule mining to land-based processing; the United States held that *only* the part of the operation in the international area should share its revenues.

Essentially as a gesture to states that did not use explicit price systems, did not recognize the concept of profits, or were simply unwilling or unable to furnish accounting data, the United States also proposed a simpler, all-royalty system. Such parallel proposals were seen as politically necessary inclusions in the text, but were the subject of little discussion in the Conference, except by Eastern Bloc countries. The United States also suggested that the Enterprise should be essentially loan-financed, with up to 10 percent of its monetary requirements to be furnished by grants from member states. The Indian proposal was silent on this question, as was Conference debate generally. The issue was simply immature.

RALLYING AROUND A MODEL

In 1976 a team at the Massachusetts Institute of Technology, led by J. D. Nyhart, obtained support from the Marine Minerals Division of the Department of Commerce's National Oceanic and Atmospheric Administration (NOAA) for the development of a computer model that could serve as a means for comparing the economic performance of a hypothetical deepsea-mining system under different conditions. Nyhart's team initiated the request; they were not in any way tied in with the LOS negotiations.

The model examined the operations of a hypothetical mining consortium operating in a near-equatorial Pacific Ocean and yielding three million tons of manganese nodules annually over a 25-year period. The model was deterministic and was driven by about 150 data values that had to be externally supplied (mainly basic cost values and future mineral prices). For any set of appropriate input values (parameters) the model generated cash flows over time. The net present value of the cash flows for the "base-case" inputs indicated that the project would break even at a (real) discount rate of 18.1 percent. It would yield a profit of $82 million at a 14 percent discount rate and lose $43 million at a 22 percent discount rate—a mildly acceptable venture, considering the risks involved. The model required cost figures on research and development, on prospecting and exploration, on capital investments (mining, transportation, and processing), and on operating costs (similarly broken down into sectors). The operating costs of each sector were then broken down for energy, labor, materials, and fixed charges. The model also demanded price figures for nickel, copper, and cobalt, and asked for detailed tax information.

A great deal of research effort was expended in providing good estimates of the 150-plus main parameter values (or vectors of values) for the model's base case. Of course, there was a great deal of uncertainty attached to many of these values. The Nyhart team's report dealt with these uncertainties primarily by sensitivity analyses for individual variables or groups of variables. Users of the model could insert their own input value assumptions into the engineering/economic framework of the model. Uncertainty was a constant theme in the team's discussions, but the model was explicitly deterministic; no formal means (such as Monte Carlo techniques) were employed to analyze stochastic elements directly. The model made scant reference to the LOS Conference, since it had not been designed for international use.

Among those at the United Nations who became interested in the MIT model was Singapore's representative, Ambassador Tommy Koh. In 1978 Koh was appointed to chair the special LOS negotiating group dealing with financial arrangements. He brought some unusual credentials to the position. Educated at Singapore, Harvard, and Cambridge, he had served as dean of the University of Singapore's law school in his early thirties. He had been the youngest ambassador ever appointed to the United Nations, had been active in the LOS Asian Group, and had been instrumental in successful negotiations on several other crucial articles of the draft convention. His appointment, therefore, raised the political level of the financial discussions, which were widely attended and translated simultaneously into the six official U.N. languages.

Koh was charged with the responsibility of producing a single negotiating text that would, after suitable modifications, generate a consensus in the overall Conference. Once the inherited text had been clarified and restructured, he needed numbers and percentages for the various fees, royalties, and profit shares. To obtain such figures, he put pressure on the participating countries to state their positions. The European Economic Community, the Soviet Union, Japan, Norway, India, and the United States all responded with new proposals. As a technique for seeking compromise, this had mixed results. Since the countries wanted their positions reflected in the text, and since Koh selected what went into it, there was some tendency for delegations to push their proposals toward the chairman's perceived zone of fairness. Of course, a request for national positions will focus attention on such positions and may serve to define an adversary process; nations can easily become committed to their stances and then require strong political reasons to move from them.

It is interesting analytically to note the similarities between a chairman-controlled SNT procedure and final-offer arbitration, where the disputing parties each offer a proposal to an arbitrator who must choose one of them without alteration. The intended effect of this arbitration method is to create an incentive for offering reasonable proposals, rather than the extreme ones that often result when the arbitrator is expected to split the difference. The LOS negotiations were a dynamic process with no clear ending, and Koh was not restricted to choosing one proposal in its entirety; but the more reasonable a proposal, the more it seemed to delegates that it might be taken into account in the text revisions.

Although the MIT model was published before the 1978 Geneva session, it was not until the negotiations in New York later in the year that it became an important topic. Early in the New York session, a seminar was held under Quaker and Methodist auspices, on neutral ground away from the United Nations. Koh had actively encouraged the seminar's sponsors and had personally urged many delegates to attend. The groups involved were generally interested in promoting world peace and had taken an early interest in the Law of the Sea questions. They had protreaty lobbying activities in Washington, had held numerous educational seminars and lunches for delegates since the 1974 sessions, and published a much-read Conference newspaper (*Neptune*) that disseminated environmental, technological, and economic information. The politically timely and obviously Koh-favored seminar was therefore extremely well attended. Known informally as the "MIT seminar," it featured the principal members of Nyhart's team, who explained their model and discussed factors affecting future deepsea-mining profitability. Seminar participants questioned many of the model's assumptions, and, in particular, its baseline values. The team's usual response to queries and challenges—an explanation of the source of assumption and a demonstration of the model's sensitivity to the factor in question—highlighted the underlying uncertainty, but also enhanced the credibility of the effort.

Attacks on the model came from the developed countries and from industry advisers to different governments. EEC members had produced a competing set of estimates—the "European Base Case"—which was much more aggregated and considerably less optimistic than the MIT study. The ire of U.S. industry was in part aroused by the fact that there was now an independent source of information for the government. Many delegates from the Group of 77, who had initially been antagonistic toward the model because it had been produced by a U.S. team, hesitatingly agreed to explore the implications of the model after they realized that it was being strongly criticized also by representatives and industrial commentators from the developed countries. Proposals by the MIT team to modify the model so that it could handle a variety of tentative financial arrangements, as well as their offers to maintain contact with the Conference members, were generally well received.

The MIT group had not planned to risk politicizing its seminar presentation by analyzing any of the existing financial-arrangements proposals; but when Jens Evensen of Norway, an influential negotiating figure, indicated his willingness to have his proposal critically examined in order to "demonstrate the model's capability," the team easily showed several economic and technical scenarios under which his essentially political compromise would badly harm the project's economic performance. At the conclusion of the presentation, Evensen acknowledged the critique, thanked the group, and indicated that he might consider modifying his proposal.

Curiosity was aroused among some of the delegates as to the economic feasibility of other proposals. In particular, the eminent Indian delegate, Satya Jagota, praised the team at the end of the seminar and inquired about India's financial-arrangements proposal. (An analysis of that proposal had been performed by the team, but the results had not been discussed at the seminar.) Not surprisingly, the financial impact of a $60 million payment some five years before commercial production was to begin, along with a 20 percent royalty, was devastating. Jagota, too, indicated that a reconsideration might be in order. In neither case did Evensen or Jagota have to admit the correctness of opponents' arguments to justify a possible move: each could point to an outside, seemingly objective analysis as a reason for considering a new position.

Evensen and members of the Norwegian delegation shortly thereafter made a trip to MIT, where they had a chance to discuss deepsea-mining economics more fully. Evensen asked Nyhart's team to analyze several alternate arrangements, and upon his return to New York he made a new proposal that leaned heavily on the

MIT analysis. All the delegates found it objectionable, but they at least considered it a more central "basis for negotiation."

Paul Engo of Cameroon, the politically adept chairman of the First Committee (which was responsible for the entire seabed regime), provided indirect but quite persuasive evidence on the extent to which the model had permeated Conference consciousness and on the way in which the locus of power seemed to be shifting to the technocrats. He lamented that the delegates had "been dragged into adopting models and systems of calculations on fictitious data that no one, expert or magician, can make the basis of any rational determination . . . We get more and more engrossed with each session and have been reduced to mere spectators in the inclusive tournament among experts."[3]

EXPLOITING DIFFERENCES AND LINKAGES

Gradually, because of the centrality of a commonly accepted (as well as commonly criticized) model, the debate shifted from vague polemical statements to harder financial tradeoffs. Still, the adversaries were far apart, and despite their common educational efforts the negotiators could not reach a compromise agreement in either the 1978 New York session or the 1979 Geneva session. Debate continued to center around the two important problems of the contractual arrangements between miners and the Authority, and the source of financing for the Enterprise's first mining efforts (which were expected to cost a billion dollars).

Although the contractual terms and Enterprise finance were debated in the same group, they were treated more or less as independent *negotiating* issues by most of the delegates. For example, it was not until the 1979 Geneva session that Koh simultaneously made proposals on both issues in the single negotiating text. Many among the Group of 77 had readily assumed a substantive link between the issues; this was reflected in an early desire to fund the Enterprise by means of revenues raised from the private side of the system. Otherwise, there was no real negotiating linkage between the issues.

3. Cited in Sebenius (1980), p. 52.

When contractual arrangements and Enterprise funding were treated as separate issues, there did not seem to be a possible zone of agreement for either issue: the scheme of taxation preferred most by the developing countries seemed to be preferred least by the developed countries. The developed countries were most reluctant, in considering Enterprise finance, to give sizable cash contributions to aid what they saw as a potential competitor with their own companies; they held the current text's provisions to be overly generous.

Compromise solutions looked dim for each issue separately. The developed countries could not accept a rigid financial-arrangement system; the developing states opposed a flexible system. The former felt that enough had been done to ensure the functioning of the Enterprise; the latter saw much more as necessary. There was constant, despairing talk of an impasse.

Linkage between contractual arrangements with the Authority and the financing of the Enterprise became a central feature of the negotiations in 1979. Meanwhile, in New York, Koh arranged for more informative seminars that were held under Methodist/Quaker auspices.

As we have seen, the potential of finding joint win-win situations depends on the exploitation of differences between beliefs, between probabilistic projections, between tradeoffs, between discount rates (a special case of intertemporal tradeoffs), between risk preferences. In the Law of the Sea negotiations ideologies clashed, and this had two contrasting effects. On the one hand, it encouraged polemics and made it more difficult to seek joint gains. On the other hand, it resulted in more extreme differences, which in turn made it easier to find joint gains—such as those made possible by the graduated-royalty scheme that eventually won consensus. One U.S. negotiator noted that "the idea of raising the figures over time was in part based on the MIT analysis, which gives far greater weight to dollars paid earlier than to those paid later in the contract. By raising the royalty rate over time, the chairman—in a constructive attempt to combine Western economics and Group of 77 politics—has created a system which requires the lowest payments at the greatest time of risk and the highest payments in the cheapest dollars."[4]

4. Katz (1979), pp. 209–222.

By linking the contractual financial arrangements with the promise by developed countries to finance the Enterprise, Koh was able to unblock earlier negotiating impasses. He could further exploit differences among the nations' perceptions of the profitability of mining operations, their attitudes toward risk and the time-value of money, and their differing political needs for making immediate symbolic statements.

The future is clouded for the overall LOS treaty, but it is interesting that the intricate compromise on the financial terms has been subject to very little criticism by the newest crop of U.S. negotiators. If in fact the treaty endures, its success will have been largely due to a few key ingredients: a remarkable chairman, the existence and acceptance of a computer model that could felicitously deflate extreme proposals and provide a proving ground for new ones, the educational seminars conducted under Methodist/Quaker auspices, the linkage between contractual arrangements to the Authority and the initial funding of the Enterprise, the creative exploitation of differences, and finally the external pressures from the United States and other developed countries that initiated legislation enabling private investment to go it alone if the Conference delayed too long. All in all, a rather remarkable achievement—no matter what the eventual outcome.

19

Fair Division

Let's look at a few mechanisms for resolving some prototypical financial disputes, such as settling estates (or divorces), allocating costs, and compensating losers in a joint undertaking. These disputes have several features in common. We'll see, first, that it's hard to come to an agreement—especially among many parties—without a "system." Second, in these negotiations there are a lot of contending systems or mechanisms for conflict resolution. Third, most of these systems are seriously flawed. Last, however, we'll see that some are much better than others, and that some are far better than unstructured improvisation.

DIVIDING AN ESTATE

Massachusetts, like other states, grants the right to individuals to specify in a will how they wish to dispose of their property at death. If an individual does not write a will, the state will write one. The laws of descent and distribution on intestacy (determining who gets the property if there is no will) specify how the estate should be split among spouse and children. "For example, if A dies without a will and is survived by wife B, and child C, and two children of deceased child D, wife B will take one-half, C will take one-fourth, and the two grandchildren will divide D's (their parent's) one-fourth equally" (Bove, 1979). There is a series of formulas that determine property shares for other interesting variations of family structure.

It would be easy to divide the estate in equal or even in well-specified unequal shares, if it consisted solely of monetary resources. But how should one decide the disposition of items that cannot be easily sold and that have sentimental value for the inheritors? The problem is not as special as it might appear: husbands and wives meet similar problems in divorce settlements; business partners in dissolving businesses; victors in dividing spoils.

Let's examine a hypothetical situation and some of the ways in which it might be resolved.[1] A father leaves his estate of four indivisible commodities to be shared "equally" among his three children. Assume that the four commodities—A, B, C, and D—have the monetary values shown in Table 24, and that the monetary worth to each of the children of any subset of the items is merely the sum of his or her monetary valuations of the individual items. Leave aside for a moment whether these monetary assignments have been strategically assessed by the individuals; assume simply that they are honest revelations and that the task is to suggest an allocation of the commodities to the children, with possible transfers of monetary amounts among them. There are three commonly proposed procedures for arriving at a solution.

Naive procedure. Allocate each commodity to the person who values it most and collect its value for the pool of money to be shared. Thus, commodity A goes to 1 for $10,000; B goes to 3 for $4,000; C goes to 3 for $2,000; and D goes to 2 for $2,000. The money collected is the sum of these amounts ($18,000), and each child gets one-third of this, or $6,000. The first child gets commodity A, less $10,000, plus $6,000—which nets out as A less a monetary payment of $4,000; the second child gets D plus $4,000; and the third child simply gets B and C. Each gets a package that has been personally valued at $6,000.

Auction procedure. Conduct the equivalent of an open ascending auction for each item; collect the payments; and share the proceeds equally. In this case, the first child gets commodity A not at $10,000 but at $7,000—the high bidder gets the commodity at the second-highest price, since the auction would stop when the maximum price of the second-to-last bidder was reached and only the highest valuer was left. Commodity B goes to 3 at $2,000 (not $4,000); C goes to 3 at $1,500; and D to 2 at $1,000. The pool would be the sum of these values, or $11,500, and each would get back $3,833.33. In this case, the first child gets A less $7,000 plus $3,833.33, or A less

1. This example is taken from Luce and Raiffa (1957), p. 366. The discussion given here is both more elementary and more extensive.

TABLE 24. *Valuation of four commodities by three legatees.*

Commodity	Monetary worth to each individual (in dollars)		
	1	2	3
A	10,000	4,000	7,000
B	2,000	1,000	4,000
C	500	1,500	2,000
D	800	2,000	1,000

$3,166.67; the second child gets D plus $2,833.33; the third child gets B and C plus $333.34. Obviously, if the parties had to choose between the two proposals on purely selfish grounds, the first child would prefer the auction proposal, the second child the naive proposal, and the third child the auction proposal.

Randomization procedure. Toss a die to determine who gets A. If the die comes up with, say, one or two dots, commodity A goes to the first child; if the die comes up with three or four dots, it goes to the second child; if the die comes up with five or six dots, it goes to the third child. Repeat the process with a new toss for B, then for C, and then for D. This procedure, while fair in some sense, may not be very efficient. For example, it may give commodity A to the second child, who values it least. But a semblance of efficiency can be achieved if the randomization process is used merely to establish an *initial* allocation of property rights; it can then be followed by open negotiations. For example, if the randomization step gives commodity A to the second child, then she could offer to sell it for a price to one of her two siblings. In this case, both 1 and 3 would be willing to offer her more than it is worth to her. If the randomization gave property rights of A to the third child, he would have only one buyer who would meet his reservation price of $7,000. One advantage of random allocation is that the commodities are divided fairly and quickly, without the requirement of any prior indication of what each item is worth to each child.

A more complicated procedure for allocation was suggested by the Polish mathematician Hugo Steinhaus, and is known as the *Steinhaus fair-division procedure*. Using the allocation shown in Table 25, we can see that, for example, Individual 1's total evalua-

TABLE 25. *The Steinhaus fair-division procedure.*

	Individual		
	1	*2*	*3*
Valuation			
Item A	$10,000	$4,000	$7,000
Item B	2,000	1,000	4,000
Item C	500	1,500	2,000
Item D	800	2,000	1,000
Total valuation	13,300	8,500	14,000
Initial fair share	4,433	2,833	4,667
Items received	A	D	B, C
Value received	$10,000	$2,000	$6,000
Excess [a]	5,567	−833	1,333
Adjusted fair share	6,455	4,855	6,689
Final arrangement	A − 3,545	D + 2,855	B, C + 689

a. Total excess = $5,567 − $833 + $1,333 = $6,067; and $6,067/3 = $2,022.

tion of all four commodities is $10,000 + $2,000 + $500 + $800, or $13,300, and that his fair share is one-third of this amount, or $4,433 (the "initial fair share" in the table). Steinhaus would give the individuals total packages (goods plus transfer payments) that exceed their initial fair shares by the same amount. Here's the way it works. The items are distributed efficiently: the first individual gets A, the second D, and the third B and C. Individual 1's excess over his initial fair share is then $10,000 − $4,433, or $5,567. The second and third individuals' excesses are, respectively, −$833 and $1,333, which makes a total excess of $6,067. As long as the individuals differ in their initial evaluations, this total excess will be positive—an important point. The total excess is divided equally: $2,022 to each individual. The first individual should thus end up with an *adjusted* fair share that is $2,022 above his initial fair share of $4,433, for a total of $6,455. This is accomplished by giving him A and asking him for a cash contribution of $10,000 − $6,455, or $3,545. Individuals 2 and 3 receive the same excess of $2,022 over their respective fair shares. Note that the monetary side payments total zero: the market clears.

Table 26 compares three of the above procedures. Individual 1 prefers the auction proposal; Individual 2 prefers the naive pro-

TABLE 26. *Comparison of naive, auction, and Steinhaus proposals.*

Individual	Items received	Side payments (in dollars)[a]		
		Naive	*Auction*	*Steinhaus*
1	A	−4,000	−3,167	−3,545
2	D	4,000	2,833	2,855
3	B, C	0	333	689

a. Total side payments for each procedure equal zero (rounding off errors).

posal; and Individual 3 prefers the Steinhaus proposal. What is fair? One way to get one's thinking straight about such alternative proposals is to see how they would perform in simpler, more transparent situations. In the simplest case, there is a single indivisible commodity to be shared between two individuals.

DIVIDING AN ENCYCLOPEDIA

Professor Brown taught physics and was an avid collector of scholarly works on modern history.[2] His friend Professor Gerschwin taught modern history, but forbore from trying to get his personal library to rival Brown's collection of outdated physics texts.

One day Brown and Gerschwin were walking to the university together through the streets of the town, when they both saw a few books strewn across the sidewalk in front of a small house. Nearby stood a medium-sized van, overflowing with material possessions of its owner. The books seemed to have come out of the back of the van. Brown stopped and picked up one of the volumes. "It's an *Encyclopedia Britannica*, Dick," he said. "Dated 1914."

"Whoever owns it must be a very careless person," said Gerschwin severely. "Those books must be of considerable value."

The front door of the house opened, and two young men came out carrying a brand new refrigerator, which they tried to put into the van. "Those damned books!" exclaimed one as he peered inside. "We have to get rid of them, or else there won't be space for the important things."

2. This case was prepared by Mr. Kalyan Chatterjee for classroom discussion. The Mr. has since become Dr. and Prof., but definitely *not* because of this case.

"Excuse me, sir," said Gerschwin eagerly. "Are you proposing to dispose of those books?"

"Yes," said the man. "I'm moving, and I have no use for those moldy old books."

"Could we then take them?" said Gerschwin.

"Certainly," said the owner of the van cheerfully, as he flung out another armful of *Britannica* volumes. Gerschwin and Brown decided to give up their walk. They called a taxi for the purpose of transporting their treasure home. The question was, whose home?

"You take it, Tom," said Gerschwin sadly. "You found it."

"No, no, Dick. It's yours. Just think of what a fine addition the 1914 edition would be to your library!"

"No, Tom. You must take it."

The discussion continued along these lines for several minutes, until the driver of the taxi, tired of circumnavigating the block, demanded to be told where to go.

"Let's take it to your place, Dick," said Brown. "We'll decide later how to share it."

"Why not toss a coin now? It's the only way I can think of to divide up this collection. We can't split the books in half. Whoever gets it must get the whole set."

"All right," said Brown, a trifle unenthusiastically.

Gerschwin tossed the coin; Brown called "heads" and won.

Later that day, at lunch, Gerschwin met his friend Professor Reif, who taught at the business school. Gerschwin described the incident to Reif.

"You tossed a coin?" asked Reif in disbelief. "Tossed a coin to decide the ownership of a valuable object?"

"Well, what would you have done?" asked Gerschwin, nettled. It had been his idea, after all, to toss the coin.

"That must wait until later," said Reif rising. "I have a class to teach. But surely, Dick, you could have thought of a better method of division. Tossing a coin, indeed!" Professor Reif left behind one puzzled and slightly displeased modern historian.

Comparing Resolution Procedures

Suppose that Brown valued the encyclopedia at $40—that is, suppose that in an open ascending auction he would bid up to a maxi-

294 / MANY PARTIES, MANY ISSUES

mum of $40 for it—and that Gerschwin valued it at $100. In the case, neither of them made this determination, since they chose instead to toss a coin; but suppose that these valuations represented their true feelings.

With the naive, auction, and Steinhaus proposals, Gerschwin gets the encyclopedia but he pays Brown different amounts: $50 with the naive proposal, $20 with the auction proposal, and $35 with the Steinhaus proposal. The calculations leading to the Steinhaus result are given in Table 27.

A little elementary algebra will show the following. Let X and Y designate two players whose valuations of a given indivisible commodity are x and y, respectively, where $x < y$. (If X is Brown and Y is Gerschwin, then $x = \$40$ and $y = \$100$.) The naive, auction, and Steinhaus proposals give the commodity to the Y-player, and the payments by Y to X are, respectively:

$y/2$ for the naive proposal,

$x/2$ for the auction proposal,

$\dfrac{x}{2} + \dfrac{y - x}{4} = \dfrac{x/2 + y/2}{2}$ for the Steinhaus proposal.

If three inheritors X, Y, and Z have evaluations x, y, and z for a single commodity to be shared, and if Z has the highest evaluation, then the Steinhaus procedure yields to each player his initial fair

TABLE 27. *Dividing an encyclopedia (E) according to the Steinhaus procedure.*

	Brown	Gerschwin
Valuation of E	$40	$100
Initial fair share	20	50
Items received	—	E
Value received	0	100
Excess [a]	−20	+50
Adjusted fair share	20 + 15	50 + 15
Final arrangement	35	E − 35

a. Total excess = − $20 + $50 = $30; and $30/2 = $15.

share (one-third of his total valuation) and an incremental bonus of

$$\frac{1}{9}\left(z - \frac{x+y}{2}\right),$$

which seems quite reasonable.

In the randomization procedure used by Brown and Gerschwin, Brown is offered a fifty-fifty lottery between a return of zero and a prize that is worth \$40 to him. His *expected value* for this lottery is \$20 (the same as his initial fair share with the Steinhaus procedure), but if he is somewhat risk-averse his certainty equivalent[3] might be somewhat less—say, \$17.

TABLE 28. *Randomization followed by bargaining for the encyclopedia.*

Recipient of the property rights	Probability [a]	Final valuation after bargaining (in dollars)	
		Brown	Gerschwin
Brown	.5	70[b]	30 (i.e., E − 70)
Gerschwin	.5	0	100 (i.e., E)
Expected value		35[c]	65[d]

a. Probabilities sum to 1.
b. This value is midway between the reservation prices of \$40 and \$100.
c. Brown's expected value is (.5 × \$70) + (.5 × \$0) = \$35.
d. Gerschwin's expected value is (.5 × \$30) + (.5 × \$100) = \$65.

Gerschwin's expected value for this lottery is \$50 and his certainty equivalent may be, say, \$45. In the above case, Brown, who valued the encyclopedia less than Gerschwin, won the toss and did not engage Gerschwin in a subsequent round of distributive bargaining. But let's look further at this possibility: randomization (to determine initial property rights) followed by bargaining. If Gerschwin is lucky enough to get the encyclopedia, no subsequent trade is possible. If Brown gets the rights to the encyclopedia, there is a bargaining zone of agreement. If both write down their true reservation prices and simultaneously disclose them, with the understanding that they will take the midpoint of the zone of agreement

3. His certainty equivalent is the minimum amount he would be willing to take for certain, in lieu of the lottery.

(if one exists), then Gerschwin will purchase the encyclopedia for $70 from Brown.[4] (Note that Brown's reservation price is $40 and that Gerschwin's is $100.) Table 28 depicts the lotteries resulting from the procedure of randomization followed by bargaining. Each protagonist's expected value is exactly what the Steinhaus procedure would give him. If Brown and Gerschwin are risk-averse, they should prefer the Steinhaus procedure.

Strategic Misrepresentations with the Steinhaus Procedure

Since strategic misrepresentation of values is not a problem to be concerned about with Brown and Gerschwin, let's imagine that the encyclopedia is jointly owned by Bea and Gary, who are involved in a hotly disputed divorce settlement and are dividing up their joint property. Let Bea's evaluation for their encyclopedia be $40 and Gary's $100. With the Steinhaus procedure, if they are both truthful, Bea gets $35 and Gary $65. If she misrepresents and he is truthful, then for every additional $4 she exaggerates, she gets an additional $1 net return—but she can't go too far. If, for example, she announces a value of $120 and he $100, then she gets the encyclopedia, which is worth $40 to her, and she must pay him $55, which results in a loss of $15 to her (see Table 29). If they both announce $100, and if the possession of the encyclopedia is then determined by the toss of a coin, she would wish fervently to lose. Notice what happens in the case where they both misrepresent and cross over: if, for instance, she announces $80 and he $60, they both share the $40 instead of the $100 total payoff.

Let's examine her strategic problem a bit more deeply. She doesn't know his true valuation and how much he might misrepresent his values. The more he misrepresents, the more dangerous it is for her also to misrepresent. So although one can't really say that the Steinhaus scheme encourages honest evaluations, in many situations it may be the pragmatic thing to do. Honesty in this case is the supercautious strategy (that is, the strategy that maximizes the valuer's minimum possible return—the so-called maximin strat-

4. The announcement of reservation prices should ideally be done *before* the randomization designates property rights: this makes it more difficult to act strategically, and the procedure is therefore less embarrassing to friends who are bargaining with each other.

TABLE 29. *Vulnerability of the Steinhaus procedure to strategic misrepresentation of values (true valuation for Bea is $40 and for Gary is $100).*

Submitted valuations		Final payoffs	
Bea	Gary	Bea	Gary
40	100	35	65
60	100	40	60
80	100	45	55
100	100	(−10, 50)[a]	50
120	100	−15	55
40	80	30	70
40	60	25	75
40	40	20	(20, 80)[a]
40	20	25	15
60	80	35	65
80	60	5	35

a. These payoffs depend on who gets the encyclopedia in case of ties. Randomization seems natural here.

egy). It is also a good strategy against an extreme or naive exaggerator. Finally, it is the easiest and most socially desirable thing to do.

Divide and Choose

If the encyclopedia were a divisible commodity, Brown and Gerschwin could divide it into two parts. Certainly it would not be optimal to give Brown volumes A to M and Gerschwin volumes N to Z, but still a divide-and-choose procedure could be used. Suppose that each puts $100 into the pot to be divided, along with a card labeled "E" for encyclopedia. A coin is tossed to determine the divider. Let's say that Brown becomes the divider and Gerschwin becomes the chooser. The divider splits the pot, consisting of E and $200, into two parts, and the chooser then selects the part he wants.

Start off with the divider (Brown) making a split that is even in his eyes: E + $80, and $120. Since Brown values E at $40, both parts are equally desirable to him and net him a return of $20 (remember he put $100 of his own into the pot). But Brown might think the chooser is much more likely to prefer E + $80 to $120. So the divider might add an amount Δ to the dollar side and split the pot into two amounts E + $80 − $$\Delta$ and $120 + $$\Delta$. The higher Δ is, the more the divider will get, as long as the chooser selects E + $80 − $$\Delta$. Hence, from a strategic point of view, the divider might want to assess a probability distribution of the chooser's evaluation of E and optimize the choice of Δ. But notice that any positive choice of Δ might entail a net return to the divider of less than $20; a choice of $\Delta = 0$ is the only way that the divider can be certain to get a net return of at least $20. Any other positive choice of Δ entails some downside risk. If the divider (Brown) splits the pot into the two amounts E + $80 and $120, then the chooser (Gerschwin) will happily choose E + $80, which is worth $180 to him and nets him a return of $80 overall.

Now suppose that Gerschwin is the divider and Brown the chooser. If Gerschwin divided the pot in a supercautious manner, he would split it into the amounts of E + $50 and $150, and in this case Brown would choose $150 for a net payoff of $50 to himself. Gerschwin's net payoff, too, would be $50.

If a coin were tossed to determine who would be the divider and who the chooser, and if the divider were to behave supercautiously, the expected-value payoffs would be once again the same as would be the case with the Steinhaus procedure, namely $35 and $65 (see

TABLE 30. *The divide-and-choose procedure with supercautious dividers.*

Divider	Chooser	Probability [a]	Net payoffs (in dollars)	
			Brown	Gerschwin
Brown	Gerschwin	.5	20	80
Gerschwin	Brown	.5	50	50
Expected value			35	65

a. Probabilities sum to 1.

Table 30). But a strange result occurs using the divide-and-choose procedure with unequal valuations: the divider will be tempted not to act supercautiously, but to try to exploit his imperfect perceptions of the chooser's valuation of E. Although it makes sense for the divider to do that, misperceptions will sometimes occur and the encyclopedia will occasionally end up with Brown rather than Gerschwin.

The general problem illustrated by our examples in this chapter is the allocation of fixed resources among several parties, where the resources are of different types and are differentially valued by the parties. This allocation is usually accomplished by means of some sort of negotiation. The more parties that are involved, the more intricate the dynamics of unstructured negotiations become, and the more desirable it becomes to adopt a formalized procedure.

20

Willingness to Pay for a Public Good

Should society expend public funds for a project that many citizens will enjoy? Certainly this should depend, among other things, on the costs of the project and on the benefits derived from it. Determining the benefits is usually tricky; one way is to ask citizens how much they would be *willing* to pay for that project. The difficulty is that the respondents will usually have only a vague idea of what the project is worth to them, and some will bias their responses—or, put less felicitously, they will misrepresent their true beliefs.[1]

PROCEDURES THAT ENCOURAGE HONEST REVELATION

A quick example will show how a small variation in a procedure for resolving a group-action problem can affect the truthfulness of responses. The twenty-one members of a finance committee of an organization (say, a union) have to decide how much money their organization should spend for some amenity (say, a library for its members). Some believe that the amount should be zero, others that it should be as much as $100,000. Assume that the procedure for resolving this conflict of opinion has been announced: a secret ballot will be conducted; each member will write down the amount that he or she thinks appropriate; and the amount that will be expended will be the average of the twenty-one amounts submitted.

Ms. Carey believes that $50,000 would be an appropriate amount. She thinks that several members of the committee will

---

1. For some recent analyses of this problem, see, for example: Ross (1974), Groves (1976), Arrow (1977), Myerson (1977), and Green and Laffont (1979).

suggest a lower amount and that some of these members, in an effort to bring down the average, will announce values that are even lower than they truly believe appropriate. So in order to bring up the average, which she thinks will be below $50,000, she decides to announce $80,000 instead of $50,000—a $30,000 exaggeration which will raise the average by $30,000/21, or $1,428.57. She would like to announce more, but a sense of propriety keeps her from exaggerating too much.

Now let's change the rules a bit. Instead of using the *average* of the twenty-one responses, suppose that the committee has decided to use the *median* response: the twenty-one values will be ordered in size and the midpoint (the eleventh value in order of size) will be taken as the group choice. In this case, does Ms. Carey gain anything by announcing $80,000 instead of $50,000? With some sets of other responses it will not make any difference whether she announces $50,000 or $80,000. But where her announcement will make a difference, she's always better off saying $50,000 instead of $80,000. If this is not readily clear, think about a few cases. There is *no* case where Ms. Carey gains an advantage by saying anything other than the $50,000 she truly feels appropriate. *The "median procedure" elicits truthful responses, whereas the "average procedure" encourages misrepresentation.*

Another simple example will also prepare the ground for our main illustration. A meteorologist—taken as one representative of a class of forecasters—has to assign probabilities of "rain" and "not rain." He truly believes that the probability of rain is .6. Now suppose that he is to be rewarded as follows: for any probability p for rain that he announces, he will get a bonus of $100p$ if it rains and $100(1 - p)$ if it does not rain. For example, if he announces $p = .8$, he will get $80 if it rains and $20 if it does not rain. Table 31 shows the rewards that the meteorologist gets with various announcements, and the *expected values* he obtains with these announcements. For example, if he announces $p = .8$ he will get $80 or $20, depending on whether or not it rains. Since his true probabilistic assessment of rain is .6, with an announcement of .8 his expected value is $(.6 \times \$80) + (.4 \times \$20)$, or $56. With this reward system the meteorologist who truly believes that $p = .6$ obtains the largest expected-value return by announcing $p = 1.0$, *not* $p = .6$. This reward procedure does not encourage honest responses.

There is a whole class of reward systems that do encourage hon-

TABLE 31. *Expected values for various probability announcements, using the rewards $100p if rain and $100(1 − p) if not rain. (The true probability belief of rain is .6.)*

Event	True probabilities	Rewards for various announcements					
		p = .5	p = .6	p = .7	p = .8	p = .9	p = 1.0
Rain	.6	50	60	70	80	90	100
Not rain	.4	50	40	30	20	10	0
Expected value (in dollars)[a]		50	52	54	56	58	60

a. The expected value is the weighted average with the true weights .6 and .4. Thus, if the announced p is .7, the expected-value return is $(.6 \times \$70) + (.4 \times \$30) = \$54$.

est revelations. Following is one such reward structure, known as the Brier Score. If the meteorologist announces that the probability of rain is p, his rewards are $\$100[1 − (1 − p)^2]$ if it rains, and $\$100(1 − p^2)$ if it does not rain. Table 32 exhibits his rewards for several announced values of p. For example, if p is announced to be .8, the meteorologist gets a reward of $96 if it rains and $36 if it does not rain. Since he truly believes that the probability of rain is .6, his expected-value return with an announcement of $p = .8$ is $(.6 \times \$96) + (.4 \times \$36)$, or $72. The announcement that maximizes the meteorologist's expected-value return is $p = .6$, his *truthful opinion*. This reward structure encourages honest revelations—assuming, of course, that the meteorologist is solely concerned with maximizing his subjective expected-value return.

Certainly, the desire to maximize monetary gains is not the only

TABLE 32. *Expected values for various probability announcements, using the rewards $100[1 − (1 − p)^2] if rain and $100(1 − p^2) if not rain. (The true probability belief of rain is .6.)*

Event	True probability	Rewards for various announcements					
		p = .5	p = .6	p = .7	p = .8	p = .9	p = 1.0
Rain	.6	75	84	91	96	99	100
Not rain	.4	75	64	51	36	19	0
Expected value (in dollars)		75	76	75	72	67	60

reason why people tell the truth. But oftentimes monetary rewards and incentives make people more conscious of their actions and, *ceteris paribus*, it is better if a system can be devised that encourages honest revelations.

> *Analytical elaboration.* The above discussion is readily generalized. Assume that one and only one of the events $E_1, \ldots, E_n$ will occur. A forecaster truly believes that the probabilities of these events are $t_1, \ldots, t_n$, respectively (where the sum of the t_i's is unity), but he may for some purpose wish to announce values $a_1, \ldots, a_n$ instead of $t_1, \ldots, t_n$. If he announces $a = (a_1, \ldots, a_n)$ and E_i occurs, let his reward be $R_i(a)$. His expected value would then be
>
> $$\sum_{i=1}^{n} t_i R_i(a).$$
>
> The problem is to find a reward function R such that his best announcement a is his true belief $t = (t_1, \ldots, t_n)$. There are many candidate solutions for this problem, including the log function:
>
> $$R_i(a) = k_1 - k_2 \ln a_i,$$
>
> where k_1 and k_2 are adjustable constants.

BARGAINING ON COST ALLOCATION

Let's consider a pervasive problem in our society: the allocation of costs for a public project. For example, should a particular park be built? If so, who should pay for it? (Instead of "park" one could substitute bridge, incinerator, library, and so on.) We can ask people how much they would be willing to pay for the park; but will they give truthful responses?

A simple three-person version of this problem will illustrate some methods of analysis. Imagine that three families—A, B, and C—share a common area which seems ideal for a swimming pool. Unfortunately, none of them has the financial resources necessary to install a swimming pool on its own. They decide on collective action. Each family ponders how it would assess the value of the pool, and the three families then meet to negotiate exactly how the cost of installing the pool ($25,000) is to be shared among them. If the negotiations break off, the pool will not be installed. Assume that there will be no restrictions on the use of the pool if it is built.

When this issue is negotiated in a laboratory setting, the subjects are divided into groups of three, and the individuals in each triplet are assigned the roles of A, B, and C. Let's say that a particular player A has received a confidential message that the pool is actually worth $12,475 to her; she would like to see the pool built if the cost to her were $12,475 or less, but she has other pressing needs and it would be nice to pay less. Indeed, she knows that for the purpose of this exercise she will be scored on the difference between $12,475 and what she actually pays.

A is told that B and C also have maximum willingness-to-pay values and that those values have been determined by independent random drawings that make each value between $5,000 and $15,000 equally likely. Her confidential value of $12,475 was drawn from this same distribution; she also knows that B and C know *how* her number was generated, but they do not know *what* particular value was drawn.

Each triplet of subjects has to negotiate whether or not to build the pool and, if the pool is built, how to allocate the costs. If A with a maximum willingness-to-pay value of $12,475 actually ends up paying $9,200, her fellow players B and C will never know that she had a buyer surplus of $12,475 − $9,200, or $3,275.

Suppose that A enters into the negotiation arena and that B opens the conversation: "I would like to see the pool built, but I'm afraid I can't offer much. I would like to hold down my contribution to $6,000. I realize that this is less than the one-third even share of $8,333, but I'm in a tight monetary situation."

"I'm short of money, too," says C. "I could pay a bit more — say, $7,500 — but I would like to get away for less."

A has a problem. Should she offer $11,500, which would bring the total to $25,000? She would be willing to pay that amount; but are B and C taking advantage of her? "Well, I guess the pool won't be built," says A, "because I was willing to offer to pay $9,000, a bit over my fair share. It's a pity that we're so close to our target of $25,000. Can't you ante up a bit more?"

After some posturing, B moves up to $7,000; C moves from $7,500 to $8,000; and A fills in the rest with $10,000. But A is still uncomfortable. She feels that perhaps she's been taken advantage of, that

C might have been able to afford $10,000 also. "I'd be furious if I were to learn that C could really afford to pay more than me," muses A. But she'll never know.

When this experiment was conducted in the laboratory, some triplets were given random numbers that totaled more than $25,000, but they did not build the pool. Other triplets were given random numbers that totaled less than $25,000, and at the end of frustrating negotiations each party felt that the pool was not built because "the other two parties were too greedy."

Simultaneous Disclosures Without a Benefactor

The allocation of costs is a particularly nasty type of negotiation. In the above simulated exercise some triplets, without any coaching, concocted the following formalized scheme for the resolution of the conflict. They mutually agreed to have each party submit a sealed announcement that would state the maximum value that that party would be willing to pay for the pool. The three announcements would then be simultaneously disclosed, and the pool would be built if the total reached $25,000. The amount to be actually paid by each would be proportional to the size of the party's announcement. For example, if A announced $12,000 and the total was $28,000, then A would be charged

$$\frac{\$12,000}{\$28,000} \times \$25,000 = \$10,714.29.$$

If A announced $10,000 instead of her true reservation value of $12,475, she would be gambling: she would end up paying less if the pool were built, but she would run an added risk that the pool might not be built, whereas it would have if she had told the truth.

Since this formal conflict-resolution procedure is so natural, I asked each subject how he or she would play in that formalized game. Subjects were asked to submit their announced bids as a function of their maximum willingness-to-pay values: What offer would they announce if their maximum willingness-to-pay value were $5,000? $7,000? $15,000? On the basis of these strategy responses, I could simulate how each subject would do against random pairings of other subjects. It turned out that subjects did not do very well with this formalized procedure; they were much better off haggling with a nonstructured format. Too many inefficiencies arose with the simultaneous-disclosure procedure, because of the considerable discrepancies between announced and true values. As was the case with an analogous simultaneous-disclosure procedure for distributive bargaining, *subjects who did best empirically were the ones who simply announced the truth*—the ones who did *not* misrepresent. The simple reason for this was that most subjects misrepresented too grossly. In this case, honesty was almost the best policy against the overzealous greediness of others.

> *Analytical elaboration.* The equilibrium analysis of this three-person game (that is, with simultaneous disclosures for announced willingness-to-pay values) indicates that each party should modestly misrepresent that party's true maximum willingness-to-pay value: each should announce a value that is modestly below his or her true value. The exact amount of this misrepresentation depends, of course, on the true willingness-to-pay value. Empirically, averaging over all the strategy responses of the subjects, the average misrepresentation was observed to be more extreme than the misrepresentation suggested by an equilibrium strategy. Hence, even leaving out any questions of ethics or morality or responsibility, I would advise a single subject playing this simultaneous-disclosure game to tell the truth, or distort only slightly.[2]

This type of problem is so pervasive in our society that it would be nice if an ingenious procedure could be devised that: (1) would encourage each party to tell the truth, regardless of how the other parties choose to behave (a "truth-dominant" procedure); or, somewhat less desirably, (2) would encourage each party to tell the truth as long as the other parties are also telling the truth (an "incentive-compatible" procedure). The procedure of simultaneous disclosures is neither truth dominant nor incentive compatible. Indeed, it is incentive *in*compatible in the sense that the more the others distort, the more you should tell the truth; but unfortunately, if they resort to honesty, then there is myopic economic incentive for you to distort, which is not what we ideally want.

2. If the other two players were to tell the truth, then on the average you could get a higher expected value by distorting a sizable amount. But now, bringing in ethical concerns, *should you want to act that way?* See Chapter 25.

It can be shown that for the cost allocation posed above, there is no truth-dominant procedure for conflict resolution. There is a complex process that achieves incentive compatibility, but it is not readily implementable because it makes strong use of the unrealistic assumption that all parties effectively choose their maximum willingness-to-pay values from probability distributions that are commonly known to all. This procedure is analogous to the one briefly described for distributive bargaining (see Chapter 4).

Simultaneous Disclosures with a Benefactor

A truth-dominant procedure does exist for a slightly different problem of cost allocation—one that involves an external banker or benefactor, such as the government. Suppose that a father has a summer home that is used by the families of his three married children. The father is contemplating installing a swimming pool that costs $25,000, but he is willing to do this only if the sum of the three willingness-to-pay values of his children comes to $25,000 or more. He asks each child to announce a maximum willingness-to-pay value. The announcements are simultaneously disclosed. A's true value is, say, $12,000. Let the sum of the announcements of B and C total x dollars. If A's announcement when added to x totals $25,000 or more, then the pool will be built; otherwise not. If the pool is built, A will not pay her announcement but will pay $25,000 - x$; that is, she will pay the incremental value that is needed to bring the total over the hurdle of $25,000. If $x = \$17,000$ (the sum of the announcements of B and C) and, not knowing x, A announces $10,000, then the pool will be built and she will actually pay $8,000 (not $10,000). If she announced her truthful value of $12,000, she would pay the same, namely $8,000. But now say that $x = \$14,000$. If A were to report honestly, the pool would be built and she'd pay $11,000. If she announced $10,000, however, the pool would not be built, contrary to her desires. It is clear that she should tell the truth, *regardless of what the other parties do*. The same applies to B and C. This procedure, by which each party pays only the actual deficit to the target, is called a Groves procedure or a Groves "mechanism" (see Groves, 1977).

What are the monetary transactions that might take place in a particular example? Let the true maximum willingness-to-pay (WTP) values be $12,000, $10,000, and $7,000 (see Table 33). Assume that A and C report honestly, but that B, who is not too bright, shades his value and announces $8,000 instead of a truthful $10,000. The pool will be built in this case, and the actual payments are shown in the far-right column. Notice that the actual amount collected from the three children is $21,000 and that a deficit of $4,000 will have to be supplied by the father. If B had reported honestly by announcing $10,000, this would have resulted in the same payment for him, but it would have reduced A's and C's payments by $2,000 each; it also would have required the father to put up an additional $4,000.

If A is solely concerned with her actual payment, if she is not concerned about the equity of payments between herself and her siblings, and if she is not concerned with the deficit her father will have to supply, then she should simply announce the truth. Of course, she can easily subvert the system by colluding with one or both of her siblings. For example, if they collusively determine that their joint willingness-to-pay values total more than $25,000, they can each jack up their true values by announcing $2,000 more than their true WTPs, which would result in a $4,000 reduction in actual payments by each and an increased deficit of $12,000 to be supplied by their father. However, there is not always honor among thieves, and one of the conspirators might renege on this socially undesirable, insecure, collusive contract. Even if A's two siblings conspire, she is still better off telling the truth. Observe that what A pays does not depend on what she says, but on what the others say; what she says, however, does influence the decision of whether or not to build the pool.

The father might trust his children not to collude, but he might suspect that they would be tempted to bias their individual announcements if they could gain by it. Hence, this scheme for generating truthful responses might be quite satisfactory to him. I don't think there is any scheme in this cost-allocation problem that can generate honest responses and be immune from collusive manipulation. The benefactor in this case is a father, but more often it is an employer or a town or a state or the federal government.

There may be schemes that are not truth dominant in the literal sense, but that may effectively reduce the size of the bias of responses. As in the case of fair-division mechanisms (Chapter 19) it may be quite complicated and financially risky to determine just how best to misrepresent. With certain complicated resolution pro-

TABLE 33. *Cost allocation using the truth-dominant procedure with an external banker.*

Individual	True maximum WTP (in dollars)	Announced maximum WTP (in dollars)	Actual payment (in dollars)
A	12,000	12,000	10,000[a]
B	10,000	8,000	6,000[b]
C	7,000	7,000	5,000[c]
Total		27,000[d]	21,000

a. A pays $25,000 − ($8,000 + $7,000).
b. B pays $25,000 − ($12,000 + $7,000).
c. C pays $25,000 − ($12,000 + $8,000).
d. The pool is built, since this value exceeds $25,000.

cedures, it may be easier simply to tell the truth. I suspect that many people may be tempted to misrepresent their true responses for their own pecuniary advantage when it is simple to do so, but that they would refrain from doing this in cloudy situations where it would require complex calculations and, especially, collusive behavior with others.

If the profits of distortion can be achieved only by detailed analysis, then some may forgo this analysis because they fear that such socially inappropriate analysis will be leaked. In summary, although it is difficult or impossible sometimes to devise resolution procedures that will guarantee honest announcements, some procedures are more effective than others in mitigating the effects of socially undesirable distortions. Researchers seek, often in vain, for ideal procedures that are truth dominant and collusion-proof; it would be fine if that ideal could be achieved, but even if it cannot be achieved in a given setting, more research should be focused on schemes that approach this ideal in practice.

Naturally, even if a resolution procedure is not truth dominant, many people will still want to reveal honest values because they perceive it to be in their social interest to do so. It may also be optimal to do so if a sense of fairness, ethics, responsibility is factored into one's overall objective function. I suspect that most people are mildly altruistic: they want to do what is socially right, as long as the selfish economic temptation is not too great. As we will see in Chapter 25, a lot can be gained in terms of efficiency if procedures are devised to exploit this limited form of altruism.

21

Environmental
Conflict Resolution

Environmental conflicts have probably always existed, but in this decade of litigation they have multiplied copiously and the courts are now clogged with such disputes.[1] Some of these disputes touch us all: the role of nuclear power, the protection of wildlife habitats, the extinction of natural species, and, more generally, the vexing tradeoffs between economic and environmental qualities of life. As an analyst, I would like to see some of this seething debate become less adversarial. We have more of a community of interest than we as a society realize, and should exploit the possibilities of joint gains. We act like a zero-sum society, when in reality there is a lot of non-zero-sum fat to be skimmed off to everyone's mutual advantage. There are an increasing number of third-party intervenors who practice various approaches to what is now being called "environmental conflict resolution." They are doing a commendable job and can point with pride to some impressive accomplishments.[2] Their efforts, though, should be bolstered by a group of problem-solving analysts who could join them in trying to find compromise solutions.

1. In this section I draw extensively from Sullivan (1980).
2. See, for example, the occasional reports of *Environmental Consensus,* published by the Conservation Foundation, 1717 Massachusetts Avenue N.W., Washington, D.C. 20036. The publications provide a forum for presenting information about the processes and activities in the field of environmental conflict resolution. The Winter 1981 issue contains, among other examples, an account of the successful mediation of the "Storm King Dispute" involving eleven utilities, environmental groups, and government agencies, including Consolidated Edison, the Natural Resources Defense Council, and the Environmental Protection Agency.

310

SITING OF FACILITIES

Let's examine one class of environmental problems: the siting of facilities for hazardous waste, for power plants, for airports, and so on. Suppose that a developer is interested in building a facility for the disposal of (low-level) hazardous waste in Massachusetts. Currently there is a vast shortage of such facilities, and a large proportion of waste is dumped illegally. Assume that it is in the interests of practically everyone (there are always exceptions) that such a facility be built somewhere in the state—as long as it is not built in our backyard! The rub is that it can't be built in some *indefinite* place; it has to be built in some *definite* place; and it is certain that the abutters—and even those farther down the road—will object, probably with good reason. If it is designated to be in our backyard, we'll complain, "Why us? Why not somewhere else?"

Let's abstract away most of the reality to get our thinking started. Suppose that a facility could be located in one of five towns: Aspen, Baileyville, Camille, Donnybrook, or Eaglestown. Contrary to reality, let's assume that each town is monolithic in its views and that each is represented by a negotiator (A, B, C, D, and E, respectively) who has full power to commit his or her town. Although each town wants the facility to be built (somewhere else), let's assume at first that the state has agreed to build and maintain the facility in any one of the five towns, but that they have to decide jointly where it is to be built. If they can't decide, it will not be built.

The five representatives bicker among themselves, but can't reach an agreement. Someone proposes using a randomized procedure to determine the location of the facility, all towns having an equally likely chance of being chosen. They all agree to this randomization procedure, and the unlucky "winner" is representative C. He can't, after the fact, suggest that he's having second thoughts about the procedure; but because he represents a rich town he is able to bargain with B, the representative of the penurious town of Baileyville, to accept the facility—for a price. B bargains hard and agrees to C's request, with a compensating sweetener of $100,000. D is furious. Why should the people of Camille get out of their obligation just because they're rich? Why should poor Baileyville always get stuck with the drudge-work of the society? "Hold on," says B. "Whom are you helping? My town is not only poor, but you won't allow us to improve our position. That's double jeopardy. That $100,000 will finance a long-needed library and a shelter for abused unfortunates."

Society has a schizophrenic attitude toward the morality of certain financial transactions. The rich are not allowed to buy themselves exemptions from the military draft; and in a college dormitory people would think poorly of an affluent student if he were to financially entice a scholarship student to swap dormitory rooms that were assigned by random numbers. But it's permissible for workers to receive premium wages for hazardous jobs.

Assume now that the five representatives have agreed to use a random drawing, but that the drawing has not yet been conducted. A knows that B would assume the obligation for $100,000; but since Aspen can only afford to pay $50,000 in order to shift the obligation to some other town, A forms a deal with E who thinks similarly. If the randomization designates A or E, they each agree to pay $50,000 to B to assume this obligation. D has second thoughts; "I don't like giving or taking compensation for this obligation, but if this is going to be the accepted norm, then I would be willing to do it for $80,000."

"That's wonderful," responds C. "Let's each put up $20,000 to give to D."

But B intervenes: "Baileyville can't afford $20,000; but we'd be willing to lower our price for accepting the facility to $75,000."

Finally E comes up with a suggestion: they should do things systematically. She presents two numbers that describe her feelings as a representative of Eaglestown: (1) the amount of compensation that Eaglestown would be willing to *give* to another town for accepting the facility (rather than not have the facility built at all); and (2) the amount of compensation that Eaglestown itself would *need* in order to accept the facility (rather than not have the facility built at all). She declares that Eaglestown would be willing to give $50,000 but would need $150,000 for acceptance.

"Let's see if I understand those two numbers," interjects C. "You see the benefits of the facility to Eaglestown, without any of the inconveniences, as worth $50,000. But the inconveniences are sufficiently high that you would need $150,000 to accept the facility, if the alternative were no facility in any of our five towns. Is that it?"

"Yes, that's it."

TABLE 34. *Compensations for a facility.*

Town	Compensation willing to give (in thousands of dollars)	Compensation needed for acceptance (in thousands of dollars)
Aspen	50	200
Baileyville	10	50
Camille	60	3,000
Donnybrook	30	80
Eaglestown	50	150

The parties agree to call the first number CWG ("compensation willing to give") and the second number CNA ("compensation needed for acceptance"). Each agrees to write down a preferred value for CWG and for CNA and to let a reputable adjudicator, Mr. X, resolve their conflict based on the ten numbers (see Table 34). The adjudicator, Mr. X, observes that the facility cannot be built in Aspen, since Aspen needs $200,000 and the other towns are willing to give only $150,000 collectively. Baileyville needs only $50,000, and the others are willing to give Baileyville $190,000. The facility cannot be built in Camille; it can in Donnybrook, and (just barely) in Eaglestown.

ADJUDICATION PROCEDURES

When this problem was used in a laboratory setting, subjects were asked to play the role of the adjudicator and to suggest resolutions of the conflict. Practically all suggested that the facility be located in Baileyville, but they differed on the compensation amounts to be paid by the other towns. According to one suggested procedure, representative B would receive 50/190ths of the CWGs of the various towns—for example, C would pay B the amount 50/190 × $60,000, or $15,790. (Some subjects preferred to interpret this number as 60/190 × $50,000.) This procedure does not give B any surplus value: it provides B just the compensation he needs for Baileyville to accept the facility.

Some subjects observed that since all parties except B were willing to pay $190,000 and B needed only $50,000, the surplus of $140,000 should be split evenly five ways, giving each a surplus of

$140,000/5, or $28,000. Thus, A and E would pay B the amount $50,000 − $28,000, or $22,000; C would pay $32,000 to B; D would pay $2,000 to B; and B would get $50,000 + $28,000 or $78,000, which is also the sum of the payments to B from A, C, D, and E.

Others felt that C should be required to pay a lot because of the excessive size of his CNA. Those who felt that a party's payment to B should depend on that party's CNA *and* CWG felt that A should pay more to B than should E.

Still other subjects felt that B should get at least $80,000, the amount of the second-highest CNA, and get still more if the traffic could bear this total. One subject collected $190,000, gave $80,000 to B, and then divided the surplus of $110,000 into five equal parts, so that B ended up with $80,000 + $110,000/5, or $102,000, for a surplus of $52,000. Some thought that this was reasonable, but that D also deserved a break: "If D's CNA were $51,000, then why should B get a surplus of $52,000 and D a surplus of only $22,000?"

If the town representatives know the scheme to be used by the adjudicator, then they can effectively misrepresent their true values to their own advantage. Notice that it becomes much harder for negotiators to strategically misrepresent their values if they don't know exactly how the announced values will be used—an important point.

There is no truth-dominant scheme for this problem; but there *is* one for an allied problem. Suppose that the state, too, is willing to pay all the necessary compensation to the towns. The state announces that the facility will be built in the town with the lowest announced CNA and that that town will be compensated (by the state) in the amount of the second-lowest announced CNA. In this case, the negotiators should announce their true CNAs. If the announced CNAs are as shown in Table 34, then B gets the facility with a compensation of $80,000. This procedure is truth dominant: no matter what the other representatives report, each negotiator should announce his or her true CNA. However, even in this case B and D could collude to squeeze more out of the state—especially if they firmly believe that the CNAs of the other three parties will be much higher than theirs.

Now let's move a bit closer to reality. The parties are no longer monolithic: the people in each town have different perceptions of appropriate CWGs and CNAs for that town. Indeed, at an Aspen town meeting, a citizen of Aspen wants to know just where the facility would be located if Aspen is chosen as the site. Assume that there are three potential sites within Aspen—A′, A″, and A‴—that could be chosen. The abutters of A′ lobby their representatives: "Not in Aspen! But if in Aspen, then absolutely not at A′!" We now have a microcosm within Aspen of the problem we posed between the five towns: the town of Aspen needs to get CWGs and CNAs from A′, A″, and A‴, and representative A is elevated to play a role analogous to that of the state. The reality probably goes further. Public opinion regarding site A′ is also not monolithic and may fractionate into A_1', A_2', and A_3'; likewise with opinions regarding the other sites.

Another complication: the proposed facility will be built by a developer who must expend time and money to produce design plans for just one site. Costs might differ widely from site to site, for such things as buying up property and obtaining building variances from the towns. It's no wonder that development projects generate litigious actions and counteractions. It may be easier not to do anything—but this is not an efficient solution: firms will end up dumping waste illegally, in part because the towns couldn't come to an agreement. What is needed is some creative side-by-side joint problem solving. These controversies should not be settled primarily in courts, because courts usually resolve disputes on narrow legalistic grounds and because judges and juries seldom seek efficient joint gains for the disputants. Of course, incentives for out-of-court settlements are enhanced by the specter of an uncertain court finding. See O'Hare (1977), and O'Hare and Sanderson (1978).

FACILITY SITING IN MASSACHUSETTS

Industry in the Commonwealth of Massachusetts currently generates 60–100 million gallons of hazardous waste each year; in-state disposal facilities have the capacity to handle less than 10 percent of this amount.[3] As a result, most of the state's hazardous wastes are either transported out of state or are improperly discarded locally. Given that other states are similarly deficient in

3. The material in this section is based on Prosnitz (1981).

waste-disposal capacity, Massachusetts' natural environment is suffering contamination.

In response to this need and to the federal Resource Conservation and Recovery Act of 1976, which requires states to develop their own programs, Massachusetts passed legislation to control the management of hazardous waste. The Massachusetts Hazardous Waste Management Act of 1979 requires regulations for the generation, transport, and disposal of hazardous waste. In addition, the Hazardous Waste Facility Siting Act of 1980 deals with the process for siting facilities within the state.

The 1980 act promotes the use of compensation for siting hazardous waste management facilities (HWMFs) in several ways. First, it provides a structure for negotiations between the developer and the host community. Compensation to the nearby communities by the developer is explicitly included in the act as a legitimate negotiating issue. This demonstrates an institutional recognition that local damages must be compensated for, in order to make proposed HWMFs acceptable to society.

Second, the act stipulates mandatory negotiations between community and developer. Developers cannot simply build facilities as soon as the proper permits are issued; nor can communities reject HWMF proposals out of hand. Both sides are compelled to come to terms with the costs and benefits of the proposed project. Local fiscal and social costs cannot be ignored. To further prevent either side from ignoring the negotiations, the act calls for binding arbitration in the event that no agreement is reached. As a result of this requirement for a negotiated or arbitrated settlement, compensation may be more frequently used, may become better understood, and may perhaps gain acceptance as a proper siting tool.

The 1980 act effectively ensures local participation in the siting process, but at the same time restricts the extent of local control in the outcome: an HWMF proposal cannot be locally vetoed. Although local fiscal and social costs are expected to be incorporated into the developer's cost structure, the burden is on the community to demonstrate the extent of those costs before an arbitration tribunal. In this respect, the developer may have an advantage, but this may be unavoidable. State residents and developers are the primary beneficiaries of the HWMFs, and the act provides a mechanism for redistributing developer benefits as well as making proposed HWMFs acceptable to all.

Can we expect that negotiations will work out to the satisfaction of community and developer? This will depend to some extent on the attitudes of the parties when they approach the negotiating table. Both parties must feel that the process is fair and that there is more to gain by cooperating with each other than not. If a community refuses to bargain with the developer in good faith, it knows that it may be worse off as a result of the arbitration process.

The amount of compensation and its exact composition are negotiable items. The developer will be primarily interested in the cost of the total compensatory package, but the community might have strong preferences regarding the composition of the compensatory package. The community's internal negotiation problem is complex, and a skillful mediator may be needed to help resolve internal disputes within the community.

The developer's reservation price for compensatory payments will depend on whether it can pass these costs on to users of the facility; this in turn will depend on the availability of other facilities, perhaps in other states. The bargaining power of the developer will also be enhanced if the developer can identify alternate communities as potential sites for the facility.

It will be fascinating to see how well this innovative program works in practice.

22

The Mariner Space Probes

In late 1980 the front pages of newspapers were excitedly reporting new discoveries about the planet Saturn. Information was being transmitted to earth by a space probe whose trajectory had been selected by an intricate arbitration procedure. Dyer and Miles (1976) give a fascinating account of the way in which collective choice theory was used to select the trajectories for the Mariner Jupiter/Saturn probes; much of what follows is based upon their account.

THE COLLECTIVE-CHOICE PROBLEM

In September 1973 the National Aeronautics and Space Administration (NASA) announced plans for two exploratory spacecraft, to be launched in August and September 1977. Their trajectories would take them past Jupiter in 1979, and close to Saturn in late 1980 or early 1981. The Jet Propulsion Laboratory (JPL), which was responsible for managing that part of the space program for NASA, attached great importance to the selection of the trajectories because the trajectory characteristics would significantly affect the scientific investigations.

NASA chose some eighty scientists, divided by specialization into ten scientific teams, to help select an appropriate pair of trajectories. Each of these teams had its own special scientific interest (radio science, infrared radiation, magnetic fields, plasma particles) and each team had its own preferences for differing pairs of trajectories. The JPL plan was to have each team articulate its own preferences for trajectory pairs and then to let the Science Steering Group (SSG) choose a compromise pair. The SSG membership comprised one leader from each of the ten teams.

Of the thousands of possible trajectory pairs, the JPL engineers, after some iterative, informal discussions with the scientific teams, reduced the competition to thirty-two contending pairs. Each group was asked first to rank these thirty-two pairs according to its own preferences (with ties between rankings allowed) and then to indicate the relative strengths of its preferences by means of a cardinal utility scale. Each team was told to scale its utility scores by giving its worst trajectory pair a score of zero and its best a score of 1.0. If a given team (say, Team E) scored trajectory pair 17 with a value of .73, then this could be interpreted to mean that Team E evaluated getting trajectory pair 17 for sure as being equally desirable (no more, no less) to getting a chance of .73 at their best alternative and a chance of .27 at their worst alternative.

In thinking about this formally, one could imagine that a decision maker is considering three alternatives—B, C, and D—which are ranked from B, the worst, to D, the best. The intermediate alternative, C, can be said to have a (utility) scale value of x relative to the reference alternatives B and D if the decision maker is indifferent between C on the one hand, and on the other a lottery that yields D with probability x and B with the complementary probability $1 - x$. In terms of this verbal convention we can say that for Team E, trajectory pair 17 is scaled at .73 relative to its worst and best trajectory pairs.

Notice how closely the format of this problem mirrors the discussion in Chapter 16. Instead of two disputants we now have ten competing teams, and instead of a single arbitrator we have an "arbitrating panel," the SSG. The one key difference thus far has to do with the status quo or no-agreement point. (In this context, a proper subset of the ten teams cannot form a coalition and exclude the other teams.) One could not very well say in this context that if the teams are unable to agree, then the space probes will be called off. But it is natural to ask each team to indicate how it feels about its worst trajectory pair relative to two standard reference points: the no-information point and its best trajectory pair. The trajectory pair representing the no-information alternative was dubbed the "Atlantic Ocean Special"—the dismal case where the two vehicles drop ineffectively into the Atlantic without ever soaring into space. Suppose, for example, that Team E scales its worst real alternative at .60 (relative to scoring the Atlantic Ocean Special at zero and its best alternative at 1.0). This would mean that in Team E's opinion, getting its worst real trajectory alternative is just as desirable (no more, no less) as getting a chance of .60 at its best alternative and a chance of .40 at no information.

Team G may think that its worst real alternative, however bad that may be, is so much better than no information that it should be scaled at .99 relative to the no-information alternative and its best real alternative. But the members of Team G may fear that if they admit this, then the SSG will not give due weight to how they feel, comparatively, about the real trajectory pairs lying between their worst and best. So instead of saying .99, perhaps they should strategically misrepresent their true feelings and say .80 or .70. After reflecting still further, Team G might think that the members of Team E will shade their values also; so in order to get their full legitimate weight, maybe they should say .30.

It was apparent to most of the scientists involved that this type of strategic game playing was going on, so the project leader intervened and gave the scientists a lecture on scientific responsibility. Even so, the scientists remained suspicious of one another and did not have complete faith that assessments would be truthfully recorded by the other teams. They felt that the comparative scalings of the real alternative trajectories would be done honestly, but they did not feel this way about the scaling of the worst real alternative relative to the reference points of no information (the Atlantic Ocean Special) and each team's best alternative.

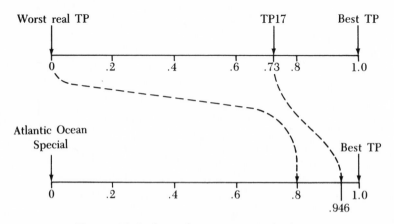

Figure 47. Scaling of trajectory pair (TP) 17.

Suppose that each team's scalings of the real alternatives relative to its worst and best real alternatives are taken as given. Assume that the project leader, in collaboration with members of the SSG, somehow assigns a value that scales each team's worst real alternative relative to the no-information alternative and to that team's best alternative. To take an example, let's say that Team E's worst real alternative is scaled at .80, relative to the no-information state and to its best alternative; and that trajectory pair 17 is scaled by Team E at .73, relative to its worst and best real alternatives (see Figure 47, top). To be consistent, it should now scale trajectory pair 17 at the value .946 (Figure 47, bottom), relative to the no-information state and its best real alternative, since .8 + .73 (1.0 − .8) = .946.

COLLECTIVE-CHOICE PROCEDURES

The collective-choice problem has now been formulated. Each of the ten scientific teams has assigned utility values to the thirty-two real trajectory pairs and to the no-information alternative (the Atlantic Ocean Special); the scales have all been normalized by giving the value of zero to the no-information alternative and the value of unity to each team's best trajectory pair. (See Dyer and Miles for the full set of data.) How should the SSG now decide? Certainly they should require efficiency: they should not recommend a given trajectory pair when there is another trajectory pair that all teams prefer.

Referring back to the discussions between the analyst and arbitrator (Chapter 16), how do you feel in this context about Nash's principle of independent alternatives? To apply this principle here, suppose that trajectory pair 17 is deemed the best overall by the SSG; then the steering group is informed by the JPL engineers that trajectory pair 28 is no longer possible. Is it conceivable that the nonavailability of 28 could cause the SSG to shift from pair 17 (which is still available) to some other trajectory pair? In this context, the principle of independent alternatives seems compelling: if 17 is best overall, it should remain best after 28 is deleted—unless, of course, the reason that 28 has been removed has implications for the desirability of 17. The Nash solution in this case assigns to each trajectory pair a "group score" that is the product of the ten team utility values for that trajectory pair, and then chooses the trajectory pair that maximizes the group score.

The Nash solution satisfies the principle of the independence of irrelevant alternatives and, in addition, it treats each team on a par. If the teams were to be randomly labeled with noninformative letters, and if each team's array of utility values for the trajectory pairs were listed, then would it be appropriate for the SSG to know the identities of the different teams? What do you think? I think that it would. After all, some scientific purposes might be more important than others. If so, then the Nash solution, which treats all teams symmetrically, *abstracts away too much*. Harsanyi (1956) gave an intuitively appealing rationalization for group-scoring each trajectory pair by taking a weighted average of the ten scores for a particular trajectory pair, and then choosing the alternative that maximized this group score (that is, the weighted average). The weights, of course, would have to be supplied by the arbitrator—or, in this case, by the SSG. They would somehow reflect the relative importance of the different scientific teams.[1]

Different collective-choice rules ranked the different trajectory pairs differently. The most commonly accepted rules (Nash and variations of Harsanyi, with some simple interteam weightings) rated three particular trajectory pairs among the top three—but with differences in the rankings of these three. The SSG examined the formal evaluations and selected one of these three top alternatives; however, it did not use any formal procedure to make this final choice. The two individual trajectories of the winning pair were labeled JSI and JSG, where J stood for Jupiter, S for Saturn,

---

1. An abstract version of the collective-choice problem is discussed in Keeney and Raiffa (1976), pp. 515–547. We think of the arbitrator as a benevolent dictator who wants to make a choice for a group of individuals, very much like the case of the SSG in the Mariner trajectories problem. We investigate a scheme that treats individuals differently (like Harsanyi's scheme, which requires interpersonal tradeoffs) and imposes the requirement of independence of irrelevant alternatives (like Harsanyi and Nash); but our scheme is also concerned about equity across individuals. For example, the group score that we would assign to the ten scores associated with a given trajectory pair would depend on the balance among the ten individual scores. If one of the ten utility values for a given trajectory pair is much higher than the others and if this individual utility value were to be further increased in size, then the group score would also go up—but *not* by much, because it would further imbalance equity among the ten utility values.

and I and G for two of Jupiter's satellites, Io and Ganymede, which were to be encountered on the corresponding trajectories.

POSTSCRIPT

In their paper, Dyer and Miles described an unusually candid review of the effect of applied work. After the final trajectories, JSI and JSG, had been chosen, they sent a questionnaire on the trajectory selection process to the members of the SSG; nine of the ten scientific teams responded. Dyer and Miles asked eighteen questions, each requiring a response on a scale from -5 to 5. Depending on the specific question, a response of -5 corresponded to "no," "not useful," "very bad," or "very unfair," while a 5 corresponded to "yes," "very useful," "very good," or "very fair." The responses that were obtained are shown in Table 35.

Dyer and Miles had some specific comments on the responses of Team 3: "Science Team 3 strongly felt that the concept of achieving complementary objectives on the two trajectories was incorrect. This science team preferred two redundant trajectories to maximize the probability of achieving the most important objectives. Thus their principal objection to the trajectory selection process was that the wrong alternatives were being evaluated. For most questions the inclusion of the responses from Science Team 3 make no significant difference in the median response. Only in Question 9 does it change the median response by as much as two units" (p. 240).

It is evident from their responses that the scientists viewed the process with some skepticism: Team 5 was obviously delighted with the process, but Teams 3 and 4 thought otherwise. Of course, in the minds of the evaluators this formal process was compared only vaguely to some "imaginary other process" for conflict resolution. The scientists felt overwhelmingly that the process was fair and that ordinal rankings of the alternatives helped in understanding and in communicating. But they thought that the cardinal utility information was a superfluous addition: with the exception of Team 5, they did not think it was appropriate to scale the worst real trajectory relative to the best trajectory—perhaps because of the mutual distrust of strategic gaming.

TABLE 35. *Responses to Dyer and Miles' questionnaire on the trajectory selection process.*

Question	Median response	Scientific team								
		1	2	3	4	5	6	7	8	9
1. Did the process of ordinally ranking the trajectory pairs aid your understanding of them?	5	5	4	-5	5	5	3	4	5	5
2. Were the ordinal rankings a useful way to communicate your preferences?	3	0	3	-5	5	4	-2	4	0	5
3. Did the assignment of cardinal utility values increase your understanding of the pairs *beyond* what resulted from the ordinal rankings?	0	-2	0	-5	-5	5	4	3	0	3
4. Did the cardinal utility values communicate useful information regarding your preferences *beyond* what was contained in the ordinal rankings?	2	-4	2	-5	-5	4	3	4	0	3
5. Was the assignment of p_ϕ^i using the "no-data" trajectory pair a useful exercise?[a]	-4	0	-4	-5	-5	5	-4	-5	-2	-5
6. Were your cardinal utility values an accurate measure of the science value of your investigation as flown on each trajectory pair?	2	5	2	-5	-5	5	-1	2	-3	3
7. Was the selected trajectory pair good or bad for your team?	3	3	3	-2	3	4	3	5	2	5
8. Were the collective-choice rules a useful way to express group preferences?	-1	0	3	-5	-3	4	-1	4	-2	-4
9. Were these collective-choice rules an accurate measure of the science value of the mission as flown on each trajectory pair?	-2	-5	2	-5	-5	4	-2	4	-2	3

Question										
10. Was the selected trajectory pair a good or bad decision in terms of the science value of the mission?	3	4	3	-2	3	4	3	4	0	5
11. Was "gaming" attempted by members of the SSG?	2	—	0	-5	3	2	2	3	5	0
12. Did "gaming" affect the selection of the trajectory pair?	0	0	-1	-5	5	0	-2	-2	5	0
13. Did the groups have a beneficial or undesirable effect on the trajectory-pair selection?	2	3	-2	0	-3	2	3	4	2	5
14. Was the trajectory-pair selection process fair?	4	4	2	0	5	4	3	4	0	5
15. Would the same trajectory pair have been selected without the development of the ordinal rankings and the cardinal utility values?	2	2	5	5	-2	-3	3	-2	2	5
16. Did the usefulness of the ordinal rankings and the cardinal utility values justify the effort required to generate them?	2[b] 0[c]	0	2	-5	5[b] -5[c]	5	2	3	0	-2
17. Would you like a similar analysis to be performed for critical mission events such as Titan encounters?	-2	0	-2	-5	-5	5	1	3	-2	-3
18. Would you like to repeat the analysis in 1977 to select the trajectory pair to be launched?	0	0	1	-5	-5	5	0	3	-5	-3

a. This question refers to the attempt to get each team to scale its worst trajectory pair relative to the no-information state and its best trajectory pair.
b. Ordinal ranking.
c. Cardinal utility value.
Source: Dyer and Miles (1976), p.239.

This was not a shining success story for formal methods, but neither was it an embarrassing failure. Like so many other experiments in the management of conflict resolution, much more work needs to be done. Dyer and Miles have started us on the right path.[2]

2. The Mariner Jupiter/Saturn 1977 Project was renamed the Voyager Project before launch. Both spacecraft successfully encountered Jupiter and Saturn. Voyager I encountered the moon Titan at Saturn, and Voyager II is proceeding on to Uranus (1986) and Neptune (1989).

23

Voting

When people disagree but must act collectively, they often resort to various voting mechanisms to resolve their conflict. There is a vast literature on voting procedures. My purpose in this chapter is to initiate readers who are not familiar with this literature to some of the intricacies of the problem. Most of the literature presents variations of an original masterpiece written by Kenneth Arrow (1951).

Let's begin with a hypothetical case study.

WYZARD, INC.

Messrs. Wysocki, Yarosh, and Zullo, joint owners of Wyzard, Inc., have to decide whether to start construction of a new Wyzard factory on a site in the town of Cohasset.[1] They all agree that it is imperative for them to start construction of the factory in the next year, but there is some debate about where the new factory should be located.

It had long been anticipated by the joint owners of Wyzard that a new factory would have to be constructed, and three years ago they purchased a plot of land in the town of Allston as a site for the factory. Just two months after purchasing the Allston property, their realtor, Mr. Pumper, told them about another property that was available in the town of Brockton; he offered them the opportunity to swap the Allston property for the Brockton property plus a commission of $5,000. This swapping deal was viewed very favorably by Wysocki and Yarosh, but unfavorably by Zullo.

As early as 1974, when Wysocki, Yarosh, and Zullo started their joint venture, they had anticipated they would have differences of

---

1. I originally prepared this case for class discussion and wonder if a variation of it has ever occurred.

opinion, and they agreed at that time to resolve disagreements by majority rule. They have great respect for one another and have never resorted to strategic voting; each issue is considered separately and voted on, and no log-rolling has ever taken place. They also agreed from the outset that if one of them was outvoted by the others, he would go along with the majority, even if he felt strongly about the issue. Since Zullo was on the losing side of the debate over the Brockton and Allston sites, he gracefully accepted the decision to pay Pumper a $5,000 commission and the three partners agreed to switch to Brockton. But Zullo did some investigating of his own, and with Pumper's help he discovered in the town of Cohasset another site, also owned by Pumper, which he thought was far superior to the Brockton site. Yarosh agreed with Zullo, but Wysocki thought otherwise. Subsequently, Wyzard signed papers with Pumper swapping the Brockton site for the Cohasset site—plus another $5,000 commission to Pumper.

Now, a year later, the three partners meet to discuss the timing for the construction of their new factory. Wysocki is uncomfortable. "I'm unhappy about our situation," he declares. "I still feel that after all our wheeling and dealing we would have been better off with the Allston site."

"What did you say?" demands Zullo. "I always wanted Allston! Why are we then going to build in Cohasset?"

"Now wait a minute, you fellows," interrupts Yarosh. "Cohasset was our agreed-upon choice. We agreed by majority vote that Brockton was better than Allston and that Cohasset was better than Brockton, and we've already paid Pumper $10,000 in commissions."

"I know that," retorts Zullo, "but I agree with Wysocki that Allston is better than Cohasset."

"Look," says Yarosh in a pained manner, "I trusted you two to vote honestly, and here you are scheming against me. Would you really pay Pumper another $5,000 so that we could go back to Allston? That's the silliest thing I ever heard of! What caused you to change your minds?"

"I don't know what you're complaining about, Yarosh. Wysocki and I aren't engaged in any conspiracy. I haven't changed my mind and I'm being perfectly honest. Do you want me to lie to you?"

"Maybe I'm to blame," says Wysocki, "because we seem to be in a ludicrous situation. I really would prefer Allston to Cohasset—but my favorite is still Brockton."

Zullo bangs on the table and says heatedly, "I formally propose that we vote on asking Pumper to give us back our original Allston site. Let's not argue. We long ago agreed on a democratic procedure for resolving conflicts: by good old-fashioned majority vote. So let's get on with it."

This illustration fuses two ideas: (1) majority rule results in intransitive group preferences if the profile of individual rankings exhibits a cyclical preference pattern; and (2) a decision agent that insists on intransitive paired preferences can become a money pump.

The preference rankings for alternatives A, B, C by individuals W, Y, Z are shown in Table 36. Using majority rule, A yields to B, which yields to C, which yields to A, and so on in a circular pattern. Wysocki, Yarosh, and Zullo are *not* strategically misrepresenting their votes; in the vernacular of political science, they are not voting "insincerely." The anomaly arises because of the voting mechanism: majority rule.

Let's change the setting. Suppose that three legislative committee members are about to recommend Bill A. One of the legislators would rather amend A so that it becomes Bill C, but he knows that C will not supplant A by majority rule. Instead, he can first suggest modified Bill B which will beat A, and then he can introduce Bill C which he thinks can beat B. The legislator honestly prefers B to A, so he is voting sincerely; but he is playing strategic games. Is this done in legislatures? I'm afraid so. The trouble is that majority rule is so vulnerable to manipulation.

A single individual can also exhibit intransitivities. There are lots

TABLE 36. *A preference profile that results in an intransitive ordering by majority rule.*

| Preference | Individual | | |
	W	Y	Z
First choice	B	C	A
Second choice	A	B	C
Third choice	C	A	B

of examples where a person might say that he or she prefers B to A, C to B, and A to C. Some of these people might change their minds once this intransitivity is pointed out to them. Others insist, however, in holding firm: "If I'm intransitive, so be it—this is how I feel." An adamant individual might even rationalize his or her preferences: "I am interested in (W)ater accessibility, the availability of a suitable (Y)ard, and in proper (Z)oning. B is better than A on the W and Y qualities; C is better than B on the Y and Z qualities; and A is better than C on the W and Z qualities. I think all qualities are equally important. So, you see, I'm not stupid after all."

Once preferences have been established, the idea of the money pump becomes applicable.[2] How much are you willing to pay to go from A to B? From B to C? From C to A? From A to B? . . .

I'm being pretty harsh on majority rule. I'm purposely leaving aside all its positive aspects, such as simplicity, impartiality, and understandability. All I want to point out here is the long-known result that sometimes majority rule can generate intransitivities in paired comparisons: B over A, C over B, and A over C, and so on. Let's look at some alternatives to majority rule—alternatives that also will exhibit anomalies.

Independence of Irrelevant Alternatives

Wysocki, Yarosh, and Zullo are still upset at their abortive attempt to find a suitable site for their new factory.[3] Their choice problem has become even more complex because their real estate agent, Mr. Pumper, has discovered two additional sites in the towns of Dedham and Essex to add to the existing potential sites of Allston, Brockton, and Cohasset.

Wysocki's daughter Pamela, an M.B.A. student, counsels her father and his partners: "You got into trouble last month because you used majority rule to compare pairs of alternatives. Why don't each of you just rank the five alternatives from best to worst, giving 5 points to the best, 4 points to the second-best, and so on? Then all you have to do is total up the points and see which site wins."

That's what the partners do. This time they're very careful about

2. See Savage (1950).
3. I myself was once faced with the following dilemma, as chairman of a nominating committee to select a president for the Institute of Mathematical Statistics.

their rankings. They take into account not only the physical environments and surrounding amenities, but also the tax structures in the different towns. Their individual rankings are as shown in Table 37; the totals are shown in the far-right column.

"Well," Wysocki says gleefully, "I guess we're going to build in Allston."

Just then Pumper rushes into the meeting and breathlessly and apologetically announces, "I hope you fellows didn't decide on Essex, because I just found out that the property is not zoned for light industry."

"No matter," explains Yarosh. "Essex was not competitive."

Zullo, feeling miserable about the loss of his preferred site, Brockton, plaintively asks Pamela, "If we knock Essex out of the competition how badly does Brockton do then?"

"Well," says Pamela, "let's see . . . Oh no!"

To everyone's surprise, it turns out that when the remaining four sites are reranked, Brockton emerges as the highest-ranked choice. With Essex out of the competition, the points range from 4 for the best to 1 for the worst. Allston gets 9 points; Brockton 10 points; Cohasset 6 points; and Dedham 5 points. So using Pamela's weighting scheme, Allston is best among the full range of competitors; but Allston falls behind Brockton if Essex is removed from the list of contenders.

This anomaly was observed long ago and is quite familiar to theorists. It's worth repeating here, though, because we're talking about mechanisms for resolving conflict and many people don't realize that it's impossible to devise a foolproof scheme.

TABLE 37. *Individual rankings of five alternative sites.*

| Site | Individual ranking (5 = best) | | | Total points (maximum = best) |
	Wysocki	Yarosh	Zullo	
Allston	5	5	2	12
Essex	4	4	1	9
Brockton	3	3	5	11
Cohasset	2	1	4	7
Dedham	1	2	3	6

Insincere Voting

Wysocki and Yarosh are still wondering how they ever got into the mess they're in. They both prefer Allston over Brockton, but Pamela's scheme seems unassailably fair and it dictates that Brockton is the winner once Essex is knocked out. Wysocki feels a bit defensive about Pamela's scheme.

"How did Zullo ever rank Dedham ahead of Allston?" Yarosh asks incredulously.

"Maybe crafty Zullo voted strategically," muses Wysocki.

"I've a great idea," exults Yarosh. "Let's tell Zullo that on reflection we absolutely agree with him that Dedham is better than we originally thought. He can't complain about that. Let's change our rankings and move Dedham right up behind Allston. Then Pamela's scheme will favor Allston."

"That's a good suggestion. But should we be doing this—acting not quite honestly?"

"Well, Zullo started it!"

It's hard enough to get voting schemes that are impervious to insincere voting by a single individual. When coalitions of voters coordinate their misrepresentations, it presents even tougher challenges to designers of voting schemes.

A POTPOURRI

Strategic voting. In Belmont, Massachusetts, twenty candidates may run for twelve open slots for town meeting member. Voters can select twelve names out of the twenty. But they can also select fewer. All selections count equally, and those twelve candidates with the highest total selections are elected. Lots of voters cast their ballots strategically. Some select only three or four candidates. The system does not encourage sincerity. It's hard for any system to do so.

The 1980 presidential election provides another example. Some people preferred Anderson over Reagan over Carter, while others preferred Anderson over Carter over Reagan. Some of these voted for Anderson, but others voted for Reagan or Carter rather than their favorite. The voting mechanism invites this voting misbehavior.

Randomization. Randomization can be used to encourage sincere voting. Let A run against B. Suppose that a candidate will be selected by a random device where the probability that A will win is equal to the proportion of votes A gets. So if A gets 60 percent of the vote, his chances of being selected are .60. (I'm not advocating this scheme—just explaining it!) But now if you favor B and think that you are in a distinct minority, you still have a motivation to vote for your preferred candidate. If this scheme were used with Anderson, Carter, and Reagan, the Anderson supporters would want to vote for their man. If Anderson got 12 percent of the vote, he could be elected with probability .12. Of course, if he were lucky, then lots of people might be very unhappy. The system wouldn't work, but still it would generate sincere voting. The message is that sincerity in voting is a desirable but not a sufficient desideratum.

Strength of preference and log-rolling. In legislatures in the United States, strengths of preference are not directly registered. If 51 percent of legislators are mildly for A and 49 percent are adamantly opposed, then A wins. This is a deficiency in the system, so legislators will try to work around the system by trading or log-rolling their votes. Some observers think that log-rolling distorts the system; others believe that it makes an intolerable system more palatable. Some want to recognize that log-rolling occurs and to institutionalize it so that legislators can fully register the nuances of their preferences—they want to establish a pseudomarket in vote trading, with tradeoffs openly posted. There are schemes like this that encourage honest revelations. To repeat: that's important, but not the only desideratum.

It would be easy to go on at length exploring the intriguing domain of collective choice voting mechanisms. The literature is vast and a good deal of it could be mentioned here, if space allowed.

When many people disagree in the course of trying to make a collective decision, and when there is no institutional mechanism for resolving their conflicts of interest, the contending parties could try to negotiate an outcome directly. They could also try to negotiate the adoption of a mechanism (for example, a voting scheme, an auction or competitive bidding procedure, a pricing system) that might facilitate the resolution of the conflict, or at least structure the ensuing negotiations. The analytical challenge is to design such a mechanism that is fair, equitable, and efficient and that will encourage honest revelations by individuals and groups.

The focus of this book is on the art and science of both negotiation and intervening in negotiations; we have seen that the intervention function includes not only facilitation, mediation, and arbitration, but also rules manipulation. Much of what I have discussed in the last five chapters could be broadly classified under the heading of rules manipulation for conflict resolution. In the last couple of decades there has been a stream of research articles on this topic by political scientists and economists, but most of it is quite abstract, academic, and mathematical. What is needed in addition is a cadre of researchers who will attempt to bridge the chasm between theory and practice. I believe that in the recent theoretical literature there is a wealth of intriguing ideas that could be of practical use to real negotiators; but the people who translate these ideas into useful handbooks will have to be just as intellectually creative as those who write for esoteric journals.

part

V

General Concerns

The final part of this book addresses two topics that apply equally well to two-party negotiations—both distributive and integrative—and to many-party negotiations. To some extent, these topics are even broader than the already broad domain of negotiation.

In Chapter 24 we'll look at some strategies for getting antagonists to talk to each other, sometimes in such a way that they will actually be negotiating without realizing it.

In Chapter 25 we'll examine ethical choices, mostly as they pertain to negotiation; but the discussion is also appropriate for decision making more generally.

In the epilogue, we'll return to the classification given in Part I. We'll see how the approach taken throughout this book—the asymmetric prescriptive/descriptive approach, with emphasis on the role of formal analysis—differs from most other treatments of the subject of negotiation.

24

Getting People to Communicate

There are many fine books that stress the psychology and sociology of negotiations: how people perceive others and are perceived by others, how they interact, how the ambience of negotiations could be altered, how trust and confidence could be established—and some on how to threaten and intimidate others. I have not stressed such "people problems" because my concern here has been to indicate how some modest *analytical* ideas can help negotiators and intervenors. But in most conflicts, the main part of the problem—and a necessary preliminary to analysis—consists in getting people to talk and listen to one another. This chapter deals with four techniques for achieving that goal.

THE OBERGURGL EXPERIENCE

When I was director of IIASA, the leader of our ecology project (one of ten projects overall) asked me to support a rather modest effort designed to show one way to bring analyst and practitioner closer together. The ecology project at that time concentrated most of its efforts on forest and salmon fisheries management. But the leaders of the project, C. S. Holling and Carl Walters of the University of British Columbia, wanted to show that the modeling of physical systems is not the final aim of analysis: those modeling efforts have to be conveyed meaningfully to practitioners. To illustrate this point dramatically, they decided to undertake a diversionary, "small but meaningful" effort in the form of a case study entitled "Obergurgl: A Microcosm of Economic Development." Obergurgl, a small alpine region in Austria (the national home of IIASA), had been rapidly and haphazardly developed under extreme pressures of tourism.

Study after study has indicated that many research modeling efforts are never implemented, because there is a lack of congruence or communication between the modeler and the intended user. Either the wrong problem is formulated, or else the problem is solved in such an esoteric fashion that the user is at a loss to see how it can be applied. Everyone talks about bringing users and modelers together, but precious little is done about it. The Obergurgl study was intended to remedy this deficiency. IIASA helped organize a series of successive workshops, each lasting several days, which examined the interrelated economic-ecological management problems of Obergurgl. The first workshop brought together for a week a small group of ecological modelers, computer specialists, experts on alpine regions, and economists with businessmen and representatives from Obergurgl: hotel managers, town and regional officials, and some plain village folk. They joined together to build a model. You can imagine the problems of communication and language— and I'm not referring to the English-German divide. The innkeeper's idea of a model, for example, was one that had bumps and curves, not mathematical variables. As was expected, the first week's work was a fiasco and the model that was developed had to be scrapped.

The skeptics at IIASA—especially those representatives from Eastern Europe—felt vindicated. But the group tried again and again (for shorter periods of time). The model improved only slightly, but something important happened: the nonscientific contributors from Obergurgl began to talk and to listen to one another. They gained deep insights into their problems and they demonstrated that those insights could be translated into operational policies. They began to communicate not *via* the model but *around* the model, and felt that the effort was worth their while. (The Obergurglians treated the foreign scientists most hospitably, and the skiers at IIASA wanted to join the project.) No papers were written about the resulting model, since none ever materialized; but months later Austria's President Kirschlager, when reviewing IIASA's impact on the country, praised the organization for the way in which it had fostered communication in Obergurgl. The exercise even won over some skeptical visitors from Czechoslovakia, who expressed interest in using similar methods in their own country.

The ecologists had started with a plan to bridge the gap between modeler and practitioner. In this, their success was limited; but inadvertently they achieved something far more important: they helped to bridge the gap between practitioner and practitioner, and that was the key to real progress.

THE COLLIERY EXPERIENCE

In the 1940s the collieries in England were in a deplorable state. Internal labor strife within each colliery was severe and resisted management's efforts toward improvement, until a new management leader named Reginald Revans devised and executed a brilliant scheme. He had each colliery organize a team whose members ranged from lowly workers to top managers. The team from Colliery A was given the task of writing a report on how to achieve better managerial rapport not within their own colliery but within Colliery B! The Colliery B team was assigned to do a similar task for Colliery C; Colliery C for D; and so on, returning finally to A. Colliery B, for example, would profit somewhat from the advice given by Colliery A. But more, much more, would be accomplished from the nonthreatening interactions among the members of Colliery B's team, as they discussed the problems of C.

The Revans Plan was designed to foster communication within each team by focusing members' attention on a problem that was removed from their own, but related enough so that the lessons articulated about that problem could trigger insights into their own. Apparently, the plan was a success.

Revans replicated his plan with a group of hospitals in England, and once again it seemed to get results. People within an organization were persuaded to talk and to listen to one another in a joint, problem-solving effort—focusing on someone else's problem to be sure, but a problem that somewhat resembled their own.

Revans then applied to a foundation for a research grant to experiment further and to document his experiences. I talked to some of the foundation officers, who wanted to know: Was this research? How was it possible to document that the plan was working? How could one be sure that some managerial innovation executed after the Revans plan had been implemented was really attributable to that plan? Today, working on analysis for conflict resolution, I admit the validity of their doubts; but I also appreciate the need for inspirational devices to induce antagonistic people to talk, listen, think, and work together. Revans deserves honorary mention, and his plan should not be forgotten by practitioners in the field of negotiation.

THE NATIONAL COAL POLICY PROJECT AND THE RULE OF REASON

The U.S. National Coal Policy Project is an effort by industrialists and environmentalists to resolve their differences over major coal-related energy policies without resorting to the courts and without exerting their influence in the legislative process. The project was viewed by its founders—principally Gerald Decker, chairman of the industrial caucus, and Laurence Moss, chairman of the environmental caucus—not as a substitute for legislation, but as a means of reaching consensus on recommendations for legislation. Representatives[1] from industry and from environmental groups spent 10,000 person-days preparing the project's first report, *Where We Agree*, published in February 1978.

The project was threatened at its inception in January 1976 by people on both sides who had a vested interest in formal adversarial procedures. The project has also been vigorously attacked by outsiders who are not industrialists or environmentalists and who feel that their voices have not been heard.

Although business can afford to support its representatives in joint activities of this kind, environmental groups are so dependent on volunteer help that it is often hard to maintain a balance in activity level. This was somewhat mitigated in the National Coal Policy Project by paying representatives an honorarium of $150 per day for their participation.

What is intriguing about this experiment is that the group agreed

1. At a planning meeting in January 1976 the following environmental groups were represented: the Environmental Defense Fund, the Environmental Law Institute, the Environmental Policy Center, the National Resources Defense Council, the National Wildlife Federation, the John Muir Institute for Environmental Studies, and the Sierra Club. On the other side were a host of industrial organizations. Funding came from four foundations, four government agencies, and fifty-nine corporations.

at the outset to abide by the code of conduct enunciated by Milton R. Wessel in his book *The Rule of Reason*. The salient points of this code are as follows:

1. Data will not be withheld because they may be "negative" or "unhelpful."
2. Concealment will not be practiced for concealment's sake.
3. Delay will not be employed as a tactic to avoid an undesired result.
4. Unfair "tricks" designed to mislead will not be employed to win a struggle.
5. Borderline ethical disingenuity will not be practiced.
6. Motivation of adversaries will not unnecessarily or lightly be impugned.
7. An opponent's personal habits and characteristics will not be questioned unless relevant.
8. Wherever possible, opportunity will be left for an opponent's orderly retreat and "exit with honor."
9. Extremism may be countered forcefully and with emotionalism where justified, but will not be fought or matched with extremism.
10. Dogmatism will be avoided.
11. Complex concepts will be simplified as much as possible so as to achieve maximum communication and lay understanding.
12. Effort will be made to identify and isolate subjective considerations involved in reaching a technical conclusion.
13. Relevant data will be disclosed when ready for analysis and peer review—even to an extremist opposition and without legal obligation.
14. Socially desirable professional disclosure will not be postponed for tactical advantage.
15. Hypothesis, uncertainty, and inadequate knowledge will be stated affirmatively—not conceded only reluctantly or under pressure.
16. Unjustified assumption and off-the-cuff comment will be avoided.
17. Interest in an outcome, relationship to a proponent, and bias, prejudice, and proclivity of any kind will be disclosed voluntarily and as a matter of course.
18. Research and investigation will be conducted appropriate to the problem involved. Although the precise extent of that ef-

fort will vary with the nature of the issues, it will be consistent with stated overall responsibility to the solution of the problem.

19. Integrity will always be given first priority.

I think that this list defines an ideal mode of behavior for congenial, civilized, cooperative, and constructive interchanges. Even if practice falls far short of the ideal, practice can be uplifted by keeping the ideal in mind.

REGIONAL INSTITUTES

Largely on the basis of my involvement with IIASA, I am motivated to suggest the following proposal: regional institutes should be created to bring neighboring, antagonistic political countries together to work on long-term mutual problems mostly of a technological kind. The problems, of course, would depend on the region, but broadly classified they could include management of common river systems and forests, the development of inhospitable areas (like deserts), the development of energy resources, the expansion and improvement of agriculture, and so on. The institutes would not concentrate on problems of the immediate present, but rather would look ahead to problems affecting local quality of life in the next quarter or half century. In the process of identifying, investigating, and partially solving such long-term problems, representatives of these antagonistic countries may well find that it is easier to talk to one another about more current problems in this less politicized milieu.

Researchers from participating countries would work together formally in interdisciplinary teams on future regional problems, rather than on the politically contentious problems of the day; but the informal agenda could include the latter issues. Depending on the ensuing political climate, the staff of the institute would shift the agenda back and forth from less to more controversial subjects. Regions where such institutes could be of use might be: the Middle East, starting from a nexus between Israel and Egypt; East Africa, including Kenya, Tanzania, Uganda, and Sudan; India, Pakistan, and Bangladesh; Central America, including Mexico; and many others.

In order to protect regional institutes from the political pressures of the moment, they should have nongovernmental status, as is the case with IIASA. Likewise following IIASA's model, the members of these institutes could be representatives of scientific institutions or universities. It's relatively easy to imagine how such regional institutes would work; it's a great deal harder to figure out, in the midst of current controversy, how such institutes could be established. External intervenors, who could also contribute financial enticements, may be indispensable. Such interventions are hard to classify. They don't fall into any standard categories such as mediation or arbitration or rules manipulation.

Skeptics might feel that nobly conceived exercises which devise idealistic futures are merely academic pastimes that may drain resources from other pressing needs. It is my conviction, however, that in these volatile times idealistic plans have to be partially prepackaged, so that contending parties can be ready if and when the window of opportunity opens ever so briefly—perhaps after a crisis.

In summary, it would make good sense if IIASA-like regional institutes could be created in various sensitive regions of the world—institutes that would be nongovernmental and somewhat buffered from today's realities; that would work on idealistic solutions of tomorrow's problems; that would induce political antagonists to work side by side on joint problem-solving tasks that are not politically threatening.

These four illustrations of the ways in which naturally antagonistic people can be brought together to talk and listen to one another are especially appealing to me. Undoubtedly, there are many other mechanisms. The challenge is not simply to think of ideas, but to wrestle with the next creative and far more difficult step: to implement those ideas.

25

Ethical and Moral Issues

Ethical concerns are sprinkled throughout this book; indeed, they are hard to avoid in bargaining and negotiating. Was Steve right when he implied that $300,000 was unacceptable for Elmtree House, when he knew that $220,000 was the value he would be willing to settle for? Are negotiators acting appropriately when they exaggerate what they are giving up on one issue in order to squeeze out a quid pro quo compromise on another issue? Is it improper for a negotiator to imply by his actions that he desperately needs something for his side, when he knows full well that he will give that up at a later stage for something else?

A subject once said to me: "In several of the role-playing exercises I was in a quandary. I didn't know what was ethically right. I was somewhat concerned about others—but how do I know where to draw the line? I didn't want to be callous, but neither did I want to be a starry-eyed, impractical idealist. How should I think about these ethically laden choices?"

Most of the subjects in our experiments had had some education in normative ethics. They had at least read excerpts from the writings of Plato, Aristotle, Augustine, Aquinas, Hume, Kant, Bentham, Mill, and others concerning normative principles of right and wrong. But knowing the distinctions between teleological (result-oriented) and deontological (duty-oriented) frameworks or between monistic and pluralistic frameworks of normative ethics may not help a subject to decide as the City representative negotiating with AMPO whether, in the case of Daniels, to lie or to be quietly misleading or to be open and honest. Normative ethical frameworks are not designed to yield definitive decision procedures, and we should not expect answers from these philosophical teachings and reflections. Indeed, some of these frameworks imply conflicting advice in negotiation contexts. People throughout the ages have worried about these moral issues; they have warred against one another and tried to exterminate one another in defense of their own moral precepts. "My way is better than your way, so take *that*"—"that" being a blow of a fist, a club, a spear, a gun, germ-laden gas, a missile, an atomic bomb, a doomsday weapon. Despite the fact that libraries are filled with books that discuss these important moral and ethical concerns, I still would like to offer some observations on how to think about ethically laden choices.

Disputants often fare poorly when they each act greedily and deceptively. In those cases it's easy to coach *all* participants: they can all jointly gain if they would be less greedy and more open and honest with one another. It's far more difficult to know how to coach one side. Would you advise Steve to tell Wilson that he would settle for $220,000 but would very much like to get $350,000?

Most negotiations are not strictly competitive: there are possibilities for joint gains. For purely selfish reasons, you as a disputant may help yourself by helping your adversaries. This is fine. But even here there is always a tension. As all parties seek joint gains, you still have a preference to favor your side. You not only would like to enlarge the pie, but you want your just share, and what you think is a "just share" may not agree with your adversaries' assessments. How far is it "right" or "appropriate" to push in favoring your own side when it may be to the disadvantage of others?

It's often said that dishonesty in the short run is a poor policy because a tarnished reputation hurts in the long run. The moral question is: Should you be open and honest in the short run because it is right to act that way, even though it might hurt you in the long run?

The hundreds of responses I have obtained to a questionnaire[1] on ethical values are instructive. The distributions of the responses from students of business administration, government, and law are reasonable. But the students do not overwhelmingly say, "That sort of behavior may be borderline in my opinion for others, but is unac-

---

1. "Devon Industries, Inc. (B)," a case study written by Gerald Allan under the supervision of John Hammond. The case describes hypothetical behavior in the construction industry, some of which is borderline or morally reprehensible. The students are asked to rate anonymously on a five-point scale whether specific behaviors are: definitely ethical, ethical so long as everyone else does it, not a matter of ethics, unethical but acceptable, definitely unethical. They are also asked: If *you* were in such a position, what do you think you would do?

ceptable to me." Most say, "If I were in that situation, I also probably would act in that borderline way"; and a few say, "I think that
that behavior is unethical, but I probably would do the same."
That's disturbing to me.

One student defended herself—even though the questionnaires
were anonymous—by stating that most business people in their
ordinary activities are not subjected to those moral dilemmas. And
although she reluctantly admitted that she would act in an unethical manner if she were unlucky enough to be in the position of the
contractor who is being unmercifully squeezed, she would try her
utmost not to get into such situations.

Let's abstract and simplify by looking at a simple laboratory exercise concerning an ethical choice.

A SOCIAL DILEMMA GAME

Imagine that *you* have to choose whether to act nobly or selfishly. If
you act nobly you will be helping others at your own expense; if
you act selfishly you will be helping yourself at others' expense.
Similarly, those others have similar choices. In order to highlight
the tension between helping yourself and helping others, let's
specify that if all participants act nobly, all do well and the society
flourishes; but regardless of how others act, you can always do
better for yourself, as measured in tangible rewards (say, profits), if
you act selfishly—but at the expense of others. Leaving morality
aside for the moment, the best tangible reward accrues to you in
this asocial game if you act selfishly and all others act nobly. But if
all behave that way, all suffer greatly.

To be more concrete, suppose that you are one player in a group
of 101, so that there are 100 "others." You have two choices: act
nobly or act selfishly. Your payoff depends on your choice and on
the proportion of the "others" who choose to act nobly (see Figure
48). If, for example, .7 of the others act nobly, your payoff is $40
when you act nobly and $140 when you act selfishly. Notice that
regardless of what the others do, if you were to switch from noble to
selfish behavior, you would receive $100 more; but because of your
switch, each of the others would be penalized by $2.00 and the total
penalty to others would be $200—more than what you personally
gain. The harm you cause to others, however, is shared: you impose
a small harm on each of many.

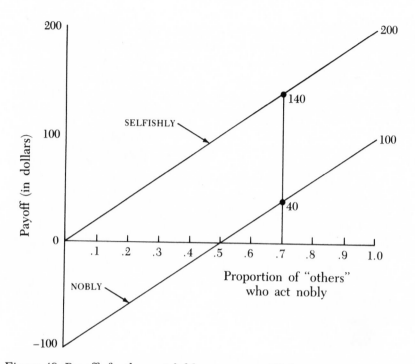

Figure 48. Payoffs for the social dilemma game. (If, for example, .7 of the "others" act nobly, your payoff is $40 when you choose nobly and $140 when you choose selfishly.)

If the others can see that you are acting selfishly, then acting un-selfishly may be your prudent action from a cold, calculating, long-term-benefit point of view. Your good reputation may be a proxy for future tangible rewards. But what if the others (because of the rules of the game) cannot see how you, in particular, behave? Suppose that all anyone learns is how many of the others chose the selfish option.[2]

I learned about this game from Thomas Schelling, who dubbed it the "N-Person Prisoner's Dilemma Game," a direct generalization of that famous two-person game. In the literature, these games are called "social dilemmas" or "social traps," and are sometimes discussed under the heading of "the problem of the commons" or "the free-rider problem." Whenever anyone uses "the commons," there is a little less for everyone else. The "commons" could be a town

2. In the laboratory version of the game I use less connotative terminology: "act cooperatively" instead of "act nobly" and "act noncooperatively" instead of "act selfishly." I'm sure that the mere labeling of these acts influences some behavior.

green, common grazing land, a common river, the ocean, or the atmosphere. Overpopulating our common planet is a prime manifestation of this problem. Whenever we enjoy a public benefit without paying our due share we are a "free rider." One variation of the free-rider problem is the noble-volunteer problem: Will a hero please step forward—and risk his or her life for the good of the many?

Subjects were asked to play this social dilemma game not for monetary payoffs, but *as if* there would be monetary payoffs. There might, therefore, be some distortion in the results—probably not much, but in any case the experimental results are not comforting. Roughly 85 percent of the subjects acted noncooperatively—acted to protect their own interests. Most subjects believed that only a small minority of the others would choose the cooperative (noble) act, and they saw no reason why they should be penalized; so they chose not to act cooperatively. They felt that it was not *their behavior* that was wrong, but the *situation* they were participating in. Unfortunately, many real-world games have these characteristics. A few subjects acted cooperatively because they were simply confused; but others—the really noble ones—knew exactly what was going on and chose to sacrifice their own tangible rewards for the good of the others, even though the others did not know who was acting for their benefit. If the rules of the game were changed to make "goodness" more visible, then more subjects would opt for the noble action—some, perhaps, for long-range selfish reasons. This suggests a positive action program: we should try to identify asocial games (social dilemmas) and modify the rules, if possible (which is easier said than done).

Now let's suppose that you are in a position to influence the 100 others to act nobly by publicly appealing to their consciences. Do you need to influence all to follow your lead? No—you will get a higher monetary return for yourself by converting 50 selfish souls to the noble cause than by joining the ranks of the selfish. But balancing tangible and intangible rewards, you might still prefer to act nobly if you could get, say, 40 conversions; with fewer conversions you might be sacrificing too much. Suppose that you are wildly successful: 75 others join your coalition. Say that 17 of these would have acted nobly anyway; 3 are despicable poseurs who join the nobles but who will defect secretly; and 55 have actually been swayed by your moral pleadings. Now you not only have benefited financially, but you feel morally righteous as well. Unfortunately, your actions have also made it more profitable for the remaining 25 who have not joined your coalition. Each conversion adds $2.00 to the payoff of each of the others, including the selfish holdouts— they've been helped by your successful proselytizing. This may really bother some of the converted ones; it's unfair, they may argue, that the selfish, undeserving ones should profit from the noble actions of the majority. (A real-world analogue is the case where most of the nations of the world might agree not to catch blue whales, and because of this pact it becomes easier for one nonco-operating whaling country to find its prey.) Some of your converts may be so bothered to see that the undeserving are doing better than themselves, that they may decide to defect. They may argue that the coalition is not working, when in absolute terms it may be working for them; but it may not be working in comparative terms. It rankles them that they are helping someone who is taking advantage of their noble behavior. So a few defect, and as a result the coalition can easily come apart.

A DIALOGUE

Once again, a troubled negotiator poses the basic question: "How should I think about ethically laden choices?"

"First of all," I say, "I think it's right that you *should* think about them. Ethical reflections should be a continuing imperative."[3]

"Fine—but how?"

"About 2,500 years ago, Tzu Kung allegedly asked Confucius whether the True Way could be epitomized in one word. Confucius replied: '*Reciprocity:* do not to others what you do not want them to do unto you.' During the reign of Herod the Great in Palestine, Rabbi Hillel repeatedly echoed this injunction, and decades later Jesus preached this as the Golden Rule."

"That still doesn't tell me whether Steve did wrong when he intimated that he would not settle for $250,000. As a City player against

3. A paraphrase from "Basic Frameworks for Normative Ethics," a case study prepared by Kenneth E. Goodpaster, p. 1. See the bibliography, under the heading "Case Studies."

AMPO, would I do wrong if I acted as if I wanted Commissioner Daniels when I secretly desired to get rid of him?"

"Well, here's a way of thinking that probably doesn't go back to Confucius: before you act, think of facing yourself in the mirror tomorrow.[4] Is this the person you would like to see? Would you feel comfortable discussing your actions with your spouse? Your children? Your friends? Let's refer to this cluster of concerns as *self-respect*."

"I'm still confused," the negotiator persists. "You're telling me to think about the Golden Rule and to think about my self-respect. You're not telling me to always obey the Golden Rule or to always honor my self-respect. How does that help Steve in his negotiations for Elmtree House?"

"I'm trying to be helpful, but it's not easy to be dogmatic about these issues," I say hesitatingly. "Unfortunately, for me, there is no overarching atomistic, moral premise from which everything else flows. Unlike Kant, I recognize no categorical imperative that I think is universally applicable. I can always think of counterexamples, such as the fact that I would lie or steal or kill to save my country or to save multitudes of innocent people. The best I can do is draw upon various schools of philosophical thought and enunciate principles that are important to reflect upon when I am at a morally intricate decision node."

"But once you have several principles of moral behavior, they may conflict in a given situation. Should you lie, or break a promise? Aren't you troubled by that?"

"Certainly I am. But before we talk about coping with inconsistencies, let's formulate a few more principles that may be relevant in bargaining and negotiating."

Another negotiator asks: "Don't you think there is enough guilt in our society? Are you telling us to be ashamed to look at ourselves in the mirror if we don't live by the Golden Rule? It seems to me that the very art of negotiation involves some amount of deception and some skillful exercise of power. Should I be ashamed of the fact that in one negotiation exercise I purposely linked two issues so that I could use the threat power of one issue to get what I wanted on the other? That's done all the time. If I'm not for myself, who will be?"

4. See Drucker (1981).

"If something is done all the time, that doesn't make it right. Certainly I would agree with you that in judging the morality of one's proposed actions, one should reflect on the norms of society. But society would change for the better if each of us tried to nudge it in more righteous ways. It's a matter of degree. Before taking an action you might ask yourself: What kind of society would we be living in if everyone acted the way I'm about to act? Or: If I remove myself from involvement in the situation and if I imagine that someone else is occupying my role, how would I as a disinterested party advise that other person to behave, taking into consideration what's right for that person, what's right for other protagonists in the negotiation, and what's right for society? There's an implicit contractual understanding in our social obligations."

The negotiator is not satisfied. "But these rights—to myself, to others, and to society—might, and usually do, conflict. That's the problem. If I'm an interested party, and if I can help myself at the expense of someone else, how should I weigh my interests against my perception of the interests of others? This is what I find hard to answer."

"You're not the only one. I, too, find the line hard to draw. But we're talking about ways to think about the problem. You might imagine yourself and the other negotiators in an original position where you as yet do not know the roles each of you will assume. In this ex ante position, what would be a reasonable contract for behavior to guide the mutual actions of all? How would you agree ahead of time that in the position you now find yourself, someone— not necessarily yourself—should act? This is something you might think about."

"Thinking is easy. Acting is hard. If I did this, and tempered my actions accordingly, I would be at a competitive disadvantage if my altruistic behavior were not reciprocated. Behave unto others as you don't expect them to behave unto you. Is that it?"

"No, that's not it! I'm trying to tell you to be conscious of and to reflect about conflicting rights—to be more conscious of others and of long-run societal interests."

Another negotiator joins the discussion. "That last piece of advice cuts two ways," she says. "An employer might want to fire a worker who is incompetent but who desperately needs the money. The employer might also empathize with the worker and decide that the bit of extra profit he could gain by the dismissal is not worth the harm that would be done to this loyal but not-too-bright worker. However, if the employer thinks of the big picture, thinks of the long-run interests of society, then perhaps he should fire the man. As a whole, society may be better off if employers were tough-minded about efficiency. If employers fire incompetents, they make places available for competent people, and with increased efficiency more jobs may be created. That's part of the free-enterprise ethic."

"I grant you the point that we sometimes have to take actions that have short-run liabilities for long-run gains—actions that appear to be hard-hearted. I agree that in thinking about society as a whole, one should think about secondary, tertiary, and long-range effects as well as immediate effects. But I would violently argue against a philosophy saying that since I can't predict what's going to happen in the long run, I might as well look after myself right now. Well-meaning people can have different assessments of long-run effects for some cases, but there are lots of other cases where the answers will be perfectly transparent. For instance, society and the free-enterprise system would be better off if people didn't tamper with the odometers of used cars before selling them, if advertisers didn't falsify information about the safety of products, if realtors informed prospective home buyers that a particular furnace or a particular roof was in poor repair."

"Wait a minute on that last one," interjects one of my interrogators. "Selling and buying is a little like the legal system. Lawyers are advocates: they select the material they choose to disclose to favor their side. It's up to the other party to protect itself. Am I, as the seller of an automobile, supposed to tell the buyer that my car is not as good as another on qualities P, Q, and R? I would rather be quiet about P, Q, and R and tell him my car is much better than the other car on qualities S, T, U, V, and W. And I might be stretching the point on qualities V and W. This is part of the bargaining game."

"I'm not sure I agree. We'd be better off if we were a lot more honest with each other in bargaining and negotiating. A lot of adversarial bickering should be replaced by collegial, joint-problem-solving interchanges. Remember those nineteen points of the Rule of Reason used in the National Coal Policy Project."

"That's fine for the National Coal Policy Project, but I'm a small businessman in the construction industry; and if I were to behave with my customers on a complete-disclosure basis, I'd be out of business in a flash. I don't lie in the factual assertions I make; but certainly I should be allowed, like everyone else, to choose material selectively to favor my side."

"I'll grant you the point that a competitive imperative may force you toward a norm of behavior that is a fact of life in marketing and advertising. But there are degrees. As a business leader, you should set higher ethical standards for yourself than you perceive are commonplace around you: exemplary behavior on your part can influence the behavior of others. You should strive by your own behavior to improve the standards of morality in business. Just as in the social dilemma game, it's not necessary for you to influence all the others to act cooperatively before it's worth your while to shift from noncooperative to cooperative behavior. And remember, there's a dynamic at play here: if you act in society's interest, others might not only follow suit but they in turn will influence others. People help create the society they live in. If they want to live in a more cooperative society, they can do so, though possibly at some cost to themselves. Most people, I believe, are willing to sacrifice a little for a more ethical world, but only so much. Many processes in our society do not exploit this limited altruism. We should seek ways to change the world, or small parts of it, to take advantage of people's willingness to sacrifice a little bit of their own comfort for the general good."

"You're saying that aspiring leaders should shun behavior that they would not respect in others—that they should be exemplars. But if someone followed that gospel, he or she probably would not become a leader. Do you know a political leader who can truthfully expose his full record? Compromises have to be made. Would you blame someone who acted improperly on a minor issue so that he could be in a position to stand up for his principles on really major issues? Are you saying that virtuous ends can't ever justify means that fail a morality test?"

"I'm not an absolutist. In special circumstances I might condone actions that, in general, I do not deem ethically appropriate; but a lot of harm comes from an overly cavalier attitude about 'ends justifying means.' I believe that many people who intuitively do this type of benefit-cost analysis do it poorly: they do not adequately consider the effects of linkages and precedents. If an immoral action (means) is adopted for glorious ends, it makes it easier for others to adopt similar actions for not-so-glorious ends. We're on a slippery slope, and it's hard to know where to draw the line."

"Exactly," says yet another negotiator. "I don't at all like your utilitarian-tradeoffs philosophy. There are certain actions that are just plain wrong in an absolute sense, and no analysis of consequences can justify them. Unless certain basic principles are inviolate, people can justify or rationalize any foul deeds."

"You're taking the strong deontologist position—that there are absolute rights or wrongs regardless of the consequences. Those who are religious believe that these are God-given. But, as I said before, I don't know of any overarching deontological principle from which all other moral principles derive. At least, I don't know of any single principle that could operationally guide my behavior, even though most of the several deontological principles that are offered seem appropriate heuristic guides for my behavior. But I must admit that I think they're appropriate because of my utilitarian calculations. If one adopts, as I do, a broad-gauged, rules-oriented, utilitarian framework, with a little deontological and contractarian reasoning thrown in, then this viewpoint, while flexible, is not operational: it does not specify appropriate actions. One needs heuristic guidelines or auxiliary principles for ethical behavior; one cannot always go back to basic principles. So as I see it, whether one adopts a deontologist or a teleologist (result-oriented) position or a mixture of the two, one must be guided by a workable, operational set of ethical principles. And one should then realize that these principles may occasionally conflict with one another. But these principles are guidelines not to be broken lightly! As Thomas Schelling so aptly put it: 'Compromising a principle sounds wrong; but compromising between principles sounds right.' And compromising, after all, is what negotiation is all about."

Another negotiator obviously thinks that we have reached the point of diminishing returns: "This conversation has meandered over a wide terrain in normative ethics. Can you summarize any insights you have from an analyst's perspective?"

"Well, as an analyst I believe that most utilitarian calculations in situational ethics are too narrowly conceived. In a loose sense, all of us are engaged in a grandiose, many-person, social dilemma game where each of us has to decide how much we should act to benefit others. The vast majority of us would like to participate in a more cooperative society, and all of us may have to make some sacrifice in the short run for that long-run goal. We have to calculate, at least informally, the dynamic linkages between our actions now and the later actions of others. If we are more ethical, it makes it easier for others to be more ethical. And, as was the case in the multiperson social dilemma game, we should not become excessively distraught if there are a few cynical souls who will tangibly profit by our combined beneficent acts.

"If you act to help others and hurt yourself in the short run, and if your act is visible to others, you may profit from it in the long run because of cyclical reciprocities. In that sense, your noble-appearing action may be in your selfish interest. But we should not demean visible acts of kindness, even though in part they may be self-serving, because your actions may make it easier for others to act similarly, and the dynamics reinforce behavior that is in the common interest. An action that represents a moderate sacrifice in the short run may represent only a very modest sacrifice in the long run, when dynamic linkages are properly calculated. And as I said before, many people are willing to make small (long-run) sacrifices for the good of others, all things considered. The visibility of beneficent acts thus plays a dual role: it reduces the tangible penalties to the actor, and it spurs others to act similarly; these two facets then interact cyclically. Finally, empathizing with others may be reflected in your own utility calculations: a sacrifice in long-range tangible effects to yourself, if it is compensated by ample gains for others, could be tallied as a positive contribution to your cognitive utilitarian calculations."

"That's wonderful," says my first questioner. "Now tell me, how do I use all this sermonizing to decide what I, as a City player, should do about Daniels?"

"That's left as an exercise."

Epilogue

It's time to take stock. I could go on to analyze other examples of negotiations: international arms-limitation talks, economic trade agreements, cartels, divorce mediation, global negotiations with developing countries, corporate takeovers, and so on. Frankly, if space and time permitted, I would be sorely tempted to include such additional material in this book, since one of my pedagogic aims is to broaden the horizons of people who think narrowly about negotiations. Executives, for example, frequently assert that they're not interested in the role of the intervenor in conflicts because that's not what they do as businessmen. It always gives me special pleasure when, during seminars on negotiation, such executives realize that mediating conflict is what they do all the time in the internal management of their organizations. Executives rarely think of themselves as mediators, even while they mediate.

Many of the ideas developed and formalized in this book are well understood by men and women of experience—but understood in the world of practice, and not in the world of thought. Practitioners often act intuitively in bargaining situations in ways that are far more sophisticated than they can conceptualize and articulate. I do believe, however, that even sophisticated practitioners of the art of negotiation can profit by contrasting negotiations in their own field with those in other fields; they can profit by reflecting about what lies within the common core of most negotiation problems, and also about what lies outside this core and is somewhat special to the narrower class of their own negotiating problems; and they can profit merely by labeling recurrent key concepts in this common core, such as reservation prices, value tradeoffs, joint gains, contingency contracts, and efficient frontiers. In this way, they gain a deeper un-

357

derstanding of what they are actually doing and can better communicate these insights to others who have been similarly sensitized.

But my aim in writing this book goes deeper. Often, disputants fail to reach an agreement when, in fact, a compromise does exist that could be to the advantage of all concerned. And the agreements they do make are frequently inefficient: they could have made others that they all would have preferred. It is here that systematic analysis can be of service to the negotiator, facilitator, mediator, arbitrator, and rules manipulator. I am not thinking of any grandiose new kind of analysis specially devised for problems of negotiation, but of simple prosaic analysis that is part of the curriculum of most schools of business and public policy: What are your alternatives? What are your objectives? How do your objectives conflict? What are your value tradeoffs? What are the primary sources of uncertainty that you face? What objective data do you have that bear on these uncertainties? How can you tap the knowledge of relevant experts, and what are their biases? Can you defer action and accumulate further information before you commit yourself?

These questions and their action implications constitute a framework of thought that applies to most decision problems. What is often overlooked is that this framework also applies to problems of negotiation. But in the subclass of decision problems that is peculiar to the domain of negotiation, a new class of concerns arises: What are the interests, motives, concerns of the other negotiating parties? What are their alternatives to a negotiated agreement? What are the opportunities for exploiting differences in values, beliefs, constraints? How should you share information for joint problem-solving without making yourself too vulnerable when the (hopefully enlarged) pie has to be partitioned? Interpersonal skills are critically important in the negotiation exchange, but so is analysis; and too many courses in negotiation stress interpersonal bargaining skills at the expense of analysis. My intention in this book is not to minimize the importance of interpersonal skills, but to balance the ledger a bit.

This is *not* a book addressed primarily to analysts and academics; it neither introduces a new, nor enhances an old, theory of the negotiation process. Rather, it is addressed to practitioners of negotiation—and they are legion. It publicizes a need and an opportunity for them to think more systematically and consciously, and in a more conceptually integrated fashion, about the dynamics of negotiation.

The principal theme of the book is that analysis—mostly simple analysis—can help. It can help a single negotiating party as he thinks reflectively about what he (prescriptively) should do, given his assessment of what others, in some quasi-rational descriptive sense, might do. Thus, the book departs from the traditional game theory approach, which simultaneously analyzes highly rational behavior of all negotiating parties who are constantly thinking iteratively about one another's thoughts. In certain highly repetitive simple problems this type of equilibrium theory, so reminiscent of game theory, is highly relevant; and even in more intricate problems for which iterative interactive thinking has its limitations and is not directly relevant to a specific case, the theory could nevertheless be of practical relevance to the rules manipulator who is concerned about how actual fallible players might play after they absorb a modicum of evolutionary learning.

The approach of this book has been asymmetrically prescriptive/descriptive: prescriptive for yourself as a protagonist when pitted against the highly uncertain descriptive behavior of others. It has also been prescriptive with regard to the intervenor, whether facilitator, mediator, arbitrator, or rules manipulator. There are, of course, intervenors who do not fit very well into any of these categories. Five important points are worth reiterating.

First, in hierarchical organizations, both private and public, the executive is often cast in the role of an intervenor in disputes. So, too, is the shop foreman, the lawyer, the newspaper editor, the university department head, the military leader—even the mother who intervenes in disputes among siblings.

Second, a negotiator, representing one side of a dispute, might simultaneously play the intervenor's role as he confronts disparate, conflicting advice from others on his side of the bargaining table.

Third, a protagonist in an ongoing negotiation may wish at some stage to suggest, or may need to react to the suggestion of, the intervention of an outside party. The protagonist should therefore be able to assess the potential implications of such a move and should be creative about the many forms that this intervention can take.

Fourth, negotiation and intervention are so intimately connected conceptually that training in one can enhance performance in the other. Thus, for example, a negotiator may suggest the adoption of a negotiation procedure that might have been suggested by an intervenor; or a negotiator might suggest a "fair" outcome that results from, and is rationalized by, an arbitration mechanism (for example, a disadvantaged player might suggest the Shapley Value outcome in a coalition-type confrontation). On the other side, an intervenor constantly has to assess the reaction of the negotiating principals to any proposal he makes; such an intervenor should understand how negotiators behave. (This is another variation of the prescriptive/descriptive dichotomy.)

Fifth, in many-party negotiations it may be desirable for one of the negotiating parties occasionally to play the role of an outside intervenor, and to move back and forth between these two roles.

In closing, let me draw an analogy. There are beautiful economic theories of the firm that explain, to a first approximation, how firms do behave or should behave. But when one gets close to the actual problems of decision makers within firms, these general theories are too vague to be operationally relevant. At the level of the firm, what is needed—among other things, to be sure—is a bag of analytical tools along with a sprinkling of specialists who know about these tools and who can interact on an ad hoc, consultative basis with decision makers. I'm thinking not only of operations researchers and decision analysts, but of analytically trained financial specialists, marketing specialists, and specialists in other functional areas of the firm.

Just so in negotiations. There are beautiful theories of the negotiation process that explain, to a first approximation, how negotiators do behave or should behave. But, as in the theory of the firm, these theories are not operational; and in spite of them, all too often no systematic analysis, or even partial analysis, is employed in practice. A certain amount of analysis can be of help to negotiators and intervenors in many different ways. The need is not for the creation of new analytical techniques specially designed for the negotiation process, but rather for the creative use of analytical thinking that exploits simple existing techniques.

Bibliography

Arrow, Kenneth. 1951. *Social Choice and Individual Values.* Cowles Commission Monograph 12. New York: John Wiley.

Ashenfelter, O. A., and G. E. Johnson. 1969. "Bargaining Theory, Trade Unions, and Industrial Strike Activity." *American Economic Review* 59: 35–49.

Astante, Samuel K. B. 1979. "Restructuring Transnational Mineral Agreements." *American Journal of International Law* 73: 335–371.

Axelrod, Robert. 1967. "Conflict of Interest: An Axiomatic Approach." *Journal of Conflict Resolution* 11 (January): 87–99.

———— 1970. *Conflict of Interest: A Theory of Divergent Goals with Applications to Politics.* Chicago: Markham.

Barclay, Scott, and Cameron R. Peterson. 1976. "Multi-Attribute Utility Models for Negotiations." Technical Report 76-1 (May). McLean, Va.: Decisions and Designs, Inc.

Bartos, Otomar J. 1974. *Process and Outcome of Negotiations.* New York: Columbia University Press.

———— 1977. "Simple Model of Negotiation: A Sociological Point of View." *Journal of Conflict Resolution* 21, no. 4: 565–579.

Beal, Edwin F.; Edward D. Wickersham; and Philip K. Kienast. 1976. *The Practice of Collective Bargaining.* Homewood, Ill.: Richard D. Irwin.

Bell, David E., and Howard Raiffa. 1980. "Marginal Value and Intrinsic Risk Aversion." Working Paper Series 79-65. Cambridge, Mass.: Graduate School of Business Administration, Harvard University.

Bishop, Robert L. 1964. "A Zeuthen-Hicks Theory of Bargaining." *Econometrica* 32: 410–417.

———— 1967. "Game Theoretic Analyses of Bargaining." *Quarterly Journal of Economics* 77: 559–602.

Blaker, Michael. 1977. *Japanese International Negotiating Style.* New York: Columbia University Press.

Bok, Sissela. 1978. *Lying: Moral Choice in Public and Private Life.* New York: Vintage.

Bove, Alexander A., Jr. 1979. Article in *Boston Globe,* Monday, July 16, 1979.

Burrows, James C. 1979. "The Net Value of Manganese Nodules to U.S. Interests, with Special Reference to Market Effects and National Security." In *Deepsea Mining.* Cambridge, Mass.: MIT Press.

Callières, François de. 1716. *On The Manner of Negotiating with Princes.* Trans. A. F. Whyte. Boston: Houghton Mifflin, 1919; originally published Paris: Michel Brunet.

Center for Strategic and International Studies. 1978. *Where We Agree.* First Report of the U.S. National Coal Policy Project. Washington, D.C.: Georgetown University.

Chatterjee, Kalyan. 1978. "A One-Stage Distributive Bargaining Game." Working Paper 78-13 (May). Cambridge, Mass.: Graduate School of Business Administration, Harvard University.

—— 1979. *Interactive Decision Problems with Differential Information.* Dissertation, Harvard University.

—— and William Samuelson. 1981. "Simple Economics of Bargaining." Distribution paper. Boston: Boston University.

Chelius, James R., and James B. Dworkin. 1980. "An Economic Analysis of Final-Offer Arbitration." *Journal of Conflict Resolution* 24, no. 2 (June): 293–310.

Coddington, A. 1966. "A Theory of the Bargaining Process: Comment." *American Economic Review* 56: 522–530.

—— 1968. *Theories of the Bargaining Process.* London: Allen and Unwin.

Cohen, Stephen P.; Herbert C. Kelman; Frederick D. Miller; and Bruce L. Smith. 1977. "Evolving Intergroup Techniques for Conflict Resolution: An Israeli-Palestinian Pilot Workshop." *Journal of Social Issues* 33: 165–189.

Contini, B. 1967. "The Value of Time in Bargaining Negotiations: Part I, A Dynamic Model of Bargaining." Working Paper 207. Berkeley: Center for Research in Management Science, University of California.

Cormick, Gerald W., and Jane McCarthy. 1974. *Environmental Mediation: A First Dispute.* Seattle: Office of Environmental Mediation, University of Washington.

Cormick, Gerald W., and Leota Patton. 1977. *Environmental Mediation: Defining the Process Through Experience.* Seattle: Office of Environmental Mediation, University of Washington.

Corsi, Jerome. 1981. Terrorism as a Desperate Game. *Journal of Conflict Resolution* 25, no. 1: 47–85.

Cross, J. G. 1965. "A Theory of the Bargaining Process." *American Economic Review* 55: 66–94.

—— 1966. "A Theory of the Bargaining Process: Reply." *American Economic Review* 56: 530–533.

—— 1968. *The Economics of Bargaining.* New York: Basic.

Deutsch, Morton. 1977. *The Resolution of Conflict: Constructive and Destructive Processes.* New Haven: Yale University Press.

Drucker, Peter F. 1981. "What is Business Ethics?" *The Public Interest* 63 (Spring): 18–36.

Druckman, Daniel. 1977. *Negotiations: Social-Psychological Perspectives.* Beverly Hills, Calif.: Sage Publications.

Duker, Robert P. 1978. "The Panama Canal Treaties: An Honorable Solution?" Unpublished paper. Washington, D.C.: National War College.

Dunlop, John, and James J. Healy. 1953. *Collective Bargaining: Principles and Cases.* Homewood, Ill.: Richard D. Irwin.

Dyer, J. S., and R. F. Miles, Jr. 1976. "An Actual Application of Collective Choice Theory to the Selection of Trajectories for the Mariner Jupiter/Saturn 1977 Project." *Operations Research* 24: 220–224.

Edwards, Harry T., and James J. White. 1977. *The Lawyer as a Negotiator.* St. Paul, Minn.: West Publishing Co.

Environmental Mediation: An Effective Alternative? 1978. Report of a conference held in Reston, Va., January 11–13, 1978. Palo Alto, Calif.: RESOLVE, Center for Environmental Conflict Resolution.

Farber, H. S. 1978. "Bargaining Theory, Wage Outcomes, and the Occurrence of Strikes." *American Economic Review* 68: 262–271.

Feuille, Peter. 1975. *Final-Offer Arbitration: Concepts, Developments, Techniques.* Chicago: International Personnel Management Association.

Fisher, Roger. 1978. *International Mediation: A Working Guide.* New York: International Peace Academy.

Fisher, Roger, and William Ury. 1979. "Principled Negotiation: A Working Guide." Unpublished manuscript. Cambridge, Mass.: Harvard Law School.

—— 1981. *Getting to Yes: Negotiating Agreement Without Giving In.* Boston: Houghton Mifflin.

Fried, Charles. 1978. *Right and Wrong.* Cambridge, Mass.: Harvard University Press.

Friedman, James W. 1977. *Oligopoly and the Theory of Games.* Amsterdam: North-Holland.

Goffman, Erving, 1972. *Strategic Interaction.* New York: Ballantine.

Groves, Theodore, and John Ledyard. 1977. "Optimal Allocation of Public Goods: A Solution to the 'Free Rider' Problem." *Econometrica* 45: 783–809.

Gulliver, P. H. 1979. *Disputes and Negotiations.* New York: Academic Press.

Harsanyi, John C. 1955. "Cardinal Welfare, Individualistic Ethics, and Interpersonal Comparisons of Utility." *Journal of Political Economy* 63: 309–321.

—— 1956. "Approaches to the Bargaining Problem before and after the Theory of Games: A Critical Discussion of Zeuthen's, Hicks', and Nash's Theories." *Econometrica* 24: 144–157.

—— 1965. "Bargaining and Conflict Situations in the Light of a New Approach to Game Theory." *American Economic Review* 55: 447–457.

—— 1977. *Rational Behavior and Bargaining Equilibrium in Games and Social Situations.* Cambridge: Cambridge University Press.

Haynes, John M. 1981. "A Conceptual Model of the Process of Family Mediation." Unpublished paper.

Iklé, Fred Charles. 1964. *How Nations Negotiate.* New York: Harper and Row.

Jackson, Elmore. 1952. *Meeting of Minds: A Way to Peace Through Mediation.* New York: McGraw-Hill.

Jenkins, B. M. 1974. "Terrorism and Kidnapping." Paper Series P-5255. Santa Monica, Calif: RAND Corporation.

Kahneman, D., and A. Tversky. 1979. "Prospect Theory: An Analysis of Decision under Risk." *Econometrica* 47: 263–290.

Kalai, E. 1977. "Proportional Solutions to Bargaining Situations: Interpersonal Utility Comparisons." *Econometrica* 45: 1623–30.

—— and M. Smorodinsky. 1975. "Other Solutions to Nash's Bargaining Problem." *Econometrica* 43: 510–518.

Karni, E., and A. Schwartz. 1977. "Search Theory: The Case of Search with Uncertain Recall." *Journal of Economic Theory* 16: 38–52.

——— 1978. "Two Theorems on Optimal Stopping with Backward Solicitation." *Journal of Applied Probability* 14: 869–875.

Karrass, Chester L. 1968. "A Study of the Relationship of Negotiator Skill and Power as Determinants of Negotiation Outcome." Dissertation, University of Southern California.

——— 1970. *The Negotiating Game: How to Get What You Want.* New York: Thomas Y. Crowell.

——— 1974. *Give and Take: The Complete Guide to Negotiating Strategies and Tactics.* New York: Thomas Y. Crowell.

Katz, Ronald. 1979. "Financial Arrangements for Seabed Mining Companies: An NIEO Case Study." *Journal of World Trade Law* 13: 218.

Keeney, Ralph, and Howard Raiffa. 1976. *Decisions with Multiple Objectives: Preferences and Value Tradeoffs.* New York: John Wiley.

Kochan, Thomas A., and Todd Jick. 1978. "The Public Sector Mediation Process: A Theory and Empirical Examination." *Journal of Conflict Resolution* 22, no. 2 (June): 209–238.

Lax, David, and James K. Sebenius. 1981. "Insecure Contracts and Resource Development." *Public Policy* 29, no. 4: 417–436.

Livne, Zvi. 1979. *The Role of Time in Negotiations.* Dissertation, Massachusetts Institute of Technology.

Lorange, Peter. 1973. "Anatomy of a Complex Merger: Case Study and Analysis." *Journal of Business and Finance* 5.

Luard, Evan. 1977. *The Control of the Seabed: An Updated Report.* New York: Taplinger.

Luce, R. Duncan, and Howard Raiffa. 1957. *Games and Decisions.* New York: John Wiley.

McCormick, B. 1977. "On Expectations, the Value of Time, and Uncertainty in the Bargaining Process." Unpublished note. Cambridge: Cambridge University.

McCullough, David. 1977. *The Path Between the Seas.* New York: Simon and Schuster.

Myerson, R. M. 1977. "Two-Person Bargaining Problems and Comparable Utility." *Econometrica* 45: 1631–37.

——— 1979. "Incentive Compatability and the Bargaining Problem." *Econometrica* 47: 61–74.

Nash, John F. 1950. "The Bargaining Problem." *Econometrica* 18: 155–162.

——— 1953. "Two-Person Cooperative Games." *Econometrica* 21: 129–140.

New York Times. 1981. "Suddenly, Heavy Weather for Talks on Law of the Sea." March 15, p. E5.

New York Times. 1981. "Law of Sea Parley in a Waiting Game." August 16, p. A11.

Nierenberg, Gerald I. 1973. *Fundamentals of Negotiating.* New York: Hawthorne.

Nydegger, R., and G. Owen. 1975. "Two-Person Bargaining: An Experimental Test of the Nash Axioms." *International Journal of Game Theory* 3: 239–249.

O'Hare, Michael. 1977. "'Not on *My* Block You Don't': Facility Siting and the Strategic Importance of Compensation." *Public Policy* 25: 407–458.

—— and Debra Sanderson. 1977. "Fair Compensation and the Boomtown Problem." *Urban Law Annual* 14: 101–133.

Owen, G. 1968. *Game Theory.* Philadelphia: W. B. Saunders.

Pratt, J., and R. Zeckhauser. 1979. "Expected Externality Payments: Incentives for Efficient Decentralization." Unpublished paper. Cambridge, Mass.: Graduate School of Business Administration, Harvard University.

Prosnitz, Eric W. 1981. "Using Compensation for Siting Hazardous Waste Management Facilities and the Massachusetts Act." Unpublished paper. Cambridge, Mass.

Raiffa, Howard. 1953. "Arbitration Schemes for Generalized Two-Person Games." In *Annals of Mathematics Studies.* Princeton: Princeton University Press.

—— 1968. *Decision Analysis: Introductory Lectures on Choices under Uncertainty.* Reading, Mass.: Addison-Wesley.

—— 1981. "Decision Making in the State-Owned Enterprise." In *State-Owned Enterprise in the Western Economies,* ed. Raymond Vernon and Yair Aharoni. London: Croom Helm.

Ramberg, Bennet. 1978. "Tactical Advantages of Opening Positioning Strategies: Lessons from the Seabed Arms Control Talks, 1967–1970." In *The Negotiation Process: Theories and Applications.* Beverly Hills, Calif.: Sage Publications.

Rao, G. A., and M. F. Shakun. 1974. "A Normative Model for Negotiations." *Management Science* 20: 1364–75.

Rapoport, Anatol. 1970. *N-Person Game Theory: Concepts and Applications.* Ann Arbor: University of Michigan Press.

—— 1966. *Two-Person Game Theory: The Essential Ideas.* Ann Arbor: University of Michigan Press.

Raskin, A. H. 1963. "The New York Newspaper Strike." *New York Times,* April 1. Reprinted in *The Fifty Percent Solution,* ed. I. W. Zartman. Garden City, N.Y.: Doubleday, 1976.

Rosenfeld, Stephen S. 1975. "The Panama Negotiations—A Close Run Thing." *Foreign Affairs* 54, no. 1 (October): 5–6.

Ross, H. Laurence. 1970. *Settled Out of Court: The Social Process of Insurance Claims Adjustment.* Chicago: Aldine.

Roth, A. E. 1977a. "Individual Rationality and Nash's Solution to the Bargaining Problem." *Mathematics of Operations Research* 2: 64–65.

—— 1977b. "Independence of Irrelevant Alternatives, and Solutions to Nash's Bargaining Problem." *Journal of Economic Theory* 16: 247–251.

—— 1978. "The Nash Solution and the Utility of Bargaining." *Econometrica* 46: 587–594.

—— 1979. *Axiomatic Models of Bargaining.* Berlin: Springer-Verlag.

Rubin, Jeffrey, and Bert Brown. 1975. *The Social Psychology of Bargaining and Negotiation.* New York: Academic Press.

Savage, Leonard J. 1950. *The Foundations of Statistics.* New York: John Wiley.

Sawyer, Jack, and Harold Guetzkow. 1965. "Bargaining and Negotiations in International Relations." In *International Behavior: A Social-Psychological Analysis.* New York: Holt, Rinehart and Winston.

Schelling, Thomas C. 1956. "An Essay on Bargaining." *American Economic Review* 46: 281–306.

———— 1960. *The Strategy of Conflict.* Cambridge, Mass.: Harvard University Press.

Sebenius, James K. 1980. "Anatomy of Agreement." Dissertation, Harvard University.

Shallert, Edwin. 1980. "Settlement of Civil Litigation in Federal Courts: The Judge's Role." Unpublished paper. Cambridge, Mass.

Shubik, Martin. 1971. "The Dollar Auction Game: A Paradox in Non-Cooperative Behavior and Escalation." *Journal of Conflict Resolution* 15 (March): 109–111.

Simkin, William E. 1971. *Mediation and the Dynamics of Collective Bargaining.* Washington, D.C.: Bureau of National Affairs.

Slichter, Sumner H.; James J. Healy; and E. Robert Livernash. 1975. *The Impact of Collective Bargaining on Management.* Washington, D.C.: Brookings Institution.

Smith, D., and L. Wells. 1975. *Negotiating Third World Mineral Agreements.* Cambridge, Mass.: Ballinger.

Stevens, C. M. 1963. *Strategy and Collective Bargaining Negotiation.* New York: McGraw-Hill.

Sullivan, Timothy J. 1980. "Negotiation-Based Review Process for Facility Siting." Dissertation, Harvard University.

Susskind, Lawrence; James R. Richardson; and Kathryn J. Hildebrand. 1978. *Resolving Environmental Disputes: Approaches to Intervention, Negotiation, and Conflict Resolution.* Cambridge, Mass.: Environmental Impact Assessment Project, Massachusetts Institute of Technology.

Tollison, Robert D., and Thomas A. Willett. 1979. "An Economic Theory of Mutually Advantageous Issue Linkages in International Negotiations." *International Organization* 33 (Autumn): 425–449.

Tversky, Amos, and Daniel Kahneman. 1974. "Judgement under Uncertainty: Heuristics and Biases." *Science* 185: 1124–31.

Ulvila, Jacob W. 1979. "Decisions with Multiple Objectives." Dissertation, Harvard University.

———— and Warner M. Snider. 1980. "Negotiation of Tanker Standards: An Application of Multiattribute Value Theory." *Operations Research* 28 (January-February): 81–95.

U.S. Department of State. 1974. "U.S. and Panama Agree on Principles for Canal Negotiations." *Department of State Bulletin* 70 (February 25): 184–185.

U.S. House of Representatives. 1975. *Congressional Record,* 98th Congress, 2nd Session (October 7), pp. H9713–25, concerning the November 1974 Panama Canal negotiations.

Vickrey, W. 1961. "Counter Speculation, Auctions, and Competitive Sealed Tenders." *Journal of Finance* 16: 8–37.

Von Neumann, John, and Oskar Morgenstern. 1944. *Theory of Games and Economic Behavior.* New York: John Wiley.

Wall, James H., Jr. 1981. "Mediation." *Journal of Conflict Resolution* 25, no. 1: 157–180.

Walton, Richard E., and Robert B. McKersie. 1965. *A Behavioral Theory of Labor Negotiations.* New York: McGraw-Hill.

Wessel, Milton R. 1976. *The Rule of Reason: A New Approach to Corporate Litigation*. Reading, Mass.: Addison-Wesley.

Wiggins, W. H. 1976. "Up for Auction: Malta Bargains with Great Britain, 1971." In *The Fifty Percent Solution*, ed. I. W. Zartman. Garden City, N.Y.: Doubleday.

Wilson, Robert. 1968. "On the Theory of Syndicates." *Econometrica* 36: 119–132.

Young, Oran R. 1967. *The Intermediaries: Third Parties in International Crises*. Princeton: Princeton University Press.

———, ed. 1975. *Bargaining: Formal Theories of Negotiation*. Urbana, Ill.: University of Illinois Press.

Zartman, I. William. 1975. "Negotiations: Theory and Reality." *Journal of International Affairs* 29 (Spring): 69–77.

——— 1976. *The Fifty Percent Solution*. Garden City, N.Y.: Doubleday.

———, ed. 1978. *The Negotiation Process: Theories and Applications*. Beverly Hills, Calif.: Sage Publications.

Zorn, Stephen. 1977. "New Developments in Third World Mining Agreements." *Natural Resources Forum* 1: 239–250.

CASE STUDIES

Graduate School of Business Administration, Harvard University:

AMPO versus City (see also Edwards and White, 1977)
  AMPO-Administration Negotiation: General Information. 3-179-163.
  AMPO-Administration Negotiation: Confidential Information for AMPO (A). 3-179-164.
  AMPO-Administration Negotiation: Confidential Information for City (A). 3-179-165.
  AMPO-Administration Negotiation: Confidential Information for AMPO (B). 3-179-166.
  AMPO-Administration Negotiation: Confidential Information for City (B). 3-179-167.
Basic Frameworks for Normative Ethics. 1-381-080.
Bobbi Barker versus Bradley Hurley
  Bobbi Barker Stores, Inc. 9-174-109. (Confidential information for one player.)
  Bradley Hurley Developers, Inc. 9-174-107. (Confidential information for one player.)
Characteristics of an Effective Negotiator. 4-179-029.
Devon Industries Inc. (B). 9-175-248.
Division of an Encyclopedia. 4-177-053.
Magnus versus Associated Instrument Laboratories
  Magnus Controls, Inc. 9-207-023.
  Associated Instrument Laboratories. 9-207-024.
  Magnus Controls—Associated Instrument Laboratories, Merger Negotiation Videotape. 9-174-121.
A Pure Coalition Game. 4-178-093.
Scandinavian Cement Company. 4-178-096.

A Simplified Highly Structured Union Management Strike Game. 4-177-112.
The Sorensen Chevrolet File. 9-175-258.
The Streaker—Buyer versus Seller
  The Streaker (Buyer). 4-179-020. (Confidential information for one player.)
  The Streaker (Seller). 4-179-021. (Confidential information for one player.)
Wyzard, Inc. (A, B, C). Unnumbered.

Kennedy School of Government, Harvard University:

Middle East Negotiations: The Camp David Summit. C14-79-261.
Panama Canal Treaty Negotiations: Concluding a Treaty. C14-79-224.
Panama Canal Treaty Negotiations: The Setting. C14-79-223.
Philippine Base (Supplementary Case). N14-79-234.
United States–Philippine Military Base Negotiations. C14-79-233.

Index